# BORDER WAR

**CIVIL WAR AMERICA**   Gary W. Gallagher, editor

STANLEY HARROLD

# BORDER WAR

## Fighting over Slavery
## before the Civil War

The University of North Carolina Press  *Chapel Hill*

All rights reserved. Designed by Courtney Leigh Baker and set in Merlo with
Barrel and Egiziano Classic Antique by Rebecca Evans. Manufactured in the
United States of America. The paper in this book meets the guidelines for
permanence and durability of the Committee on Production Guidelines for
Book Longevity of the Council on Library Resources. The University of North
Carolina Press has been a member of the Green Press Initiative since 2003.

Library of Congress Cataloging-in-Publication Data
Harrold, Stanley.
Border war : fighting over slavery before the Civil War / Stanley Harrold.
p. cm. — (Civil War America)
Includes bibliographical references and index.
ISBN 978-0-8078-3431-2 (cloth: alk. paper)
1. Slavery—United States—History—19th century. 2. Antislavery
movements—United States—History—19th century. 3. Fugitive slaves—
Legal status, laws, etc.—United States. 4. Slavery—United States—Legal
status of slaves in free states. 5. Slavery—Law and legislation—Untied
States. 6. Border States (U.S. Civil War) 7. United States. Fugitive slave law
(1850) 8. United States—History—Civil War, 1861–1865—Causes. I. Title.
E449.H2985 2010
973.6—dc22    2010018133

14 13 12 11 10   5 4 3 2 1

FOR BILL AND DARLENE

I like middles.
It is in middles that extremes clash,
where ambiguity restlessly rules.

JOHN UPDIKE, 1966

# CONTENTS

# ILLUSTRATIONS AND MAP

ILLUSTRATIONS

# PREFACE

A brutal system of race-based slavery shaped life in the United States for generations prior to the Civil War. Black bondage controlled the South's economic, social, and political structure. It encouraged white racism and demands for black subordination throughout the country. As the cultivation of cotton expanded during the nineteenth century, many northerners believed their welfare depended on the perpetuation of slavery. But, as economics and racism tied the North to the South, other considerations encouraged disagreement. Fear that slavery threatened northern interests and freedom accentuated the impact of a moral campaign against slavery and pushed the sections apart.

Nowhere were tensions between forces binding the sections together and those pulling them apart stronger than in the North-South borderland. In this region stretching westward in a broad uneven band from the Atlantic coast to the Kansas plains, sectional identities, economies, and moralities intermeshed, interacted, and clashed. Although the border region is variously defined, I follow the pre–Civil War custom of including the entire area encompassed by what contemporaries called the "border free States" and the "border slave States." The former included New Jersey, Pennsylvania, Ohio, Indiana, Illinois, and—by 1846—Iowa. The latter included Delaware, Maryland, Virginia, Kentucky, and Missouri.

Many miles and some cultural differences set the northern portions of the border free states, or Lower North, apart from their southern portions. But these states functioned as political units and differed demographically, historically, economically, and culturally from their neighbors to the north as well as the south. Similar divisions existed in the border slave states. Southern Maryland's tobacco counties, southeastern Virginia's cotton counties, and Kentucky and Missouri's hemp counties relied more heavily on slave labor than did other parts of these states. Yet, like the states of the Lower

North, the border slave states functioned as political units and constituted a region distinguishable from others in their section.

Robert J. Breckinridge, a mildly antislavery Kentucky clergyman, recognized the distinctiveness of the North-South borderlands and their centrality in the nation's struggle over slavery. In January 1860, as civil war approached, Breckinridge placed responsibility for sectional antagonism on the Border South and Lower North. The key issue, he contended, was northward escape of African Americans from slavery. He declared, "It is Maryland, Virginia, Kentucky, and Missouri that have borne all the losses and annoyance," and he held the Border North responsible. As "the border free states" pondered the consequences of their aid to fugitive slaves, Breckinridge warned, they "ought to remember that their borders are as much exposed as ours." Omitting sparsely settled Iowa and tiny Delaware, he charged, "Posterity will hold these six border free States and four border slave States responsible for the fate of this nation in the present crisis."[1]

Although Breckinridge correctly evaluated the role of slave escape in worsening sectional relations, he misjudged posterity. As it turned out, later generations did not hold the border region responsible for the Civil War. Most of the border slave states stayed in the Union, and the Lower South received most of the blame for starting the war. Decades of fighting over slavery in the North-South border region, nevertheless, had a profound impact on American life, culture, and politics. It helped shape the sectional struggle, the Civil War, and how that war proceeded.

I portray the North-South border conflict comprehensively. Bravery, brutality, fear, and anger helped shape the story. Moral principle, altruism, self-interest, political calculation, and emotion all had roles. Obscure as well as famous people acted in a huge and complex geographic region. The border struggle's development, its forms of engagement, and its relationship to larger sectional forces require close analysis. Therefore, this book's organization is topical as well as chronological. Developments on each side of the North-South divide require separate chapters that overlap chronologically. In all cases, I move the story along, while neglecting neither analysis nor dramatic incidents.

VIOLENT CLASHES over slavery in the North-South borderlands were sporadic. Compared to the War for Independence, the War of 1812, and battles against American Indians, fighters and casualties were few. With major exceptions, especially during the 1850s, weapons consisted of small arms. But fighting in the Lower North and Border South lasted much longer than the nation's wars. Violence grew out of the proximity of free- and slave-labor societies. Those who experienced that violence used the term "border war," either to describe what they observed or predict its result. African Americans and their northern white neighbors had good reason to regard kidnapping into slavery and enforcement of the fugitive slave laws as war against freedom. White southerners had good reason to regard assisted slave escape as war against their economic and social order. Although proximity shaped the struggle, other factors intensified it. Among them were the antislavery movement, the proslavery reaction to it, party politics, and the nature of American journalism.

From the late eighteenth century, and especially during the decades after 1810, a variety of reform movements dedicated to religious, moral, educational, and health issues flourished in the United States. Antislavery became the largest and most influential of these movements, although its more dedicated adherents—abolitionists—were relatively few. With roots in the American Revolution, black resistance to slavery, and activist religion, abolitionism was strongest in the Northeast. But it had a major impact on conflict over slavery in the border region.

By the 1830s, abolitionists advocated immediate emancipation of the slaves and equal rights for African Americans. But they disagreed regarding how these objectives could be achieved, and by 1840 there were three factions. The American Anti-Slavery Society, led by William Lloyd Garrison, rejected all violent means, denounced churches and the U.S. Constitution as proslavery, and called for separating the North from the South as the best means of ending slavery. The American and Foreign Anti-Slavery Society, headed by Lewis Tappan, sought to expand abolitionism in the churches. The tiny Liberty Party aimed to end slavery through the political system. Slavery's defenders often overlooked these factional divisions in portraying abolitionists as a united, ubiquitous, and powerful threat to the white South.

Party politics had begun in the United States during the 1790s. From that decade through much of the 1810s, the aristocratic, nationalistic, moralistic, and sometimes antislavery Federalist Party opposed a (Jeffersonian) Republican Party representing agrarianism, state sovereignty, individualism, and slaveholders. As the Federalist Party declined following the War of 1812, and the Republican Party divided into nationalist and state-rights wings, a second American party system emerged. In this new system, shaped by univer-

sal suffrage among adult white men, the Whig Party advocated national pro-
grams for economic development; the Democratic Party stood for the white
northern masses and increasingly for southern slaveholders. In the North
during the 1830s and 1840s, Whigs—more than Democrats—sympathized
with antislavery efforts. In the Border South, Whigs tended to advocate the
eventual abolition of slavery and colonization of former slaves outside the
United States, while Democrats usually defended perpetual slavery.

In 1848 most Liberty abolitionists joined with minorities of northern
Whigs and Democrats to form the Free Soil Party. As members of a much
larger third party than the Liberty Party had been, Free Soilers sought
mainly to stop the expansion of slavery, rather than to end it. By early 1856,
more northern Whigs and Democrats had become disenchanted with what
seemed to be proslavery politics. They joined with Free Soilers to form a
new Republican Party, which replaced the Whig Party in the two-party system. Through all of this, a small group of Liberty abolitionists remained independent. Best known as radical political abolitionists, they believed slavery could never be legal, that slaves had a constitutional right to escape, and
abolitionists had a duty to help them.

All of these developments—reform movements, disagreement over slavery, and partisan politics—encouraged journalists to take sides on issues
facing the nation. Most newspapers and periodicals made no pretense of
neutrality. They displayed sectional, political, moral, religious, and ethnic
prejudices openly and proudly. Bias shaped journalists' choices of articles
to publish as well as the editorials they wrote. Reliance on volunteer correspondents, rather than professional reporters, led to error, exaggeration,
and misinterpretation. Even when journalists sought accuracy—which they
often did—they lacked the technology required to guarantee it. Newspapers therefore accentuated sectional division, fear, and suspicion.

Newspapers nevertheless are an essential source for information concerning the struggle over slavery. They are especially valuable in revealing attitudes and perceptions on each side of the North-South line. Yet, because
of their bias and frequent inaccuracy, newspaper reports must be carefully
evaluated. In many cases, the reports can be placed in contexts provided by
updated accounts in the newspapers themselves, competing periodicals,
court records, and government documents.

Other historical sources raise more profound difficulties. This is especially
the case for material related to the underground railroad. There should be
no doubt that organized biracial networks designed to help slaves escape

existed in the Lower North. Some of them extended into the Border South and beyond. But overreliance by historians, during the late nineteenth and early twentieth centuries, on imprecise and sometimes self-serving reminiscences of elderly white abolitionists have led to a scholarly reaction that either denies the networks existed or that white abolitionists participated in them. Therefore, when discussing slave escapes, I have not used sources dependent on old memories—black or white—unless they are supported by contemporary evidence.

BECAUSE THIS STUDY covers a large geographic area and a long period of time, I have frequently relied on the work of other historians. I owe a great debt to accounts of local events published in historical journals, state histories, and larger interpretive studies. The work of several historians has been especially helpful. William W. Freehling's long-term investigation of the role of the Border South in the secession movement has in many ways shaped my interpretation of conflict across the North-South line. David Grimsted's analysis of mob violence before the Civil War, and Paul Finkelman's wide-ranging studies of legal issues related to the fugitive slave laws have been very helpful. Nicole Etcheson's *Bleeding Kansas* is crucial to my portrayal of events in that border conflict.

Professors Freehling and Etcheson are among the historians who have generously devoted time and thought in evaluating draft chapters of this book. Others who have read one or more of the chapters and provided suggestions are Richard J. M. Blackett, Douglas R. Egerton, William C. Hine, John R. McKivigan, and Stacey M. Robertson. Although I am solely responsible for factual and interpretive errors, these scholars clarified my interpretation, improved my prose, and tightened my organization. I have also received advice on various aspects of the *Border War* project from J. Michael Crane, Merton L. Dillon, Dan Green, and Randall M. Miller. I thank as well David Perry of the University of North Carolina Press for his steadfast support. And, as usual, I owe a great deal of thanks to Judy Harrold and Emily Harrold for their technical help and patience.

Archivists and librarians also helped. Among archivists, I am indebted to the staffs at Hill Memorial Library, Louisiana State University; the Library of Virginia; the Maryland State Archives; the Rare Book and Special Collection Library, Duke University; the State Historical Society of Missouri; and Wilson Library, University of North Carolina at Chapel Hill. The staffs of two departments at the University of South Carolina's Thomas Cooper Library deserve special thanks. I am impressed by how quickly the Interlibrary Loan Department is able to locate and loan rare materials. The Government Information, Microforms, and Newspapers Department has an extensive collection of nineteenth-century documents and provides a wonderful working environment.

Finally, I am grateful to the National Endowment for the Humanities, from which I received a Faculty Research Award in 2005. The award funded a year of uninterrupted research and writing.

# INTRODUCTION

## Perception of War

"A fierce border war is evidently to be the only protection and hope of the Southern States," declared the *Richmond Enquirer*. Physical conflict over slave escapes from Maryland, Virginia, Kentucky, and Missouri into the border free states of Pennsylvania, Ohio, Indiana, and Illinois had disillusioned the editor of this influential Virginia newspaper. Shortly after Congress passed the draconian Fugitive Slave Law of 1850, he warned, if "the people of the Northern borders" could not respect the new law, they would face "the law of the sword, the rifle, [and] the tar barrel." Just as "the people of the Southern borders" had "slaughtered the Indians who stole their cattle," they would "shoot the Yankees who steal their negroes."

The slavery issue created a crisis in 1850 over more than northward escapes. Northerners and southerners clashed regarding human bondage in Washington, D.C. and its expansion into the southwestern territories recently taken from Mexico. But, for the editor of the *Enquirer* and thousands of others who lived on the South's northern periphery, slave escape constituted the most pressing and dangerous issue. Rather than affecting pride of place or distant territories, slave escape involved tangible concerns, including financial loss, threats to the social order, race loyalty, and public safety.

Slave escape and northern sympathy for the escapees, the editor feared, could wreak havoc in the Border South and required a forceful response. He suggested "a foray into Pennsylvania or Ohio, with burnings to the ground of a few such towns as Harrisburg," where a white judge and a predominantly black mob had obstructed two Virginia masters' attempt to recover three escaped slaves. Such a raid, the editor bitterly predicted, "Would soon teach the amalgamationist inhabitants of Pennsylvania and Ohio, that the stealing of their thick-lipped relations and superiors in the South is not the delightful amusement they now take it to be." A few weeks earlier, the Baltimore correspondent of the *New York Tribune* had predicted "open border warfare" over slave escapes.[1]

In fact, conflict had long existed on what the *Baltimore Patriot* referred to in 1837 as "the Middle Ground"—the borderland where the wage-labor and slave-labor sections of the United States met.[2] Fighting over slavery extended in attenuated form throughout the country. But it centered on the North-South line and the states abutting it. Major events in the struggle— such as resistance to the Fugitive Slave Law, Bleeding Kansas, and John Brown's raid—are well known. But until now, there has been no exploration of the conflict in its entirety, in its depth, breadth, complexity, drama, and impact. This book describes and analyzes the roots and development of "border war," the hopes and fears it engendered, the various forms of violence that characterized it, attempts to end it, and its impact in the border region and the nation.

Contrasting societies, economic forces, state and national governments, the wider sectional struggle, and the political power of slaveholders all had roles in borderlands fighting. Three groups, however, were directly involved. African Americans sought freedom by escaping northward. Abolitionists and other residents of the Lower North helped them. Border South masters and those aligned with them attempted to recapture fugitive slaves or preserve slavery in their region. On each side of the sectional divide, people feared the struggle might end in destruction of their labor system, values, and independence. The border clashes of the 1840s and 1850s had a significant role in the sectional controversy that led in 1861 to the Civil War. They helped shape the course of the Border South as the war began and thereby affected its outcome.

BORDERLANDS ARE contiguous regions where contrasting economic, political, and cultural forces compete, interact, and clash. They are most volatile when residents on each side of the border may easily pass to the other. This was the case along the Mason-Dixon line, the Ohio River, and northern Mississippi river, which together marked the North-South boundary prior to the Civil War. The origins of the boundary were political, and no natural barrier blocked movement between the Lower North and Border South.

Surveyors created the Mason-Dixon line in 1767 to clarify where Maryland and Pennsylvania's authority began and ended. In 1786, Pennsylvania and Virginia extended the line across the Allegheny Mountains. A year later, the Northwest Ordinance began a process that in a quarter century made the Ohio River another boundary between free-labor and slave-labor regions.

And in 1821, the admission of Missouri to the Union as a slaveholding state gave the Mississippi River a similar role. But none of this prevented interaction. Concerning the Mason-Dixon line, Pennsylvania's antislavery poet John G. Whittier observed, "Our own broad state and the slave region along its southern border are not even 'lands intersected by a narrow firth,' nor have so much as a solitary 'mountain interposed' to wall them off."[3] Meanwhile, the Ohio River served as a route of travel and commerce intertwining the interests of Ohio, Indiana, and Illinois with those of Virginia and Kentucky. The Mississippi River linked Illinois and Missouri.

In addition to travel and commerce, demographic and cultural ties spanned the sectional boundary. During the eighteenth century, people from Pennsylvania settled large portions of Maryland and Virginia, and Virginians settled in southwest Pennsylvania. White "upland southerners," from Virginia, Maryland, North Carolina, Kentucky, and Tennessee predominated among settlers in southern Ohio, Indiana, and Illinois. They brought southern farming techniques, styles of architecture, and racial attitudes. During the early years of the nineteenth century, many of them were poor and illiterate, as well as independent and self-sufficient. Many of them—and many white Pennsylvanians—sympathized with slaveholders. Although they lived in the North, they admired what they regarded as the orderliness and hospitality of southern society.[4]

As these observations suggest, residents of the Lower North and Border South had more in common economically, demographically, and culturally than those who lived farther from the sectional boundary. On each side of the Mason-Dixon line and each bank of the Ohio River, agriculturally oriented rural economies existed symbiotically with centers of commerce and modernization. Slaveholding Baltimore had an economic hinterland overlapping Philadelphia's. Pittsburgh channeled western Pennsylvania's and eastern Ohio's agricultural and mineral products down the Ohio River toward the southern port of New Orleans. Cincinnati performed a similar function for western Ohio and Indiana. By 1860, Wheeling, located in Virginia's narrow northern panhandle extending between Pennsylvania and Ohio, had become the Old Dominion's second largest city, surpassed only by Richmond. Farther west, the Border South cities of Lexington, Louisville, and St. Louis hoped to challenge Cincinnati as America's largest inland port.[5]

An expanding network of steamboats, turnpikes, canals, and, by the 1830s, railroads facilitated intersectional economic expansion. Cooperative efforts linking federal and state governments with private enterprise built turnpikes, canals, and railroads. The National Road, begun near Cumberland, Maryland, in 1811, passed through Pennsylvania to Wheeling in 1818. It reached its terminus at Vandalia, Illinois, in 1852. During the 1830s, civic boosters in Kentucky and southwestern Ohio dreamed of linking Cincinnati by rail with Charleston, South Carolina. The Baltimore and Ohio Railroad, begun in 1828, reached Harpers Ferry, Virginia, by 1834 and the Ohio River by 1852. Other rail lines tied Baltimore and points south with Philadelphia and points north. In 1853 William Harned, a white abolitionist who had moved from New York City to a farm near Wilmington, Delaware, described society near that slave state's boundary with Pennsylvania as "neither southern or northern."[6]

Commerce gave slaveholders great influence in the Lower North's urban areas. As a Cincinnati journalist noted in 1838, southerners were that city's best customers. They purchased provisions, slave clothing, bagging and rope for cotton, as well as mules and horses. Following a proslavery and antiblack riot during September 1839, local abolitionist Gamaliel Bailey complained, "Cincinnati is the outpost of the Anti-Slavery cause—and more beset by pro-slavery influences than any other spot in the free states."[7] Philadelphia and Pittsburgh's economies also depended on the South and slavery.

BECAUSE OF THE Lower North and Border South's interaction, historians often regard them as moderate regions caught between Upper North and Lower South radicalism. As historian Edward L. Ayers puts it, "The people of the border did not start the fight that became the Civil War. Indeed, they prided themselves on their restraint in the face of what they saw as provocation by extremists above and below them." Delaware, Maryland, Kentucky, Missouri, and parts of Virginia have been described as outposts of slavery. In portions of these states, slavery had never been extensive, had not expanded, or had declined. During the late eighteenth century, the natural-rights ideology of the American Revolution and a shift from planting tobacco, which required a year-round labor force, to planting wheat, which did not, led many Chesapeake masters to manumit slaves. Manumissions in turn created a much larger free black population than existed in the rest of the South. By the 1810s, a tendency of Chesapeake masters to migrate southwest with their bond people or to sell them to cotton producers led some to believe borderland slavery was declining.[8]

Yet, contrary to a recent contention that the Border South would be better understood as the "Border North," no one in antebellum America doubted that Delaware, Maryland, Virginia, Kentucky, and Missouri were southern, while New Jersey, Pennsylvania, Ohio, Indiana, and Illinois were northern.[9] Despite interconnectedness, fundamental differences divided the Lower North and Border South, and predisposed them to conflict. Much more than in those areas of the Lower North settled by upland southerners, the Border South maintained a structured society and conservative culture. Premodern values associated with agrarianism predominated. Commercial development and population growth lagged.

Virginia had strong ties to regions farther south. Although the state adopted democratic forms for white men, powerful planting families controlled it. Even its mountainous northwestern portion had a "centralized and undemocratic political structure" that encouraged hereditary power. Kentucky's dominant Bluegrass planters, who produced hemp for bagging cotton bales, also identified culturally and economically with the Lower South. They lived in "stately brick mansions," observed aristocratic customs, and bred racehorses. Solidarity with cotton planters and a powerful master class set Missouri—the most exposed of slave states—apart from Illinois, its neighbor to the east.[10]

Most important, slavery's decline in the Border South during the decades prior to the Civil War has been exaggerated. Delaware's tiny slave population and Maryland's much larger one diminished between 1830 and 1860—Delaware's drastically and Maryland's significantly. The declines were greatest in Delaware's two northern counties and in Maryland's counties bordering Pennsylvania. Still, 87,189 slaves lived in Maryland in 1860, with 14,227 of them in its northern-tier counties. In Virginia, Kentucky, and Missouri, slave numbers *increased* throughout the antebellum period, although they declined as a percentage of total population.

Virginia retained the largest slave population in the United States throughout the antebellum decades. There were 469,757 slaves within its boundaries in 1830 and on the eve of the Civil War there were 490,865. The state's northwestern counties bordering Pennsylvania and Ohio never had many slaves, and their number declined by over 50 percent between 1830 and 1860. But Virginia's Potomac counties just south of Maryland maintained stable slave populations between 1830 and 1850; they had declined only slightly by 1860. During the same period, Kentucky's total slave population grew from 165,213 to 225,483. Even in its counties bordering the Ohio River, the number of slaves increased from 35,645 to 52,552, although most of the growth occurred in newly settled areas south of Indiana and Illinois, where slaves engaged in clearing fields as well as planting. Numbers of slaves declined slightly in Kentucky counties just south of Ohio, nevertheless over 10,000 lived in this area in 1860. Missouri held 25,091 slaves in 1830.

By 1860 there were 114,931, although in large areas of the state there were very few. In Missouri, as well as in Maryland, Virginia, and Kentucky, slavery remained a viable institution, which would have endured had it not faced external foes.

The Border South's economic stake in unfree labor guaranteed that most of its internal opposition to slavery was mild and qualified. Demographic considerations also discouraged emancipation. By 1850, African Americans—slave and free—constituted 37 percent of Virginia's population, 28 percent of Maryland's, 22 percent of Delaware's and Kentucky's, and 13 percent of Missouri's. In these states, both slavery's staunch defenders and the overwhelming majority of its critics regarded such large black populations as threats to white security. Members of each group feared slave revolt. But they also feared that unrestricted emancipation would produce an uncontrollable free black class. Therefore, except for a few individuals influenced by northern abolitionism, those who claimed to oppose slavery advocated only prospective, gradual emancipation linked to the removal of free African Americans.[11]

Following slave preacher Nat Turner's 1831 uprising in southern Virginia, that state and neighboring Maryland strengthened their slave systems rather than pursue emancipation plans. In 1833, Kentucky's legislature banned the importation of additional slaves as a defensive measure against revolt. But disinclination to enlarge the state's free black population and hemp production, which seemed to require slave labor, more than offset antislavery sentiment. By 1849, when the Kentucky legislature repealed the ban on slave imports, one-third of the state's residents owned slaves. In 1860, Kentucky had the third largest number of slaveholders in the country. Far fewer Missourians—one-eighth of the state's families—owned slaves that year. But Missouri slave owners profited from hemp and tobacco, received additional income from sales of excess slaves to traders, and wielded great political power.[12]

In contrast to the Border South, very few slaves and small numbers of free African Americans lived in the Lower North. In 1850 black people constituted 4.9 percent of New Jersey's population, 2.3 percent of Pennsylvania's, 1.3 percent of Ohio's, 1.1 percent of Indiana's, and .6 percent of Illinois's. After Pennsylvania initiated gradual abolition in 1780, human bondage steadily declined within its jurisdiction, although white farmers in the southeastern portion of the state continued into the 1820s to employ black indentured servants. By 1840 only sixty-four Pennsylvania slaves remained; there were none in 1850. New Jersey initiated gradual abolition in 1804 and slavery remained significant in that state into the 1830s. Even so, by 1840 there were just 674

New Jersey slaves, and 236 in 1850. Similar conditions existed in Ohio, Indiana, and Illinois. Although, as in Pennsylvania, white farmers in southern portions of the Old Northwest held small numbers of African Americans as indentured servants into the 1820s, the great majority of residents regarded slavery to be an economic, political, and moral evil. Most of those who had southern backgrounds believed black slaves marginalized white laborers.

Tiny black populations in the Lower North did not prevent prejudice. Like their counterparts in the Border South, many white border northerners regarded free African Americans to be shiftless, lazy, unintelligent, and immoral. They were, it seemed, a degraded race not fit to participate in white society. As the black populations of Pennsylvania, Ohio, Indiana, and Illinois grew after 1810—in part because white southerners forced out free African Americans—white residents sometimes reacted negatively. They enacted legislation to curtail black settlement and limit black citizenship. A few resorted to mob violence. In 1848 a Democratic congressmen from Ohio suggested if slaveholders in Kentucky and Virginia continued to force free African Americans northward "the banks of the Ohio [River] (a mile wide) would be lined with men with muskets on their shoulders to keep off the emancipated slaves."[13]

But because white people in the Lower North had less to fear from African Americans than white border southerners, racial laws north of the sectional boundary—known in the Old Northwest as "Black Laws"—were relatively mild. Despite racial bias, the border free states treated African Americans as human beings, in contrast to the border slave states' definition of them as property.[14] Many white residents of the Lower North sympathized with fugitive slaves and free African Americans, some of whom were servants in their homes or hired hands on their farms.

DESPITE THE PERMEABILITY of the Mason-Dixon line and the Ohio River, antebellum travelers recognized they separated distinct societies. When English visitor Harriet Martineau journeyed south from Philadelphia to Baltimore and Washington, D.C., in 1835, she remarked changes in food, manners, and living conditions. But the pervasiveness of slavery struck her most forcibly. Fifteen years later, as Jane Grey Swisshelm, an antislavery journalist from Pittsburgh, traveled to Washington, she observed that Maryland suffered for its reliance on slave labor. Inactive farms stretched "out in primitive wilderness or exhausted barren wastes." Even prosperous Baltimore, where there were relatively few slaves, had a southern demeanor. British traveler James Dixon, who visited the city in 1848, perceived "an air of aristocracy" lacking in northern cities. "We were now, indeed, in one of the slave-holding States," he commented, "and from the specimen given in this and other places visited, it is pretty apparent, that the system of slavery tends to produce this spirit." Southerners too recognized a sectional divide. When David Aiken of South Carolina visited Cincinnati in 1850, he noticed widespread antislavery sentiment. The people who lived in the city, he reported, were "as ignorant of the . . . South [and slavery] . . . as if a Great Desert lay between Cincinnati and the Kentucky shore."[15]

Early nineteenth-century travel accounts contrasting the free-labor and slave-labor sides of the Ohio River are common. In 1812, Scottish mapmaker John Melish journeyed down the river from Pittsburgh to beyond Marietta. The settlers on the Ohio side, he noted, were "in the most comfortable circumstances." They had no difficulty providing travelers with food and lodging. In contrast, travelers could get neither of these on the Virginia side, and Melish attributed this difficulty to "the effects of slavery." Anticipating northern antislavery tracts, he maintained that, because white Virginians relied on the "exertions" of slaves, they were "miserable and wretched, and poor, and almost naked." Ohioans, on the other hand, worked for themselves, which increased wealth, population, and "domestic comfort."[16]

During the early 1830s, Alexis de Tocqueville reacted similarly as he voyaged down the Ohio. He declared, Kentucky and Ohio "differ only on a single point: Kentucky has accepted slaves, the state of Ohio has rejected them all from its midst." That particular difference had a profound effect. In Kentucky, Tocqueville observed, "The population is sparse; . . . the primitive forest constantly reappears; one would say that society is asleep; man seems idle." White men in Kentucky preferred "idle ease," "hunting and war," and "the most violent exercises of the body" over productive labor. In Ohio, however, "a confused noise . . . proclaim[ed] from afar the presence of industry; rich harvests cover[ed] the fields; elegant dwellings announce[d] the taste and care of the laborer." According to Tocqueville, an Ohio man "obliged to live by his own efforts . . . placed in material well-being the principal goal of his existence."[17]

Martineau's, Swisshelm's, Dixon's, Melish's, and Tocqueville's observations reflect antebellum opinion concerning cultural boundaries in the North-South borderlands. In Cincinnati in 1838, a Democratic candidate for Congress contrasted "happy and flourishing" Ohio with Kentucky's "poverty . . . sterility, and squalid wretchedness." At about the same time, Benjamin F. Wade, a member of the Ohio legislature, declared, "The beautiful

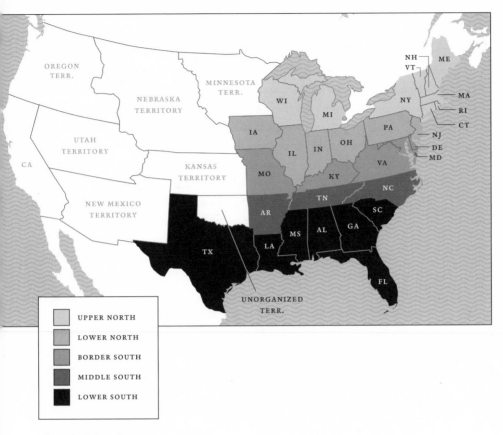

The United States in 1854

river Ohio, like the fabled Styx, was forever to separate the land of darkness, slavery, and oppression, from the Elysium, beyond, of virtue, happiness, and universal liberty."[18]

Marylanders, Virginians, and Kentuckians often affirmed that slavery negatively affected their economies and moralities, but they resented northern criticism. Like their counterparts farther south, many in the border slave states believed greed and duplicity inspired northern enterprise and attitudes. By the 1820s, Kentuckians referred to Ohio as "the Yankee State," using "Yankee" as a pejorative to suggest unwanted materialism and sharp dealing in financial affairs. In 1841 the *Louisville Public Advertiser* contended that the thousands of northern women working as seamstresses were worse off than slaves.[19]

SPORADIC CONFLICT BETWEEN the two regions began shortly after 1780, when Pennsylvania's initiation of gradual emancipation made the Mason-Dixon line a sectional boundary. By the early 1800s, violent incidents occurred in the region bordering the Ohio River. By the 1820s, fighting over slavery had spread to the Mississippi River boundary between Illinois and Missouri. In the Lower North, masters fought to recapture fugitive slaves and to keep slaves whom they brought with them into the region. Free African Americans fought against kidnappers and slave catchers. White residents might be drawn in on either side. In the Border South, masters and their allies fought against absconding slaves and those who aided the fugitives.

Physical clashes in the North-South borderlands became more numerous after Congress in 1808 banned the importation of slaves from Africa and the West Indies. The ban increased the value of slaves in the United States and encouraged kidnappers from the Border South to prey on free African Americans in the Lower North. Conflict increased again after the mid-1830s as demand for slaves in the cotton-producing Old Southwest encouraged masters in the Border South to sell more slaves south, more slaves to head north, and kidnappers to expand their activities. A vicious circle developed as slaveholders sold slaves south to prevent escape and slaves escaped to prevent sale south. In July 1845, "A Baltimorean" reported slave traders were "very rife" in Maryland. Estimating that "3000 [slaves] have been sent out from this state since January," he contended, "not a few slaves have fled to escape such a lot."[20]

Many white residents of the Lower North regarded renditions of slaves to be little different from kidnapping. They held both practices to be threats to state sovereignty, free society, and safety. In 1842, Ohio's excitable former Democratic U.S. senator, Thomas Morris, denounced the kidnapping of African Americans as a potential "cause of war." Morris might be dismissed as a hothead, if four years later the Ohio legislature had not threatened to go to war against Virginia if it did not extradite four of its citizens accused of kidnapping three *white* Ohioans.[21] Other northerners charged that armed bands of slave catchers and those who abducted free African Americans into slavery might place portions of New Jersey, Pennsylvania, Ohio, Indiana, and Illinois under southern control. The result, they worried, would be moral, economic, and political disaster.

In January 1842, political abolitionists at a Liberty meeting in western New York claimed that white southerners had "for nine long years filled our borders with persecution, violence, and terror." Southerners, the abolitionists charged, had launched attacks on northern communities. They had "plucked up our rights on our own soil. . . . kidnapped hundreds of our free colored citizens and consigned them to perpetual bondage. . . . mobbed our assemblies, assaulted our wives and daughters, burnt down our halls, blown up our churches, sacked our houses, broken up our presses, set prices on the heads of our clergy, shed the heart's blood of our philanthropists."[22]

Initially, most of the cross-border conflict occurred in the Lower North. But by the mid-1830s, escape networks extending into the Border South had become more common. Many in the Border South believed northerners invaded their land, endangered their property rights, insulted their honor, and threatened war. Toward the end of the nineteenth century, historian Hermann von Holst looked back on Maryland, Virginia, and Kentucky during the decades prior to the Civil War and observed, "Slaveholders look[ed] forward to the future with gloomy anxiety." They became, in historian Barbara Jeanne Fields's words, "especially overbearing, arbitrary, and vindictive." As early as 1839, Kentucky slaveholder Henry Clay—leader of the Whig Party, perennial presidential candidate, and sectional moderate—warned that a "collision of opinion" between abolitionists and slaveholders would "be quickly followed by the clash of arms." Clay contemplated a war that would produce "desolated fields, conflagrated cities, murdered inhabitants, and the overthrow of the fairest fabric of human government that ever rose to animate the hopes of civilized man."[23]

Similarly, the *Lynchburg Virginian* declared that if the "governments of the nonslaveholding states" did not protect slave property, the border slave states "must take their defense into their own hands." They might have to "'carry the war into Africa,'" by going north to abduct "negro stealers" for trial and punishment in the Border South. In 1845 a Maryland correspondent warned *New York Tribune* editor Horace Greeley that most southerners were "descendents of the countrymen of [John] Hampden and [Algernon] Sydney [Puritan martyrs of the English Civil War]." "We can be persuaded," the correspondent asserted, "but not driven, unless vanquished by numbers."[24]

As time passed, the Border South grew more apprehensive than the Lower North that it faced defeat. The region's leaders preferred to rely on local or state action to protect slavery. They amended slave codes, expanded patrols, formed vigilance associations, and threatened abolitionists. They sent diplomats to border free-state capitals seeking legislation to curtail northward escapes and aid masters in apprehending fugitives. When, during the 1840s, the last of the diplomatic efforts only increased antislavery sentiment, they sought federal protection.

Following a spate of mass-escape attempts, border slave-state congressmen led in formulating the Fugitive Slave Law of 1850. In a radical departure from the Fugitive Slave Law of 1793, they made the U.S. government responsible for slave rendition and quelling resistance in the North. Yet the law produced greater violence. In 1852, Free Soil congressman Joshua R. Giddings of Ohio claimed the law caused the "murder of three white men and four colored men in Pennsylvania." "Civil War," he asserted, "may be said to exist on the borders of that State." In 1855, citizens of Salem, Ohio, collected money to purchase arms "for self defense" against slave catchers. One white resident asserted, "I am for open hostility."[25]

By that year federal support for Missouri's effort to prevent slave escapes across its western border ignited guerrilla war between proslavery and antislavery forces in Kansas Territory. In this perspective, John Brown's 1859 raid on the federal arsenal at the Virginia border town of Harpers Ferry in a failed attempt to spark slave revolt escalated an old conflict. Years before the raid, a conviction had emerged throughout the white South that if African Americans continued to escape, slavery could not long survive on the section's northern periphery. In an alarming scenario similar to that imagined in the twentieth century's Cold War domino theory, Lower South politicians and journalists foresaw one tier of southern states after another falling to the forces of black freedom.

Well before Brown's raid, the Lower South's more radical leaders concluded their states had to secede to stop northern aggression, keep the Border South from slipping away, and prevent loss of proslavery political power. Many in the border slave states agreed. But, when the Lower South states left the Union following the November 1860 election of Republican Abraham Lincoln to the presidency—and the Middle South states followed after Fort Sumter—most of the border slave states remained in the Union. Their declining fortunes in the long border struggle convinced white majorities in most of them that only federal protection could save slavery in the region. That decision deprived the Confederacy of vital resources it needed to win the Civil War.[26]

THE DEBATE OVER the causes of the Civil War began before the war. Republican politicians emphasized an irrepressible conflict between the interests of slaveholders and slave labor on the one side and free white wage laborers on the other. They portrayed a struggle between America's founding commitment to republican government and the political demands of aristocratic slaveholders. In contrast, southern politicians and journalists emphasized an underlying northern antipathy to slavery and southern civilization that emerged in resistance to the Fugitive Slave Law, opposition to slavery's territorial expansion, and interference with slavery itself. Observing this growing division, moderate politicians and journalists in each section complained that radical agitators, rather than fundamental differences, drove the sections toward a needless conflict.[27]

During the century and a half since the war ended, historians have often centered on the issue of whether or not it could have been avoided. From the late nineteenth century into the early twentieth, the dominant interpretation held that the war was inevitable and in the best interest of the nation. Then from the 1920s through most of the 1950s, a group of pro-southern revisionists claimed it had been a needless tragedy that kept the white South from dealing effectively with slavery and race. In the early twenty-first century, most historians once again place slavery at the center of fundamental economic, cultural, and ideological forces that brought on a necessary war. Only a small minority argues that a breakdown in the two-party system, caused by issues other than slavery, led to an avoidable war.[28]

Despite their differences, each of these groups of historians describes the approach of war in terms of a series of sectional clashes. They usually begin with the crisis posed by Missouri's application in 1819 to join the Union as a slaveholding state and end with the Republican victory in the presidential election of 1860. The tendency is to regard northern efforts to stop slavery's territorial expansion as key to driving the Lower South to secession. Over the years, however, individual historians have studied a variety of underlying factors in the sectional conflict. Among them are class conflict between southern planters and northern capitalists; a northern free-labor ideology that regarded slavery and slaveholders' political power as threats to the rights and interests of free white men; a white southern perception that the North sought to deny the right to hold property in slaves; and the interrelated impact of slave resistance and white southern commitment to racial dominance.[29]

The proposition that fear in the Lower South of losing the Border South was a major cause of the Civil War is compatible with all of this, unless slavery expansion is interpreted as the only determining issue. Since the 1970s, William W. Freehling has most thoroughly studied the role of Border South slavery in the events that led to secession and war.[30] Freehling emphasizes internal developments—including what he regards as "peaceful" slave escapes—in a decline of slavery in the region. This book owes a considerable debt to Freehling's insights. But it emphasizes a violent and often external threat to a viable slave system.

Parts of this interpretation are not new. In 1898, historian Wilbur Siebert declared, "It is safe to say that the Underground Railroad was one of the greatest forces which brought on the Civil War, and thus destroyed slavery." More recently, Keith P. Griffler placed slave escapes and their ramifications at the center of Civil War causation. Griffler notes the warlike nature of the struggle in the Ohio Valley between fugitive slaves and their abettors on the one side and their erstwhile masters on the other.[31] No book before this one, however, has integrated events in the Lower North and Border South in a narrative of extended cross-border conflict.

THE STRUGGLE CENTERED on African Americans, slave and free. Black men, women, and children catalyzed physical conflict as kidnap victims and self-emancipated slaves. Small black communities and isolated families along the North-South border harbored fugitives and saw them on their way north. Black men and women participated in underground-railroad networks that assisted escapees. The numbers involved in northward escapes have sometimes been exaggerated. More African Americans who fled slavery remained in the South than headed to the free states and Canada. In the Border South, manumissions and sales south very likely had a greater negative impact on slave populations than did escapes.[32] But the phenomena were interrelated, and escape disturbed masters and shaped northern impressions of a brutal slave system.

Although escape might seem to have been a peaceful means of saving individuals from bondage and weakening slavery, fugitives often carried weapons and fought masters who pursued them. Among many examples, two young black men who escaped in 1840 from their master's Maryland plantation drove a hack toward the Mason-Dixon line. When slave catchers on horseback overtook them, the pair used pistols to drive them off. Six years later, a fugitive slave from Maryland, who had reached Somerset County, Pennsylvania, used "a long knife" to kill a slave catcher. In some instances, armed bands of escapees reached impressive size. Pursuers, including masters, professional slave catchers, local men seeking rewards, constables and other law enforcement officials, also carried weapons.[33]

Even when escaping slaves suffered defeat and recapture, abolitionists expressed admiration for their determination to be free. "There is much in these cases to alarm the oppressor and encourage the advocates of the oppressed," declared the *Philanthropist* in 1836. Some nonabolitionist white residents of the Lower North who were not overtly hostile to slavery or its westward expansion joined in this admiration. When a fugitive slave in

Dayton, Ohio, killed himself rather than be returned to Kentucky, a white resident compared the black man to Patrick Henry. In 1845, Chicago abolitionist Zebina Eastman declared that nothing in the "anti-slavery controversy" attracted more attention "than escapes, attempted and successful, of slaves from the southern States."[34]

Except for Quakers, who constituted an important part of underground-railroad escape networks in the North-South borderlands, few abolitionists by the late 1830s objected to escaping slaves' using force.[35] Abolitionists often celebrated the manhood of black men who fought on behalf of themselves and their loved ones. No one gained greater notoriety than Congressman Giddings for his advocacy of black men killing their would-be captors. In 1846 on the floor of the House of Representatives, Giddings, who was then a Whig, endorsed providing weapons to fugitive slaves. Two years later, he contended slaves had a right to free themselves by any means that God placed in their hands. The *Congressional Globe* reported Giddings declaring, "If a slave killed his master in a struggle to prevent his arrest in Ohio, he would be justified in the eye of the law, and he (Mr. G.) would call him a good fellow." Giddings was not alone. The *Pittsburgh Gazette* represented many in the Lower North when it responded to the passage of the Fugitive Slave Law of 1850 by advising black men in the region "to arm themselves and fight for freedom, if need be, but not to run away."[36]

SOPHISTICATED NATIONAL DEBATE over slavery, its territorial expansion, or the relative political power of each section in the U.S. government were not the fundamental causes of conflict in the North-South borderlands. Neither was abolitionist propaganda nor formal white southern defenses of the "peculiar institution." Instead, the physical proximity of the Lower North and Border South, combined with the regions' divergent economies, cultures, moralities, and—especially—their opposing views of slavery, led to physical clashes and expectations they would spread. Improved transportation, weak state authority, a law enforcement system dependent on private initiative, and a code of masculine honor encouraged the clashes.

Whittier, writing in the *Pennsylvania Freeman*, recognized the impact of location on experience and attitude. Pennsylvanians' "sympathies," he observed in 1839, "are constantly appealed to by the hunted fugitive, flying from the grasp of the slave-trader. They see the frightful atrocities of slavery written in the whip-scarred backs of these wretched men and women. They see the kidnapper pursuing. . . . They cannot look upon it as mere abstraction." In 1841 a similar proximity to a slave state led a Cincinnati "gentleman" to declare that Kentucky and Ohio "must . . . be constantly exposed to sudden and violent interruptions," because human nature required the rescue of slaves "from southern bondage."[37]

Arguing on behalf of the view that a political party breakdown rather than fundamental differences between the North and South caused the Civil War, historian Michael F. Holt contends that prior to 1861 slavery-related sectional differences "had existed for decades without causing a shooting war."[38] Regarding government-directed military campaigns involving the mobilization of armies much larger than those that fought in Kansas Territory beginning in 1855, Holt is correct. But regarding groups of armed men shooting at each other, he is not. For over seventy years prior to the outbreak of the Civil War, Americans—northern and southern, black and white— fought and sometimes killed each other over slavery. When state efforts to quell the violence failed, Congress passed the Fugitive Slave Law of 1850 as part of an effort to avoid civil war. But nothing could stop slaves from escaping, slaveholders from pursuing them, and black and white residents of the Lower North from helping the escapees.

# ONE

## Early Clashes

On Sunday morning, September 17, 1826, Edward Stone of Paris, Bourbon County, Kentucky, and three other slave traders steered their flatboat southwest on the Ohio River. They had a cargo of seventy-five or seventy-six slaves—"males and females, and of various ages"—destined for sale in Mississippi or Louisiana. Having purchased the slaves in Maryland and Kentucky, Stone and his associates anticipated profits on reaching their destination in the Old Southwest. Instead, 100 miles down river from Louisville, twelve of their human cargo attacked them and a white passenger, killed all five, and used weights to sink their bodies in the river.

The slaves then piloted the boat to the river's northern bank, split into two groups, and headed north. The larger group, numbering fifty-six, had "marched" five or six miles into Indiana when, near the town of Rome, its leaders asked directions from a white man. After the fugitives passed on, the man organized a posse that captured all of them "after an obstinate fight on the part of one or two." Within a few days, the posse apprehended most of the smaller group and took all of the captives to Hardinsburg, Kentucky, where local authorities confined them in Breckinridge County Jail. On November 20, a jury found five of the slaves guilty of murder and a judge sentenced them to be hanged. The jury "cleared" seven of the slaves whom newspapers claimed were "strongly suspected of being guilty." According to local tradition, those seven and about thirty-eight others resumed their melancholy southward journey. About twenty-four others returned, at least temporarily, to Paris.[1]

Inhabitants of Kentucky and Indiana knew the slaves who rose up against Stone and his companions were not the first to seek freedom through violence. There had been eighteenth-century slave revolts, black men had fought for freedom on the British side during the War for Independence, and in 1800 Gabriel's failed revolt conspiracy near Richmond, Virginia, put masters on guard. Gabriel, a literate, enslaved blacksmith cognizant of revolutionary events in the Atlantic world, had hoped to end slavery in central Virginia. Over a dozen years later, during the War of 1812, black men again fought on the British side. But, on a river that served as a sectional boundary, the slaves on Stone's boat killed more white Americans during peacetime than had any other black group since slaves in New York City killed nine in 1712. The casualties on the Ohio River increased in 1829, when near Greenupsburg, Kentucky, far to the east of the earlier uprising, four slaves killed their master while he transported them downriver. Observers at the men's execution reported, "They died with astonishing firmness." One of them yelled from the gallows, "Death—death at anytime, in preference to slavery."[2]

As these Ohio River uprisings suggest, enslaved African Americans recognized the significance of the boundary formed by the river in the region west of the Appalachian Mountains. Earlier they had similarly become aware of the importance of the Mason-Dixon line. Some black men, and lesser numbers of black women, fought and killed to cross these boundaries. They hoped to avoid sale south, leave masters and traders behind, and enjoy the limited degree of freedom available to them in the North. But they did not know the land into which they escaped and required help to avoid recapture. The people from Edward Stone's boat failed to find such help and those at Greenupsburg never got a chance to seek it. Others did, and by the mid-1810s significant numbers had reached Canada.[3] The disputed legality of the aid they received, its sometimes-violent character, and charges that government officials in the Lower North tolerated it had important consequences. The aid, along with the fugitives themselves, was at the center of a conflict that began along the North-South border during the 1780s and ended during the Civil War.

During the first four decades of this conflict, conditions and law determined that clashes over slavery occurred almost invariably in the Lower North. Masters and their northern henchmen usually fought to recover fugitive slaves. In other cases, masters struggled to keep slaves they brought north. And kidnappers ripped free African Americans from their northern homes to take them south into slavery. During the early 1820s, some southern settlers in Indiana and Illinois attempted to legalize slavery in these new states—with violent results in the latter. Almost everywhere, antislavery forces acted on their own ground.

STARTING WITH PENNSYLVANIA in 1780, state action mandated the gradual or immediate abolition of slavery in the Northeast. But the ordinance passed by Congress in 1787 to organize the Northwest Territory provided less assurance regarding slavery's fate in that large region. Although the ordinance banned the introduction of additional slaves, it allowed the few residents who owned human beings to keep them. Those who arrived later could hold black people in virtual slavery as indentured servants. In addition, the ordinance did not deny states created from the territory the power to legalize slavery and therefore did not guarantee the Ohio River would become a sectional boundary. In some cases, masters in Kentucky and Missouri rented slaves to farmers in Ohio, Indiana, and Illinois. As late as 1819, a slave trader had his headquarters in southern Illinois, across the Mississippi River from St. Louis.[4]

In 1802, the Ohio constitutional convention rejected in committee a proposal to permit slavery, ending the slight chance that Ohio would become a slave state. Two decades later in Indiana and Illinois, more determined efforts to legalize slavery organized. Indiana in 1816 and Illinois in 1818 had adopted constitutions allowing only limited amounts of forced labor. By 1820, there were only 190 slaves in Indiana out of a total population of 147,178. In Illinois there were only 1,107 out of 55,211. Yet proslavery forces in each state demanded a convention to write a new constitution that would legalize human bondage. In August 1823, an Indiana referendum peacefully and decisively rejected holding such a convention by a vote of 11,991 to 2,601. In contrast, Illinois, which after mid-1821 had the slave state of Missouri on its western border, engaged in a violent struggle, during which proslavery rioters, shouting "Convention or death," marched on the residence of antislavery governor Edward Coles. Thereafter, Conventionists fought anti-Conventionists in mortal combat. Proslavery forces harassed antislavery leaders and kidnapped African Americans. In December 1823 a proslavery mob burned the statehouse at Vandalia and fruit trees on Coles's farm at Edwardsville.[5]

In August 1824, Illinois voters rejected holding a constitutional convention by a vote of 6,822 to 4,950, narrow in comparison to the margin in Indiana.[6] The election ended the chance that Illinois would become a slave state. Proslavery and antiblack sentiment remained strong, however, in the southern portion of Illinois for the next four decades. The area became a battleground with slave catchers, kidnappers, and transient masters on one side and slavery's black and white opponents on the other.

Even so, the antislavery victory in Illinois completed the boundary between the free and slave states demarcated by the Mason-Dixon line, the Ohio River, and the Mississippi River. North and east of the boundary, three varieties of white opinion existed concerning slavery and black efforts to resist it. First, Quakers, members of antislavery societies, and many of those who employed fugitives opposed slavery and helped escapees. Second, considerably more residents disliked slavery and had some sympathy for black refugees. But, while they did not help slave catchers, they provided limited aid to fugitive slaves. They disparaged African American character, saw no place for free black people in American society, and did not want black neighbors. Such sentiments even affected Quaker abolitionist Benjamin Lundy. When Lundy warned Illinoisans in 1824 against legalizing slavery, he did so in part because he considered African Americans "degraded beings, almost as ignorant as the beasts of the field, but far more vicious and mischievous." Those representing the third variety of white opinion in the Lower North went further. They were like the man who encountered the slaves escaping from Stone's flatboat. They sympathized with slaveholders and helped apprehend fugitives, often in hope of collecting reward money.[7]

Less division of white opinion existed in the Border South. Many doubted the morality of the slave trade and held its practitioners in low regard. The Lexington, Kentucky, *Western Luminary*, which reported the deaths of Stone and his associates, observed that Stone had a bad reputation, stemming from his harsh "treatment of the poor negroes who have passed from his hands." The *Luminary* reminded its readers that men engaged in buying and selling slaves risked God's wrath. But white border southerners almost unanimously regarded slave escape and free African Americans as threats to their interests and safety. Very few sympathized with fugitive slaves. Fewer still aided them on their northward journeys.[8]

IF LEGISLATION and differing attitudes concerning slavery created the sectional border, common law and constitutional provisions facilitated proslavery intrusion beyond it. The common law, as historian Don Fehrenbacher points out, recognized a right of individuals "to recover property wrongfully taken [including slaves who *took* themselves] so long as the execution did not cause 'strife and bodily contention, or endanger the peace of society.'" From the start, legal experts assumed this "right of recaption [recapture] was . . . extrajurisdictional." Masters could cross state and sectional lines to reclaim their human property. They might recruit northern constables, sheriffs, and magistrates in fugitive slave renditions. But they could also recover slaves on their own.[9]

Pennsylvania's gradual abolition law recognized this "right of an out-of-state owner to recover a fugitive." The Northwest Ordinance combined its ban on the introduction of slaves into the territory north of the Ohio River with a proviso that slaves escaping to it "may be lawfully reclaimed and conveyed to the person claiming his or her labor." The fugitive slave clause of the U.S. Constitution, written the same year as the Northwest Ordinance, had a similar intent, although—unlike the Pennsylvania law and the ordinance—it limited state sovereignty. The clause provided that persons held to "service or labour," who escaped from states upholding slavery into those banning it, could not, "in consequence of any law or regulation therein, be discharged from such service or labour, but shall be delivered up on claim of the party to whom such service or labor may be due." Although the clause suggested that state authorities had to "deliver up" alleged fugitive slaves, it left the initiative to slaveholders. It assumed masters could cross state lines to "claim" escapees without help or interference from the local authorities.[10] No one anticipated federal legislation to enforce the clause. But a series of cross-border incursions between Pennsylvania and Virginia and southern charges of clandestine aid to escaping slaves led Congress in 1793 to pass its first fugitive slave law.

During the 1770s, John Davis's master brought him from Maryland to what the master believed was western Virginia. In 1779, commissioners representing Virginia and Pennsylvania agreed the region belonged to Pennsylvania, and it became that state's Westmoreland and Washington counties. When Pennsylvania's legislature adopted gradual abolition in March 1780, Davis's master missed a November deadline to register Davis as a slave he intended to keep. The master also missed an extended deadline of January 1783, and Davis became free under Pennsylvania law. Nevertheless, in early 1788 his master took him to Ohio County, Virginia, and hired him out to a neighbor. Shortly thereafter, white abolitionists affiliated with the Pennsylvania Abolition Society (PAS) traveled to Virginia, located Davis, and brought him back to Pennsylvania. In an early reference to what later became known as the underground railroad, officeholders in Virginia called those who engaged in such activities "the negro club." The "club," according to the Virginians, "seduced" slaves away from their owners and "concealed" them in Pennsylvania.[11]

In May 1788, three Virginia bounty hunters "violently" recaptured Davis and returned him to slavery. According to the PAS, the Virginians, "with force and arms and a strong hand, assaulted, seized, imprisoned, bound, and carried" Davis away. The bounty hunters claimed to be exercising the right of recaption recognized by Pennsylvania law and the U.S. Constitution. But if Davis was free, they had kidnapped him. They faced punishment under a Pennsylvania law passed two months earlier that prohibited "by force or violence [to] take and carry . . . or . . . by fraud seduce . . . any negro or mulatto . . . with a design and intention of selling and disposing, or of causing [her or him] to be [held] as a slave." In November a Washington County grand jury indicted the three Virginians under this law. When the men failed to surrender and the PAS demanded action, Pennsylvania governor Thomas Mifflin initiated extradition proceedings in May 1791 to bring them to trial and liberate Davis.[12]

The following July, after Governor Beverly Randolph of Virginia refused to extradite the men, Mifflin wrote to slaveholding president George Washington, urging federal action to facilitate delivery of fugitives *from justice*. As Washington referred the matter to Congress, some Virginia legislators defended the men, claiming the Pennsylvania government had permitted the "negro club" to commit "robberies . . . on the innocent citizens of Virginia." According to assemblymen from Ohio County, the "Negro Club" and the PAS consisted of "evil disposed persons" and "robbers acting under the sacred cloak of religion." The bounty hunters were, in contrast, upstanding citizens who had "rescue[d] the property of their fellow-citizen from these artificers of Hypocrisy and fraud." Other western-Virginia assemblymen claimed Pennsylvania abolitionists had either "forcibly seized" or "seduced" slaves from their constituents as they passed through Pennsylvania.[13]

Because rendition of fugitives from justice and fugitives from labor intertwined in the Davis case, between late 1791 and early 1793 Congress produced a statute dealing with both issues. It clarified the criminal extradition process and formalized the right of recaption by authorizing masters or agents to apprehend alleged fugitive slaves, take them before a federal judge, state judge, or local magistrate to present evidence of ownership. If the evidence satisfied a judge or magistrate, he could issue a certificate endorsing the return of the fugitive to the state from which he or she had fled. What became known as the Fugitive Slave Law of 1793 also provided that a master or agent could sue for up to $500 anyone who interfered with rendition. The law accorded persons accused of being fugitive slaves no right to testify in their defense, have a lawyer present, or have a jury trial. As the PAS complained, the law had insufficient safeguards against fraudulent affidavits and testimony.

But it did not deny states' power to guard against such abuses. Neither did it deny the power of states to pass laws against kidnapping.[14]

Most significant, the Fugitive Slave Law introduced national government intervention on behalf of slaveholders in what had been purely interstate disputes. It anticipated Border South efforts during the 1840s and 1850s to seek more active federal protection for slave property against escape and those in the Lower North who assisted it.[15] Yet, from 1793 to 1850, the U.S. government had a minor role in renditions. Clashes over slave escape during this long period occurred between private groups or states and private groups, not between U.S. civil servants or military officers and private groups.

The 1793 law failed to alleviate conflict over slavery in the Lower North. Many masters and agents continued to capture black men, women, and children without legal process. The law did not address the issues raised by kidnapping or when slaves were held by masters in transit. More important, so long as slaves escaped and found sympathetic northerners to help them, so long as masters brought slaves into the Lower North and pursued fugitives, so long as kidnappers preyed on free African Americans, no legislation could prevent legal, political, and violent clashes.[16]

FROM THE 1780s into the Civil War years, white southerners denounced aid in the Lower North to fugitive slaves and the separation of transient slaves from their masters. They regarded as outrageous that some northern state and local officials condoned such practices. In 1827 a Louisiana master charged, "The experience of a number of years has convinced them [white southerners] that the non slave holding states which are contiguous to the slave states abound with swarms of self styled philanthropists . . . [who] think themselves justified in the use of every possible means by which they can rob a southern master of a slave."[17]

Maryland and Pennsylvania became antagonistic as abolitionists affiliated with the PAS persisted, despite the 1793 law, in helping slaves get away from their masters. In November 1796, William Handy complained to Maryland's House of Delegates that during a visit to Pennsylvania, "the abolition society, in conjunction with the civil officers . . . [deprived] him of his negroes, and arrested his person." At a time when many Marylanders expected slavery to recede from their state, the House of Delegates declined to enter this case. It suggested instead that Handy seek federal assistance. But, as the number of cases mounted, the delegates in December 1798 declared Maryland slaveholders "were subjected to great loss and inconvenience for the escape of slaves to Delaware, Pennsylvania, and New Jersey, where they remained concealed and protected by the whites." Initiating what became a major but ultimately unsuccessful form of proslavery interstate diplomacy (see chapter 4), the House of Delegates asked that the governor of Maryland negotiate with his counterparts in these states "to stop such abuses."[18]

Of the three states, Pennsylvania aroused the greatest anger. During late 1815, residents of Maryland's western border counties—Allegheny and Washington—and St. Mary's County on the Potomac River called for action to prevent escapes across the Mason-Dixon line. Subsequently, Maryland's House of Delegates, the lower house of the state assembly, called on Pennsylvania to "prevent the employment or harboring of runaway negroes" and "facilitate the regaining [of] them by their real owners." In early 1816, this resolution failed in the Maryland Senate. But in January 1818, the assembly ordered Governor Charles Ridgely to send a similar resolution to the governors of Pennsylvania and Delaware. In his letter to Governor William Findley of Pennsylvania, Ridgely added, "The mischief[s] complained of in the resolution, although in contravention of your laws are . . . often practised, and so justly complained of by the people of Maryland."[19]

Thereafter, Maryland slaveholders contended they suffered "great imposition and serious inconvenience from the constant and ready protection afforded their runaway negroes by the citizens of Pennsylvania." In 1820 the Maryland Assembly declared, "Whenever a runaway slave is pursued and found in Pennsylvania, every possible difficulty is thrown in the way, so as to prevent the recovery of such slave; there are persons always ready to lend every practicable aid in thwarting the just and legal efforts of the owner. . . . If . . . legal proceedings fail [to help the fugitive], force is not unfrequently resorted to."[20]

A year later, a Baltimore County member of the assembly complained that when he exercised "the provisions of the act of Congress for the capture of fugitive slaves," residents of York County, in southeastern Pennsylvania, aided the fugitives and threatened him with "personal violence." He gave up attempting to recover his slaves, he reported, when "civil authorities" threatened to imprison him and try him "under a State law against kidnapping." Other masters more successfully engaged the Pennsylvania legal system to recover escaped slaves. But this case convinced many Marylanders that "sundry citizens" of Pennsylvania and some in Delaware aided fugitive slaves *and* that such aid had increased to an "alarming . . . degree." In 1836 a Pennsylvania jurist confirmed this point of view. During the first two decades of the nineteenth century, the jurist maintained, the right of recaption in his state "was often attended with hazard . . . disputes, violence, bloodshed, and rescues often ensued."[21]

As Marylanders accused Pennsylvanians, Virginians took preventive action. In 1798 the Virginia Assembly restricted black travel on river and seagoing vessels. Following Gabriel's conspiracy in 1800, it bolstered militia and slave patrols. In 1805, Virginia increased penalties for aiding slave escape and in 1817 provided bounties for fugitive slaves captured "north of the Potomac." Yet in 1822, Congressman Thomas L. Moore of Fauquier County claimed his district "sustained an annual loss of four or five thousand dollars by runaway slaves." Moore charged that the federal Fugitive Slave Act of 1793 "was inadequate to the object it proposed to effect," which encouraged his state to continue to strengthen its preventive laws.[22]

RECORDS OF PHYSICAL CONFLICT arising from slave escapes from western Virginia and Kentucky into Ohio or from Kentucky into Indiana and Illinois do not date as far back as those for more easterly regions. Frontier conditions discouraged escapes across the Ohio River into the Old Northwest. American Indians, who prior to 1795 controlled most of what became Ohio, Indiana, and Illinois, sometimes welcomed fugitives who reached their villages. But reaching them was difficult and involuntary servitude existed on the north shore of the Ohio River into the early 1800s.[23]

Yet flight from western Virginia and Kentucky became an issue immediately after Ohio joined the Union in 1803. As historian Stephen Middleton points out, one of the reasons the Ohio Assembly passed the "Black Laws" of 1804, which limited African American citizenship rights, was to pacify slaveholders. The assembly hoped to discourage northward black migration so that conflict between those in Ohio who sheltered fugitive slaves and those who sought to recapture them would not damage "commercial relations with southern states." A potentially deadly confrontation at a Dayton tavern on January 30, 1806, suggested what could happen as long as black migration continued. Ned and Lucy Page, who were at the center of the clash, were not fugitive slaves. Rather they were free under Ohio law because their master had brought them illegally from Kentucky. When two armed men from Lexington entered the tavern seeking to capture the black couple and Ned Page waved a pistol in self-defense, two-dozen local white men supported him. They arrested the Kentuckians and charged them with breach of peace.[24]

The following year, as masters in Virginia and Kentucky complained about slave escape and threatened action, the Ohio Assembly amended the Black Laws to make northward migration even more difficult for African Americans and recapture easier. Speaker of the state house of representatives, Philemon Beecher, used the threat of border conflict to justify the legislation. He warned, "The owners of these persons will [otherwise] take measures to reclaim them, and by the event may involve our frontiers and perhaps the nation, in troubles which prudent measures in proper season may prevent."[25]

The futility of Beecher's legislation became evident three years later. In February 1810, slave catcher Jacob Beeson arrived in Marietta seeking Jane, a slave from Wellsburg, Virginia. Jane, condemned to death for theft, had escaped jail and fled across the Ohio River to Marietta where she found employment as a domestic servant in the home of a prominent family. When the family and others in Marietta prevented Beeson from capturing Jane, he complained to Ohio governor Samuel H. Huntington. Beeson told the governor, "It is with great concern that the people of Virginia (who reside on its western extremity) look forward to the evils that will grow out of this course of conduct pursued by the people of your State residing on or near the Ohio [River]. The idea of emancipation is propagated, and . . . will fire the breast of every slave no one will doubt."[26]

More sectional friction occurred as a result of Indiana's insistence, beginning in 1816, that masters and slave catchers must follow legal procedures. Despite harboring racial prejudice at least as ingrained as in southern Ohio, Indiana's legislature, hoping to discourage kidnapping, mandated jury trials for persons claimed as fugitive slaves. Two years later, Kentucky's assembly instructed Governor Gabriel Slaughter to contact Indiana governor Jonathan Jennings "concerning the difficulty said to be experienced by our citizens in reclaiming their slaves, who escaped into your state." In a manner similar to that of Virginia and Maryland governors who had complained about Pennsylvania's procedures, Slaughter accused Indiana magistrates of "prejudice against slavery."

Indiana's response to Slaughter had more in common with Pennsylvania's response to Virginia than Ohio's to Virginia and Kentucky. A legislative committee claimed two types of Kentuckians criticized the state's rendition process. Some, the committee maintained, had been disappointed in attempts "to carry away those whom they claimed as slaves," because they had not followed "the preliminary steps required by law." Others were "unprincipled individuals [kidnappers] who have attempted . . . to seize and carry away people of color, who were free and as such entitled to the protection of the laws as any citizen of Indiana."[27]

Back in 1792, Governor Thomas Mifflin of Pennsylvania made a similar point regarding John Davis. Since the Pennsylvania General Assembly had "benevolently" passed a law by which Davis "obtained his freedom," Mifflin argued, "it is surely incumbent on the power that bestowed the blessing, to protect him in the enjoyment of it."[28] Despite racism in the Lower North, despite its physical proximity to the Border South and cultural overlap between the two regions, the degree to which the Mason-Dixon line, by the 1790s, and the Ohio River, by the 1810s, had become boundaries in racial thinking is striking.

WHEN ORGANIZED AID TO fugitive slaves began in Ohio, Indiana, and Illinois is unclear. Prior to the 1820s, there is no direct evidence in these states for the operation of groups like the PAS or "Negro Club." Historians, however, have concluded aid began during the mid-1810s. In his *History of the Rise and Fall of the Slave Power*, published during the 1870s, former U.S. vice president Henry Wilson claimed residents of Ohio's Western Reserve helped fugitive slaves "as early as 1815." Four decades later, Edward Channing contended that during "the fifteen years prior to 1830" white settlers in Ohio and Indiana "welcomed fugitives from across the Ohio River and passed them along on their journey toward Canada." More recently, Keith P. Griffler wrote, "The Cincinnati press began to take note of [free] African Americans' involvement in the runaways' cause as early as 1815."[29]

It seems likely that small black communities north of the Ohio River led in early physical aid to fugitive slaves. In 1846, Joshua R. Giddings recalled an incident in May 1810, when he was fifteen. It involved a Kentucky master and several associates who attempted to recover a slave family in Giddings's hometown of Jefferson, located in northeastern Ohio. Aided by a local white informer and armed with bowie knives and pistols, the slave catchers located the family, captured it, and headed south. Within a few miles of the village, according to Giddings, "some fifteen or twenty colored men" armed "with guns, pistols, and other weapons" overtook the Kentuckians and their captives. Surrounded throughout the night, the Kentuckians agreed to a local white attorney's suggestion that they present their claim to a magistrate. When they did, the official summarily rejected it and charged them with assault. They had to post bond before returning home. Five years later, Canada began encouraging former slaves to settle on its southern border. In January 1821, William Brown of Harrison County, Kentucky, presented a memorial from his state assembly to Congress. It called on the U.S. state department to negotiate for the return of the "many negroes and persons of color" who had settled in that British colony.[30]

During the 1820s, aid in the Old Northwest to fugitive slaves and resistance to slave catchers became more common. In 1822, when John Rankin, a white, Presbyterian minister from Tennessee, settled in the Ohio town of Ripley, located on the north shore of the Ohio River, he observed some residents helping fugitive slaves. By 1829, Rankin and his family's engagement in these activities, and slave catchers' threats against their lives, led him to move out of town to a protected hilltop location. Levi Coffin, a North Carolina Quaker, who settled the west-central Indiana town of Newport in 1826, had a similar experience. He later claimed that within a year of his arrival he joined free black families to help fugitive slaves and encouraged other Quakers to join in. As a result, Coffin recalled, "Slave-hunters. . . . often threatened to kill me, and at various times offered a reward for my head." At one point, he received "letters warning [him] that [his] store, pork-house, and dwelling would be burned to the ground." Quaker Coffin did not personally resist his enemies. Instead he relied on neighbors to protect him and arrest anyone who attacked him.[31]

AFRICAN AMERICANS had to be especially well prepared to deal with attacks. They could expect varying degrees of support from white people but had to be ready to protect themselves. This was the case for fugitive slave John Read on the evening of December 14, 1820, when Samuel G. Griffith and Peter Shipley of Baltimore broke into Read's home at Kennett Township, in southeastern Pennsylvania. Griffith, who claimed Read as his slave, and Shipley, who was an overseer, carried between them three pistols, a whip, handcuffs, and rope. As the pair forced open his door, Read yelled, "It is life for life!" Within seconds, he shot Griffith to death and used a club to wound Shipley mortally. Because it was unclear whether or not a fugitive slave had a right to defend himself in his home against individuals seeking to return him to slavery, Read faced two charges of murder. But he had enough white support to avoid the death penalty. The jury in the Griffith case acquitted him. In the Shipley case, he was convicted on a lesser charge of manslaughter and received a sentence of nine years. Neither verdict satisfied Maryland authorities.[32]

Not long after the deadly encounter at Read's house, a larger confrontation at New Albany, Indiana, demonstrated a more pronounced determination among white border northerners to protect an African American threatened with return to slavery. In 1820 a white Kentuckian named Case had brought a black man named Moses to New Albany—located across the Ohio River from Louisville, Kentucky—to free him. A year later, after

Moses had gained a good reputation in the town, Kentuckians who had monetary claims against Case sent an agent to seize the black man. When local authorities required the agent to appear with Moses in court, the agent brought "forty-three ably bodied men" from Kentucky with him, ostensibly as witnesses. The county sheriff reacted by assembling twenty militiamen. As the judge declared Moses free, the Kentuckians seized him. Bystanders then attacked the Kentuckians. When the judge called for order, a Kentuckian knocked him down and the militia charged with fixed bayonets. They "badly" wounded several of the Kentuckians, forcing them to release Moses and retreat south of the river.[33]

Four years later, fighting between white residents of Meigs County, Ohio, and Mason County, Kentucky, demonstrated how slave escape could produce more extended and dangerous cross-border clashes. The origin of the conflict lay in slaves hiring men to guide them north. Similar to modern "coyotes" operating on the U.S.-Mexico boundary, the guides took advantage of borderlands conditions to make a dangerous living. During the summer of 1824, Hamilton Carr, a white Kentuckian acting as the agent of eight enslaved black men, employed John Adams Smith, a young white man who lived on the north shore of the Ohio River, to guide the men from western Virginia to Columbus, Ohio. That October, after Smith had successfully carried out his mission, four white Virginians crossed the river into Ohio, arrested him without a warrant, took him to Virginia, and jailed him at Point Pleasant.

Within six weeks, a half-dozen white Ohioans, with their faces "blackened" and "armed with hunting rifles and pistols," went to Point Pleasant. They threatened the men who guarded the jail, broke down Smith's cell door with an axe, and released him. As the Ohioans ran off, the guards opened fire, wounding one. In August 1825, Governor Jeremiah Morrow of Ohio, acting on a requisition from Governor James Pleasants of Virginia, issued warrants that led to the arrest of three of the Ohioans and their imprisonment in the Point Pleasant jail. Two months later, Virginia authorities—seeking to avoid continued and perhaps escalating conflict—arranged for the acquittal of two of the men and a fine of thirty dollars for the third.[34]

KIDNAPPING OF free African Americans differed from slave renditions, although the distinction between the two depended on point of view and circumstances. What in John Davis's case appeared to Pennsylvanians to be a kidnapping, seemed to white Virginians to be recovery of property. A master seeking to recapture a fugitive slave could face kidnapping charges, and rendition could degenerate into attempted kidnapping. In addition, kidnapping was not entirely an intersectional crime; free black people who lived in the Border South faced abduction. Nevertheless, many in the Lower North regarded as especially egregious aggressive efforts to take indisputably free African Americans from their region for the purpose of enslaving them.[35]

Like slave escape, kidnapping began as a sectionally divisive phenomenon during the 1780s. In 1789, J. P. Brissot de Warville reported to the French Société des Amis des Noirs that gradual emancipation and the abolition of the slave trade in Pennsylvania led local slave traders to kidnap free African Americans and ship them to the West Indies. A decade later, as the destination of kidnap victims shifted to the Lower South, the Reverend Absolom Jones and seventy-three other black Philadelphians charged that the victims were "fettered and hurried into places provided for this most horrid traffic, such as dark cellars and garrets." In 1801 the American Convention of Abolition Societies declared, "The inhuman crime of kidnapping . . . has increased to an alarming degree."[36]

The crime became even more common after 1808, when Congress abolished the external slave trade. The incidence of kidnapping increased again during the late 1820s as demand for labor in the cotton-growing states mounted. Abductions of this sort were especially common in Pennsylvania. In 1817, kidnappers based in Maryland burst into a free black woman's Philadelphia home, beat her husband, threatened to harm anyone who interfered, and seized her and her sons. More often, kidnappers employed subterfuge to entice victims—especially boys—onto schooners, packet-boats, and sloops bound from Philadelphia for Baltimore. According to the PAS, kidnappers maintained "a regular chain of communication and barter from Philadelphia to the Eastern shore of the Chesapeake." In early 1826, Baltimore's *Niles Register* declared, "This most abominable trade . . . has been much revived of late," adding that its chief victims were children. The *Genius of Universal Emancipation*, *Freedom's Journal*, and the *African Observer* reported similarly. Looking back from 1899, W. E. B. Du Bois concluded that Philadelphia became "the natural gateway" through which passed "a stream of . . . kidnapped colored persons toward the South."[37]

FROM ITS BEGINNING in 1775, the PAS worked for the "relief of free negroes held illegally in bondage." During the late 1780s, the society established— in historian Carol Wilson's words—"satellite organizations" in Delaware, Maryland, and the District of Columbia to assist in tracking kidnapping victims and their abductors. Members of these organizations served as a fifth

Four white men forcefully kidnap a free black woman and her child from their home in 1817. Woodcut from Jesse Torrey Jr., *American Slave Trade* (London: J. M. Cobbett, 1822).

column south of the Mason-Dixon line. Slaveholders regarded them as foreign agents, the mirror image of kidnappers and slave catchers in the Lower North. During the first three decades of the nineteenth century, two Quakers—Isaac Hopper of Philadelphia and Elisha Tyson of Baltimore—were the most prominent PAS agents in the borderlands. In some cases, they brought abductors to justice and rescued their victims.[38]

Hopper and Tyson's religious views prevented them from initiating violent action. Instead, in a manner similar to that used by Levi Coffin to protect himself in Indiana, they relied on civil authorities to arrest and punish kidnappers. The two men were nevertheless courageous. In 1802, when a slave trader produced a pistol and vowed to shoot him, Hopper responded, "I only prevent Southern marauders from robbing people of their liberty." A decade later, Tyson went alone to a Baltimore tavern where five traders held six free African Americans pending sale south. As one of the traders threatened him, Tyson declared, "Shoot if thee dare . . . but thee knows, that the gallows would be thy portion." In another instance, prominent Baltimore slave trader Austin Woolfolk claimed he would send Tyson "to hell for interfering with his *property*," whereupon Tyson "coolly exposed his breast, telling him [Woolfolk] that he dare not shoot."[39]

Between 1815 and 1829, the PAS had to deal with the Cannon-Johnson gang of kidnappers and murderers. Patty Cannon, her husband Jesse Cannon, and their son-in-law Joe Johnson headed the gang. They lived on the border between Maryland Eastern Shore and Delaware, using access to intercoastal waters to pray on young black Philadelphians. Although gang members carried weapons, they, like earlier maritime kidnappers, used deception rather than force to lure their victims onto vessels in the Delaware River. A black man named John Purnell was especially effective in enticing young men and boys onboard. In response, the PAS and local officials created a network of informers and a variety of nonviolent strategies to rescue the victims. In the best-documented incident, which took place in August 1825, several gang members, including a white woman and a black man, kidnapped five boys and a "half-blind" young woman and sold them in Louisiana. In an extraordinary combined effort, Philadelphia's mayor, the city constable, and local black leaders recovered most of the boys, although one died shortly after his return. Louisiana magistrates and some masters cooperated with the recovery, but Chesapeake juries refused to convict the gang members. Murder charges filed in Delaware in 1829 finally broke up the Cannon-Johnson gang, not legal or extralegal tactics originating in Pennsylvania.[40]

The PAS and similar organizations concentrated most of their energies on vigilance, court action, and petitioning state and federal governments for stronger antikidnapping laws. This left African Americans to undertake most of the forceful resistance to kidnappers. Philadelphia's Free African Society, formed in 1787, had a central role. But so did informal groups of neighbors. By 1804, a growing black community and a series of abductions in Columbia, Lancaster County, made this southeastern Pennsylvania town a center of resistance. In one instance, a group of African Americans caught a kidnapper, "stripped him of his clothing and whipped him soundly with hickory-withes."[41]

As kidnapping spread to the Old Northwest, it became more open and violent. In 1818 at Corydon in southern Indiana—not far from where the Ohio River uprising took place eight years later—three armed white men from Kentucky "knocked down a negro woman in the street," threatened "death to any person that should interfere," and "carried her off." When it published the story, the Niles Register predicted, "Such infractions of the law . . . if not checked, will produce very unpleasant collisions among our western brethren." Many in the Old Northwest agreed. Indiana had passed an antikidnapping law in 1817, and Ohio adopted a similar one in 1819. Following the Corydon incident, an Indiana legislative committee declared the state had a duty "to defend [African Americans] against the grasp of miscreants, who have, in repeated instances, attempted to carry them away from our shores into perpetual slavery." A year later, Indiana strengthened its law against kidnapping by mandating public whipping as punishment for "man-stealing."[42]

DESPITE EARLY PHYSICAL, judicial, and legislative resistance to rendition and kidnapping, most residents of New Jersey, Pennsylvania, and the Old Northwest remained, into the 1840s, rhetorically and legally conciliatory toward slaveholding interests. There were in the Lower North many pro-slavery legislators, judges, magistrates, and constables. Even slavery's stronger opponents in the region, and elsewhere in the North, were publicly cautious. In 1820 an abolitionist journal published in southwestern Ohio asserted that, while it was immoral for newspapers to publish "runaway" advertisements, they should not encourage "negroes to run away from their masters." With notable exceptions, this remained the dominant abolitionist position through the 1830s. They rejected contact with slaves, illegal tactics to help escape, and antislavery violence.[43]

But, as the borderlands environment often prevented effective enforcement of laws designed to protect black residents, more white people became concerned. As early as 1821, William Foster of Vincennes, Indiana, declared, "We hear many sad stories of kidnapping. I wish some active benevolent people could induce every person of color to remove away from the river, as it gives wicked, unprincipled wretches the opportunity to get them into a boat and carry them off to [New] Orleans or Missouri." Four years later, four men from Lexington, Kentucky, outraged many in Cincinnati when, "with arms and bludgeons in their hands," they waylaid free black man John Lewis on a Cincinnati street "and carried him away with impunity, to the land of slavery." The *Cincinnati Advertiser* called for state "interposition and punishment" of "banditti from Kentucky" who had violated "the protection which the constitution holds out to individuals."[44]

The *Advertiser* reflected distrust in the Lower North of the Border South, when it observed in regard to the Lewis case, "Every freeman, who values liberty must feel himself degraded and sunk by the conduct of these man stealers." Luckily for Lewis—who had lived in or near Cincinnati for thirty years—two white clergymen from the city visited Kentucky not long after he had been abducted. They recognized Lewis as his mounted captors led him on foot through a village with a rope around his neck, his hands cuffed, and his arms bound. The clergymen hired an attorney, arranged for witnesses from Cincinnati to come to Kentucky, and secured Lewis's freedom, $100 in compensation, and safe return.[45]

During the mid-1820s, after thirty years of cross-border conflict, the sectional struggle over slave escape, renditions, and kidnapping remained in its infancy. As yet, the relatively primitive state of American journalism, moderation among abolitionists, and intersectional commercial interests limited the struggles' political impact. Although southerners complained early on of interference, during this period they were more likely than northerners to cross the sectional border on missions related to slavery. Consequently, the great majority of clashes occurred in the Lower North. Masters believed they had the law on their side and had not become as defensive as they would during the following decades. Nevertheless, antislavery forces won a great, if predictable, victory in making Illinois a free state. The determination of African Americans, slave and free, to fight to achieve or defend their freedom and the willingness of white border northerners to provide assistance were equally important in shaping the border struggle.

# TWO

## Fear and Reaction in the Border South

In 1842 the *Louisville Journal* published an article entitled "Abolitionists Beware—Atrocious Outrage." Graphically and chillingly, it described how some white border southerners reacted to a supposed northern menace. As the steamboat *Corsair* moved "up the Ohio" before dawn on a Saturday in May, someone on board saw a small sailboat heading from Illinois toward Kentucky. Because "there had recently been a number of slaves stolen from Kentucky by the Abolitionists of Illinois," the steamboat's captain "hailed" the sailboat, ordering its single occupant to "'heave to.'" When the "mysterious gentleman" refused to obey, some crew and passengers brought out "guns, pistols, and other deadly weapons." They fired "several shots . . . apparently without effect," as what appeared to be a black man kept the sailboat on course.

The captain, hoping to capture the man, ordered the steamboat's "yawl to be manned; and the crew having armed themselves sufficiently, set out in full pursuit." As if to accentuate danger through exaggeration, the article described the black man as "a powerful athletic personage, weighing at least three hundred pounds." When the yawl overtook the sailboat and crew members thrust a "noose" over the man's head, he resisted and "nearly overpowered" them. Once onboard the steamboat, he disengaged himself and sprang to its boiler deck, frightening passengers who had gathered there to watch the spectacle. Within seconds, a crewman, who approached the black man from behind, struck him "with an axe on the back of the head with such force as to cause instant death."

Then "enraged" crew and passengers hung up the black "villain" and "skinned and quartered him as they would have done an ox." Suggesting that the black man, rather than his white antagonists, had committed an "atrocious outrage," the article concluded that he was the son of a man from Illinois who had "been committing depredations in that vicinity for some time."[1]

Well before this gruesome event, white residents of the border slave states had become more defensive than they had been during the 1820s. Many of them expressed fear, hatred, and contempt for abolitionists, black northerners, northern politicians, and northern law enforcement officials. They charged that free black troublemakers and northern interlopers *seduced* their content and loyal bondpeople into revolt or escape. Slavery was resilient in the Border South. But the masters' fears were not groundless. Slaves escaped from the region, northerners aided them, and they had weapons to defend themselves against recapture. As white border southerners perceived themselves to be under attack, they organized in self-defense and engaged in sectionally divisive actions.

SINCE THE early eighteenth century, white southerners regarded slave unrest to be the greatest threat to social order and safety. When, during the 1790s, the Haitian Revolution developed into a race war won by slaves, fear of a similar uprising in the American South spread. This was especially true of the Chesapeake where a large free black population sympathized with its enslaved brethren, had ties to Haiti, and access to revolutionary currents of thought in the Atlantic World. After the revelation in 1800 of Gabriel's revolt conspiracy, the Virginia, Delaware, and Maryland legislatures passed laws designed to control free African Americans as well as slaves. When Kentucky and Missouri became states, they adopted similar measures.

Some of this legislation sought merely to bar free African Americans from social, economic, and political participation. Other laws aimed to prevent slave escape, conspiracy, and rebellion, as well as more mundane black market and criminal activity. There were laws *against* slave meetings and *for* the formation of semimilitary organizations, such as slave patrols, sheriff's posses, urban police, and vigilante associations that could be mustered to meet domestic and external threats. Nat Turner's 1831 revolt in Southampton County, Virginia, and the rise of the northern movement for immediate emancipation heightened anxiety among white southerners. Many in the Border South held abolitionists responsible for the "excitement" among African Americans that preceded Turner's uprising.[2] Combined with fear of slave revolt and intrusive northern abolitionists, escapes—which at times resembled revolts—encouraged the assumption that the Border South faced great danger.

# HORRID MASSACRE IN VIRGINIA·

The Scenes which the above Plate is designed to represent, are—Fig. 1. a Mother intreating for the lives of her children.—2. Mr. Travis, cruelly murdered by his own Slaves.—3. Mr. Barrow, who bravely defended himself until his wife escaped.—4. A comp. of mounted Dragoons in pursuit of the Blacks.

"Horrid Massacre in Virginia" illustrates scenes from Nat Turner's 1831 slave revolt in Southampton County, Virginia. Figure 1 shows "a Mother entreating for the lives of her children." Figure 2 shows slaves killing their master. Figure 3 shows a master "bravely" defending himself. Figure 4 shows "mounted Dragoons in pursuit of the Blacks." From *Authentic and Impartial Narrative of the Tragical Scene which was Witnessed in Southampton* [1831], Library of Congress.

Masters and other white border southerners linked instances of physical intervention with a more comprehensive abolitionist campaign, including petitions for the abolition of slavery in the District of Columbia, criticism of the interstate slave trade, and distribution in the South of antislavery propaganda. Starting shortly after 1800, peaking in 1835, and continuing at a high level thereafter, northern abolitionist organizations sent antislavery publications into the South—especially the Border South.

By 1804, PAS agents "carefully" distributed antislavery addresses to white and free black people in the Chesapeake. During the late 1820s, *Freedom's Journal*—the first African American newspaper—circulated in Maryland and Virginia. In 1831, William Lloyd Garrison's *Liberator* reached black audiences in Baltimore and Washington. Southern hysteria occasioned by Turner's revolt prompted an abolitionist pledge to deal only with masters. Nevertheless, in 1835 the American Anti-Slavery Society (AASS), headquartered in New York City, launched its Great Postal Campaign. The 175,000 pieces of antislavery propaganda the AASS sent south that year reinforced an image of fanatical abolitionists taking aggressive action against the South. That summer, southern journalists and politicians raised a tremendous outcry against abolitionists and their *emissaries*. They called on northern state governments to suppress antislavery sentiment, offered rewards for the capture of abolitionist leaders, demanded disunion or a boycott of northern products, and endorsed vigilante action against what they portrayed as threat to their safety.[3]

In the Lower South, where few abolitionists ventured, suspicions spread among white residents that antislavery emissaries and free African Americans plotted servile insurrection and race war. Postmasters confiscated and burned antislavery literature, and mobs beat, humiliated, and executed suspects who were almost always innocent. Slavery's defenders in the Border South acted with greater restraint, even though they had more reason to fear abolitionist agents. They fought not only against rumors and innocent outsiders but real northern abolitionists, escaping slaves, those who helped fugitives, and a few white natives who challenged the slave-labor system.[4]

Negative southern responses to the Postal Campaign did not end the abolitionist propaganda effort in the Border South. During the late 1830s, Benjamin Lundy of the *National Enquirer* and Joshua Leavitt of the *Emancipator* continued to mail copies of their newspaper to white southerners. Leavitt declared rhetorically that of all the slave states, "Kentucky must be the *battle ground* of abolition." Charles B. Ray, editor of the *Colored American* had southern subscribers in 1840, and later that decade the *Pennsylvania Freeman* circulated in Maryland and Virginia. African Americans in Baltimore and Washington received antislavery literature—including the publications of black abolitionist Frederick Douglass—through the 1850s.[5]

Continued circulation of antislavery materials in turn helped perpetuate charges from slavery's defenders in the Border South that northern abolitionists encouraged slave resistance. Contending that "incendiary missionaries" turned slaves against masters, the *Richmond Enquirer* declared in 1837, "The South must take her stand. Her safety calls for new and strong measures against fanatics." The following year the editor of the Frankfort, Kentucky, *Commonwealth* wrote of the *Emancipator*, "We say now, of that paper, that it is better calculated to work ruin in the South, than all the rest of the [abolitionist] machinery put together. It is conducted with singular ability."

In 1840 the *Baltimore American* declared, "Roguish *fanaticism*" led to interference "with other people's conscience and affairs, and to the grossest violation of territorial rights and property." Early in his career, even Kentucky abolitionist Cassius M. Clay called his northern counterparts a "horde of fanatical incendiaries."[6] Because of the propaganda campaign, masters anticipated less slave productivity and more resistance, escape, and perhaps rebellion. These concerns led to tighter controls, more slaves sold south, and increased vigilance. Masters did not always achieve their objectives. But they galvanized the region in defense of the social and racial order.

HISTORIAN PETER H. WOOD OBSERVES, "No single act of self-assertion was more significant among slaves or more disconcerting among [southern] whites than that of running away." But there is considerable disagreement concerning the phenomenon. Some historians regard escape as mainly a form of resistance *in* the South, involving "lying out" near a plantation, forming maroon settlements in inaccessible regions, or taking refuge among free black urban communities. They insist that northward escapes, even in the Border South, "were of minimal significance to the survival of slavery."[7] Others contend that mounting northward escapes during the late 1830s and 1840s had a major impact as they encouraged abolitionists to become more aggressive in helping fugitives and contributed to declining slave populations in the Border South. People living in the North-South borderlands between 1835 and 1861 agreed with the latter interpretation. They portrayed the late 1830s and early 1840s as a time of surging northward escapes from Virginia, the District of Columbia, Delaware, Maryland, Kentucky, and Missouri.[8]

Nevertheless, estimates of the number of slave escapes varied widely as shifting arguments among slavery's opponents and defenders influenced them. Depending on circumstances, each side produced figures that were either too high or too low. When abolitionists sought to depict African American resistance to a brutal system and demonstrate how northern antislavery tactics encouraged resistance, they found that large numbers of slaves escaped north. When slavery's defenders sought to show how aggressive abolitionism justified retaliation, they found large numbers as well. The same figure might serve each side's purpose. In 1841 the proslavery *Observer and Reporter* of Lexington, Kentucky, quoted the *Montreal Courier's* claim that there were 20,000 fugitive slaves in Canada. Proslavery and antislavery newspapers used that number for a decade. In 1849, black abolitionist Josiah Henson asserted there were 50,000 fugitive slaves in the free states. Ten years later, John A. Quitman, governor of Mississippi, contended abolitionists had abducted 100,000 slaves over the past forty years.[9]

But sometimes abolitionists and slavery's defenders rejected high escape estimates. In 1850, Gamaliel Bailey, who had moved from Cincinnati to Washington, D.C., wanted to assure white northerners that antislavery tactics would not encourage massive black migration to their section. So he ridiculed an estimate that 61,624 slaves had escaped north during the past forty years. According to the AASS, he pointed out, only about one-tenth of that number had done so. Similarly in 1853, leading southern journalist J. D. B. De Bow used his position as U.S. Census superintendent to produce a figure of just 1,011 slave escapes in 1850, so as to demonstrate how content the great majority of African Americans were in bondage.[10]

Historians too have been inconsistent regarding the number of northward escapes. The 1860 Census, as well as that of 1850, suggested that about 1,000 slaves escaped each year. But in 1906, historian Albert Bushnell Hart concluded that a better estimate was 2,000 escapes per year between 1830 and 1860, for a total of 60,000. He contended that 10 percent of the escapees remained in the South, 10 percent reached Canada, and the rest settled in the North. Some investigations have produced higher estimates. Writing during the late 1950s, Kentucky historian Thomas D. Clark estimated that 20,000 slaves escaped each year to the north *from just his state*.

A reaction began during the 1960s as scholars, relying on the Canadian as well as U.S census reports, concluded that relatively few fugitive slaves headed north. The 1,000 per year figure seemed reasonable to them. Nevertheless, wide disagreement continues, in part because the census figures are questionable. In 1999, John Hope Franklin and Loren Schweninger, emphasizing that most escapees remained in the South, held that 50,000 left their masters each year. In 2001, William W. Freehling estimated 5,000 slaves per year, or 150,000 between 1830 and 1860, reached the North.[11]

All the historians' estimates take into consideration the large numbers of slaves sold south. The domestic slave trade, encouraged by economic change and demand for labor in the cotton-producing Old Southwest drained slaves from the Border South. Baltimore, Maryland; Alexandria, Virginia; and Lexington, Kentucky had thriving slave markets. Slave dealers also operated in the region's smaller cities and towns. In 1840, Robert Wickliffe, Kentucky's largest slaveholder, estimated that 60,000 slaves had been sold south from his state during the past seven years. In July 1844, the *Pennsylvania Freeman* claimed "probably 3000" had been sent out of Maryland "since January."

Seven years later, Joshua R. Giddings reported that an estimated 25,000 had been "sent south" from Virginia the previous year.[12]

Unlike contemporary figures regarding escapes, these numbers for sales south are consistently too low. According to recent analyses, between 1820 and 1860 "at least 875,000 American slaves" went south with their masters or were sold to traders. Therefore, it is likely that a significant portion of the slaves, whom contemporaries estimated to have escaped north, instead went south. Nevertheless, as discussed in the introduction, the two phenomena interacted. Masters sold slaves south for fear they would escape; slaves headed north to avoid sale south.[13]

Despite these losses, slavery maintained a tenacious hold on the Border South, especially prior to 1850. Delaware's tiny slave population declined by 49 percent between 1820 and 1850, Maryland's by 16 percent, and the District of Columbia's by 42 percent. But during the same period, Virginia's large slave population increased by 16 percent, Kentucky's by 66 percent, and Missouri's—which was initially very small—by 855 percent. Border *counties* had similar experiences. Between 1820 and 1850, the number of slaves in Delaware's and Maryland's exposed northernmost counties suffered absolute declines of 66 percent and 24 percent respectively. Virginia's northwestern counties, where slaves had never been numerous, lost 32 percent. But the number of slaves in Kentucky's border counties *increased* by 77 percent during the same period. The slave populations in counties immediately south of Ohio increased 14 percent and those in counties immediately south of Indiana increased by 51 percent. In counties immediately south of Illinois, a small enslaved population increased by 280 percent.[14]

In all, escapes and sales south posed a threat to slavery in the Border South, as did changing economic conditions. But, except in Delaware and the District of Columbia, black bondage remained the predominant interest in the region. And, perhaps because they benefited financially from sales south, the great majority of people who lived in the Border South concentrated their fear and anger on northward escapes. This was especially the case in the region's northernmost counties.

Those who advocated gradual emancipation joined with those who demanded perpetual slavery to advocate measures to reduce escapes and punish groups and individuals they presumed to be responsible. White border southerners claimed they only wanted to be left alone and had been goaded into action. As the *Commonwealth* put it, "Abolitionism . . . running wild like a prairie fire, threaten[ed] destruction to all that is desirable in the land."

During the fall of 1835, Thomas Ritchie of the *Richmond Enquirer* warned that, although the South could not prevent all cross-border intrusions by "emissaries," it would "arrest their publications," and wreak "fiery vengeance . . . upon the head of the incendiary." In early 1841, the moderate *Louisville Journal* threatened to hunt "like midnight wolves" northern advocates of slave revolt if they ventured into the South.[15]

LIKE ESCAPES THEMSELVES, abolitionist involvement in them has been a contentious issue. Historians often describe white southerners' hyperbolic portrayals of northern contact with slaves as gruesome fantasies based on "a pathological fear of servile insurrection." According to David M. Potter, southern journalists "transformed into 'news items' the fantasies of a society obsessed with fears of slave insurrections and with apocalyptic visions of terrible retribution." Larry Gara adds that the southern press misinterpreted infrequent arrests of northerners who helped slaves escape "as unquestionable proof that abolition emissaries were engaged in large-scale organized operations." John Hope Franklin and Loren Schweninger make the important point that slaveholders resorted to a "conspiracy theory" concerning the influence of abolitionist agents to convince themselves that "despite the profusion of runaways in their midst . . . blacks were [not] resisting slavery."[16]

It is essential, nevertheless, to distinguish between fear of abolitionist emissaries in the Lower South, where they were very rare, and in the Border South, where they were relatively common. Since colonial times, fugitive slaves in the latter region had enjoyed the aid of black and Quaker communities. The AASS, from its organization in 1833, recognized slaves' natural right to escape. And, in January 1842, the New York Liberty Party adopted Gerrit Smith's "Address to the Slaves," which endorsed helping slaves exercise that right. Abolitionists, Smith declared, had made a "great and guilty error" when in response to southern charges of complicity in Nat Turner's rebellion, they had forsworn contacting slaves and vowed to deal only with masters. Noting an increased willingness of "the people of the border free States" to aid fugitives, Smith proclaimed the right and duty of northerners to communicate with slaves. Rather condescendingly, he announced, "The abolitionist has perfect moral right to go into the South and use his intelligence to promote the escape of ignorant and imbruted slaves from their prison house."[17]

People living north of the sectional boundary had for years acted on this theory. By the mid-1830s, antislavery activists in southwestern Ohio maintained contacts with free African Americans who helped slaves escape from Kentucky. In September 1835, four white men from Ohio crossed the Ohio River to Kanawha Springs, located near Parkersburg, Virginia, to persuade "several slaves to leave their masters." Late in the 1830s, abolitionists centered in upstate New York and western Illinois initiated similar tactics. In 1839, New York's nonabolitionist governor, William H. Seward, refused to extradite from his state three black sailors who had helped slaves escape from Virginia. That same year, authorities in Washington, D.C., arrested black abolitionist Leonard Grimes on charges that he had assisted slaves escaping from Virginia, and the predominantly black Philadelphia Vigilance Association began forwarding fugitive slaves from Virginia and Maryland to New York and Canada. In 1841, abolitionists helped former slave Madison Washington return from Canada to Virginia to rescue his wife. Captured, reenslaved, and shipped south onboard the brig *Creole*, Washington led a successful and well-publicized revolt on that vessel.[18]

Because he established a long-standing escape network stretching from the Chesapeake to Albany, New York, Abel Brown's activities are especially important. In 1838, Brown, a white Baptist minister from western New York and an associate of Smith, became pastor of a church at Beaver, Pennsylvania, just across the Ohio River from Virginia's northern panhandle. Brown, who faced local antiabolitionist mobs, helped fugitive slaves who reached his church. He claimed "almost daily [to] see the poor heart-broken slave making his way to a land of freedom." Brown also traveled to Baltimore where, by prearrangement, he met an enslaved "young girl" from Alexandria, D.C., conveyed her by carriage to York, Pennsylvania, and arranged for her transportation to Canada. Slaveholders apprehended Brown and charged him with helping the girl escape, only to have a jury acquit him.[19]

As railroads extended their lines during the 1830s and 1840s, slaves relied on them to speed escapes. In December 1841, two enslaved women departed Richmond via the Fredericksburg Railroad on the first leg of their successful attempt to reach Philadelphia. A year later, John T. Mason, a member of Congress from Hagerstown, Maryland, lost twelve slaves. He contended that "for some time" railroad conductors from Pennsylvania had been involved in "a well-concerted scheme for the escape of slaves from this neighborhood." Escapees, he charged, crossed "over the Maryland line on foot" and then boarded trains "at or near Chambersburg," Pennsylvania. This gave "them a start of [*sic*] their pursuers, difficult to overcome, and thus the losses [were] fast becoming very numerous."[20]

Northward slave escapes in the Border South had the same role in causing conflict in that region as kidnapping and slave catching had in the Lower North. Escaping slaves often carried guns, knives, and improvised weapons. Sometimes they used them to kill or disable those who pursued them. In May 1833, two white men from Morgantown, Virginia, came to Uniontown, Pennsylvania, seeking a black man they claimed as a slave. When the Virginians attempted to apprehend him, he fought back with a knife, wounding one of them so severely that intestines protruded through the man's abdomen. In October 1837, the *Baltimore Patriot* reported that three enslaved men, who had escaped from Frederick County, Virginia, bludgeoned one pursuer nearly to death.[21]

Stories like these intimidated slave catchers *and* contributed to the perception among white border southerners that they were under attack by abolitionists whose misguided sympathies and agitation—rather than oppression—instigated slave escape and violence. During the mid-1830s, as the Postal Campaign got underway, reports of abolitionist emissaries in contact with slaves were common. In October 1837, the *Maysville Eagle*, of Maysville, Kentucky, claimed Ohio had a "class of fellows" who either stole slaves for profit or helped them escape. The following year, after a band of Kentuckians arrested a prominent abolitionist in Ohio for helping slaves who reached that state, the moderate *Commonwealth* warned, "As the fanatics grow stronger they increase their demands, and speculative opinion is now giving way to positive action. KENTUCKY, it seems, has been selected by them as the point of attack. Organized societies are upon the border, encouraging the slaves to run away, and furnishing them with every faculty for escape." Cincinnati abolitionists, the *Louisville Public Advertiser* added, conducted "war" against the slave states. In 1839, Professor J. C. Cross of Kentucky's Transylvania University warned against the "dark and bloody spirits of abolitionism," who could lay southern "hearths . . . desolate." [22]

Similar charges and admonitions circulated in other border slave states. In 1835, Thomas Ritchie, of the *Richmond Enquirer*, predicted Virginia, like Kentucky, would be on the front line in a civil war against "fanatics" who interfered with its "domestic institutions." Three years later, the *Gazette* of Parkersburg, Virginia, complained of numerous escapes during the previous three months. "An organized band, residing in Ohio," it alleged, "are constantly guilty of inducing, abetting and aiding these escapes." The newspaper's editor called on "reflecting" Ohioans to consider the commercial and political costs of such behavior. He warned, "The worst period of the French Revolution, would be peace and harmony, compared with the state of society" resulting from continued assisted escapes. In late 1839, the *Times* of Centreville, Maryland, asserted that, by helping slaves escape, white abolitionists and free African Americans threatened the existence of slavery in all regions "contiguous to nonslaveholding states." The *Baltimore American* agreed, contending that "roguish fanaticism" employing "free negroes" as agents had "overrun" Maryland and spread to Virginia. Organizations in Pennsylvania and New Jersey, it maintained, "seduced away" slaves and employed vessels on Chesapeake Bay to transport them to the North.[23]

Border South politicians seconded these assertions. In December 1835, Virginia congressman Henry A. Wise threatened, "If violence or intrusion upon our rights be persisted in and pursued, gentlemen will find Union men and nullifiers of the South *all united* on the subject,—ready ripe for revolution." In February 1839, Missouri's legislature complained that interference from nonslaveholding states into the border slave states was "well calculated to disturb their domestic peace, light up the torch, and plunge them amid the horrors of servile insurrection and war." Northern interference with slavery, the legislature charged, would disrupt interstate relations "and ultimately destroy their union." The "southern and south-western States," it declared, had to defend their "domestic institutions from wanton invasion . . . 'peaceable [*sic*] if they can, forcibly, if they must.'" That month, Representative Robert Craig of Montgomery County, Virginia, warned that if Congress abolished slavery in the District of Columbia, "Virginia must either emancipate her slaves or 'stand upon her arms.'"[24]

Northern governors' refusals to extradite those accused of helping slaves escape encouraged such outbursts. In February 1840, the *American Farmer*, a periodical published in Baltimore, claimed lack of northern cooperation had in effect dissolved the Union. It declared, "There remains to the Southern Planter nothing but shameful and ruinous submission; or self protection by the means of retaliation or defense." Slavery declined in Maryland, the magazine's editor contended, not through a defect in it as a labor system but because of "interference of numerous and vexatious drawbacks on the efficiency and happiness of the slave—such as the number of free Negroes—their agency in the schemes of abolitionists—the proximity of the states of Pennsylvania and New Jersey, where infamous organizations exist for their seduction and concealment."[25]

Prior to the passage of the Compromise of 1850, few in the Border South went further than the editor of the *Lynchburg Virginian*. In late 1842, he declared the time had arrived "to convince our Northern brethren that the provisions of the Constitution [in regard to fugitive slaves] must be adhered to by them, or that they will no longer be regarded as binding upon us; and that further aggression on their part will be met by resistance on ours."[26]

PERCEPTIONS AMONG Border South residents of organized assaults on their interests and safety produced action as well as rhetoric. The region's slave patrols, law enforcement officers, and volunteer military companies turned their energies toward preventing escape. Meanwhile, local vigilance associations proliferated, as masters and their allies sought means to protect their interests, and proslavery mobs threatened abolitionists.

Slave patrols, dated to the seventeenth century in the Chesapeake, spread throughout the South, and constituted an "ongoing paramilitary counterinsurgency campaign." In Virginia, they began as an arm of the militias in which all white men served. As threats from American Indian and European nations declined during the late eighteenth and early nineteenth centuries, so did compulsory militia service. But the patrols survived as white residents continued to fear slave unrest, escape, and revolt. They consisted of four to six men chosen every three or four months at the increasingly social militia musters. As historian John Hope Franklin observes, Virginia's "militia-controlled patrol system helped create a warlike atmosphere in times of peace." Beginning in 1811, St. Louis and other Missouri cities had patrol systems. In 1825 the state's general assembly gave county courts and townships the power to establish slave patrols patterned on Virginia's.

Similar semimilitary institutions developed elsewhere in the Border South. Although some evidence indicates patrols declined in Kentucky during the late 1830s, they continued to operate in urban as well as rural parts of the state. The Louisville patrol, established in 1809, went out each night. It visited taverns and inns seeking information about fugitive slaves. Patrols in the area also sought to block escape routes across the Ohio River to Indiana and Ohio. Immediately following Nat Turner's revolt, the Washington, D.C., patrol, "armed with *two* pieces of cannon, guns, pistols, swords, daggers, clubs and *whiskey*" beat, imprisoned, and robbed black men and women. In 1852 a Louisville mob whipped a white man for selling fake passes to African Americans that enabled "them to escape patrols." Patrollers did not, however, always enjoy physical superiority. In March 1840, "the county court of Fairfax, Va." sentenced "two negro slaves" to death for "maliciously assaulting and beating the patrol with intent to kill."[27]

As time passed, law enforcement officers acquired duties previously performed by patrols. In Maryland, constables had led the patrols since 1723. When Congress organized the District of Columbia in 1801, the city of Washington required its police force to capture and whip fugitives, although a separate slave patrol continued in the city until the 1830s. In 1838 the city's white residents called for more police officers, because they feared free and enslaved African Americans plotted revolt. Beginning during the early 1840s, police in Washington and Baltimore routinely searched homes of African Americans for fugitive slaves. To block northward escapes, they patrolled steamboat landings, railroad depots, and roads. By 1828, Richmond, Virginia, had a "public guard" to "keep order among Negroes." In 1848 it proposed to create a school to train young men to serve in the guard.[28]

During the 1830s and 1840s, more explicitly military organizations emerged to protect slavery in the Border South. As the militia declined throughout the country, volunteer companies bearing such names as "Union Guards," "National Blues," "Independent Grays," and "Invincibles" replaced it. These private military units attracted men who could afford to purchase uniforms and other martial gear. They became a major part of antebellum America's public ceremonies and celebrations. "Independent military companies" from the Old Northwest and Border South periodically gathered in "grand military encampment[s]" to display "the strength and chivalry of the west and south." But states also employed volunteer companies to guard prisoners, maintain order at public executions, and to put down riots. In the Border South, they defended slavery by "watching the Negroes," arresting suspected abolitionists, and destroying antislavery publications. When sheriffs summoned "large part[ies] of armed citizens" to pursue escapees and/or their northern abettors, they relied on these organizations.[29]

Well before private military units became popular, masters in the Border South organized vigilance associations. In July 1827, slaveholders in Mason County, Kentucky, located across the Ohio River from the abolition center of Ripley, Ohio, met "for the purpose of better security of their property." A decade later, Gamaliel Bailey, writing in the *Philanthropist*, used a similar phrase to describe efforts in Kentucky and Virginia to prevent northward escapes. Masters in these states, he observed, "are beginning to hold meetings for the purpose of devising means for the better security of slave property."[30] Similar to the antislavery vigilance associations in northern towns and cities, such Border South defensive organizations proliferated during the mid-1830s.

This was the case in Virginia. In 1835 the Fairfax County court appointed a three-man committee for each of the county's militia districts "to detect and bring to speedy punishment all emissaries who may be found . . . giving circulation to the papers or pamphlets put forth by the Abolitionist Associations of the North, agitating the question of slavery, and therefore endangering the peace and tranquility of our land." The *Richmond Enquirer* portrayed such "voluntary associations of citizens" as a moderate means of protecting slavery and white supremacy because they did not advocate disunion. But such organizations certainly aimed to use force against fugitive slaves and those who assisted them. At a meeting held in the Parkersburg courthouse in 1837, J. J. Jackson demanded "immediate, united and active exertions on the part of every Virginian in sustaining their [constitutional rights]." He called for measures "to repel the aggressive interference of unauthorized associations of individuals in . . . the State of Ohio, called Abolition Societies" and "more effectively recapture . . . decoyed and runaway Slaves." During the late summer of 1844, the Sussex County, Virginia, "vigilance committee" had 163 members organized into "sub-committees by location."[31]

Three years earlier, masters in Kenton County, Kentucky, just south of Cincinnati, organized to secure "the possession of their servants," and recover "such as abscond[ed]." They claimed they had "been driven to this step by the excessive arrogance to which they are continually subject, in the escape of their slaves to the opposite side of the river, where they are harbored and aided in their further escape to Canada by a band of infamous fanatics." Cassius M. Clay reported in 1843 that a group had formed in Lexington, Kentucky, to "lynch abolitionists." Clay also charged that gangs of white men, calling themselves "police assistants," terrorized free African Americans to drive them from Kentucky.[32]

In St. Louis, during October 1835, after two white men helped several slaves escape to Illinois, a mass meeting called for creating associations in the city's wards and surrounding townships. Each group had the responsibility of driving out nonresident African Americans, reporting white abolitionists to local authorities, and—if necessary—engaging in violence. In 1841, vigilance associations organized in a nearby county to "examine strangers who could not well explain their business and expel them and threaten them with 50 lashes if they returned." But St. Louis remained the center of activity in Missouri. In 1843 the city's association proposed to kidnap an Illinois abolitionist for each slave who had assistance in escaping to that state.[33] In 1846 "a mass-meeting" of masters in St. Louis sought to devise "ways and means to protect their slave property in this city and country."[34]

Abolitionist Charles T. Torrey remarked in 1842, "The 'eternal vigilance' with which . . . proud plunderers of the poor watch against the remotest approach of danger to their unholy gains." Because Torrey ventured into the Chesapeake, he knew better than most northerners that vigilance associations had become the most common form of armed defense in the Border South.[35]

COMPARED TO SLAVE PATROLS, volunteer military companies, and vigilance associations, antiabolitionist mobs existed for days, not years. They appeared in response to specific threats, or *perceived* threats, and disbanded once a crisis passed. In the Border South, fear that legal and political institutions could not preserve established social, racial, and sectional relations produced these extralegal bodies. They undertook preventive violence and were more likely than the vigilance committees to resort to lynch law.

From 1835 onward, the region's mobs were large, well organized, and well armed. The "most respectable" citizens—including militia officers—led them. Unlike mobs in the Lower South, they responded to real threats, faced significant opposition from legal authorities, and drew criticism from progressive elements. Unlike antiabolitionist and antiblack mobs in the Lower North, those in the Border South during the 1830s and 1840s never had to fight on equal terms against their adversaries.[36]

The first major antiabolitionist mobs in the Border South arose during 1835 at the beginning of the Postal Campaign. In March of that year, James G. Birney, a former Alabama slaveholder turned abolitionist, organized an antislavery society at Danville, Kentucky, southwest of Lexington. A few months later, he caused a reaction after he announced his intention to publish an antislavery newspaper, *The Philanthropist*, in the town. A committee of thirty-three prominent slaveholders, many of whom favored gradual emancipation and colonization, notified him that if he published "incendiary" material he might face violence. When another local group supported Birney's right to publish, the committee held a meeting that attracted a crowd of 500. Those assembled passed resolutions declaring that Birney intended "a direct attack upon, and a wanton disregard of our domestic relations." On July 29, the mob forced Birney's printer to sell his business, and Birney decided to publish the *Philanthropist* in New Richmond, Ohio, near Cincinnati.[37]

During 1835, three other Border South mobs did more than threaten violence. That August a mob formed in Georgetown, D.C., after constables arrested Reuben Crandall, a New York City physician who had come to the district to lecture on botany. Authorities charged Crandall with circulating publications "encouraging the negroes to insurrection." After it failed to wrest Crandall from jail, the mob spent nearly a week vandalizing black churches, burning other black-owned buildings, and forcing local black abolitionists to flee for their lives. This large and well-armed mob "face[d] down" a force of "about fifty" commanded by militia general Walter Jones, and it took a detachment of federal troops to restore order. As it turned out, Crandall had abolitionist publications in his possession but did not intend to distribute them.[38]

Fear during 1835 that white abolitionists sought to encourage slave violence also produced mob action in Virginia and Missouri. On September 4, dozens of rioters at Kanawha Salines in western Virginia arrested four Ohioans, whom they accused of encouraging slaves to escape. After an informal trial, "Judge Lynch" sentenced two of the Ohioans to thirty-nine lashes and expulsion from the county. The *Lynchburg Democrat* characterized the mob leaders as "gentlemen of the first respectability," who found statute law inadequate "to the protection of their fire sides and property . . . [against] such high-handed and dangerous acts." A month later, antislavery journalist Elijah P. Lovejoy, who published *The Observer* in St. Louis, reported that, following the "abduction of several slaves" from a town near the city, "about sixty of our 'most respectable' . . . citizens" seized two men, took them "about three miles back of the city, and there whipped them, as near as can be ascertained, one hundred and fifty or two hundred lashes each."[39]

This incident encouraged more bloodshed. Tensions along the Missouri-Illinois border had been rising for months as white Missourians feared abolitionists from Illinois would cross the Mississippi River to instigate black revolt. In these circumstances, Lovejoy feared he too might be tarred and feathered, or "*hung up.*" Then on April 28, 1836, a white mob burned to death black boatman Francis J. McIntosh, after McIntosh stabbed one St. Louis policeman to death and wounded another. As Judge Luke E. Lawless blocked the effort of a grand jury to indict members of the mob, he blamed the incident on abolitionists in general and Lovejoy in particular. Men like Lovejoy, Lawless charged, caused black rebelliousness "and civil war." On July 21, Lovejoy responded that Lawless's ruling encouraged "the perpetuation, by a congregated mob . . . of every species of violence." Shortly thereafter, approximately 200 men broke into the *Observer* office, inflicted $700 worth of damage, and convinced Lovejoy to leave the city. Later, a few members of the mob followed him to Alton, Illinois, and joined the attack on his press that led to his death (see chapter 3).[40]

Meanwhile, another Missouri mob's actions had cross-border repercussions. On May 1, A. C. Garratt had arrived from New York at Marion College. Abolitionist minister David Nelson served as president of the college, which was located near Palmyra, one hundred miles north of St. Louis. Garratt brought with him "a company of young men who expected . . . to enter the college," a "respectable colored young man; and a colored boy, both from New York City," and a "library" of antislavery books.

On May 16, news of what many white Missourians regarded as a biracial abolitionist invasion of their state led about 200 mounted Palmyra men to visit the college. Armed with "pistols, dirks, &c., and the most of them also . . . clubs," they captured Garratt, some of his companions, and a local abolitionist named Williams. They burned Garratt's books and threatened to whip him and Williams 200 lashes each, but dropped the threat when the two men agreed to leave the state.[41] A few days later, about ninety men meeting at Palmyra praised the mob for defeating an attempt "to instruct our slaves to rebellion by the use of incendiary pamphlets." The men resolved, "Our county is one among the selected theatres of action . . . of the antislavery associations . . . [which pursued] objects . . . incompatible with the peace, happiness, and security of our citizens, as members of a slaveholding community." Those in attendance declared that because of the inadequacy of statute law, the community had to defend itself.[42]

On May 22, as Nelson presided over a religious meeting at a nearby campground, an argument between an advocate of compensated emancipation and a defender of perpetual slavery led to more violence. The emancipationist, armed with a knife, severely wounded the perpetualist, armed with a sword and pistol. Meanwhile, after students at Nelson' college vowed to continue their antislavery efforts, "a company of forty-two left [Palmyra] for the College on horseback." Fearing for their lives, Nelson and his family fled across the Mississippi River to Quincy, Illinois. There, within a year, Nelson confirmed the Missourians' suspicions about abolitionists by establishing the Mission Institute and encouraging his divinity students to help slaves escape.[43]

In July 1841, three of the students—Alanson Work, James E. Burr, and George Thompson—sailed a skiff across the river and attempted to entice away five slaves. The slaves reported the intruders to their master, who— with several neighbors—ambushed and captured the students. That September, amid riotous conditions, a jury found the three guilty of slave stealing, and they each received a twelve-year sentence in the Missouri Penitentiary. None of the students denied the charges against them. Rather, they asserted, Christian duty required them to help slaves escape, and they pledged to encourage slaves they met in prison to do so. Work wrote in his journal, "We believe that our being here will spread the knowledge that there is a road to LIBERTY." Many northern abolitionists praised the students as "noble-hearted martyrs in the cause of suffering humanity." In contrast, Palmyra's prosecuting attorney denounced them as "notorious land pirates," and the *St. Louis Republican* called them "emissaries of mischief." In Kentucky, the *Louisville Public Advertiser* used the term "deluded criminals." Rumors spread in Palmyra of abolitionist plans to rescue the three men by force. According to Thomson, local white women lived in fear of racial and sectional violence.[44]

BY THE EARLY 1840s, similar fear, as well as anger and resentment, extended throughout the Border South. The great majority of white residents believed those in the Lower North who opposed slavery, aided fugitive slaves, or, worst of all, interfered across the sectional boundary had to be punished. Perceptions of a faltering slave economy and racial insecurity had caused the border southerners to overreact. But they were not irrational. They had reason to be defensive and organize forceful means to protect their way of life. They failed to recognize, however, that their defensive efforts accentuated longstanding insecurities in the Lower North.

## THREE

# Southern Aggression in the Lower North

"Along the border line, on both sides of it, there is a set of vicious, degraded, crazy scoundrels, whose sole business it is to arrest fugitives," declared Charles T. Torrey in 1844. Torrey, who helped slaves escape from Maryland, Virginia, and the District of Columbia, called his adversaries "border miscreants." They were, he contended, ignorant, impoverished, and "comparatively harmless," unless "invested with police offices" or employed by slaveholders "to kidnap some poor fugitive." One of them, Torrey declared, was a constable—"a low lived creature from Gettysburg, who received $200 for his base services." A few weeks later, Torrey's black associate, Thomas Smallwood, reported "a group of knaves" who lived three miles north of "'Mason & Dixon's Line' on the west branch of the Susquehanna River." They were, in Smallwood's opinion, "a set of careless scoundrels, whose chief business is man-hunting, and whose occasional amusements are counterfeiting, steeling sheep, stabbing, killing men, and debauchery in its lowest forms." They associated with "females, not a whit more elevated in moral character." Like his friend Torrey, Smallwood believed these criminals were "convenient tools of the refined, genteel slaveholders." They were "a scourge and terror" to African Americans and to local white farmers who employed black labor. The farmers, Smallwood reported, "Fear[ed] to prosecute . . . lest the vengeance of these wretches should fall on them."[1]

Northerners used similar terms to describe several other border gangs. In 1827, Philadelphia mayor Joseph Watson called the Cannon-Johnson gang (see chapter 1), which operated from a hideout on the Delaware-Maryland boundary, "desperadoes" who stole slaves in Maryland and Virginia at the same time they kidnapped black children from his city. In 1840, well after the demise of the Cannon-Johnson gang, the *Baltimore Sun* reported a similarly located "gang of scoundrels" engaged in kidnapping. Six years later, the *Pennsylvania Freeman* complained that slave-catching "pimps" existed "in all the towns along the Pennsylvania Line." During the early 1850s, the "Gap Gang" kidnapped, hunted fugitive slaves, and the robbed over a large portion of southeastern Pennsylvania.[2]

Farther west, criminal organizations used cross-border tactics on the Ohio River to steal slaves in Kentucky and kidnap free African Americans in southern Ohio, Indiana, and Illinois. In 1846, Ohio attorney William Johnson charged, "A horde of pirates . . . infest[s] the waters of the Ohio on both its banks, and make man-catching a trade. . . . they are the enemies of the human race." Johnson warned Kentuckians that the pirates "will steal your slave from you today and sell him to you tomorrow." He told those north of the river, "If you were on the southern line of Ohio, you would almost imagine you were on the slave coast of Africa."[3]

The river pirates and other criminal groups co-opted law enforcement officers, such as the Gettysburg constable Torrey mentioned, to give legal veneer to their activities. This sometimes led to charges against the officers. As early as 1820, a Clark County, Indiana, justice of the peace had to resign following charges "that he did 'willfully and corruptly aid, abet and assist in unlawfully arresting, imprisoning and running out of the state one Isaac Crosby, a man of color.'" In 1851 a Philadelphia jury convicted former constable George F. Alberti for abducting a black baby to Maryland. His record as a kidnapper in the Philadelphia vicinity stretched back to 1815.[4]

The popular view in the Lower North of "border miscreants" who kidnapped, caught fugitive slaves, and corrupted officials, foreshadowed how free-state settlers in Kansas Territory during the 1850s regarded the Missouri border ruffians, whom they described as dirty, immoral, and illiterate "pukes." Border miscreants also lived on in southeastern Pennsylvania memory. As late as 1911, a local historian portrayed them as "seemingly organized bands of kidnapers and slave-hunters who lived along the border of Maryland and Pennsylvania and followed the business of recapturing escaped fugitives from Virginia and Maryland, or kidnapping by force and violence free negroes." The historian recalled that the gangs still operated during the first year of the Civil War when one of them burned the barn of a man who had gone to Baltimore to rescue a free black man a gang had kidnapped.[5]

Chapter 2 investigated border southerners' perceptions of and reactions to slave escapes and northern aggression during the 1830s and 1840s. This chapter deals with proslavery initiatives in the Lower North and their impact on the views of border northerners during the same decades. Those who kidnapped African Americans into slavery epitomized proslavery aggression. But many residents of New Jersey, Pennsylvania, Ohio, Indiana, and Illinois barely distinguished between kidnappers and those who sought legally to recapture fugitive slaves or brought their human property north. Men and women who one way or another expanded slavery into the Lower North appeared to jeopardize the peace, morality, stability, rights, interests, and independence of free-labor society. For African Americans and their white allies, sporadic antiblack and antiabolitionist riots on the northern side of the sectional line accentuated this distressing state of affairs.

ANTISLAVERY JOURNALISTS INSISTED that a violent proslavery culture dominated southern portions of Pennsylvania and the Old Northwest. In 1844, Chicago abolitionist Zebina Eastman identified in the region just north of the Ohio River "a murderous, mobocratic spirit." Eastman caricatured white southern migrants in the area as debased failures who had fled north because they could not compete against slave labor. He claimed they brought with them poverty, illiteracy, ignorance, intemperance, and the "grossest vices." They had no respect for "good order, virtue, and freedom" and blamed "niggers," Yankees, and Mormons for "all their evils."[6]

Within this population were individuals who had much in common culturally with gangs on the North-South line and engaged in racially motivated violence. Three cases among many illustrate what had by the late 1830s become frequent occurrences. In June 1838, at Bear Creek, Illinois, located not far from the Mississippi River, fifteen local white men, hoping to gain a reward, attacked two fugitive slaves from Missouri and killed one. Two years later, a gang of inebriated white men in Ross County, Ohio, assaulted the home of a Portuguese man married to a woman of African and American Indian descent. The gang threw fence posts through windows, broke down the kitchen door, and later shot to death the couple's son. At Indianapolis in 1845, "a gang of drunken ruffians," motivated by racial hatred viciously murdered a black man as a white crowd stood by.[7]

Many others in the Lower North supported laws designed to discourage black immigration, called for expelling African Americans, and aided slaveholders. In 1838 a Jacksonville, Illinois, jury took twenty minutes to allow a slaveholder, who lacked a warrant, to take a black man named Robert into slavery in Kentucky. That same year the learned and moderately antislavery Charles Hammond, who edited the *Cincinnati Gazette*, claimed that free states on the border of slave states had a moral duty to protect a master's right to his human property. As late as 1856, the *Richmond Enquirer* complimented Pennsylvania and the southern counties of the Old Northwest for their proslavery sentiment.[8]

To a degree, white abolitionists of the Lower North accommodated themselves to this climate of opinion. In August 1842, Gerrit Smith, who led New York's Liberty Party, called the Cincinnati-centered Ohio Liberty Party a "selfish scheme." According to Smith, the party's white leaders only wanted to keep their "own neck[s] from under the yoke of slavery." Smith charged that white abolitionists in Cincinnati with refused to cooperate with African Americans. Cincinnati abolitionists were, he contended, less likely than white abolitionists in New York to help slaves escape, and Cincinnatians distinguished "between the rights of a colored man and a white man." This seemed to be the case for Thomas Morris, a Liberty abolitionist who lived in Cincinnati and had been a Democratic U.S. senator from 1833 to 1839. In November 1838 and again in February 1839, Morris had spoken against admitting "the Negro . . . to the enjoyment of equal, social, or political privileges, with the white race, nor to sit at the same table, or enjoy the social comforts of the same fireside."[9]

Yet Smith erred. Stories of black resistance to kidnappers, slave catchers, and masters led many white people in the Lower North to reconsider racial stereotypes. When confronted with aggressive southern action against African Americans, many white residents sympathized with the victims. This was especially the case when the African Americans involved were their employees or neighbors, had established themselves as productive community members, displayed courage, or suffered severe mistreatment. Many white people of the Lower North recognized that African Americans—impoverished, uneducated, and alien as they might be—shared their values and interests. White abolitionists in the region led in this empathy. In Cincinnati, they supported African Americans on the issue of taxation without representation, helped them recover kidnapping victims, and provided aid to black schools. The Liberty Party, not only in Ohio but throughout the Lower North, always opposed Black Laws. A black man addressed an abolitionist Wesleyan Methodist convention held in Pittsburgh in May 1843. White abolitionists attending the Southern and Western Liberty Convention in Cincinnati in June 1845 ate and slept in black churches.[10]

Morris supported black rights much more often than he suggested during the winter of 1839–1839 when he misrepresented himself in a futile effort to convince the Ohio Legislature to reelect him to the U.S. Senate. Before and after his uncharacteristically racist remarks, he vociferously denounced proslavery aggression against the Lower North's black residents. He condemned the Fugitive Slave Law of 1793, kidnappers, and slave catchers. He sacrificed his political career when he responded in the Senate to John C. Calhoun's radical proslavery views and defended abolitionists against Henry Clay's criticism. Black people, Morris contended, should enjoy the same guarantees as white people regarding life, liberty, property, happiness, and safety. Free African Americans should not be subject to a "system of kidnapping and sale." Morris was only the most prominent of many white border northerners who, despite their biases, detested race-based kidnapping. Much proslavery sentiment existed in southern Illinois, but as Zebina Eastman observed in 1842, more of that state's white residents helped fugitive slaves than assisted slave catchers.[11]

NEVERTHELESS, southward abductions of African Americans began another round of expansion after the mid-1830s. Benjamin Lundy, writing in Philadelphia in 1837, attributed the increase in abductions to high cotton prices and "the prospective opening of the *Texas Slave Market*," following Texas's successful war for independence from Mexico. Kidnappings in the border region, he observed, were "never before known to be so brisk." Abductions, the *Cincinnati Gazette* observed in 1843, had increased "all along the borders of the free states." Four years later, the *Pennsylvania Freeman* claimed, kidnappers were in a "perfect frenzy."[12]

Although the greatest danger existed on the North-South line, kidnapping occurred with appalling frequency throughout the Lower North and extended into New York and New England. Most incidents went unreported, in part because commercial newspapers avoided the subject. But, when victims resisted and called for help, they attracted neighbors who in various ways perceived threats to themselves.[13]

Perpetrators included professional criminals—such as Torrey's "border miscreants"—law enforcement officers, and individuals seeking to recover former slaves freed by their relatives. During the 1830s and 1840s, Philadelphia, Pittsburgh, and Cincinnati were notorious for kidnapping due to their large black populations, proximity to the Border South, and the publicity abolitionist newspapers generated. In 1836, Lundy portrayed a Philadelphia burdened by a "slave-trading establishment," supported by "kidnapping gentry," and linked to slave purchasers in Baltimore and Washington, D.C. Southern Illinois also gained a reputation for frequent kidnappings.[14]

Kidnappers operating on the north bank of the Ohio River, especially in Cincinnati, continued to be more brutal than those in Philadelphia, and they compromised numerous law enforcement officials. In August 1837, two

Cincinnati constables helped "a band of desperadoes" from Kentucky, who had neither a certificate nor a warrant, break into the home of a "respectable" black man and seize a black woman. A month later, an atrocious attack occurred at Ripley, approximately forty miles upstream from Cincinnati. Four white men—including a Mason County, Kentucky, master, another Kentuckian, and two Ohioans—broke into the home of Eliza Jane Johnson at a time when her husband was away. On the assumption that Johnson had escaped years earlier from the master's father, the men "whipped her severely to make her submit," and took her without a warrant to Kentucky. When a Mason County judge determined Johnson was not the woman who had escaped, he nevertheless sent her to jail on suspicion that she had been "stolen" from the captain of a steamboat. If the captain did not claim her within two months, she would be sold into slavery to pay for the cost of jailing her.[15]

Two similar cases occurred in Cincinnati the following year and a third in 1841. In June 1838, the captain of the steamer *London* learned that "a young colored man, about seventeen years old," who had boarded at Cincinnati, did not have his free papers. Although the young man had been born in Brownsville, Pennsylvania, and was traveling to his parents' home in Pittsburgh, the captain, seeking a reward, took him to Newport, Kentucky, as a fugitive slave. That December a river pilot, angry over the disputatious deportment of Alexander Johnson, a free black boatman from Portsmouth, Ohio, lured Johnson to the Cincinnati ferry landing. From there, several men took Johnson to Covington, Kentucky, and had him jailed as a fugitive slave. In the 1841 case, crew from the steamer *Commodore* seized a black boy who had been standing on the quay, procured a yawl, and sailed him to Covington. The men implausibly claimed that the boy had escaped from slavery in New Orleans.[16]

The immediate issue kidnapping raised in the Lower North was the safety of African Americans. In some instances, black and white witnesses stood by as kidnappers dragged people off. In others, they sought peacefully to secure the return of those who had been abducted. In Eliza Jane Johnson's case, white abolitionists in Ripley mounted a courtroom effort to have her freed. When this tactic failed, the Ohio General Assembly appealed to Governor Joseph Vance to ask his Kentucky counterpart to intervene in her behalf, which resulted in Johnson's return to Ohio in 1838.[17] In the case of the young man from Brownsville, abolitionists located his free papers, brought them to Newport, and immediately secured his release. But Alexander Johnson's fate is unknown. And, when abolitionist Cornelius Burnett "sued out a warrant" for the arrest of the steamer's captain in regard to the black boy on the quay, a deputy U.S. marshal did not enforce it. The local justice of the peace refused to grant another.

THE MEANING OF law and order became a contentious sectional issue. Widespread disregard for black rights in the Lower North did not prevent support for laws that protected black freedom. South of the North-South line, however, many believed a master's interests should override the law. In regard to the Eliza Jane Johnson case, a correspondent of the *Maysville Eagle*—a moderate Kentucky weekly—claimed that in a "*case [that] appeared so plain*," the "high sheriff" of Mason County had authority to send men to Ohio to capture Johnson without taking "the usual legal steps." The *Cincinnati Journal* responded that no "*high station*" empowered an individual to act "above the laws of the land." In August 1845, when Marylanders hired a disreputable Pennsylvanian to abduct a recently manumitted black mother and her children from Bendersville, the *Pennsylvania Freeman*, stressed the act was in "open defiance of law and order."[18]

Abolitionists and others who sought to shape public opinion in the Lower North were especially careful to publicize how southern disregard of the law affected *white* northerners. They did this in part to promote white empathy for suffering African Americans. But they also encouraged sectional antagonism by warning white people that their loved ones too might be kidnapped into slavery. James G. Birney observed in his *Philanthropist*, "If slavery endure, poor *white* children, as well as the *colored*, will soon become the victims of its hopeless horrors." Relying on a northern stereotype of southern immorality, Birney also suggested white women might be kidnapped, enslaved, and forced into prostitution. He reminded his readers, "There are in the South, already, slaves as white as any of us, who have in our veins the purest Saxon blood. . . . The whiter the slave—especially if it be a female— the more extravagant the price—the more desirable the victim." Three years later, Gamaliel Bailey, who succeeded Birney as *Philanthropist* editor, asked white parents, "Are not your daughters already kidnapped by the harpies of northern licentiousness? . . . Is slavery more chaste, more scrupulous in these matters?" In 1845, Chicago's *Western Citizen* responded to a Democratic newspaper's objection to interference with southern slave catchers. Not to interfere, the *Citizen* warned, risked exposing the "whitest and best known free child in the city" to kidnapping.[19]

More frequently than abolitionists warned about the threat to white women and children, they publicized how kidnapping affected white safety and property rights as armed men invaded their homes in search of African

Americans. Lundy reported in December 1836 how "five or six" men, with drawn pistols but no search warrant, forced their way into the home of a Salem, New Jersey, Quaker who employed "two or three colored men." Although the would-be kidnappers did no major damage and did not find the black men they sought, Lundy declared, "The question, here presented, is a *serious one*. . . . Shall a set of kidnapping marauders . . . [be] suffered thus to trespass upon quiet unoffending citizens? WHERE ARE WE! Do we inhabit a land of '*constitutional freedom*?' or, rather, is our lot cast in a region where lawless freebooters and midnight prowlers are the 'sovereigns of the country,' who may violate the sanctity of our private dwellings, to carry men and women into southern bondage?"[20]

In 1848 a woman in Downington, Pennsylvania, bluntly portrayed the threat kidnappers presented to white security. "Three white men, ruffians indeed," had invaded her home, abducted a "young colored girl," frightened the woman's sister, and knocked down her father. "This deliberate invasion of our house is a thing unimagined," she asserted. Subsequently, as if to clarify what the incident had meant to her as a white northerner, she wrote of her "burning desire" to provide "what will be the most service to the cause — not their [black] cause — ours — that of our own race." Two years later, white residents of Athens and Gallia counties in southeastern Ohio complained to the state legislature because the "extensively prevailing" kidnapping of African Americans "grossly infringed" on the "rights of peaceable, law abiding [white] citizens." The petitioners charged, "Prevailing ignorance respecting the lawful power of slaveholders" had led justices of the peace to issue what amounted to general search warrants for "*stolen slaves*" and "*certain negroes claimed as slaves*."[21]

Nothing so humiliated white people in the Lower North as invasions of their homes and violent treatment of white women. But the rare, forceful cross-border abductions of white men raised more direct challenges to state sovereignty that had frightening implications. In December 1838, a "committee" from Guyandotte in western Virginia crossed the Ohio River to arrest an Ohio man charged with being "a modern abolitionist." The vigilantes took the man to Guyandotte, tarred and feathered him, and rode him on a rail. Seven years later, a band of slaveholders captured three white Ohioans, who had been helping fugitive slaves on the *west* bank of the river, and took them to jail in Parkersburg, Virginia. As public meetings in Ohio declared "the dearest rights of our citizens have been violated and our State sovereignty shamefully outraged," the state's Whig governor, Mordecai Bartley, intervened on the men's behalf.[22]

The inability of Border North states to protect their residents, black and white, aroused anger and some interracial solidarity as well as fear. In November 1842, a half dozen "white villains" from Kentucky forced their way into the home of Vincent Wigglesworth, a black farmer who lived east of Cincinnati in Clermont County. The Kentuckians bound Wigglesworth and kidnapped his wife and children. After the Ohio Senate's judiciary committee failed to act in the case, Morris called on Ohio's Democratic governor, Wilson Shannon, to open negotiations with his Kentucky counterpart for the family's return and offer a reward to bring the kidnappers to Ohio justice. Meanwhile, Clermont county resident Robert Fee, supported by a group of Wigglesworth's white neighbors, searched for the black man's wife and children. By early 1843, he found them and two of their kidnappers in Missouri. But despite an indictment and a requisition from Shannon demanding that the governor of Missouri extradite the criminals, Fee failed to reunite the family. Concerning the abduction, Morris declared, "Between nations such an act might be considered a good cause of war." Southerners, he complained, demanded that Ohioans uphold slavery, "while the negro hunting tribe . . . break open our dwellings and steal our people." He asked, "Will the time never come when we shall wake up to the preservation of our rights and the sovereignty of our State![?]" [23]

Similar emotions existed in Pennsylvania. Following the 1845 Bendersville abduction, the *Freeman* declared, "Pennsylvania, the *boasted* 'Keystone of the Federal Arch,' [sh]ould hide her head in shame at being thus insulted and bullied by Southern blackguards, and her people laughed and jeered at as a set of cowards and poltroons." Although the *Freeman* aligned with the pacifistic Garrisonian wing of the abolitionist movement, it concluded, "We deserve to be hewers of wood and drawers of water to our . . . Southern Masters if we thus suffer our citizens to be taken from among us without resisting unto the death."[24]

By 1850, sectional animosity had intensified to such a degree that when armed men from Kentucky kidnapped eight black children from their home in the Ohio River town of Ironton, Ohio's proslavery Democratic governor Reuben Wood declared that his state's sovereignty had been "wantonly violated," by an act of "aggression."[25]

DURING THE same years that many residents of the Lower North perceived an increase in kidnappings, they also complained of being "plagued with" what they called "slave catchers," "man hunters," or "nigger hunters," who sought to recapture fugitive slaves. Among the slave catchers were border miscreants, poor white southerners, and some African Americans. There were also constables, marshals, slaveholders, and members of slaveholding families. They carried guns and knives, and employed men from the Lower North to assist in arresting suspects and in transporting them south. There seemed to be so many of them that a Delaware County, Ohio, resident contended in October 1838 that the state had become "a mere race-ground between the slave states and Canada . . . run over, by the slaveholders and their hirelings."[26]

African Americans, of course, were the targets of slave catchers, just as they usually were of kidnappers. Most renditions took place without excessive force and attracted little attention outside black communities.[27] But, because fugitive slaves were on guard and better prepared to resist than free black abductees, their struggles against violent attempts to reenslave them burned heroic as well as brutal images into collective memories. Accounts of the capture of Benjamin "Big Ben" Jones of Bucks County, Pennsylvania are especially graphic.

Described as a "man of giant stature and Herculean strength," Jones, who was six feet ten inches in height, had escaped from slavery in York, Maryland, during the early 1830s. In March 1844, as Jones chopped wood with two other men, William Anderson, his former master, and four other Marylanders arrived. A struggle ensued as Jones, with his axe, fought the slave catchers armed with clubs and pistols. He knocked all of them to the ground and wounded two before they overpowered him, "beat him over the head and shoulders," and dragged him to a carriage. Witnesses claimed that as the captors and their victim headed south to Philadelphia, where they boarded a vessel bound for Baltimore, "their carriage could be tracked by the blood which dripped through its bottom."[28] In Baltimore, Anderson lodged Jones in slave trader Hope H. Slatter's notorious slave prison, pending sale south to New Orleans.

The Jones capture aroused local indignation, and some of his white neighbors joined with Philadelphia abolitionists and underground railroad operative Torrey in purchasing Jones's freedom for about $700. Jones, who never fully recovered from his injuries, remained for years a living reminder of southern brutality. While he was still in Baltimore, a group of his neighbors resolved, "It is the duty of every one to do all that he constitutionally can to defeat and baffle the slave catcher, to protect his prey from his grasp, and to hold up to public scorn . . . the infamous conduct of . . . northern men, who sell their principle, and barter the rights of their fellow men for southern gold."[29]

Fugitive slave renditions, like that involving Jones, encouraged the belief that the Lower North was under attack. And, because the Fugitive Slave Law of 1793 recognized the legality of recaption, the practice raised more political and constitutional, if not moral and emotional, issues than kidnapping. In October 1838, five slave catchers legally seized a woman and several children in Peru Township, Delaware County, Ohio, and returned them to slavery in Mason County, Kentucky. Shortly thereafter, a correspondent of the *Philanthropist* declared, "Ohio has no sovereignty, no independence, such as southrons claim and enjoy. She is but a kind of hand-maid to the South, and wishing to do her duties well, she loves and serves and obeys." In November 1839, following a similar rendition in Illinois, that state's antislavery society asserted that slavery had made "rapid encroachments upon the liberties of the free states." Five years later, as the Illinois Assembly considered legislation designed to make capture of fugitive slaves easier, Zebina Eastman lamented it would turn the state's "officers of justice into blood-hounds."[30]

That masters and constables, who had legal authority to search for fugitive slaves, were more likely than kidnappers to break into homes of white people helped spread such impressions. In November 1838, a resident of Clinton County, Ohio, complained that while he was away his house "was forcibly entered by a band of ruffian slaveholders and their hirelings, seven in number." That the slaveholders had a warrant from a Cincinnati justice of the peace did not keep them from frightening his family. During the 1840s, similar incidents occurred in Oberlin and Butler, Ohio; Doylestown, Pennsylvania; and South Bend, Indiana.[31]

Because the Fugitive Slave Law of 1793 required state and local officials to help masters and their agents, many residents of the Lower North, black and white, held the officials responsible for such break-ins. Despite the fact that officials in the Lower North often repulsed slave catchers' demands, abolitionists and others assumed slaveholders controlled the officials. In October 1837, prominent abolitionist Henry C. Wright labeled judges "tools of slave catchers." Nine months later, a Quaker from Pennsylvania's contentious Chester County charged a local constable and an "associate judge" with helping a "gang of Southerners" capture "a most estimable young colored man." These "ministers of the law," the Quaker contended, were "participants in a crime . . . much more heinous than robbing a man of his purse."[32]

In October 1841, a resident of Mercer County in northwestern Pennsylvania reported in the *Spirit of Liberty* "a gross outrage . . . upon the feelings of this community . . . by a gang of negro catchers from Virginia, two constables from Pittsburgh, and their abettors in this place." According to the

This woodcut portrays the states of Ohio and Indiana as slave-catching bloodhounds. It appeared in the *Philanthropist* on August 13, 1839.

*Spirit's* correspondent, the slave catchers, acting on a warrant from a Pittsburgh alderman, had forcefully arrested a black man while the constables threatened other black men who attempted a rescue. The *Spirit's* editor, asserting that the warrant was illegal, commented, "Are southern[ers] . . . to be permitted . . . to regard our laws as a dead letter? Are their northern abettors, the sneaking jackals of slavery, the hireling whippers-in for the man thieves of the south—to be suffered to trample with impunity upon the laws they have sworn to defend?" The editor wanted "negro hunting constables . . . marked by a virtuous community."[33]

In November 1844, the *Indiana Freeman* denounced the 1793 law for establishing slavery in Indiana. The law, the *Freeman* charged, allowed the slaveholder to "prowl over *this* state, in pursuit of his fugitive slaves, to issue process and warrant to kidnap innocent persons flying for life and liberty." Conditions in Indiana, the *Freeman* charged, were worse than in slave-catching regions of West Africa.[34]

WHY, CRITICS DERISIVELY ASKED, did abolitionists preach against slavery in the North where there were no slaves and not go to the South to make their case? One abolitionist response was that there *were* abolitionists such as Torrey in the South. Another response, more relevant to this chapter, was that there *were* slaves in the North.[35] And they were not all fugitives or persons kidnapped into bondage. In numerous instances during the three decades prior to the Civil War, southerners openly or through a variety of subterfuges introduced slave labor into the Lower North. More frequently, masters brought slaves with them as they visited in or traveled through the region.

These practices threatened to undermine the Lower North's free-labor character. When in 1837 a woman from Maryland kept two or three slaves as "apprentices" at the southeastern Pennsylvania town of Downington, one of her neighbors charged she had committed "a most flagrant outrage, not only upon justice and humanity, but upon the spirit of our laws." The woman was not alone. "Hundreds in the Southern counties of the state," the neighbor reported, "are guilty of the same evasion of the law; and their example and haughty tyrannizing spirit are poisoning the minds of their neighbors." He admonished the "children of [William] Penn" not to allow "this contagion to spread among us."[36]

Later that year, a contributor to Elijah Lovejoy's *Alton Observer* chided the editor for not publicizing the existence of slavery in southwest Illinois along the Mississippi River. The contributor reported that several hundred persons were "held in perpetual and absolute servitude" in the area. He emphasized that the relatively small number did not make the practice "less pernicious . . . nor less criminal in its principle, nor less productive of misery and debasement." Not only was it "a glaring injustice in the practice and laws of a free people," it laid "the foundation of slavery throughout the State." In one instance, Porter Clay, brother of Henry Clay, brought slaves Robert and Emily to Jacksonville, Illinois. In April 1838, after the pair sought freedom under state law, Clay family members "bound and gagged" Robert and placed him on a steamboat for Kentucky.[37]

That same year, John Burns brought "a few slaves" from Maryland to Union County in central Ohio. Burns, unaware that Ohio law "would not allow him to hold them in involuntary servitude one day," informed his neighbors that he planned to free the slaves in five years. When one of the slaves attempted to escape, Burns hired two men to bring him back, tied him up, placed him in a wagon, and drove him to a slave market for sale. If Burns could do these things, Gamaliel Bailey asked, why could not others? "And then what would become of that glorious provision against slavery?" Most threatening was that several men in Union County believed Burns had a right to sell the black man. "There are thousands of windy patriots in this state," Bailey observed, "that know no more and care no more about the principles of civil liberty and the constitution and laws of Ohio, than the said John Burns."[38]

Cincinnati was particularly susceptible to slaveholding because of family ties between its residents and Kentuckians. Some who lived in the city owned slaves south of the river. Some Kentucky masters rented their slaves to people in the city. Others brought slaves to Cincinnati as domestic servants. In one case, a black family of seven arrested as fugitive slaves a few miles north of the city turned out to be the human property of a wealthy young man who had lived there before marrying a Kentucky woman. Because Ohio banned black testimony against white people, writs of habeas corpus often failed to free those held illegally in bondage.[39]

Yet people held as slaves for months or years in the Lower North had the law on their side. Slaves brought by masters who briefly visited or traveled through free states had a more complicated status. Considerable legal opinion assumed the U.S. Constitution's privileges and immunities clause and its requirement that each state recognize the laws of other states established a right to bring slaves temporarily into the North. Masters traveling west with slaves on the National Road or, later, by railroad through Pennsylvania, Ohio, Indiana, and Illinois depended on these provisions to retain title to their human property. The same was true in Cincinnati and other ports on the north bank of the Ohio River. For many years, courts, legislatures, and popular opinion in the Lower North, for the sake of interstate comity and economic self-interest, upheld this right. The Pennsylvania Assembly, when it initiated gradual abolition in 1780, allowed "persons, visiting or traveling with slaves . . . to hold their slaves for six months." In 1831, the Indiana Assembly passed a statute protecting the right of masters to travel inside the state's boundaries so long as there was "no unnecessary delay." Throughout the region, state law punished anyone who urged such slaves to leave their masters or intervened physically in their behalf. In 1837, Charles Hammond of the *Cincinnati Daily Gazette* noted that for thirty years Ohio courts had ruled that slaves in transit who escaped must be delivered up to their masters under the Fugitive Slave Law. Those who helped the slaves get away, Hammond observed, violated the law.[40]

Abolitionists, however, barely distinguished between employing slave labor in the Lower North and bringing slaves through the region. The latter, Bailey declared in February 1838, was "one of the numerous ways in which slavery depraves the moral and political principles of the border free states. . . . [It] at once outrages and corrupts our feelings." John H. Purdy of the *Xenia Free Press* agreed, linking the admission of slaves to Ohio with a "decline of moral principle, of patriotism, and of regard for the laws of the land." As the practice most affected Ohio, increasing numbers of the state's inhabitants endorsed this argument. Even before Bailey wrote, Hammond admitted, "To carry slaves into free states is a great wrong in many points of view, and the subject should attract more attention than has, as yet, been paid it."[41]

In May 1841, the Ohio Supreme Court—in a case arising out of forceful abolitionist interference with Virginia master Bennett Raines, his family, and four slaves passing west through Ohio's Warren County—adopted the abolitionists' point of view. Many commentators regarded Ohio Supreme Court justice Ebenezer Lane's opinion in the case as *obiter dicta* or "*extra judicial.*" Lane nevertheless set a precedent in declaring, "If the owner of a slave *voluntarily* bring him into this State or permit him to come, although it should only be for the purpose of *visiting*, or traveling through from one State to another, the slave in such cases becomes a *free* man the moment he touches the soil of Ohio." Following a brief abolitionist James G. Birney and antislavery lawyer Salmon P. Chase had developed, Lane ruled the Fugitive Slave Law of 1793 only applied to slaves who had escaped *into* Ohio not those who escaped while passing through the state. Particularly important for physical conflict in the border region, Lane went on to declare that an attempt by a master to retain a slave brought voluntarily into Ohio by removing the slave "into a slave State . . . is an offense against, or violation of, the laws of Ohio, (the law against kidnapping)." In such cases, Lane ruled, "*any citizen* has a right to prevent, *even by such force as is necessary to rescue him* [the slave] *from* such illegal custody of any person in whose possession he may be found."[42]

Many Ohioans and many more Kentuckians objected to this reasoning. Lane's decision helped provoke a proslavery riot in Cincinnati the following September, and masters continued to bring slaves to the state and kidnap former slaves who had become free under its laws. Pennsylvania's March 1847 repeal of its six-month transit rule similarly failed to stop these practices. So did legislation Indiana passed in 1851 and Illinois in 1853 banning the entry of all African Americans, slave or free. Still, Ohio's judiciary and Pennsylvania's, Indiana's, and Illinois's legislatures encouraged physical interference with those who brought slaves across the Mason-Dixon line and the Ohio River.[43]

MEANWHILE, mobbings of African Americans and abolitionists in the Lower North contributed to perceptions of southern aggression. Between 1829 and 1849, four major riots occurred in Cincinnati and six in Philadelphia. Scores of other mob actions took place throughout the region. In 1836, white men from Kentucky had a central role in a Cincinnati mob. The following year, white Missourians led rioters in Alton, Illinois.

In Cincinnati, during July 1836, men from Kentucky and city residents

On the evening of November 7, 1837, a mob, including men from Missouri, attacked the Alton, Illinois, warehouse in which Elijah P. Lovejoy stored the printing press for his anti-slavery newspaper, *The Observer*. This woodcut is from [William S. Lincoln], *Alton Trials of Winthrop S. Gilman . . . for the Crime of Riot* (New York: John F. Trow, 1838).

of southern background attacked black neighborhoods and Birney's *Philan-thropist* printing office. The mob, angered by abolitionist activity and a black Independence Day parade, enjoyed support from south of the Ohio River, including a $100 reward for anyone who delivered Birney's dead body. Riot-ers threw his press in the river and destroyed black businesses and homes. Abolitionists claimed "the commercial and slaveholding aristocracy of the south" in league with the city's "kindred commercial aristocracy" planned the attacks.[44]

In Alton, during October 1837, "armed ruffians" from Missouri led mobs that destroyed two of Elijah P. Lovejoy's printing presses. Journalists in nearby St. Louis justified the violence, based on Alton's commercial ties to the South and the passage of southern immigrants, with their slaves, through the town. That November, a similarly composed mob attacked a warehouse, where Lovejoy, his friends, and family maintained an armed guard over a third press. The battle began with coordinated "volleys of stones" from the mob. It escalated to burning the warehouse and finally to exchanges of rifle fire that mortally wounded one of the rioters and killed Lovejoy. For at least a month thereafter, a proslavery mob controlled Alton. Although Lovejoy's friends and enemies all faced criminal charges, local courts found no one guilty.[45]

The Cincinnati and Alton mobs were exceptional in their southern character, as the great majority of antiblack and antiabolitionist rioters in the border free states were white northerners. This was the case in the infamous May 1838 burning of Philadelphia's newly opened Pennsylvania Hall, dedicated by abolitionists to freedom of speech. In addition, no southerners participated when the following year a mob from Zanesville, Ohio, threatened abolitionists meeting in nearby Putnam, burned buildings, and fought volunteers from Putnam on a bridge connecting the two towns. Neither the rioters in Philadelphia nor Putnam required southern leadership to attack African Americans and abolitionists. Instead, local "gentlemen of property and standing" led shopkeepers and laborers. The wealthy leaders believed abolitionist interference with slaveholders threatened commercial prospects and black assertiveness undermined social order. Their poorer followers despised African Americans as economic competitors. They hated white abolitionists for favoring African Americans.

When in February 1841 Morris blamed slaveholders for a Dayton, Ohio mob, which threw rocks at him and burned a black neighborhood, Bailey disagreed. "A certain class of population in the free states," he contended, "needs no stimulus to the indulgence of their lawless propensities." Earlier, John G. Whittier of the *Pennsylvania Freeman* portrayed Philadelphia's white mobs as unwittingly undermining their own rights. Yet the riots and Lovejoy's death helped convince many throughout the North that bloodthirsty slaveholders threatened Pennsylvania, Ohio, Indiana, and Illinois.[46]

Proslavery journalists in the Border South, by praising the rioters, encouraged this point of view. The *Richmond Compiler* portrayed the burning of Pennsylvania Hall as "an index of the proper state of public sentiment on the subject of Abolition." Noting that white women and black men had intermingled in the hall, the *Richmond Whig* declared, "If ever there was a case in which a community should be excused for using violence to . . . enforce the observance, of the canons of decency and a well ordered society, the case was made out for the citizens of Philadelphia in their late proceedings."[47]

ABOLITIONISTS LED in linking kidnapping, slave catching, slaveholding in the North, and riots to "foreign" efforts to control the Lower North. They pioneered rhetoric that later became characteristic of the Republican Party, which by 1856 controlled Ohio and Pennsylvania and, by 1858, Indiana and

Illinois. Morris denounced "riots, burning, and murders," and attempts to transform human beings into property. "The Bowie-knife and the pistol," he claimed in January 1838, are "substituted for reason and argument, usurping the power of law." If the free states were to remain free, he warned, they had to prevent masters from abducting African Americans and bringing slaves into the North. Unless northerners acted to confine slavery to its constitutional limits, masters would "make war upon and destroy every obstacle in [their] path." Seven years later, the Pennsylvania Liberty Party advised white southerners, "If you chose to cling to such a system—cling to it; but you shall not cross our line; you shall not bring that foul thing here. We know . . . we have no right, as well as no power, to alter your State laws. But remember, that slavery is the mere creature of local or statute law, and cannot exist out of the region where such law has force. . . . You shall not force the corrupted and corrupting blood of that system into every vein and artery of our body politic."[48]

A newspaper published in Indianapolis during the 1844 presidential campaign demonstrated that a less noble version of such attitudes extended beyond African Americans and abolitionists. It showed that fear of southern aggression and antiblack prejudice were compatible. Each major party in 1844 had nominated a slaveholder for president. Democratic nominee James K. Polk of Tennessee unabashedly defended slavery and its territorial expansion. Whig nominee Henry Clay of Kentucky advocated eventual abolition and tried to avoid the expansion issue. Yet Clay insisted on keeping slavery for the foreseeable future. In an ill-chosen phrase, he contended on behalf of white southerners, "If we could not have *Black Slaves* we must have *White Ones*." This led the *Indiana State Sentinel*, a Democratic journal aligned with Polk, to warn its readers that Clay as president "would make *you* slaves, had he not 'sleek and fat' negroes sufficient to do his bidding." Beneath a crude illustration depicting Clay ordering a black couple to abuse a white couple, the *Sentinel* placed these words: "See how calmly the would-be President looks on! See the dandy nigger, with uplifted whip, obeying the orders of his *master*, and applying the lash to the *white* slave? . . . See a charming *white* girl under the control of a black wench. . . . Look! Freeman? Look!"[49]

FROM THE MID-1830s into the mid-1840s, people on each side of the sectional line had reason to believe they suffered from aggressive action against their way of life, interests, rights, and sovereignty. In the Border South, slave escapes, assistance for them, and the circulation of antislavery literature spread fear among the white majority of financial loss and black rebellion.

The *Indiana State Sentinel*, a Democratic newspaper, published this crude woodcut on May 23, 1844. In it, slaveholding politician Henry Clay of Kentucky (right) orders slaves to whip a white northern couple.

The region's journalists and political leaders often exaggerated these threats, stoked emotions, and threatened violent reprisals. In the Lower North, slave escape also had a central role. Small black communities that identified with the escapees sheltered them. A minority of white people—abolitionists, farmers who employed black labor, neighbors of black families—helped them avoid recapture. Many others either witnessed the sometimes-brutal actions of kidnappers and slave catchers or observed masters introducing slaves into a free-labor state. They observed proslavery mobs killing and burning. They worried about their rights, interests, and safety. Border slave state governments underestimated the impact of such worries in the Lower North, when—concerned with mounting northward slave escapes—they launched a series of diplomatic initiatives that had unintended results.

# FOUR

# Interstate Diplomacy

Kentucky governor James Clark announced in December 1838 that he had a "painful and unpleasant but necessary duty" to call attention "to a subject of vast importance to the peace and tranquility of society, as well as to the security of those rights that belong individually to the citizen." The "infuriated fanaticism" of abolitionists and their "wild and illegal projects" against slavery, he asserted, had brought "this happy land" to "the brink of a fearful convulsion." Assisted slave escapes, he warned, threatened Kentucky's entire "north-western boundary," as abolitionists extended "their operations so far as to mingle, personally" with Kentucky slaves. "There is," he charged, "a spirit of Abolition now abroad in the land, that threatens fearfully the overthrow of all social intercourse between neighboring states." Claiming Kentucky had "exercised too much forbearance," he called for "capital punishment" for those convicted of "aiding or assisting a slave from this to any other State." If that were not enough to stop abolitionist aggression, Clark— who belonged to the Whig Party—promised to "call into requisition every power" that Kentucky's constitution and laws invested in him.[1]

Although incidents dating back to the 1810s influenced Clark's angry words, the September 1838 arrest of white abolitionist John B. Mahan at Sardinia, Ohio, by a mounted posse from Mason County, Kentucky, prompted his radical outburst. Mahan, a "muscular, rawboned, and stalwart" Methodist minister, helped organize the Ohio Anti-Slavery Society. He also led armed bands in southern Ohio to help slaves escape and protect African Americans from kidnappers and slave catchers. Charges that he collaborated with a black barber in Maysville, Kentucky, to aid slave escapes led to his arrest.[2]

To avoid the convulsion Clark warned of, the Kentucky legislature in January 1839 sent diplomats to negotiate with the Ohio General Assembly. The resulting Ohio Fugitive Slave Law temporarily lessened white Kentuckians' concerns while heightening those of many Ohioans. They believed William Greathouse, who led the posse that captured Mahan, was a slave catcher engaged in "marauding expeditions" from Kentucky into their state. They charged that Ohio governor Joseph Vance—who like Clark was a Whig—should not have approved serving a Kentucky warrant against an Ohio citizen. They regarded Ohio's new fugitive slave law as an insult to the state's sovereignty.[3]

This Kentucky-Ohio controversy exemplifies how conflict over slave escapes drew in state governments, encouraged exaggerated claims to state sovereignty, and led border slave states to launch diplomatic efforts. On two prior occasions Maryland had sent commissioners to Pennsylvania to protect slavery and quell violence. But by the time Kentucky launched its diplomacy, the stakes were higher. It came at a time when Georgia and Maine, Virginia and New York, and Virginia and Ohio confronted each other. Maryland's earlier interstate efforts had not achieved their objectives, and Kentucky's effort shared a similar fate. The circumstances that led to these initiatives—especially Kentucky's—reveal a great deal about the border conflict. In addition, the Ohio Fugitive Slave Law, its results, the complicating role of party politics, and the failure of interstate diplomacy shaped the national Fugitive Slave Law of 1850 and anticipated the northern reaction to it.[4]

THE EARLIEST ENGAGEMENTS between southern and northern state governments had been less volatile. During the early 1790s, governors of the resolutely proslavery Commonwealth of Virginia and the pro-emancipation Commonwealth of Pennsylvania corresponded regarding interference with rendition of slaves. The futility of this correspondence led Congress to pass the Fugitive Slave Law of 1793 in an influential but unsatisfactory attempt to end disputes (see chapter 1). During a second round of diplomacy, beginning in 1818, Maryland's governor corresponded with his Pennsylvania and New Jersey counterparts. After several missteps, this effort led in early 1826 to seemingly successful contacts between the Maryland legislature and those of Pennsylvania and Delaware.

Marylanders always believed Pennsylvanians were the major culprits in assisting fugitive slaves. And the Maryland-Pennsylvania diplomacy set important precedents affecting the interstate clashes of the 1830s. But escapes and kidnappings also frayed Maryland's relations with slaveholding Delaware and pro-emancipation New Jersey, which had gradually been ending slavery within its bounds since 1804. Therefore, on January 5, 1826, the Maryland Assembly commissioned a "deputation" consisting of state senator Ezekiel F. Chambers and delegates Archibald Lee and Robert H. Goldsborough to travel to Dover and Trenton, as well as Harrisburg. They had authority to "negotiate" in each state "for the purpose of procuring such aid by legislative provisions, or otherwise, as may be most effectual for the recovery of persons bound to, or owing service or labour, to citizens of Maryland, who have heretofore absconded, or who shall hereafter abscond."[5]

Because the New Jersey legislature was not in session, the Maryland commissioners never visited Trenton, and their missions to Dover and Harrisburg had differing results. On January 19, 1826, the Delaware legislature adopted the commissioners' proposal as "An Act Relating to Fugitives from Labour." It committed judges, justices of the peace, and other local officials to issue, on application by masters or their agents, warrants directing sheriffs and constables to arrest alleged fugitive slaves. It required the officials, when they received a minimum of proof, to authorize removal of the captive to the state or territory from which "he or she fled." The act followed the Fugitive Slave Law of 1793 in providing for the punishment by fine, imprisonment, and civil damages of anyone who "shall aid or abet in the rescue of such fugitive," or assemble to "interrupt" rendition. The act also imposed penalties for helping slaves escape by water routes, with a stipulation that African Americans who did so could be whipped.[6]

Delaware, although a slave state, was contested borderland. Two weeks after it adopted its fugitive slave act, citizens gathered in Wilmington to protest. Their views anticipated responses in the Lower North, as they appealed to "universal justice and invaluable rights of man" and claimed that outside interference threatened their state's sovereignty and dignity. The act, they asserted, imposed on Delaware's citizens the "degrading office of assistants to the dealers in human flesh, and . . . jeopardize[d] their own freedom and property at the mandate of a sister republic." It "prostrate[d] the rights of our own citizens, white as well as black."[7]

Amid reports of Delaware's submission and resulting protests, Maryland's diplomats attracted attention as they traveled during late January from Dover to Harrisburg. They met with Pennsylvania governor John Andrew Shulze on February 2. Shulze in turn communicated the object of their mission to the legislature, which appointed a joint committee "to consider the subject, and to hear the commissioners." Decidedly more hostile to proslavery initiatives than their Delaware counterparts, Pennsylvania legislators recast the issue presented to them. Even those who favored conciliating the Marylanders believed Pennsylvania had an obligation to protect black residents. Meanwhile, African Americans, Quakers, and the PAS lobbied against the commissioners on behalf of fugitive slaves and free black people. Consequently, in contrast to what happened in Dover, the committee reported a bill on February 7 that was not what the commissioners hoped for.[8]

According to one of its more conservative supporters, the bill, which passed on March 25, provided "for the peace, honor, & dignity of the commonwealth. . . . secure[d] the *rights* of the free negroes . . . & . . . g[ave] to the unfortunate fugitives themselves, whom we are [constitutionally] *bound* to deliver up—all that we *can* give them."[9] The resulting act failed to provide for jury trials. But it denied masters or their agents the right to recapture alleged fugitive slaves without a Pennsylvania warrant and rejected the oaths of claimants as evidence in removal hearings. It extended protective custody to alleged fugitive slaves, and gave them time to gather evidence on their behalf.

The leading authority on what became known as the Law of 1826, states, "While ostensibly designed to assist slaveholders to recover their slaves; [the law] actually made recovery virtually impossible." One of the Maryland commissioners declared the law was "worse for the Slave holders than no Law at all." Yet, another commissioner interpreted it as "a pledge that states will adhere to the original obligations of the confederacy." Over a decade later, when the fugitive slave and kidnapping issues had become more divisive and dangerous, some leaders in the Border South looked back to the efforts of the Maryland commissioners as successful. Through ignorance or for propaganda they claimed states on either side of the North-South border had in 1826 "cheerfully" sought to cooperate and establish "harmonious relations."[10]

AFTER 1826, kidnapping, assisted escapes, and resistance to slave catchers continued in Pennsylvania and throughout the Lower North. Yet not until the late 1830s was there another round of interstate diplomacy. Events leading to it began in March 1837 when attorney Edward Prigg and three other men from Baltimore arrived in York County, Pennsylvania. They intended to capture Margaret Morgan on behalf of a woman who claimed her as a slave. A local justice of the peace issued Prigg an arrest warrant. But when Prigg returned with Morgan, the justice refused to grant authority to remove her to Maryland. Frustrated and angry, Prigg took Morgan without authority on April 1, 1837, leading a county grand jury to indict him and his companions for kidnapping. Mildly antislavery Pennsylvania governor Joseph Ritner then sought to extradite the four men from Maryland.[11]

When Maryland's Whig governor, Thomas W. Veazey, received Ritner's extradition order, he recognized "he was bound under the federal constitution to render the persons demanded." He and other Maryland officials concluded, nevertheless, that if they complied with Pennsylvania's demand they would weaken the ability of masters to reclaim slaves. They feared they would also "to a great and injurious extent admit the power of the non-slaveholding states in effect to nullify that article of the federal constitution which recognizes the relation of master and slave, and guaranties [sic] the right of property in persons held to service." Faced with this dilemma, Veazey turned, as his predecessors had, to diplomacy.[12]

In November 1837, he dispatched "a deputation to the executive of Pennsylvania, hoping to induce him to withdraw the demand." As this undertaking yielded only delay, a Maryland House of Delegates committee proposed an initiative patterned on that of 1826. The committee suggested appointing three legislators, "whose duty it shall be immediately to proceed to Harrisburg, and to confer with the legislature now in session at that place, and demand from them the dismissal of the indictments now pending in York county . . . and such modification of the laws of that state relating to negroes as will effectively recognize the right of the master to arrest and bring away his absconding slave."[13]

In March 1838, consultations between the Maryland House of Delegates and Senate altered this proposal. The new version directed Governor Veazey to chose a single commissioner, who would "repair to Harrisburg . . . and endeavor to procure the dismissal of the prosecution pending against" Prigg and the others "or to make such arrangements as may be necessary to refer the questions involved, to the Supreme Court of the United States, without compromising the liberty of the accused and obtain such modification of the laws of Pennsylvania, as will preserve the rights of slaveholders, and cherish good will between the two States."

Although Jonathan Meredith, the Maryland commissioner, arrived in Harrisburg too late in the legislative session to accomplish anything in 1838, the second alternative in the legislature's plan of action led to an agreement reached in early 1839. Under it, Veazey extradited the accused Marylanders to stand trial in York County, where they were convicted on May 22, 1839, and the Pennsylvania Supreme Court upheld the conviction so that the U.S. Supreme Court could definitively decide the role of states in recaption.[14] The resulting case, *Prigg v. Pennsylvania* (1842), recognized the constitutionality of the Fugitive Slave Law and rejected state interference in renditions. It thereby redefined the relationship between state governments and enforcement of the fugitive slave clause. The ruling influenced other interstate disputes and provoked a new round of state legislation. It *did not* quell a border struggle based on issues profoundly resistant to legislative and judicial solutions.

AS THE PRIGG CASE UNFOLDED, controversies involving states far from the border region contributed to a sense of crisis during the late 1830s that encouraged additional interstate diplomacy. Each dispute centered on refusals of northern governors to extradite men accused in the South of having helped slaves escape. The controversies raised the specter of physical interstate conflict. They also accentuated sensitivity concerning state sovereignty and strained sectional relations. Georgia and Maine engaged in the first controversy, which only indirectly affected the borderlands.

On May 4, 1837, just over a month after Edward Prigg took Margaret Morgan from Pennsylvania, a slave named Atticus sailed from Savannah, Georgia, on a schooner bound for Thomaston, Maine. Atticus's masters, James and Henry Sagars, who had access to "a fast sailing pilot-boat," pursued the schooner to Thomaston, found Atticus hiding in a barn, and "without any legal process or authority" took him to Savannah. Shortly thereafter, the Sagars charged two Maine citizens—Daniel Philbrook, captain of the schooner, and Edward Kellerman, its mate—with felonious abduction of human property. For their part, the seamen contended that Atticus had concealed himself on board, that they had not discovered him until they were at sea, and therefore they were not responsible for his escape. When two successive governors of Maine used technicalities to reject an extradition order for Philbrook and Kellerman, the Georgia legislature, supported by South Carolina, entered the dispute, which continued into late 1839.[15]

In December 1838, the legislature charged Maine's chief executive with failing to observe the courtesy that should exist "between sister states." It denounced "the machinations of certain fanatics of the north" and accused Maine of encouraging "wanton depredations upon our property." It anticipated arguments for passing the Fugitive Slave Law of 1850 by warning that, unless Congress gave U.S. Courts greater authority in such cases, war must result as southern states had to protect their "*own* people." The Maine Anti-Slavery Society reacted with sarcasm to Georgia's threat. "To send her chivalry into Maine, and carry off the men by force," it observed, "would be a rather delicate affair."[16]

Observers in the Lower North and Border South took the threat more seriously. In Cincinnati, Gamaliel Bailey claimed Georgia had approached declaring "war against a sister state." In regard to Maine, he asked, "What state, having any regard for its honor or security, would consent to abandon the right to protect its own citizens, . . . sacrifice state sovereignty on the altar of slavery, and convert the federal courts into engines of the grossest oppression?" In Baltimore, the proslavery *American Farmer* asserted that if northern governors did not extradite men accused of helping assisting escapes, "there remains to the Southern Planter nothing but shameful and ruinous submission; or self protection by the means of retaliation or defense."[17]

Before the Georgia-Maine controversy ended without resolution, a more dangerous dispute began between Virginia, the largest border slave state, and New York, the home of abolitionists who advocated aggressive action in the South. In July 1839, Norfolk, Virginia, authorities charged three black sailors, all of whom were New York citizens, with aiding in the escape of a slave on the schooner *Robert Center*. When the vessel reached New York City, three Virginia officers carrying "pistols and dirks" came on board. They recovered the escapee and put him on a vessel bound for Norfolk. They also arrested the three sailors and had them jailed in New York on a Virginia warrant. At a habeas corpus hearing, however, the Recorder of New York discharged the sailors. They had not, he ruled, taken the slave against his will, did not know he was onboard their schooner, and were jailed without an examination as required by New York law.[18]

Therefore, the sailors were not in custody when one of the Virginia officers traveled to Albany that July to deliver an extradition order from his state's lieutenant governor Henry L. Hopkins to New York governor William H. Seward. In his initial rejection of the order, Seward—a Whig—merely contended he had not received sufficient evidence the men were guilty of the charges against them. Two months later, after Hopkins pressed him for a fuller response, Seward asserted that he had to protect the "civil liberty" of New York citizens and, since neither New York nor international law recognized slavery, he was not constitutionally bound to extradite the men. The extradition clause, he argued, did not prevent states from acting as "independent, equal and sovereign communities." This remark, and the New York legislature's passage in May 1840 of a law requiring jury trials in fugitive slave cases, produced a furious reaction in Virginia and several other slave states.[19]

That October, Hopkins informed Seward that New York had no constitutional authority to dispute the legitimacy of Virginia law and warned, "*Virginia knows her rights and will at all times maintain them.*" Two months later, Virginia governor David Campbell called on his state's House of Delegates to take action against New York, suggesting the Old Dominion might have to assert its "original rights and the law of self-preservation." The delegates then warned "the non-slaveholding states that they may find, when it is too late, that the patience of the south . . . from repeated aggressions will become exhausted."[20]

As Seward defended his actions, the Virginia General Assembly in February 1841 ordered inspection of all New York vessels leaving Virginia ports. The inspections began in May 1842, after Seward failed to extradite the men and the New York legislature failed to repeal the jury-trial law. A similar extradition controversy between Georgia and New York led the Georgia legislature that December to require vessels from *all* northern states to post bonds against removing slaves from its waters. Shortly thereafter, South Carolina initiated searches of New York vessels. The Virginia-New York and Georgia-New York disputes ended when Seward left office in late 1842. At that point, Georgia repealed its restrictions on New York shipping, and Virginia followed in 1846.[21] Nevertheless, interstate relations across the sectional boundary had deteriorated.

Each side emphasized the other's threat to state sovereignty and alluded to impending conflict. Northerners maintained that Virginia, Georgia, and South Carolina had unconstitutionally attempted to regulate interstate commerce and Virginia and South Carolina had violated the constitutional ban on state alliances. As early as January 1840, the *Pennsylvania Freeman* perceived an impending "interstate war." Two years later, Pittsburgh's *Spirit of Liberty* characterized the governor of South Carolina as "ready for a declaration of war against New York." Threats and warnings also circulated in the Border South. Thomas Ritchie of the *Richmond Enquirer* reminded his readers that Virginia had "not yet parted with the powers of self-defense." Shadrack Penn of the *Louisville Public Advertiser* charged that New York, in refusing to extradite the men and in passing the jury trial law, could do "nothing more . . . in the way of Abolition without invading the Southern States and exciting servile war."[22] In this atmosphere of mutual hostility, distrust, and suspicion, the sovereign states of Kentucky and Ohio engaged in the borderland's most dangerous diplomacy.

THE ACTIONS OF John B. Mahan and his Brown County associates sparked Governor Clark's angry words of December 1838, recounted at the beginning of this chapter. But long-existing tensions between the Old Northwest on the one side and Kentucky and Virginia on the other provide a broader context for the outburst. In 1817, the Kentucky General Assembly called, without success, on its Ohio counterpart to act against slave escapes. Five years later, the assembly suggested, "One or more commissioners . . . be appointed on the part of each state [Kentucky, Ohio, Indiana, and Illinois] to meet at such time and place as may be agreed upon, in order . . . to recommend . . . such laws that may be calculated to . . . secure the rights of [slaveholding] citizens and perpetuate that harmony, which is so desirable between different states." The Ohio General Assembly agreed to appoint two commissioners to meet with those from Kentucky. But nothing came of this initiative, and in 1831 Ohio strengthened its antikidnapping law. The new act made apprehension of fugitive slaves more difficult by prohibiting "carrying out of this State any black or mulatto person," without first taking her or him before a "judge or justice of the peace" to present proof of ownership.[23]

On each side of the Ohio River, the September 1838 arrest of Mahan seemed to fit into a threatening pattern. By the mid-1830s, some Kentuckians believed as many as 20,000 slaves escaped each year across the river. A correspondent of the *Maysville Eagle* claimed some Ohioans made a business of "stealing our negroes" and that "negro-stealing rascals" had attacked him as he traveled in that state.[24] The cross-border abduction in 1837 of Eliza Jane Johnson from her Ripley, Ohio, home to Mason County, Kentucky, (see chapter 3) also had repercussions that worried white Kentuckians. As Governor Vance intervened to secure Johnson's freedom, a rumor spread that Thomas Morris—who was then Ohio's Democratic U.S. senator—had asserted during a visit to Ripley "that war ought to be immediately declared against Kentucky; that perfect non-intercourse should take place, and that every Kentuckian should be *shot* down so soon as he set foot on the Ohio side." One Kentucky resident declared, if Morris had spoken in this manner, the nation had to prepare "to see our glorious stripes and stars wink amid the din of civil war."[25]

At about the same time, a public meeting held in Brown County, Ohio, on November 1 passed resolutions claiming that for six months "negro hunters" had watched houses, searched barns and outhouses, plundered grain fields, and threatened to whip or shoot residents. In at least two instances, Kentuckians had broken into homes of white residents in search of fugitive slaves. Ohio abolitionists also emphasized the Mahan incident's negative impact on state sovereignty and individual rights. They thought Vance should have blocked the arrest as had the governor of Maine in a similar circumstance.[26]

Race and party politics had a role in Ohio. Some journalists regarded the abduction into Kentucky of a white man, such as Mahan, to be more threatening than the frequent taking of black men, women, and children.

Charles Hammond, of the Whiggish *Cincinnati Gazette*, exclaimed regarding Mahan's capture and imprisonment, "Irons on a citizen of Ohio, the victim of perjury! What say our fellow citizens?" Shortly thereafter, the Mahan incident had a crucial role in state elections scheduled for late October. Unlike Hammond, many Whigs only reluctantly admitted that Vance's compliance in the capture of Mahan encouraged invasions of Ohio and threats to its white citizens. That attitude allowed Democrats, who were usually more supportive of southern rights, to use the incident to attract abolitionists by portraying Vance and other Whigs as "tools of the slaveholders." Samuel Medary, the distinguished editor of the *Ohio Statesman*, claimed Democratic gubernatorial candidate Wilson Shannon would protect those who aided fugitive slaves. In contrast Vance, according to Medary, sought "to gratify 'the dark spirit of slavery.'" Ohio voters seemed to agree when they elected Shannon to replace Vance.[27]

A few weeks after the Ohio election, a Mason County jury found Mahan not guilty, because although he had helped slaves escape in Ohio he had not done so within Kentucky's jurisdiction. This verdict relieved some Kentuckians. "Our fellow citizens of Ohio will perceive, from the results of this trial," wrote Lewis Collins of the *Maysville Eagle*, "that there is no disposition on our part to interfere with *their* rights or to encroach upon the sovereignty of their State." But many more believed the jury had freed Mahan on a technicality and thereby encouraged abolitionist assaults. Many also held, contrary to the jury, that the trial proved Ohio abolitionists interfered with slaves in Kentucky. They continued to call on Ohio's government take action against the practice.[28]

Even Collins contended that, in return for leniency toward Mahan, Ohio must "frown down the disposition manifested, by a portion of its citizens, to intermeddle with our rights, by inciting, aiding and abetting the escape of our slaves, which we esteem *property*, and the possession of which is guaranteed by a common constitution." Another Kentucky editor declared, "The anger of Kentucky is waxing warm," and demanded "healing measures" from Ohio. Clark's message that December reflected this outlook. Some went further. The *Warsaw Patriot* claimed only fear would curb abolitionist "demon spirits." It advocated capital punishment for anyone convicted of circulating antislavery documents.[29]

As Kentuckians threatened, Ohioans backtracked. Mahan and other abolitionists disingenuously denied they helped slaves escape or that an escape network existed.[30] Hammond asserted in late November that no one doubted "a number" of Ohioans aided "runaway slaves in escaping from

their masters." He insisted that, because of Ohio's constitutional obligation to protect masters' property rights, it must make aid to fugitive slaves
within its boundaries a "felonious misdemeanor." Even Thomas Morris, in
his failed attempt to gain reelection by the Ohio assembly to the U.S. Senate, endorsed passage of a state law providing for the rendition of fugitive
slaves.[31]

Governor Vance's final annual message, delivered on December 4, 1838,
embodied this moderating trend. On the same day Clark issued his belli-
cose warning, Vance emphasized preserving "peace and harmony." To fail "to
deliver up" fugitive slaves or to interfere "with the domestic institutions of
our neighboring States," he warned, risked "convulsions, anarchy and civil
war." He called on Ohio's General Assembly to enact measures to "secure the
peace and tranquility of our border population and the rights of individuals
in adjoining States."[32]

VANCE'S MESSAGE ENCOURAGED the Whig-controlled Kentucky Assembly's
decision—mentioned at the start of this chapter—to seek a diplomatic so-
lution. The assembly had for years favored resumption of interstate contacts
regarding slave escapes and renditions. In December 1836, it asked Clark to
correspond with the governors of Ohio, Indiana, and Illinois seeking "appropriate legislation." A year later, Clark opened the correspondence, predicting it would produce "prompt legislative notice of the evils complained
of, and the passage of such laws as will prevent their recurrence," but he
made no progress.[33]

Following the Mahan incident, the Kentucky Assembly became more
assertive. Led by Adam Beatty of Mason County, it declared that, without
"concurring legislation on the part of its free state neighbors," Kentucky's
laws punishing those who enticed slaves to escape and resist rendition "cannot be effectively enforced." To encourage Ohio to pass such legislation, the
assembly voted on December 28, 1838 to send two commissioners "forthwith" to Columbus.[34] The assembly contemplated sending commissioners
to Indianapolis as well, but decided to concentrate on Ohio after Indiana's
legislature began on its own to consider resolutions condemning interference with slavery. In early January, former governor James T. Morehead—
a Whig—and Colonel J. Speed Smith—a Democrat—agreed to carry out
the Ohio mission. The *Commonwealth* welcomed this effort, citing a need to
protect "our line of coast between Cincinnati and Louisville" against what it
claimed were thousands who banded together to destroy a large portion of
Kentucky's property.[35]

Ohio's leading journalists, if not most of its citizens, acquiesced to Kentucky's diplomatic venture. They respected slaveholders' rights and wanted to preserve peace. Medary advised embracing the commissioners "unless the time has arrived when all our obligations as confederate states are to cease, and that we are hereafter to be the mere plunderers of each others' acknowledged property and rights." The choice, he asserted, was to remain at peace with Kentuckians "or become their most dangerous enemies." Hammond, who found much "good sense" in Medary's words, declared, "The Kentucky move is a proper one." He praised its "statesman-like spirit" and advised Ohio to make "large concessions" directed at restraining "our citizens from interference with the slave property of Kentucky." He compared the diplomacy involved to that undertaken by the United States and Canada to settle border disputes. The similarly obsequious *Ohio State Journal* remarked, "If the Commonwealth on our southern border, felt aggrieved at the conduct of citizens of Ohio, we know not what method she could have pursued to open a correspondence with Ohio more appropriate than the appointment of honorable legislative commissioners. The method is most respectful, and withal direct."[36]

Based on the responsiveness of the Ohio press and fears concerning the alternatives to diplomacy, most white Kentuckians hoped the state to their north would warmly greet the diplomats. The *Maysville Monitor* declared, "We have no doubt her sense of justice, will prompt her to grant all that in reason our legislature can ask." The *Commonwealth* believed that Kentucky, by sending the commissioners, had shown "the most marked courtesy to a sister State." It expected, "They will be received with every mark of courtesy, and the measure will tend in a great degree, to allay all excitement, and place the future relations of the two States, upon that amiable basis which has long characterized them." A few Kentucky leaders, however, emphasized the profound differences between their state and Ohio. They predicted Morehead and Smith would face resentment, insult, or worse. The *Louisville City Gazette* wrote, "We are not very sanguine. It will be an arduous business." Penn of the *Louisville Public Advertiser* opposed the mission, denying it would "be productive of any very important result."[37]

The method the Ohio government adopted to greet the commissioners and regulate their dealings with the state legislature briefly strengthened this pessimism and exposed the fragility of trust between the states. Kentuckians had assumed the ambassadors, in a manner similar to the Maryland mission to Pennsylvania in 1826, would address the Ohio Assembly and negotiate directly with its members. Instead, prior to their arrival in Columbus on January 20, the Ohio House of Representatives and Senate appointed a joint committee of six to meet them. Subsequently, the Kentucky envoys channeled written communications through Governor Shannon to the Ohio legislature.[38] Collins of the *Eagle* interpreted these developments as "manifestly discourteous to the state of Kentucky." For the commissioners to receive "a respectful hearing," he argued, they had to be "invited, or at least *permitted*, to address the Legislature." Unless sufficient cause existed for the apparent insults, Collins called on Morehead and Smith to "abandon their mission, and return forthwith to Kentucky." Similarly, the *Lexington Observer* perceived in the proceedings at Columbus "a sullen resolution on the part of Ohio to disregard the complaints of Kentucky."[39]

As it turned out, the commissioners *preferred* the mode of communication adopted in Columbus because not all Ohioans welcomed them. Penn, who had no hope for the mission, reported in early February, "For weeks the lobbies of the Senate and House of Representatives of Ohio had been thronged with negroes, presenting petitions, pressing to be placed on grounds of perfect equality with white citizens, and watching [from the galleries] the actions of members on their memorials." The morning after Morehead and Smith arrived, members of the General Assembly presented "no less than sixteen petitions" related to slavery and repeal of Ohio laws discriminating against "colored persons." Not only were these scenes abhorrent to white Kentuckians—scenes never to be permitted in Frankfort—but, noted Penn, "The negroes have their [white] backers and champions—many of them men of smartness," who might subject the commissioners' speeches to misinterpretation and caricature. Therefore, "written communications were required, because they would show, now and hereafter, the real positions taken by the commissioners, as well as the true motives governing members of the Legislature." In early February, the *Commonwealth* decided the commissioners had been received in Columbus "with distinguished courtesy" and written communications were "most respectful, and in strict conformity with diplomatic usage."[40]

For the next several weeks, it seemed nearly everyone agreed the commissioners had succeeded wonderfully in their endeavor. On January 21, 1839, Shannon sent to the Ohio Assembly Kentucky's request for two measures. The first sought to "prevent evil disposed persons" from "enticing away" slaves in Kentucky and "aiding and assisting, or concealing them" in Ohio. The second aimed to facilitate recovery of slaves. On January 26, Shannon transmitted the commissioners' justification for these measures, which reflected the framework established by the Maryland commissioners of 1826 in regard to interstate cooperation to protect masters' rights. The Democratic leadership of an almost evenly divided Ohio legislature then passed, with considerable Whig support, legislation that *seemed* to meet Kentucky's wishes. On February 9, the house approved the bill by a vote of fifty-four to thirteen. The senate took it up on February 15 and, after defeating several amendments, passed it on February 22 by a vote of twenty-six to ten.[41]

The resulting Ohio Fugitive Slave Law, popularly known as the Black Law or Black Act, assured masters in "a spirit of just compromise" that Ohio sheriffs and constables would "seize and arrest" individuals claimed as slaves. It banned jury trials for the accused. It disallowed the increasingly successful strategy, employed by lawyers who defended fugitive slaves, of demanding proof of slavery's legality in a claimant's home state. It imposed ample penalties on those who enticed slaves from other states, helped them on their way once they reached Ohio, interfered with the arrest of fugitive slaves, or rescued them from custody. Anyone convicted of these offenses could be fined up to $500 and jailed for up to sixty days.[42]

A day after the Fugitive Slave Law passed, a "large and respectable body" of Ohio politicians held a "collation" at a Columbus restaurant for the departing commissioners. The event centered on a "festive board sumptuously laden" and decorated with patriotic emblems and mottoes. The first among many toasts pronounced "Kentucky and Ohio—united in interest, affiliated in blood, endeared in the recollections of a common military glory: may the cement of their union endure till the materials are dissolved." Morehead spoke for three-quarters of an hour on the "delicacy" of his and Smith's mission and "the great importance of a continuance of friendly feeling and intercourse between the States, and the preservation of their noble union." The *Statesman* declared the passage of the Fugitive Slave Law a victory for "the *friends of the Union* against the *separatists!*" The Georgetown, Ohio, *Standard* claimed, "Something of this nature has been long needed to prevent abuses and preserve harmony and order."[43]

White Kentuckians expressed similar optimism. When Morehead and Smith, en route to Frankfort, reached Maysville on February 27, the *Eagle* rejoiced: "The commissioners, so far from having been met with coolness, or discourteously treated, were received with marked kindness and entertained with distinguished hospitality." The newspaper's editor regarded Ohio's Black Law to be "all that Kentucky could reasonably ask in reference to her absconding slaves." In the editor's estimation, "a matter . . . fruitful of heart-burning and discord" had been removed and peace assured "between the two commonwealths." The *Western Citizen* of Paris, Kentucky, declared,

"The act is all that Kentucky could ask, and is what Ohio should and did cheerfully grant." Yet, like the Pennsylvania law of 1826, the Ohio law turned out to be no boon for slave catchers. In contrast to the national Fugitive Slave Law of 1793, it allowed legal representation for the accused and sixty days to produce evidence of freedom. The law also retained Ohio's longstanding antikidnapping ordinance, prohibiting attempts "to carry out of this state" persons claimed as fugitive slaves, "without first obtaining sufficient legal authority." Most important, it aroused widespread resistance.[44]

Bipartisan support in Ohio for the Fugitive Slave Law and relieved self-congratulation among Kentucky leaders testified more to the depth of the crisis the states faced than to the law's potential effectiveness. The Kentuckians' relief explains their failure to scrutinize the Black Law and grasp how little their diplomats had gained. Supporters on each side of the river also discounted those who opposed the law. Among prominent journalists, only Bailey and Penn predicted trouble. Few heeded Bailey when he warned Ohio Democrats that their role in passing the Black Law "would forever make them infamous, and bring down a crushing odium on their party." Nevertheless, ample signs indicated trouble lay ahead.[45]

From the start, abolitionists emphasized Kentucky's threat to Ohio's sovereignty and dignity. Bailey characterized Clark's message and outbursts in the Kentucky press as expressions of "a disposition on the part of slaveholders to bully the people of Ohio." He asked mockingly, "Will not Ohio . . . tremble . . . when the anger of Kentucky waxes warm?" After the commissioners arrived in Columbus, others called for open opposition. A man from southern Ohio correctly asserted that compliance with Kentucky's proposals might "accelerate, but cannot possibly retard" antislavery activism. Kentucky, he charged, had sent "bands of armed men into . . . [Ohio] to seize and insult our citizens and even females." They forced "white citizens to flee from their own dwellings to save their lives." Rather than obey laws enacted at Kentucky's request, the man suggested, "It is time that these insulting demands of the slaveholders were met with counter demands—their boasting and menacing threats with manly and dignified defiance."[46]

A minority of Whigs in Ohio's legislature agreed with abolitionists concerning Kentucky's diplomacy and slave renditions. Little opposition to the Fugitive Slave Law emerged in the state house of representatives. But a band of eleven Whigs, led by Benjamin F. Wade of Ashtabula, obstructed its progress in the senate. Wade called the commissioners' justification of their mission "a base libel on the people of this state." He proposed printing 10,000 copies of the justification so Ohioans could see what the commissioners demanded. In a speech that began at 2:00 A.M. on the day the bill passed, he declared his belief in "universal liberty," equality, and justice, and his determination "to resist oppression to the death." Pointing out how "haughty, arrogant" Kentucky slaveholders had to beg Ohio for help in catching "runaways," he predicted they would not get that help because the proposed law was "mean, deceptive, unworthy of the dignity of this State."

No decent man, Wade declared, would support unchristian oppression of "the weak and defenceless." Yet, in denouncing "this aggressive movement of Kentucky," Wade noted fugitive slaves were *not* defenseless. He asserted, "Every slave in the South has an unalienable right to his liberty, and a right to defend that liberty against all aggression, if need be, even unto the death of the assailant. Should a slave, then, escaping through this State, turn upon his pursuer, and in defence of his liberty cleave him to the earth, he is guiltless before God and your own constitution."[47]

Wade's speech inspired others. On March 1, he presented a petition from twenty-eight Licking County residents suggesting—in a parody of the Kentucky mission to Columbus—that the Ohio Assembly send "a delegation" to Frankfort to, among other things, request, "As slavery is likely to be the occasion of continued turmoil between the two States . . . the Legislature of Kentucky . . . take measures for its *speedy abolition*." In April the Stark County Anti-Slavery Society vowed to treat public officials who attempted to enforce the law with "contempt." A few weeks later, the Fayette County society declared Ohioans must obey "the law of the MOST HIGH" in "bidding defiance to the *Black* law of Ohio." In June the state antislavery society described the law as "a dead letter in the statute book."[48]

Soon claims that the law should not and could not be enforced spread beyond Wade and abolitionists. Ohio's former chief justice, Joshua Collett, vowed he would continue to provide food and directions to "colored person[s]" who reached his door. An *Ohio State Journal* correspondent claimed nineteen out of twenty Ohio citizens agreed with Collett. It had been a "farce," wrote the correspondent, to pass the law "at the dictation of foreign slave holders." In a series of addresses in Cincinnati that attracted enthusiastic nonabolitionist audiences, Morris claimed the Kentucky commissioners should have been imprisoned when they reached Columbus. Ohio, according to Morris, had no constitutional duty to return fugitive slaves. He favored passing a law to punish those who "in any way" aided recaption. In June a correspondent of the *Ohio Atlas* claimed the Black Law established "quasi slavery in Ohio." He asked, "Shall we obey?" and answered, "No! No!"[49]

Although many Ohioans supported the law and slave catchers from Kentucky and Virginia briefly became more aggressive, predictions of resistance proved correct. Enforcement became spotty and difficult as slaves continued to escape and Ohio residents helped them. In April 1839, the *Cleveland Observer*, a New Light Presbyterian weekly, reported that a band of thirty slaves had passed through the state on its way to Canada. A few months later, the same newspaper declared in response to an alleged escape of sixteen slaves from Wheeling, "The fugitive law of Ohio, in practice is a nullity. It cannot be generally executed." Meanwhile, the proslavery *Painesville Republican* claimed sixty-four "runaway slaves" from Virginia had, during the preceding weeks, passed through Ashtabula County. In August the *Colored American* reported, "In some few places, attempts" had been made to enforce the Black Law "but never with entire success." By early 1840, the *New Lebanon Aurora* estimated 800 fugitive slaves had crossed Ohio during the previous year and 4,000 Ohioans had aided them. "What a satire. . . !" the *Aurora* declared, "More than two slaves everyday transfer themselves across some portion of the BLACK state [Ohio], and yet no lawyer is feed, no jury tries, no judge condemns, no jail encloses those numerous offenders against the Morehead and Smith law."[50]

When prosecutions occurred, the law's provisions ensured they usually did not turn out well for slaveholders. During the summer of 1839, Adna Van Bibber of Kanawha, Virginia, captured a black man named William Mitchell and brought him before Judge Ozias Bowen at Marion. Bowen allowed Mitchell the requisite forty days to prove he was free, and at a heavily attended trial decided the case in Mitchell's favor. When, after the verdict, Van Bibber and a band of Virginians attempted to seize Mitchell, angry spectators knocked them down and local officials charged them with kidnapping. The following February, Vivian Crosthwait of Warren County, Kentucky—acting under the Black Law in behalf of his father's estate—arrested Jesse Jackson, a black resident of Columbus. A panel of three judges allowed Crosthwait sixty days to gather evidence. Six attorneys volunteered to represent Jackson. After hearing conflicting testimony, the judges freed Jackson, ruling amid applause from spectators, that even if Jackson were a slave, Crosthwait "had no shadow of a right to set up claim to him."[51]

In October 1840, abolitionist Abram Brooke relied on the Black Law to bring about the arrest of a Virginian who was transporting six slaves across Ohio on his way to Missouri. When the case went to court, the judge ruled in favor of the Virginian and a mob attacked Brooke and his supporters. But this was not the way Kentuckians expected the law to be used! Five months later, Kentucky slave catchers stormed the home of a white Oberlin resident and captured a black man. Soon all involved faced charges under the Black Law. The homeowner was indicted for harboring, the black man was jailed pending trial, and the Kentuckians were accused of kidnapping. When the case reached court the following August, the judge ruled against the Kentuckians. Despite the wording of the law, he held they had not proved slavery existed legally in their state. In May 1841, an Ohio circuit court discharged Brooke and fifteen other abolitionists who had been convicted under the Black Law in late 1839 for helping four Virginia slaves escape as they passed through the state with their master, Bennett Raines. "Liberty," the court ruled, "is the fundamental law in Ohio" (see chapter 3).[52]

Kentuckians disagreed among themselves concerning these developments. Whigs and those Democrats who had supported sending the commissioners sought to avoid conflict with Ohio. They claimed, despite evidence to the contrary, that the Ohio Fugitive Slave Law had succeeded. In June 1839, the *Commonwealth* praised the law for its positive impact on the "public mind" in Kentucky by "allaying those angry feelings which threatened to disturb the peace of two neighboring commonwealths." Six months later, Charles A. Wickliffe, who became acting governor that August on the death of Clark, made similar remarks in his annual message. He claimed the law promoted greater security for slave property and had "obviated and suppressed" the "difficulties and practices which threaten to disturb the peaceful relations of the citizens of Kentucky and Ohio, residing upon the Ohio [River] border of the two States."[53]

Most Kentucky Democrats were less accommodating. As early as May 1839, Penn reminded his readers that abolitionists remained active in Cincinnati and across the North. A month later, the *Western Citizen* of Paris reported, "The law recently enacted by Ohio for the protection of the slave property of Kentucky, is not doing much good."[54] However, aware of rising anger in Ohio and the political risks Ohio Democrats had taken on behalf of slaveholders, Kentucky Democrats did not advocate action against their neighbor to the north. Instead they followed Robert Wickliffe in seeking to strengthen slavery in Kentucky by repealing its 1833 law banning slave importations.

This oblique approach led some frontline slaveholders to rely on their own resources. In August 1839, a Covington master captured an escaping family of seven near Cincinnati and returned the family to Kentucky without the judicial hearing the Black Law required. In November 1841, citizens of Kenton, Kentucky—located just south of Cincinnati—angered "by the excessive annoyance to which they are continually subject, in the escape of their slaves to the opposite side of the river," organized a vigilance association to undertake recapture. In December 1842, men from Kentucky kidnapped from Clermont County, Ohio, the wife and four children of Vincent Wigglesworth, angering his nonabolitionist neighbors (see chapter 3). Although Hammond and Morris differed considerably in their views on slavery, they agreed that "rash and unwise conduct" by Kentuckians increased after the passage of the Black Law.[55]

THE KENTUCKY COMMISSIONERS, resistance to the Black Law, and an apparent upsurge of incursions from Kentucky contributed to a dawning awareness among Ohio politicians that subservience to slaveholders' demands threatened their electoral prospects. In October 1839, the *Painesville Telegraph* reported, "Thus far every member of the legislature from the [Western] Reserve, who voted for the infamous *black law* of last winter, has been dropped [for renomination] by common consent; while several of those who went against it, are nominated already for re-election." In December 1840, the *Philanthropist* added that of "the seventy-eight members" of the Ohio Assembly who voted for the Black Law "ONLY FIVE" had regained their seats.[56]

Calls for repeal of the Black Law accompanied these developments. Within a few weeks of its passage, citizens of Bellefontaine circulated a petition against it. Within a few months, repeal became a theme among Ohio abolitionists and Quakers. Nevertheless, Democrats, who emphasized economic issues, performed well enough in the 1839 elections to retain control of the General Assembly. Consequently, the legislature's Select Committee on Petitions refused to endorse repeal of the law or amendment of it to provide jury trials. The committee maintained reasonably enough that the law "had thus far operated without abuse or oppression" and "time alone can determine" if it were the best means of achieving its object. Following a Whig victory in the fall 1840 elections, which gave the party control of the governor's office and the legislature, more anti–Black Law petitions reached Columbus. But, once again the legislature rejected repeal, this time arguing the Black Law provided protections for alleged fugitive slaves that did not exist under the federal law of 1793. Instead of repeal, Albert A. Bliss, a Whig who represented Medina and Lorain Counties, reported a bill from the house judiciary committee to amend the law so that it would provide for jury trials for accused fugitive slaves. On March 18, 1841, the house postponed the bill indefinitely by a vote of thirty-five to thirty-two. A similar bill in the senate failed by a vote of twenty-four to eight.[57]

A year later, the U.S. Supreme Court decision in *Prigg v. Pennsylvania* hampered further efforts to amend the Black Law, since the court implied the law violated the U.S. Constitution. In suggesting that *any* state legislation affecting recaption was null and void, *Prigg* also mortally wounded interstate diplomacy as a means to deal with the fugitive slave issue. In November 1842, a Granville, Ohio, judge freed a black man claimed as a slave by a Clark County, Kentucky, master. The judge contended *Prigg* made the Ohio Fugitive Slave Law unconstitutional.[58]

Nevertheless, the interrelated party politics of Kentucky and Ohio led to legislative repeal of the law rather than judicial nullification. Kentucky Democrats and Whigs each supported slaveholding interests and the Union. But Kentucky Democrats portrayed Whigs as either allies or dupes of abolitionists, while Whigs portrayed Democrats as South Carolina-style nullifiers. In Ohio, Democrats and Whigs each revered the Union and defended state sovereignty. But Democrats charged Whigs with abolitionism, while Whigs charged Democrats with subservience to the South.[59] In 1840 and 1842, the attributions remained the same in Kentucky but reversed in Ohio, as in each of these years Kentucky slaveholders campaigned in Ohio for Whig candidates against the very Democrats who had championed the Black Law.

In 1840 the campaign for Whig presidential candidate, William Henry Harrison, led prominent Kentucky Whigs to head north as Harrison spokesmen. As soon as such powerful Whig slaveholders as former Kentucky commissioner Morehead, former governors Thomas Metcalfe and Charles A. Wickliffe, and Congressman John Chambers reached Ohio, Ohio Democrats lost enthusiasm for the Black Law. They lost more when Whigs won that year's elections in Kentucky, Ohio, and nationally. Feeling betrayed by slaveholders he had helped, one Ohio Democrat said, "He would not give a pin if the Black law were repealed." Others lamented "the ingratitude of the slaveocracy." They pledged, "Never [to] lift a finger again to help them put down the fanatics."[60]

Democrats took control of the Ohio House of Representatives in the fall 1841 elections. The next year, Ohio Whigs undertook an effort to regain the house and retain the governorship. But when they brought Henry Clay— their party's prospective presidential nominee for 1844—and other prominent Kentuckians to speak at a huge barbeque in Dayton on September 29, 1842, Ohio Democrats called Ohio Whigs traitors. Medary charged that the Whigs had invited "into this sovereign and independent state . . . a mob of Kentucky mercenaries, political desperadoes and demagogues." He advised voters to join the Ohio Democrats "in support [of] the constitution of their state, the integrity of their free institutions." A "gentleman in Cincinnati" promised that when Democrats won in Ohio they would provide the justice Kentuckians "seem to merit, *the repeal of all laws in Ohio, that are intended to protect their rights, acquired under the peculiar institution of their State.*" Another Ohio Democrat went so far as to appeal to the "Slaves of Kentucky" to resist their masters. There were other issues in the Ohio election of 1842. But, when the Democrats elected Shannon and gained control of the state legislature with a margin of twenty-three to thirteen in the senate and forty to thirty-two in the house of representatives, they made repeal of the Black Law a priority.[61]

On December 6, twenty-five-year-old Democrat James B. Steedman—one of two members who represented Ohio's newly organized northwestern counties, and a future major general in the Civil War—introduced a bill into the state house to repeal the Black Law. Steedman was no abolitionist or advocate of black rights. Instead, he believed Kentucky had insulted Ohio's sovereignty and hurt his party. After Ohio had been good enough to pass the Black Law at the "insistence of the State of Kentucky," he complained, "The people of that State had sent agents here to interfere with our own domestic concerns." Therefore, "he thought it nothing but justice to let them take care of their own negroes, without calling for the aid of a party which has been treated in bad faith." Not all Ohio Democrats favored repeal. Steedman's bill passed the house by a vote of forty-six to twenty-four, with the majority made up equally of Democrats and Whigs. On December 17, the senate passed a slightly amended version of the bill by a twenty-five to eleven margin, with Democrats accounting for ten of the eleven dissenters. The amended bill became law when the house passed the senate version on January 19, 1843.[62]

The likelihood that *Prigg* had doomed the Black Law and Kentucky's failure to object to repeal of a law that had not benefited slaveholders suggests anticlimax. Abolitionists and some Whigs characterized the Ohio Democrats' motives as political and selfish. Yet, Democratic leadership for repeal demonstrates the depth of animosity in the Lower North toward the Border South. That the Democratic-controlled legislature responded to charges that Oberlin College was a "thoroughfare for slaves en route to Canada" by *refusing* to revoke its charter, and that Steedman's bill maintained Ohio's 1831 antikidnapping law underlines this fact. Ohio chief justice Reuben Wood, a Democrat, later ruled the antikidnapping law unconstitutional under *Prigg*. But after 1842, no Ohio legislature dared to facilitate slave renditions. This was the case throughout the rest of the Lower North as well.[63]

THE KENTUCKY COMMISSIONERS had urged, and the Ohio legislature had passed, the Fugitive Slave Law of 1839 to protect slavery and halt a downward spiral in relations between the two states. But the law did not prevent slaves from escaping or people north of the Ohio River from helping them. Like Maryland's earlier initiatives in Pennsylvania, Kentucky's in Ohio indicated—well beyond the *Prigg* decision—the ineffectiveness of border slave-state diplomacy in dealing with conflict over slave escape and slave catching. Never again did a slave state send emissaries to negotiate with northern neighbors.

The failure of interstate diplomacy helps explain the leadership exercised in 1850 by otherwise moderate politicians of the Border South in Congress's passage of a new *national* fugitive slave law that relied on U.S. marshals for enforcement. During 1850 and ever since, critics have noted how the law's stringent, unfair, and invasive provisions guaranteed northern resistance and heightened sectional animosities. The provisions contributed to the coming of the Civil War and destruction of the institution the law sought to protect. Yet, based on experience, most leaders in the Border South believed they had little choice. They believed they had to seek active national protection to preserve slavery in their region. A large minority in the Border South, however, had learned a different lesson. Only expanded "border war," they contended—not federal legislation—could protect against slave escape and abolitionist incursions. Of course, the expanded war that came in 1861 did not go as they hoped.[64]

# FIVE

# Fighting against Slavery
# in the Lower North

In December 1844, the *Telegraph* of Georgetown, Ohio, reported an "affray" between "some Kentucky negro-hunters and a number of abolitionists" at the racially integrated Red Oak settlement. Located west-northwest of Ripley, Georgetown and Red Oak were way stations on the underground railroad in heavily abolitionized Brown County. Colonel Edward Towers, who led the Kentuckians, had learned that two white men, Robert Miller and Absalom King, had taken into their homes six slaves from his Mason County estate. Towers's party found two of the slaves at Miller's house. As Miller attempted to protect the slaves, "the incensed Kentuckians" knocked him down and stabbed him several times. He "lingered but a few moments, and died." Neighbors spread an alarm, so that when Towers and his band reached King's house, they faced "four or five armed men, who declared their determination to resist any search of the house." One of Towers's sons died in the ensuing battle, and another of the Kentuckians, firing into the house through a window, mortally wounded King as he reloaded "some of the fire-arms." With remarkable dispatch, a posse led by the county sheriff intervened to stop the fighting and arrest the "ringleaders of each party." Yet "another band of Kentuckians," led by the Colonel's brother, captured and hanged one of the fugitive slaves, burned Miller's and King's houses, beat a white man, and retreated south across the Ohio River.[1]

Aside from a high mortality rate and a peace officer's evenhanded response, the fighting that December was not extraordinary on the North-South border. It was neither the largest nor longest skirmish between antislavery and proslavery forces in the Lower North during the three decades preceding the Civil War. William Lloyd Garrison exaggerated when he characterized this "bloody tragedy, enacted on the free soil of Ohio, by a gang of

Kentucky slaveholders" as "probably, but 'the beginning of the end.'" The proslavery *New York Sun* similarly overemphasized the confrontation's impact when it blamed abolitionists for the violence and declared, "This is but the precursor to more sanguinary contests." In reality, rather than mark a turning point, the deadly fighting at Red Oak exemplified endemic borderlands violence between proslavery and antislavery forces during the 1830s and 1840s. Each incident made peaceful state-level solutions less likely. According to the *Observer*, of Lexington, Kentucky, northern "slave-stealing miscreants," like those at Red Oak, had to be taught "a lesson which they will not forget."[2]

Where chapter 2 discusses the threat posed by antislavery forces to the Border South, and chapter 3 the proslavery threat to the Lower North, this and the following chapters focus on violent resistance to these threats. This chapter investigates the nature of the fighting in the Lower North, the motives of black and white northerners involved, the role of abolitionists, and the impact of the violence on local officials and slave catchers. It categorizes and analyzes the forms of physical conflict that occurred, and concludes with a description of a series of clashes in southwestern Ohio.

MANY OF THOSE throughout the Lower North who opposed slavery faced and employed deadly force. Sometimes antislavery fighters relied on improvised weapons, including stones, axes, pitchforks, plowshares, scythes, handspikes, tongs, and broomsticks. In other instances, they used clubs, pistols, rifles, double-barreled shotguns, and a variety of knives. They often relied on improvised weapons *and* firearms, as in late 1836 when a black mob at Swedesboro, New Jersey, unleashed "a discharge of musketry and volleys of clubs and stones" in an attempt to free a family captured by slave catchers.[3]

During the late 1830s, antislavery violence became more organized as vigilance associations dedicated to protecting African Americans against kidnappers and slave catchers formed. The first of these appeared in New York City in 1835, and others followed in cities of the Lower North. Vigilance associations operated in Philadelphia by 1837, in Cincinnati by 1838, and in Pittsburgh by the end of the decade. White abolitionists, following Elijah P. Lovejoy's violent death at Alton, Illinois, in 1837, formed a military company. By 1840 there were rural vigilance associations in several western Pennsylvania counties. The associations usually had biracial memberships, although African Americans often served most actively. These groups fought northerners as well as southerners. At Harrisburg, Pennsylvania, during September 1849, African Americans defending a fugitive slave defeated a sheriff's posse. Shortly thereafter, a white volunteer company—marching to fiefs and drums—attacked the black men as they defended their homes.[4]

Compared to fighting between military units in the Mexican War and Civil War or to the slaughter involved in Nat Turner's revolt and aftermath, casualty rates in these conflicts were low, reflecting the relatively small numbers engaged, the use of improvised weapons or unreliable firearms, and poor marksmanship. There were, nevertheless, many wounds and occasional deaths. Black men and women risked beatings and death, and—as the Red Oak engagement indicates—white people who harbored fugitive slaves faced similar danger. When black and white antislavery vigilantes confronted bands of slave catchers backed by local constables or militia, casualties increased. Yet invading slave catchers suffered the most.[5]

SOMETIMES BLACK INDIVIDUALS, households, or fugitive bands fought on their own against slave catchers or kidnappers to preserve their freedom or that of the people they harbored. Other times, fugitive slaves, kidnapping victims, or slaves in transit sparked violence between opposing white groups. Violent encounters also occurred between black or integrated antislavery vigilante bands and men from the Border South and/or their northern proslavery allies. Often, close-quarter fighting that began indoors among a few individuals led to wider confrontations involving mobs or posses combating—usually smaller—bands of slave catchers or kidnappers.

The motivation of African Americans who fought is clear. Black men and—less often—women defended themselves and their community. They realized slavery, discriminatory legislation, and southern white violence threatened their freedom, well-being, and lives. Formal membership in antislavery organizations and involvement in underground railroad activities helped motivate such black leaders in the Lower North as Robert Purvis of Philadelphia and Martin R. Delany of Pittsburgh to engage in illegal and risky conflicts. But necessity and visceral reaction to physical threats sufficed to motivate the majority of black participants. A few African Americans, either for money or self-preservation, helped slave catchers. But black people overwhelmingly regarded masters and their agents as deadly enemies.

The attitudes of white people in the Lower North regarding slave catchers, kidnappers, and their allies were more complicated than those of their black counterparts. Most white residents, regardless of their views on slavery, race, and the U.S. Constitution, avoided involvement in physical struggles. Others who recognized a constitutional right to recapture human property and bring slaves temporarily into free labor states supported the masters. Among them were the "gentlemen of property and standing" who led antiabolitionist mobs in defense of the social order. Businessmen who depended on trade with the South, day laborers fearful of competition with African Americans, members of conservative churches, and most Democrats also sided with the South. In addition, there were white men, known disparagingly as "*volunteer* agents" or "hirelings," whom slave catchers paid to assist them.[6]

Arrayed against these groups was a minority of white men—and far fewer women—who risked life and injury to protect fugitive slaves from recapture or to free slaves whom masters brought into the North. Because Quakers and abolitionists welcomed African Americans to their communities, employed them, or helped them on their way, they sometimes found themselves standing between slave catchers and their prey. Newspaper accounts identify abolitionists and Quakers as prominent among those who turned out to defend African Americans, often by overwhelming numbers rather than open violence.[7]

Law enforcement officials—city police, constables, sheriffs, and deputy sheriffs—frequently became involved in fights over slave renditions. Depending on their bias, local climate of opinion, or which group reached them first, they sided with slave catchers or with African Americans and their white supporters. Because of the nature of law enforcement in much of early nineteenth-century America, once a judge, justice of the peace, or other magistrate issued a warrant for an alleged fugitive slave, the claimant or his agent had the responsibility to enforce it. Those who secured a writ of habeas corpus on an alleged fugitive's behalf had the same responsibility. But the Fugitive Slave Law of 1793 encouraged masters or their agents to recruit law officers to accompany them. Those who defended African Americans did so as well. So many town, city, and county officials had authority to issue "legal process" that slave catchers and their opponents could each have forces in the field, armed with deadly weapons and legal authority backed by law officers.[8]

In some cases, white residents of the Lower North, who were not Quakers, abolitionists, or law officers, became involved in confrontations. They were often neighbors or employers of black men and women accused of being slaves. In other instances, brutal and illegal methods employed by slave catchers provoked them. The nonabolitionist *Cincinnati Daily Gazette* supported the slaveholders' right, "which the law guarantees," to recapture slaves. But its editors criticized masters and their agents for relying on "*open force*" rather than "legal process." Ohioans, the editors warned, would not consent to "scene[s] of lawless violence, or brutal assault."[9]

Sometimes, natural-rights doctrines inspired violent resistance among individuals who had no particular animosity toward slavery. During a stage-coach ride from Pittsburgh to Erie, a white Pennsylvanian told the editor of the *Pittsburgh Witness* that, although he was "'no abolitionist . . . when he saw a man in pursuit of his liberty . . . he needed no labored and long-winded argument to convince him that the fugitive had a right to himself.'" Northerners also objected to what they regarded as "arrogance" among masters seeking to retrieve a fugitive slave. This was especially the case among African Americans, as white southerners refused to recognize what limited citizenship rights they enjoyed, invaded their homes, and assaulted them. But many white people resented the masters' behavior, especially when they hired northern "scum" to help them.[10]

Lower North abolitionists encouraged such attitudes. As early as 1834, the leaders of an antislavery mob in a town northeast of Pittsburgh proclaimed a Christian duty to release alleged fugitive slaves from custody. In 1838, after fugitive slaves in Illinois used guns to defend themselves, Gamaliel Bailey declared, "Success to the runaway! God bless the runaway!" At Indiana, Pennsylvania, a white abolitionist armed two fugitive slaves he employed on his farm. When slave catchers arrived in the vicinity in April 1845, the abolitionist warned them "to be careful how they interfered with any negroes in Indiana, as they were armed, had guns and knives . . . and most likely would fight." Less than a year later, another white abolitionist praised the "colored population" of Chester County, Pennsylvania, for turning out "en masse" against "hunters."[11]

In a manner similar to critics of Ohio's Black Law, those who advocated violent resistance to kidnappers and slave catchers appealed to state pride and sovereignty. Following the May 1839 recapture of a slave at a cabin near Camden, New Jersey, a local man declared, "We are quite tired of having our territory invaded by these myrmidons of the South." He hoped, "The day will come when the genius of liberty, planting her feet on Mason and Dixon's line, will say to these savage hunters of men, 'thus far shall ye go, but no further.'" In October 1842, Zebina Eastman commented, "Hundreds of those who would shrink from the epithet of abolitionist" helped fugitive slaves because they resented Illinois being a "hunting ground for Missouri slave catchers." There were calls to protect Ohio's sovereignty against "broadcloth gentlemen" and guard Illinois from "marauders from the State of Missouri."[12]

In this climate of opinion, local officials who accommodated masters risked condemnation. In October 1841, the *Western Press* of Mercer, Pennsylvania, admonished two Pittsburgh police officers and a local justice of the peace for aiding two Virginians who sought three fugitive slaves. The *Press* asked its readers, "Are the . . . northern abettors, the sneaking jackells of slavery, the hireling whippers in for the man thieves of the South—to be suffered to trample . . . upon the laws they have sworn to defend?" The *Press* wanted such men "marked by the virtuous community." In many localities, this was already the case. A year later, when a "mostly black" Pittsburgh mob prevented two constables from apprehending a suspected fugitive slave, the city's mayor, aldermen, and police force refused to help the constables.[13]

Such attitudes reached the highest levels of government. In March 1846, Ohio governor Mordecai Bartley charged William Henderson, a Columbus justice of the peace, with "aiding and assisting" in the kidnapping of a black man, because Henderson had issued a warrant for his arrest. Jailed pending trial, Henderson wrote an open letter to the man's master, threatening, "Unless you aid and assist us, you may rely on it that you never need expect an officer in this section of the country ever again to touch anything of the kind for fear of the Penitentiary." African Americans who surrounded courthouses or crowded into courtrooms during rendition hearings added to the pressure on officials. Torrey exaggerated in 1844 when he reported that antipathy to slave catchers had become so intense that few officers in Pennsylvania remained willing to arrest fugitive slaves or those who helped them. Yet masters often had to deal with unsympathetic law officers and magistrates.[14]

IT MIGHT BE supposed that nonabolitionists were more likely than abolitionists and Quakers to resist slave catchers because of the association of these groups with pacifism. But most abolitionists were not fundamentally opposed to violent means, and even those who were, including Quakers, professed varying degrees of pacifism. In late 1836, following what he called the "unfortunate affray" between African Americans and slave catchers, Quaker abolitionist Benjamin Lundy declared, "The violent proceedings on the part of the colored people, are not by any means whatsoever to be justified." He suggested nevertheless that "KIDNAPPING deeds" mitigated the sinfulness of forceful resistance. Charles T. Torrey more actively relaxed his nonviolence in response to conditions on the North-South border. Many other abolitionists, including John Rankin, maintained a traditional Christian acceptance of defensive violence.[15]

Even nonviolent abolitionists could act aggressively. In November 1841, about forty of them at Portersville, Pennsylvania, surrounded six armed slave catchers and convinced them to release their captives. Perhaps the southerners were not sure the abolitionists were pacifists. When a local "squire" dropped kidnapping charges against them, the slave catchers "hastened away." Six years later when "Southern gentry" attempted to recover alleged fugitive slaves from a house at Randolph in Portage County, Ohio, between 100 and 200 townspeople surrounded the house. "Though they did not threaten any violence, nor appear at all excited," the locals "quizzed" the southerners "most unmercifully" until they gave up the recovery effort. A similar strategy undertaken by approximately 150 abolitionists in Hamilton County, Indiana, in May 1845 had the same result.[16]

When fighting over slavery occurred in the Lower North, it took a variety of forms. Most common were isolated incidents when black individuals or small groups turned on their pursuers with guns, knives, or improvised weapons. Sometimes these efforts failed; other times they succeeded. At Mount Vernon in southern Indiana during October 1836, a black man tried to use a rifle to protect his wife and child against a "gang" of Kentuckians, only to be knocked down and beaten until his breastbone broke. In June 1838, two black men armed with rifles, who had escaped from Missouri to Quincy, Illinois, were about to eat a hog they had killed when a dozen local men, seeking a reward, surrounded them. The ensuing gunfight left one of the slaves dead with a bullet in his "bowels," one of the slave catchers near death with a wounded leg, and the surviving slave in custody. In Somerset County, Pennsylvania, during July 1846, "a wagoner from Ohio," named Holland attempted to capture a fugitive slave from Maryland. Holland hoped to gain a $150 reward. But as the two men fought at a tavern, the slave stabbed Holland in the heart with a "long knife" and escaped into the night.[17]

No wider conflict resulted from these incidents. In many other cases, masters, their agents, or bounty hunters captured suspected fugitives with little or no force, took them before compliant officials, and headed south. But in scores of localities across the Lower North, attempts to apprehend alleged escapees, whether carried out to the letter of the law or in disregard of it, sparked enough physical opposition to convince contemporaries they were at the center of a large violent sectional struggle. Three types of engagements predominated. There were *confrontations* at the scenes of abduction attempts that pitted neighbors and/or abolitionists against slave catchers. There were *pursuits* of slave catchers and their victims undertaken by either vigilantes or posses. And there were courtroom or jailhouse *riots* designed to rescue alleged fugitives if a judicial ruling favored those who claimed them. In another category were *liberations* of slaves in transit as black or abolitionist groups, either by force or threat, freed slaves who accompanied their masters on visits to or trips through the Lower North.

Confrontations over fugitive slaves, such as the one at Red Oak, occurred in black or racially integrated communities and the homes of white people who harbored or employed black men and women. Although the numbers of people involved in confrontations were smaller than in pursuits or riots, they were at times substantial enough to attract attention in the commercial as well as antislavery press. Black people were their own first line of defense. But white antislavery activists also stood against slave catchers and law officers.

Such interaction abounded in Brown County, Ohio. Five years prior to the fighting at Red Oak, "the colored settlement on Brush Creek" endured a much longer but less deadly struggle between pro- and antislavery forces. On Sunday, April 7, 1839, five mounted "*volunteer* agents of Kentucky kidnappers" from nearby Georgetown rode to Brush Creek seeking Thomas Fox. His cries for help "brought to his assistance several of his neighbors; one of whom was a white man." When the volunteers could not produce a warrant, the neighbors drove them off and freed Fox. A week later, the volunteers returned with reinforcements, a constable named Valentine Carberry, and a warrant for the arrest of the neighbors on charges of assault and battery. The reinforced volunteers entered the settlement's church, dragged Moses Cumberland from his pew, and fought their way to their horses through a group of angry parishioners, among whom Sally Hudson was most aggressive.[18]

Before the volunteers headed with Cumberland toward the home of a local justice of the peace, one of the church members went to the nearby white abolitionist center of Sardinia, seeking help. Immediately, fifteen Sardinians set off on horseback for Brush Creek "to render such assistance as might be necessary in the maintenance of good order." The Reverend John B. Mahan, who a year earlier had been abducted from Ohio to Kentucky to stand trial for helping slaves escape (see chapter 4), led the Sardinians, who brought their own constable and justice of the peace. Mahan's band and some black men encountered the volunteers about two miles from Bush Creek. Carberry later testified that the Sardinians carried pistols and threatened to use them if he did not release Cumberland. Apparently fearing for his life, Carberry "put spurs to his horse, and left the black man with his abolitionist friends."[19]

The next day, Monday, April 15, Carberry had Mahan and five other Sardinians arrested and brought to Georgetown on charges of riot and assault. A magistrate released three of them for lack of evidence. Mahan and two others posted bond pending a trial in September. The following Sunday, the men from Georgetown, joined by other volunteers from New Hope, returned to Brush Creek but could not locate "the person they attempted to kidnap, or any of those who had defeated them in that attempt." When on Tuesday, April 30, eighteen volunteers "armed with guns and pistols" tried again, "a number of colored persons, and two or three whites . . . assembled" to stop them. During a fierce struggle, the volunteers picked out Sally Hudson and beat her. When she tried to run away, one of them mortally wounded her with a pistol shot to her back. This ended the fighting as both sides recoiled at the cowardly act. Although a Brown County grand jury refused to indict Hudson's killer, that September a Georgetown jury convicted Mahan and the other two Sardinians. They received sentences of ten days in jail on bread and water, and relied on technicalities to have their convictions reversed.[20]

At Brush Creek, African Americans and white abolitionists demonstrated their willingness to fight slave catchers. In Chester County, Pennsylvania, during early April 1844, they won a more decisive victory. Located close to the North-South line, and home to several black settlements and plenty of abolitionists, Chester County—like Brown County—was a prime location for sectional conflict. At dawn on April 1, a band of five Marylanders and two "Chester Country *volunteers*," carrying "pistols, dirks, and handcuffs, &c." arrived in East Caln, near Coatesville. There, without legal authority, the slave catchers attempted to capture "a colored man" named Tom who lived with his wife on the premises of a white man named Michael Myers. As the men entered his home, Tom "seized an axe which lay under his bed, and immediately gave battle." He drove the Marylanders outdoors and continued to get the best of them until one of the volunteers grabbed him from behind. At that point, Tom's wife picked up the axe. Hoping to frighten her or hurt Tom, a Marylander fired his pistol only to wound one of the volunteers. Meanwhile, Tom's cries for help brought a group of neighbors, "both white and black armed with guns, pistols, forks, and hoes." Several Marylanders "hastily decamped," either to get medical help for the volunteer or out of fear for their lives. That left two of their comrades, "pistol[s] in hand, guarding their prey, and threatening death to the man who should interfere." Soon, a black man "with a pistol in one hand, and with the other grasping a knife" freed Tom.

According to an account published in the *Pennsylvania Freeman*, the "feelings of the outraged assemblage" that gathered around the Marylanders "and particularly [of] the colored portion, were wrought up to a pitch beyond endurance." A "constable who was present cautioned them [the Marylanders] to beware how they talked and goaded an outraged community." They might, he warned, be treated "as roughly as they had handled Tom, if not more so." By the time another constable arrived to arrest them, the Marylanders had begun to plead with the white portion of the crowd for protection against the black portion. The *Freeman's* correspondent reported, "I have heard several [of the white neighbors] declare, who have always manifested great bitterness toward the colored class and their advocates, that they would have been glad to have seen them [the slave catchers] shot dead." The correspondent concluded, "Thus ended this shameful affair . . . and *worse*, will it be for the *man*, or *men*, who shall dare hereafter to venture a repetition of such an outrage in this county; for a feeling pervades it throughout that needs but the enactment of a similar scene to drive it to acts of terrible retribution."[21] This prophecy proved all too true at nearby Christiana in 1851 (see chapter 7).

There were in the Lower North during the 1840s other confrontations with black and white residents on the one side and slave catchers on the other. In Pittsburgh in July 1845, when a man attempted without a warrant to "seize" a black woman at her home, her husband "gave the alarm" and neighbors arrested the slave catcher. Slightly less than two years later in the same city, a "large crowd . . . principally of colored men" forcibly rescued a man who had been "seized by officers" employed by a Winchester, Virginia, master. In November 1847 in Dauphin County, located just to the north of Harrisburg, Pennsylvania, a confrontation between a white man, who harbored ten fugitive slaves, and the slaves' Maryland masters led each side to send for reinforcements. Nearly forty "mostly colored men," arrived on horseback from Harrisburg, but were too late to prevent the Marylanders from recovering six of the slaves. The following June, three Kentuckians and one local white man seeking a fugitive slave invaded the home of a black couple in Cincinnati. When the black man forced the slave catchers to retreat to his yard, a crowd gathered "in rather dangerous multitudes." Angry black women appeared first. When black men and white people joined them, the Kentuckians gave up.[22]

In some cases, white abolitionists intervened without black support on behalf of fugitive slaves, as at Red Oak, or defended themselves against proslavery reprisals. Near midnight on September 12, 1841, six young men from

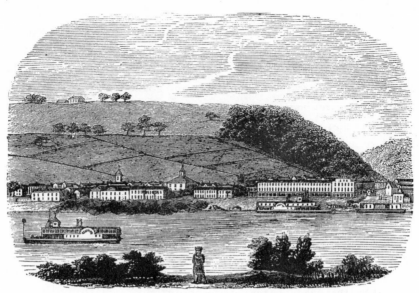

*Drawn by Henry Howe, 1846.*

This 1846 drawing of Ripley, Ohio, shows abolitionist John Rankin's house perched on the hill beyond the town. Each night, the Rankin family hung a lantern as a beacon for escaping slaves. From Henry Howe, *Historical Collections of Ohio: An Encyclopedia of the State*, centennial ed., 2 vols. (Norwalk, Ohio: State of Ohio, 1896).

Kentucky attempted to burn down John Rankin's house, located on a hill above the town of Ripley, Ohio. The Kentuckians hoped to punish Rankin for his long career as an underground-railroad leader. In anticipation of such a reprisal, Rankin had acquired "a number of fire arms" for his large household. When Rankin's son Calvin "heard a low whistle," he and his cousin John R. Rankin "seized each two loaded pistols and ran out . . . without so much as waiting to put on their shoes." As soon as he stepped outside, a bullet grazed Calvin's shoulder. Returning fire, he wounded his assailant, who "cried murder and fled." John R. then shot and mortally wounded another of the Kentuckians, who stumbled away from the house. After "six or seven" additional shots, all of the Kentuckians fled, and eluded a pursuit undertaken by "many of the citizens" of Ripley.[23]

Fifty miles west of Ripley in October 1847 at a village in Butler County, Ohio, "about a dozen" men from Kentucky broke into the home of a white abolitionist. When they discovered he was not home, one of them pointed "a six barreled revolver . . . at the breast of" his wife, threatening to kill her if she did not "divulge the hiding place of the slaves." As "alarm spread through the neighborhood, and a large number armed with rifles began to assemble," the Kentuckians "decamped, threatening, however, they would return with a much stronger force." Eight months later at a village near Sparta in southwestern Illinois, two Missourians had less luck. First, white men prevented them from manacling a black man. Then, when the Missourians presented "a double barreled shot gun" and threatened an invasion that would send the village "to hell," they were arrested.[24]

PURSUITS WERE less common than confrontations, but involved larger numbers and covered more territory. In contrast to the Rankin incident, they usually were not responses to assaults on white abolitionists but to abductions of black men, women, or children. They involved black and white men who sometimes acted together and sometimes independently. In some instances, coordinated but separate black and white bands took up pursuit. The readiness of communities in the Lower North to engage in this activity suggests the warlike conditions in which they lived.

The antislavery stronghold of Oberlin, Ohio, home of racially and sexually integrated Oberlin College, had since the mid-1830s drawn the hatred and disdain of slavery's supporters. In late February 1841, a band of Kentuckians—armed with bowie knives, pistols, and a writ from a Pittsfield, Ohio, justice of the peace—arrived in the town, along with a Lorain County, Ohio, constable. They "attacked" the home of white abolitionist Leonard Paige, assaulted him, threatened to spill his "heart's blood," captured a black man and woman, and set off for Pittsfield. Accounts of what followed vary. An abolitionist correspondent of the *Philanthropist* contended, without reference to racial identity, that a village meeting sent thirty-eight men in pursuit. According to the *Cleveland Advertiser*, a newspaper aligned with the Democratic Party, African Americans "let slip the dogs of war" as the slave-catching party left Oberlin. In this version of the story, black men, joined by white college students and citizens, pursued the Kentuckians and attacked them with guns and clubs.[25]

The accounts agree the pursuers forced the constable and Kentuckians to seek refuge in a house two miles from town, "where they barred the doors and windows and prepared for a deadly conflict." By morning, the mob surrounding the house had increased—the *Advertiser* claimed it numbered "about five hundred"—and antislavery Whig attorney Edwin S. Hamlin arrived from Elyria. Although the *Advertiser* characterized Hamlin as "an anarchist, a fanatic, and a red hot Abolitionist," he saved the slave catchers by convincing them to submit to a hearing at Elyria. In a courtroom crowded with black and white people from Oberlin, a judge questioned the legitimacy of the Kentuckians' warrant, but granted them a continuance to April 30 and had the alleged fugitives jailed. Shortly thereafter, the Kentuckians and the constable were arrested for assaulting Paige. On the following day in the same courthouse, a justice of the peace ordered them, on bonds of $500 each, to appear at the next session of the Loraine County court. After men from Oberlin and Elyria used saws and axes to break the alleged fugitives out of jail "and [carry] them off in a carriage," the Kentuckians forfeited bond, believing themselves "fortunate in being permitted to return home with whole [skins]."[26]

Pursuits also occurred in southeastern Pennsylvania and southern Illinois. In Pennsylvania, a few months after the events in northern Ohio, a Maryland man persuaded two Lancaster County "police officers" to help him capture a "fugitive female slave" in what turned out to be Chester County, where the police lacked authority. After the capture of the woman, five or six black men caught up to the officers' carriage and stopped it by clubbing the horses that drew it. The police opened fire, wounding one of the black men, before the rest beat the officers until they released the woman.

The Illinois pursuit began during September 1843 at Jacksonville, located in the west-central portion of the state. A professional bounty hunter named Calvert and two associates had seized a young black woman. The woman, Lucinda Lea, had "escaped from her master" and found employment in a home at Jacksonville. As the slave catchers left town with their victim, residents incorrectly assumed they had ridden northwest toward the Missouri River. Therefore, "a party of colored people started [from Jacksonville] pretty much on their own hook, for Naples; and another [party] of four whites, went to Meredosia, to head [off] Calvert." The white group learned at Meredosia that Calvert would most likely delay a few days and then head south for St. Louis. This knowledge allowed a third group, headed by attorney L. L. McConnel and armed with guns and "legal process," to catch up to Calvert at Carlinville, located south of Jacksonville. When Calvert threatened to defend himself with "an eight barreled pistol and two bowie knives," McConnel, claiming "he didn't mind a little shooting, on such an occasion, stepped up . . . and arrested him," freeing Lea in the process.[27]

Records of pursuits in which only white men participated are typical of areas bordering the north shore of the Ohio River. Although the level of violence in these pursuits was usually low, they contributed to tensions between the Lower North and Border South. An early instance involved the Posey

County, Indiana, black man whose breastbone had been broken in October 1836 by those who abducted his wife and children. Despite his injury, the man walked ten miles to the town of Mt. Vernon, where his family had been put on a Ohio River ferry, seeking help. In response, two white men boarded a "steamboat in pursuit of the villains." They captured two of the gang at Shawneetown, Illinois, only to have them slip away. Farther down river, at New Madrid, Missouri, a larger group from Mt. Vernon apprehended one of the gang following a gunfight, but by then the woman and children had been sold south.[28]

Another pursuit initiated and carried out by white men had even less success. It began at Peru, a Quaker settlement in Delaware County, Ohio. A black family of four and a single black man, all of whom had escaped from slavery in Mason County, Kentucky, had settled in the town. During October 1838, three men from Mason County captured the woman and children while the men were away and hired a local man to transport the captives in his wagon. When the woman "shrieked," Quaker neighbors "mustered in considerable force, and gave chase." They got a warrant for the Kentuckians' arrest and a constable to enforce it. But when they cornered the slave catchers on the National Road in Jefferson County, the constable accepted the Kentuckians' claim that the woman wanted to go back to her master. At that point, the Quakers gave up and returned home.[29]

OF THE THREE TYPES of engagements in the Lower North, the courtroom and jailhouse riots were the most violent. In some cases—as at the Elyria, Ohio, courthouse—a pursuit led to the riot. In most cases, antislavery mobs, which were comparable in size to the more famous antiabolitionist mobs, acted in response to news that African Americans faced hearings or trials that might lead to enslavement. At least three such mobs, including the one at Elyria, arose in the Old Northwest. But most of them were in Pennsylvania or adjacent portions of New Jersey. In contrast to antiblack and antiabolitionist mobs, antislavery mobs only incidentally damaged property. They nevertheless threatened masters and their agents.[30]

Perhaps the earliest such mob arose in September 1834 at Brookville, Venango County, in west-central Pennsylvania. That month, masters from Jefferson County, Virginia, captured two slaves who had settled near Brookville. A judge issued a warrant to return the slaves, and the masters lodged them, "lightly ironed," in the county jail. Soon Elijah Heath, "an associate-judge," and his brother-in-law James M. Steedman, "a justice of the peace," instigated mob action that freed the fugitives. Heath told a gathering crowd it had a "Christian duty to release the negroes from bondage." The fugitive slave clause of the U.S. Constitution, he said, should be "'nullified.'"[31]

As locally prominent white men who led an antislavery mob, Heath and Steedman were the equivalent of the gentlemen of property and standing who led proslavery mobs. They used their social status to instigate illegal and violent actions on the part of younger white men. But, in most of the subsequent antislavery courthouse riots east of Ohio, African Americans took the lead. They participated in the riots at a much larger numbers than they did in confrontations or pursuits. The size of the mobs, the emotions stirred by rendition cases, and the refusal of either antislavery forces or slave catchers to accept magistrates' rulings that went contrary to their wishes produced volatile situations.

Sometimes, overwhelming numbers of antislavery activists achieved their objective with little violence. The famous case of Basil Dorsey, a fugitive slave from Frederick, Maryland, and a far less prominent case in Pittsburgh demonstrate the quelling effect antislavery mobilization had on slave catchers. Dorsey's master captured him in July 1837 and brought him to Doylestown in Bucks County, Pennsylvania, for a hearing. Shortly thereafter, a crowd of white abolitionists and "colored people" gathered. When the judge accepted the defense attorney's absurd but common argument that the claimants had not proved slavery was legal in Maryland and released Dorsey, the mob prevented the master from recapturing him. Then, under the leadership of black abolitionist Robert Purvis of Philadelphia, the rioters kept the master and his henchmen busy while a horse and wagon transported Dorsey to safety. In the June 1845 Pittsburgh case, a "man-stealer" from Louisville, Kentucky, seized an eighteen-year-old black "lad." Within minutes, a racially integrated mob, led by a white exchange broker, forced the Kentuckian to take his captive to the mayor. Then, as they climbed the stairs to the mayor's office, the mob helped the "boy" escape.[32]

In other cases, governmental intervention peacefully subverted or forcefully prevented rescues and mob violence. At Burlington, New Jersey, in August 1836, a black mob, estimated to have been as large as 500, used minimal force to prevent slave catchers from placing fugitive slave Severn Martin on a steamboat destined for Philadelphia. But when Burlington's mayor persuaded the mob to disperse, the slave catchers proceeded with their plan. Ten years later in Philadelphia, police assembled at the city courthouse stopped several hundred African Americans from rescuing a black man ruled to be the property of a Kent County, Maryland, master. In November 1847, at the largely Quaker community of Mount Holly, New Jersey, a detachment of "some sixty or seventy" state militia "marched into the Court House" to stifle a rescue after a jury awarded custody of "two men and a woman" to another Maryland master.[33]

On several occasions, however, considerable violence resulted when slave catchers or those who sympathized with them defied antislavery mobs. At Swedesboro, New Jersey, on a December evening in 1836, African Americans gathered after a professional Philadelphia slave catcher, named Donahee or Danahower, imprisoned a black family in the basement of a tavern. At 11:00 P.M., forty black men, armed with muskets, clubs, and stones, attacked the tavern. "The windows were broken out, and the building riddled by bullets and large musket shot." The tavern keeper, as he tried ineffectively to protect his property, used "a light fowling piece" to wound "one or more" of the mob and—by accident—an elderly English peddler.[34]

A journalist, implying this was not the first time African Americans gathered at Swedesboro against slave catchers, called on the New Jersey government to end "these incessant tumultuous assemblages." Yet the Swedesboro riot shrinks in comparison to events at Carlisle, Pennsylvania, in June 1847 and nearby Harrisburg in August 1850. At Carlisle, masters from Hagerstown, Maryland, had followed escaping slaves north into south-central Pennsylvania. James H. Kennedy claimed two of the fugitives, a woman and girl, and a Colonel Hollingsworth claimed the third, a man. After the Marylanders captured the escapees, a Carlisle justice of the peace upheld their claims, and local abolitionists responded with a writ of habeas corpus requiring an appearance at the county courthouse. The abolitionists also had the Marylanders charged with kidnapping, and African Americans "assembled in large crowds in the courtroom and around the building."

When the judge ruled in favor of Kennedy and Hollingsworth, "constables and officers of the Court, cleared the Courtroom," hoping to prevent a rescue. Outside "the crowd of colored people, men, women, and children" grew to "several hundreds." White abolitionist students from nearby Dickinson College joined them, along with Professor John McClintock. Southern students attending the college came to support Kennedy and Hollingsworth. Several witnesses reported that when the masters and their reclaimed slaves emerged from the courthouse "the rush was made." "Paving stones, brick-bats, missiles of all kinds from the hands of women, as well as men, fell in a perfect shower." A ferocious struggle followed. "Many of the negroes were severely wounded," including women with head injuries and a "boy" who soon died. Kennedy, struck on the head and stabbed in the neck, also expired. His slaves escaped before authorities restored order. In contrast, Hollingsworth survived and returned with his slave to Maryland. A Cumberland County grand jury indicted thirty-six of the rioters. Juries convicted eleven who received sentences of three years in prison, but the Pennsylvania Supreme Court reversed their convictions after they had served eight months.[35]

Three years later at Harrisburg, the outcome might have been more deadly than at Carlisle had militia not intervened. Two masters from Clark County, Virginia, accompanied by ten "assistants" arrived in the city, where they captured three black men, charging them with escape and the theft of the horses they rode. At a habeas corpus hearing, a judge ruled the masters had sufficient proof of escape and theft, but ordered the black men "discharged from confinement" on a variety of technical points. By then, "a great crowd [composed mainly of black men and women] . . . had . . . assembled in front of the jail," and when the Virginians attempted to recapture the men as they exited the building, "a general melee commenced." Although the fugitives "fared decidedly the worst," one of them escaped. As fighting spread beyond the jail's vestibule—and Irish laborers intervened on the Virginians' side—the judge had the Virginians, the remaining fugitives, and ten rioters arrested. When this failed to end the conflict, he ordered the militia "with muskets and bayonets fixed" to disperse the mob.[36]

The less numerous antislavery riots west of Pennsylvania unfolded similarly to those in that state and New Jersey. Among the more significant were those at Marion, Ohio, in August 1839 and South Bend, Indiana, ten years later. The extensively reported Marion riot began when Adna Van Bibber and seven other citizens of Kanawha Court House, Virginia, captured a fugitive slave named William "Bill" Mitchell, who had lived in Marion County for about a year. As Mitchell's trial began on August 26, white abolitionists and other residents crowded the Marion courtroom "to overflowing." In an effort to avoid trouble, Judge Ozias Bowen delayed his decision until the following morning. But when he ruled against Van Bibber, the Virginians "seized the prisoner" and "presented pistols, bowie knives, dirks, etc." As they dragged Mitchell through the streets to the office of a justice of the peace, where they hoped to receive a more favorable ruling, "the populace became enraged and attacked with stones and whatever missiles they could get hold of." As these improvised weapons failed to secure Mitchell's release, some of the rioters broke into a state arsenal to get muskets. Now better armed and led by an associate judge, they burst into the justice of the peace's office to liberate Mitchell "in defiance of cocked pistols and flashing steel." Even then, the Virginians did not give up. Two of them pursued Mitchell only to be knocked down and beaten. Mitchell escaped, eight arrested rioters gained release on bond, and the Virginians hastened home.[37]

Similar events occurred at South Bend. In October 1847, a family of six escaped from Boone County, Kentucky, into Indiana. Their master, John Norris, and forty other men spent two months searching for the family before temporarily giving up. Nearly two years later, Norris and eight other men captured the mother and three boys in Michigan. When on their way south the Kentuckians reached South Bend, 140 residents, some armed with guns and others with "bricks, stones, or clubs rallied against them." Local abolitionists, with the help of the county sheriff, secured a court order to release the fugitives. In a familiar southern response, Norris and his associates drew pistols, and threatened to shoot anyone who interfered. Although Norris succeeded in having the woman and children jailed, he faced arrest warrants for kidnapping in Michigan and for assault and riot in South Bend. To make matters worse for him, between 75 and 400 armed black men arrived. They "entered the village in companies, some of them bearing firearms, and almost all had clubs." Faced with this force, Norris gave up his attempt to recover the family, and—perhaps in recompense—a local grand jury failed to indict him and his associates. In early 1855, Norris won a federal legal suit for damages.[38]

FORCEFUL RESISTANCE in the Lower North to the recapture of fugitive slaves constituted a major aspect of cross-border skirmishing during the 1830s and 1840s. Thousands of people in the region fought against what they regarded as brutal, inhumane, unjust, and intrusive efforts to reenslave men, women, and children. The aggressiveness and arrogance of masters and their agents shocked many white residents who were not otherwise sympathetic to African Americans or hostile to slavery. In turn, as masters risked injury, death, arrest, and imprisonment, in attempts to recover bondpeople, they came to regard the Lower North as a hostile, perplexing, and alien land where they faced judicial chaos as well as mobs. Officials often charged masters with kidnapping and assault, and they had to post exorbitant bonds to remain free. Even when there were no legal charges, the masters' journeys consumed time and money. As abolitionist John Cross reported in December 1839, a failed attempt by a band of Missourians to capture a fugitive slave at Joliet, Illinois, cost between $500 and $600. The Missourians had to pay for transporting witnesses from St. Louis, four weeks room and board at a hotel, the local "rabble" who helped them, lawyers, court costs, and horses.[39]

Some towns, counties, and sub-regions were especially dangerous. In August 1837, after a crowd and judge foiled a recaption in Bucks County, Pennsylvania, a local Quaker declared, if the "friends of the oppressed" remained vigilant "not many runaway slaves will be reclaimed from this county." Cross claimed that Missourians' intrusions had "practically abolitionized the village of Joliet—secured the supreme contempt of every body whose opinion is worth a brass farthing." Others issued broader warnings. In October 1847, the *Pennsylvania Freeman* observed, "Constitutional barriers and legal protections" were not enough to protect against the "plantation" spirit. During preliminary congressional debate over what became the Fugitive Slave Act of 1850, Joshua R. Giddings announced, "I am free to say, that if there be a crime for which I would hang a citizen in our State [Ohio], it is that of aiding the slaveholder to seize his trembling victim upon soil consecrated to freedom. . . . Sir, we ought not to deceive Southern men. We should say to them, in all frankness and sincerity, that the day for arresting fugitive slaves has gone by forever."[40]

NOTHING BETTER ILLUSTRATES the divide between the Lower North and Border South than a series of events that unfolded in southwestern Ohio between 1839 and 1841. It began with a forcible and successful abolitionist attempt to free slaves in transit, included a confrontation at an abolitionist's home, and culminated in a spectacularly ugly Cincinnati riot that produced a consensus against slave catchers and altered the city's relationship with Kentucky.

On the evening of November 5, 1839, Bennett Raines, his wife, their two children, and "two colored women and two children," whom Raines claimed as slaves, camped near Wilmington, Ohio, located to the northeast of Cincinnati. The Raines party, traveling from Virginian to Missouri, attracted the attention of seventeen abolitionists from nearby Oakland. The following night near Springboro, the abolitionists, led by Abram Brooke, rode into Raines's camp, informed him they "had come with the full determination and power to see that these colored people should not, without their consent, be conveyed beyond the limits of this state."[41]

The accounts provided by the abolitionists and the Raines family, concerning what followed, differ. The abolitionists maintained that, without violence or "any incivility," they helped the black women and children leave Raines. The Raineses claimed Brooke and the others "stole" their slaves, took $1500 in gold and notes, and knocked down Raines's daughter. In October 1840, a common pleas court convicted Brooke and sixteen others of riot but acquitted them of assault and grand larceny, as the claim they had taken money proved false. An appeal of the riot conviction on a writ of error resulted in the Ohio Supreme Court decision of May 1841 (discussed in chapter 3) that slaves brought voluntarily by masters into the state were automatically emancipated and Ohioans could use force to free them from "illegal custody."[42]

Southern newspapers charged that the Ohio court had "nullified" the privileges and immunities clause of the U.S. Constitution. Moderates in Cincinnati assured Kentuckians they could safely continue to bring their "servants" with them on business and shopping trips to the city. One mildly antislavery city resident wrote, "Nine-tenths of the citizens of Cincinnati. . . . sincerely seek and desire to enjoy friendly and social intercourse with their Southern fellow-citizens." But local abolitionists demanded "more manliness among us."[43]

Physical conflict broke out in the city during late June, with a "serious fracas" between a white family harboring a fugitive slave and a master backed by local law officers. Julius McCauley of Fayette County, Kentucky, had gone to the proslavery Cincinnati magistrate Squire William Doty to get "process in due form" for the rendition of McCauley's recently escaped slave, George. Accompanied by city police officer Robert Black and three constables, McCauley proceeded to the home of Cornelius Burnett, an English immigrant, prosperous candy manufacturer, and president of the city's vigilance association. According to the *Cincinnati Republican*, a conservative daily newspaper, when McCauley's party reached Burnett's home "a serious personal conflict took place between officer Black . . . and Mr. McCauley of the one party, and Burnett, his son and one or two other abolitionists of the other party." The *Republican* reported, "Blows were freely passed, several violently floored, pistols drawn, &c. &c. Mr. McCauley was seriously injured, and the officer slightly." The law officers captured George, and arrested Burnett and his companions. That night, city police prevented a proslavery mob from destroying Burnett's house.[44]

During the following weeks, Kentucky newspapers warned masters they might lose their servants if steamboats on which they traveled stopped at Cincinnati or if they visited the city. Soon the Democratic and proslavery *Cincinnati Enquirer* advised its readers that abolitionists had to be "quelled" to avoid hostility on the part of "our southern neighbors." The newspaper alleged abolitionists had recently attempted "to steal away some negroes from Boone county," Kentucky. It complained that "ladies" from Kentucky who visited Cincinnati not only risked losing their carriage drivers and servants, but were "assaulted by a posse of buck negroes, or persons of lighter skins—but darker principles."[45]

Meanwhile, a series of brawls between African Americans and Irish immigrants culminated on September 3 in a planned attack by a white mob—numbering between 2,000 and 3,000 and including men from Newport and Covington Kentucky—on black-owned shops and houses. In self-defense, black men opened fire with rifles and muskets, injuring several of the rioters and killing a Kentuckian. At one point, the mob brought up a cannon, which—according to the more trustworthy accounts—African Americans captured before it could be used. The following morning, as city authorities persuaded black men to disarm, the mob renewed and expanded its attack. With a company of Kentucky militia on the scene, rioters assaulted black men, killed at least one, and raped several black women. They also wrecked Gamaliel Bailey's *Philanthropist* office and Burnett's bakery.

Bailey and the *Cincinnati Daily Times* emphasized the role of Kentuckians in the attacks. The *Times* charged, "The most forward and efficient leaders of the rioters were volunteers from Kentucky, urged on by a feeling of revenge, created by the actions of the abolitionists in relation to the runaway slaves who take refuge in this city." Bailey characterized Cincinnati as "a conquered province of the slaveholders." The riot ended during its third day as Ohio governor Thomas Corwin, a moderately antislavery Whig, personally organized volunteer companies to stop the violence.[46]

The riot encouraged some Cincinnati residents to organize an antiabolition society, and the viciousness of the mob daunted some abolitionists, including Bailey. When he resumed publication of the *Philanthropist*, he issued a disclaimer "to allay unnecessary excitement, and place ourselves in our proper position before the community." He denied abolitionists advocated race-mixing or helped slaves escape, and he claimed emancipation would reverse northward black migration. But, as historian David Grimsted notes, the riot expanded abolitionist and antisouthern sentiment in Cincinnati. Of the city's four commercial dailies, all but the *Enquirer* condemned the mob, as did local religious papers. Although the twenty-eight men convicted on charges of riot received token punishments from a Democratic judge, it is significant that they were tried at all. Overtly racist Democrats retained political power in the city into the Civil War years, but many nonabolitionist white residents recoiled at the violence inflicted on African Americans by "a drunken mob 'led by a corps of Kentucky negro-whippers.'"[47]

Events during the following two summers demonstrated the new Cincinnati posture toward Kentucky and the South. In August 1842, city magistrate E. V. Brooks ruled in favor of a Kentuckian who claimed a black "occasional resident" of Cincinnati as his slave. But when a band of slave catchers hurried the black man toward the Ohio River, "a party of constables with a bail piece" overtook them at the Covington ferry landing. The constables followed the Kentuckians onboard, attempted "to seize the negro," and the fight continued "to the Kentucky side." In the end, the Kentuckians retained control of their captive, placed him "in the Covington negro depot," and returned to Cincinnati "to have another brush with the Constables." The city's law officers had nevertheless demonstrated a new attitude toward slave catchers. By August 1843, when a Louisiana man raised an antiabolitionist mob to recapture a nine-year-old girl who had slipped away from a docked steamboat, he had no success. The mob numbered about 100 and included many Kentuckians. But when the rioters attacked Burnett's house, neighbors drove them away with an onslaught of bricks, and fourteen armed abolitionists patrolled the city's streets. There were no more antiblack or antiabolitionist mobs in Cincinnati.[48]

VIOLENT RESISTANCE in the Lower North to slave catchers, kidnappers, and masters passing through with slaves characterized the region during the 1830s and 1840s. Led by African Americans and abolitionists, armed struggle influenced and engaged other elements of the population, including government officials and law officers. Isolated incidents, confrontations, pursuits, riots against masters, and opposition to proslavery mobs discouraged masters in the Border South and the white South generally. Combined with the failure of interstate diplomacy to end assistance to fugitive slaves, fighting in the Lower North helped convince masters they needed stronger methods to keep their human property and defend themselves.

# SIX

# The Struggle for the Border South

Cassius M. Clay of Lexington, Kentucky, was not, by northern standards, a radical abolitionist. He did not quite advocate immediate emancipation and, although he sympathized with African Americans, he emphasized how slavery prevented nonslaveholding white southerners from advancing politically, economically, and intellectually. Unlike Garrisonian abolitionists, he rejected neither defensive violence nor union with slaveholders. He *was* a slaveholder until 1843. Unlike New York Liberty abolitionists, he advocated neither the universal illegality of slavery nor helping slaves escape. Nevertheless, throughout the 1840s and 1850s, Clay maintained contact with northern abolitionists of all persuasions and enjoyed their support. He gained their admiration to such a degree that slavery's defenders justly included him among the emissaries of abolitionism in the Border South.[1]

Clay, a Whig prior to 1848 and a cousin of Henry Clay, had emerged in 1841 as an antislavery voice in the Kentucky Assembly and a dangerous defender of his constitutional rights. He described himself as "impulsive, hot-headed, reckless, and passionate." By June 1845, when he began publishing his weekly *True American*, his proslavery enemies agreed with this assessment. More than any other native-born white southerner, Clay personified the worst fears of the slaveholding gentry: one of their own in league with northern abolitionists and African Americans.[2]

In August 1845, Clay outraged slave-state sensibilities concerning class and race. First, he published an anonymous article advocating equal political rights for free black men. Then, weakened and perhaps deranged by typhoid fever, he declared in an editorial directed at slaveholders, "Remember, you who dwell in marble palaces, that there are strong arms and fiery hearts and iron pikes in the streets, and panes of glass only between them and the silver plate on the [side]board and the smooth-skinned woman on the otto-man." Clay continued, "When you have mocked at virtue, denied the agency of God in the affairs of men, and made rapine your honeyed faith, tremble! for the day of retribution is at hand, and the masses will be avenged." Fi-nally, Clay issued a handbill appealing to "laborers of all classes," and asking them "where will you be found when this battle between *Liberty* and *Slavery* is to be fought?" He so intertwined class and race that the Kentucky gentry first assumed he advocated slave revolt rather than, as he explained later, an uprising of the white masses. Thereafter, the gentry charged he sought to arouse white workers *and* black slaves against the social order.[3]

On August 18, a crowd "of several thousands" met at Lexington Court-house in opposition to the *True American*. Its leaders, including a former governor, intended to go beyond statute law. Thomas F. Marshall presented an address justifying the suppression of Clay's newspaper under "the highest of all laws, the law of self-defense." Marshall, a nephew of U.S. chief justice John Marshall, was a former Whig congressman who had joined the Demo-cratic Party to support the annexation of Texas as a slave state. In regard to Clay, he favored "force . . . without judicial process" because "the fullest evi-dence" linked the journalist to northern abolitionists. Marshall accurately charged such northerners with believing "the negro slave here is an American born, entitled to the full benefits and blessings of republican freedom. . . . maintain[ing] for him the right of insurrection." Clay, Marshall contended, was an "agent" of this "incendiary sect," who would force on Kentucky "prin-ciples fatal to her domestic repose, at the risk of his own life and the peace of the community." Clay kindled "horrible fires" in the slave's "already fiery heart." Marshall and a committee of his associates therefore "determined no longer to endure the presence of an armed abolitionist, hurling his fire brands of murder and lust into the bosom of a peaceful and polished city."[4]

Clay refused to accede to what Marshall termed the committee's "won-derfully mild request" that he discontinue his weekly. Clay called the com-mittee a "secret conclave of cowardly assassins." Fearing its members had "a six-pound cannon and some sixty or one hundred balls . . . ready to bat-ter down" his office, he prepared to defend it with his own cannon and a booby-trapped keg of gunpowder. To Marshall, this meant Clay was either "a madman, or that he . . . ha[d] prepared himself for a civil war, in which he expected the non-slaveholding laborers along with the slaves, to flock to his standard, and the war of abolition to begin in Kentucky." Thomas H. Waters, another committee member, said Clay insanely used "the principles of the 'Declaration of Independence'" to link white nonslaveholders with slaves in a "war for universal liberty." Clay caused great excitement "by inflammatory publications, addressed to all the passions of our slaves . . . against the settled institutions of the country, and the safety and the peace of our wives and daughters." Dread of central Kentucky's large black population inspired these charges, and white rioters "brutally attacked . . . several free negroes" on the city square.[5]

Clay's illness forced him to offer concessions to the vigilantes, and he failed to defend his press when on August 19 a "committee of sixty" dismantled and shipped it to Cincinnati. Even so, many white Kentuckians assumed Clay had escalated the border struggle. Like others before him, Marshall alluded to a pressing need to defend slavery on its northern periphery. He declared, "On the frontier of slavery, with three free States fronting and touching us along a border of seven hundred miles, we are peculiarly exposed to the assaults of abolitionists." But, he added, "The plunder of our property, the kidnapping, stealing and abduction of our slaves, is a light evil in comparison with planting a seminary for their infernal doctrines [the *True American*] in the very heart of our densest slave population."[6]

Just as during the 1840s antislavery forces in the Lower North defended African Americans and state sovereignty against slave catchers, Border South proslavery groups were vigilant against abolitionism and slave escapes. New antislavery newspapers in the region, well-publicized underground-railroad ventures, and a series of mass slave escapes encouraged insecurity among masters that led to additional protective measures. By the decade's end, and as the nation faced a major sectional crisis, Border South leaders urged federal action to stop escapes.

CLAY'S *TRUE AMERICAN* was not the first abolitionist publication in the Border South. Gradual abolitionist newspapers had existed in the region during the 1810s and 1820s. Except for Benjamin Lundy's *Genius of Universal Emancipation*, they were short-lived. All of them, including Lundy's, either had failed or had been suppressed by the time of Nat Turner's rebellion. As noted in chapter 2, a committee of slaveholders in Danville, Kentucky, had in 1835 threatened mob a action to dissuade James G. Birney from establishing an antislavery newspaper in that town. Yet, less than a decade later, several high profile abolitionist weeklies appeared in Border South cities. Although they by no means ignored the sinfulness of slavery and the oppression of African Americans, most of them—like the *True American*—emphasized the interests of white nonslaveholders and advocated class-based antislavery political organization.

In August 1843, Joseph Evans Snodgrass, like Clay a former slaveholder, transformed his *Baltimore Saturday Visiter*, initially a literary journal, into a moderate advocate of abolition and the rights of free African Americans. When Clay, who had revived the *True American*, left Kentucky in mid-1846 to fight in the Mexican War, John C. Vaughan, a native of South Carolina and a resident of Cincinnati, edited the paper until a dispute with Clay's proslavery brother, Brutus, led to its suspension. After raising money among northeastern abolitionists, Vaughan in June 1847 initiated the *Examiner* in Louisville as a more moderate antislavery journal. Six months earlier, Gamaliel Bailey moved from Cincinnati to Washington, D.C., to establish the well-financed *National Era*. Between 1847 and 1860, it advocated in turn the Liberty, Free Soil, and Republican parties. It called for abolition in the district, equal rights for local African Americans, and abolition in the South through state legislation. The *Era* absorbed the *Visiter* during the summer of 1847, and Snodgrass became one of its correspondents.[7]

Zebina Eastman, from his vantage point in Chicago, described these antislavery journals in the Border South as "outposts of the Empire." Their animosity to slavery and links to northern abolitionism would have disturbed proslavery interests in any case. As their publication coincided with slave unrest and a series of abolitionist forays into the Border South, they seemed especially dangerous. All of the journals' editors rhetorically opposed slave revolt, abolitionist appeals to slaves, and intrusions into the South to help slaves escape. Many Whigs in the Border South were willing to grant them freedom of the press. But slavery's stronger defenders agreed with Eastman's characterization of the newspapers. In early 1845, when the Maryland House of Delegates rejected legislation to suppress the *Visiter*, the *Marlboro Gazette* called for "*summary steps*" to shut it down. Even judicious Vaughan faced charges in Louisville that he threw "firebrands into this community."[8]

Of all the antislavery journalists in the Border South, Clay and Bailey were the most formidable, particularly in their class appeal to the interests of non-slaveholding white southerners. Clay—who for a time was the darling of the northern abolitionist press—was a large, muscular, and pugnacious brawler who in self-defense used a bowie knife to maim one proslavery opponent and kill another. In the first issue of his *True American*, he warned Robert Wickliffe, against whose son he had fought a duel and whose henchman he had nearly killed, "If you still thirst for bloodshed and violence, the same blade that repelled the assaults of assassin sons, once more in self-defense, is ready to drink of the blood of the hireling horde of sycophants and outlaws of the assassin-sire of assassins." One of Clay's proslavery enemies responded,

"The hemp is ready for your neck. Your life cannot be spared. Plenty thirst for your blood."[9]

In contrast to robust and threatening Clay, Bailey was frail, nonviolent, and diplomatic. Having faced several proslavery mobs in Cincinnati, he came to Washington determined to charm opponents and appeal to white southerners "as men who have minds to be reasoned with, sensibilities to be respected." Yet, like the *True American*, the *National Era* encouraged class struggle in the Border South by calling for the overthrow of "the ruling caste, the Slave Power" so that white men could get better wages and the region progress economically. As a newspaper conducted by a talented journalist in a federal district more subject to northern political influence than a border slave state, the *National Era* appeared to proslavery leaders to be a supremely "mischievous enterprise." After reading the newspaper's first issue, the Georgetown, D.C., city council declared the existence of "such a paper in our midst . . . undoubtedly . . . calculated to arouse the worst feelings of our peaceful population and its vicinity, and thereby tend very greatly to endanger the peace and harmony of the community."[10]

By no means had Bailey, Clay, or the other Border South abolitionists of the 1840s originated the class argument against slavery and slaveholders. During the 1820s, Lundy had used it against slavery in Virginia and Maryland. In 1835, Birney wrote to Gerrit Smith, "The contest is becoming — has become, — one not alone of freedom for the *black*, but freedom for the *white*. . . . There shall be no cessation of the strife until Slavery shall be exterminated, or liberty destroyed." Like Lundy and Birney before them, Bailey, Clay, Snodgrass, and Vaughan claimed slavery hurt wages, economic development, education, land values, respect for the law, and public and private morality. They called for political action in the Border South to bring about its abolition in the near future.[11]

WHAT THE Border South's abolitionist journalists advocated might not seem far removed from the professed views of many white leaders in the region. Following Nat Turner's revolt, the Virginia and Maryland legislatures discussed gradual abolition. The Delaware legislature nearly adopted gradualist plans in 1803 and 1847. Proposals for one form of prospective emancipation or another affected Kentucky's legislature from the early 1830s until 1849. The great majority of masters in all these states, and in Missouri as well, defended slavery as a "necessary evil" rather than as a "positive good." They realized large sectors of their state economies depended on commerce with the North, wage labor was often more profitable than slave labor for the types of crops produced at their latitude, and nonslaveholders embraced free-labor values. Cities such as Washington, Wheeling, Louisville, Richmond, St. Louis, and especially Baltimore acted as wedges for the North's free-labor economy.[12]

Because of these and other developments, knowledgeable people throughout the United States assumed slavery faced inevitable eventual termination in the Border South. Abolitionists—based on their interpretation of public opinion, acts of manumission, escapes, sales south, and the effectiveness of their propaganda—expected state legislation to end slavery in the region. Slavery's fiercest Lower South defenders shared this perception of slavery's weakening in the Border South and parts of the Middle South. How long, one of John C. Calhoun's correspondents asked in 1848, would Maryland, Kentucky, western Virginia, eastern Tennessee, and western North Carolina "feel it in their interest to retain slaves?"[13] Abstractly, the issue was not the demise of slavery in the region, but how and when it would perish.

Yet, during the three decades prior to the Civil War, virtually all white border southerners retained binding economic, political, economic, and cultural commitments to slavery. Racism, family ties, and a tradition of deference linked most white nonslaveholders to slaveholders. The great majority wanted slavery abolished only in the distant future—perhaps in seventy years.[14] Slavery's so-called opponents joined its strongest defenders in regarding free African Americans as idle, disruptive, and dangerous. They believed that if slavery ended in the near future without a plan to remove former slaves, the result would be social and economic disaster. Therefore, unlike abolitionists and free black leaders, they insisted that plans for gradual abolition had to be linked to colonization of former slaves in Africa, Haiti, or some other location outside the United States.[15] They believed slave escape, abolitionist propaganda, antislavery journalists, and political organizations must not be allowed to undermine the existing system. Like slavery's defenders throughout the United States, they contended abolitionists misled otherwise content bondmen into rising up against masters.[16]

Border South Democrats, seeking political gain during the 1840s, exaggerated their Whig opponents' commitment to emancipation and ties to northern abolitionists. Shadrack Penn of the *Louisville Public Advertiser* charged that those in Kentucky who favored prospective gradual emancipation differed from northern fanatics only because they were "not ready to say to the slave '*strike!*'" Penn asked, "Are Kentuckians willing to sanction negro stealing, to act with men engaged in such business, or support politicians and newspapers that indirectly encourage such a crime?" In Penn's view, the mildest criticism of slavery amounted to "jumping . . . into the ranks of the Abolitionists of the North, who are waging an implacable war upon the South." Robert Wickliffe lamented, "While nineteen twentieths of the slaveholders are violent against negroe [*sic*] stealers, none but Democrats vote against negroe stealing and the combination of the negroe party of the North and the Whigs of the South." How, Democrats asked, could individuals who called slavery a "withering pestilence" and an "unmitigated curse"— as Whig gradualists did—consistently criticize "negro stealers?"[17]

ALTHOUGH CHARGES OF "negro stealing" dated to the late eighteenth century and increased during the late 1830s, several well-publicized cases suggested a mounting threat during the 1840s. One involved the arrest on September 28, 1844, of a white couple in Kentucky. Calvin Fairbank, a twenty-eight-year-old Methodist minister from Ohio, and Delia A. Webster, a twenty-seven-year-old teacher from Vermont, helped a black man named Lewis Hayden, his wife, and child escape by carriage from Lexington, Kentucky, to Hopkins, Ohio. Fairbank had contacts with black abolitionists in Oberlin and white abolitionists in Cincinnati. Armed with "a Colt's revolver," he had helped slaves escape from Kentucky and points farther south since 1837.

In the Hayden case, prominent Cincinnati abolitionist Jonathan Blanchard sent Fairbank to John Rankin in Ripley. From there, Fairbank went to Lexington, where he persuaded Webster to join him. As the pair returned to Lexington from Hopkins so that Webster could continue in her teaching position, a posse intercepted and arrested them. At their separate trials, Fairbank admitted his guilt under Kentucky law and Webster pleaded innocent. Although a jury found Webster guilty, she served just two months of a two-year sentence before being pardoned in return for denouncing abolitionists and "what is termed '*Negro Stealing*.'" Fairbank received a fifteen-year sentence at hard labor. He served until 1849, when Hayden—who had moved to Boston—raised money to compensate his former master in return for a pardon for his rescuer.[18]

As northern abolitionists praised Fairbank and Webster for their efforts in Kentucky, white border southerners condemned them. The *Lexington Gazette* declared, "Their crime is evidently the result of deep seated fanaticism." The *Observer and Reporter* accused Fairbank of plotting to take Hayden's money and sell him and his family back into slavery. Kentucky governor William Owsley initially refused to pardon Webster, stating, "We insist upon her punishment not only on account of the offense she has committed, but because of her sex, which she has desecrated."[19]

Evidence produced in Fairbank's and Webster's trials confirmed that escape networks located in the Old Northwest extended into the Border South. More significant in sectional politics, however, was a network extending north from the Chesapeake through Philadelphia, New York City, and Albany to Canada. Utilizing this route, Charles T. Torrey struck at slavery in the strategic region centered on Washington, D.C. He arrived in that city during December 1841 as the congressional reporter for Abel Brown's *Tocsin of Liberty* and several other abolitionist newspapers. During the spring of 1842, he joined forces with former slave Thomas Smallwood to guide escapees north on what they called their "new underground railroad."[20]

Antislavery attorney and journalist Stephen Pearl Andrews called Torrey "the regular Rob Roy MacGregor of dare-devil philanthropy." Smallwood was similarly audacious. Although each of them had a wife and young children, they risked their lives organizing escapes in an attempt to drive slavery out of the Chesapeake. In February 1844, Torrey forcefully echoed a key phrase in Gerrit Smith's "Address to the Slaves." "Too long," Torrey declared, "have we delayed assaults on slavery in her own dark dominions. The spirit of cowardice has infested us, and we call it 'prudence.'" He and Smallwood—in a form of psychological warfare—sent accounts of their activities to masters whose slaves they helped. The two men taunted police officers in Baltimore and Washington. They threatened to kill black informers and white constables who hindered their activities.[21]

Torrey spent most of 1843 in Albany as editor of the *Weekly Patriot*, which succeeded the *Tocsin of Liberty*. Smallwood ran the southern end of the network until October of that year when Washington police closed in, forcing him to flee to Toronto. A month later, the two men reunited in New York and returned to Washington hoping to lead another group of slaves north. Instead, the police captured the would-be escapees, arrested a black collaborator, and nearly caught the two ringleaders. Smallwood escaped on foot to Baltimore and on to Toronto, never returning to the Chesapeake. Torrey, who foolishly revealed his identity to police, remained in the region, expanded his operations into Virginia's Shenandoah Valley, and boasted of plans for wider operations. His efforts at Hope H. Slatter's Baltimore slave market on behalf of Benjamin "Big Ben" Jones led to his arrest in June 1844. Convicted of slave stealing and sentenced to six years in Maryland Penitentiary, Torrey—like Work, Burr, and Thompson before him—instructed slaves he met in prison regarding how to escape. Although Torrey died of tuberculosis in May 1846, Chesapeake masters continued to attribute escapes to his influence.[22]

Some abolitionists, including more than a few on the North-South border, called Torrey's actions "imprudent." But most, including an obscure Ohio resident named John Brown, regarded him as a Christian hero and prophet of future attacks on slavery. Another abolitionist observed that if more of his coadjutors were like Torrey, "We might storm the infernal castle of slavery in the next twelve months, and make the blood-stained soul of the guilty slaveholder 'quake with more terrific fear.'" In November 1848, the nonviolent *Anti-Slavery Bugle* of Salem, Ohio, reported, "Torrey's example was contagious." The newspaper's editor declared, "Never, until since his conviction and suffering, had there been so many open, bold attempts to aid slaves in their escape. . . . 'The blood of the martyrs is the seed of the church.' The South will learn ere long the truth of this, and will see within her very borders bold, widely-diffused actions against slavery, which the oppressors can neither control nor escape."[23]

Torrey and Smallwood were certainly more aggressive than most others who had helped slaves from the Border South escape through the North to Canada. But they were not alone. White southerners had long recognized that assisted escape threatened slavery on its northern periphery. By the early 1840s, the generic name for northward escape networks was the "underground railroad," although, as one abolitionist noted, much aid was "above-the-ground" in plain view.[24]

Some abolitionists claimed Torrey invented the underground railroad. In fact, he and Smallwood refined an escape network that for years had extended north from the Chesapeake. As early as 1833, a Fauquier County, Virginia, master charged northeasterners with "monstrous injuries" stemming from their cooperation with free African Americans in the creation of "a perfect system of plunder and robbery" by which fugitive slaves traveled by carriage from Baltimore to Philadelphia. Even earlier, other networks helped slaves who reached "frontline" towns and cities in western Pennsylvania, Ohio, Indiana, and Illinois. Since about 1800, there had been a "maritime underground railroad" stretching along the Atlantic coast from North Carolina to Massachusetts.[25]

Participants in these networks invoked the Biblical injunction, "thou shalt not deliver unto his master the servant who has escaped unto thee," to justify their actions. They also appealed to the golden rule and universal natural rights. In a revealing August 1842 statement, Gamaliel Bailey declared Ohio abolition would "open its doors" to "the wretched, starving, fugitive slave."

It "would spread its table for him; it would clothe him; it would crowd his wallet with provisions for his journey; it would be eyes and feet to him, and raise a shout of triumph when it saw him safe beyond the reach of his pursuers." William Elder of Philadelphia put it more bluntly in 1845. He told Salmon P. Chase that abolitionists were "disposed to steal, and aid in receiving the stolen goods and chattels that think fit to steal away."[26]

Open aid in Illinois to fugitive slaves attracted considerable comment. Although the *Peoria Register* in September 1842 expressed doubt concerning the existence of "a regular succession of harbors extended from Missouri to Canada," it noted a "brisk business in the way of moving slaves through this part of our state . . . with little concealment." Nine months later, a grand jury indicted abolitionist Owen Lovejoy of Princeton, located southwest of Chicago, for helping slaves escape. As news of the indictment spread, an Illinois correspondent of the *Emancipator* boasted that Lovejoy's "*Canada line of transportation* runs night and day, and is in full tide of successful experiment." The correspondent compared Owen Lovejoy to his martyred brother Elijah, and concluded "*acting*" was better than speaking. The proslavery *New Era* of St. Louis complained, "There are in Illinois associations, as well as individuals, who have established a correspondence and chains of communication, by which negroes, can be conveyed with speed and certainty from one corner of the State to the other." Many of the fugitives, the *New Era*, reported, reached Chicago and Detroit, where "it is said . . . any effort to reclaim them, except by stealth, would be hopeless. The anti-slavery feeling is so intense and defused that after every legal impediment to the restoration of the runaway fails, the inevitable recourse is to the sympathies and violence of a mob."[27]

Abolitionists often published exaggerated accounts of the underground railroad as propaganda designed to create an image of massive escapes and aggressive challenges to slavery throughout the South. In 1847, the *Pennsylvania Freeman* described fugitive slaves "pouring into and through the North" and referred to "a friend of ours, who is a large stock holder and forwarding agent in a certain mysterious rail-road whose extremes are Texas and Canada." Despite this exaggeration, by the mid-1830s slavery's opponents and defenders regarded as fact the existence of widespread organized assistance to fugitive slaves. The *Alexandria Gazette*, responding to a *Boston Journal* report on how abolitionists helped fugitive slaves reach Canada, observed that this was a way they "*rob* . . . the Southern people of their property!" The *Gazette* declared, "The South will not, cannot, ought not to stand these things."[28] Helping slaves escape challenged masters' property rights, slave catchers' guns, the U.S. Constitution's fugitive slave clause, and Congress's Fugitive Slave Law of 1793. Slaveholders found all the more threatening the wide tolerance in the Lower North for such activities.

NOT LONG AFTER Governor Clark of Kentucky warned in December 1838 of conflict on his state's northern border (see chapter 4), the Missouri General Assembly resolved that the "numerous" efforts to interfere with slavery in "the southern and southwestern States" would cause a "dreadful crisis." Each state, the assembly declared, "Must look out means adequate to its own protection.... 'peacefully if they can, forcibly, if they must.'"[29]

By the mid-1840s, such insecurity pervaded the Border South. During the summer of 1845, Cassius M. Clay contributed to intensified fear in Kentucky. George D. Prentice, the moderately antislavery editor of the *Louisville Journal*, reported during a trip to Lexington, "The conduct of the slaves in Fayette [County] is said to have changed since the publication of the True American." He "heard . . . that the slaves in the factories and in the farms had refrains set to words, which they were singing to the praise of Cassius M. Clay, boasting that he was about to break the chains of their bondage, and would by the force of his character and influence elevate them to an equality with their masters." "The slaves," Prentice informed his readers, "have lately become idle and insolent, and, in some instances, had refused to labor." Fear of "negro violence" spread among white residents."[30]

That same summer, an abolitionist, who had been "traveling through all the northern slaveholding States," reported from Paris, Kentucky, "No one can fail to be convinced that the crisis is rapidly approaching, that the great final battle between Liberty and Slavery must soon be fought." It would be a battle, the abolitionist claimed, between "truth, justice, and eternal right" on the one side, and "Satan and slavery" on the other. A year later, a Baltimore correspondent of New York City's *Christian Advocate* claimed the battle had begun in the Chesapeake. Maryland, he wrote, was in a difficult position. It had to punish Torrey because he "declared *war against the State*, invaded her territory, and *plundered her citizens*." But when Torrey died, the abolitionists made him a martyr. Others warned similarly that killing Cassius M. Clay— or someone like him—would anger northerners and increase pressure on the Border South."[30]

Sometimes advocates of gradual emancipation and colonization of African Americans used the crisis atmosphere to justify their moderate outlook. In 1849, the *Louisville Weekly Courier* called for eventual emancipation as an alternative to "making Kentucky a frontier slave State, to fight the battles of the South."[32] Usually, however, as slave escapes and perceptions of northern aggression proliferated, those in the Border South who favored gradual emancipation joined with those who defended perpetual slavery to threaten physical resistance and retaliation. Despite slave-catching forays into the North, they portrayed themselves and the entire white South as grievously wronged victims.

Therefore, during the 1840s, Border South slaveholders sought means, beyond slave patrols and vigilance associations, to protect their human property. Maryland masters, who felt especially vulnerable, led the way. In January 1842, a "highly distinguished" group convened in Annapolis. Those assembled called on Maryland's legislature to offer "large rewards for the detection of any person who induces or aids a slave to run away, [to] employ bailiffs to watch the arrival and departure of every steamboat and railroad car," and pay the legal expenses of Marylanders engaged in northern slave cases. The slaveholder convention also called for legislation to expel "free people of color," ban manumission, and facilitate prosecution of those who possessed "seditious publications." The Maryland House of Delegates passed legislation in compliance with the convention's demands, but the state senate defeated it by a vote of fifteen to six. Even so, the slaveholders did not give up. In 1844, the legislature established a system of rewards for slave catchers, including payments of $100 to those who returned fugitive slaves from free states.[33]

In 1846, masters in Kent County, Maryland, formed a "Mutual Protection Society." Members pledged to recapture escapees, sell out of state those they caught, and use the proceeds to reimburse each other for losses. The next year, Baltimore County slaveholders organized against free black support of slave escapes. In 1849 a similar group of slaveholders in Frederick County "banded together for the purpose of mutual protection in the matter of their absconding chattels." Shortly thereafter, they hired a man to pursue a fugitive slave to New York City. By the summer of 1850, as escapes from Maryland mounted, a meeting in Baltimore County proposed a "detective police to secure runaways." Those attending threatened "woe to any of the abolitionists caught in the act . . . of aiding slaves in their flight." A correspondent of the *New York Tribune* reported, "New fuel" had been added "to the indignation of the 'flesh and blood' owners and traders" of Baltimore.[34]

AS HAD BEEN the case during the 1830s, proslavery defensive measures during the 1840s included mob violence. In addition to action against the *True American*, notable Border South riots occurred at Covington, Georgetown, and Frankfort, Kentucky, as well as in Cecil County, Maryland. In a rare event, a mob in Covington, during March 1841, confronted about seven members of the Cincinnati Vigilance Association. The abolitionists had pursued into Kentucky a Missouri woman who had brought two enslaved women to Cincinnati and refused to surrender them under a writ of habeas corpus. The Covington mob, armed with "bowie knives, clubs, and pistols," prevented the apprehension of the Missouri woman and the release of her slaves. But there was no "affray" because the Cincinnatians had at least "two pistols" among them.[35]

The other Border South riots were more conventional. At Georgetown in August 1845, local vigilantes, in sympathy with the Lexington attack on Clay, attempted to suppress Evan Stevenson's *Christian Intelligencer*. Stevenson, who refused to leave town and continued to publish his weekly for nearly a year thereafter, persevered by denying he was an abolitionist. At Frankfort in October 1846, a band of men armed with knives threatened to kill Ohio abolitionist reverend Isaac Wade for visiting underground-railroad operative Calvin Fairbank at the Kentucky Penitentiary. In Cecil County during September 1847, approximately thirty-five men attempted to disrupt a meeting organized by Snodgrass on the Maryland-Pennsylvania border. Led by the Honorable William Bailey Biles, the vigilantes dragged from bed the man who owned the land on which the meeting took place and wrecked the speaking stand. The next day, they threatened Snodgrass but gave up after the local sheriff refused to sanction their actions.[36]

Northern abolitionists who traveled openly in the Border South might also face mobs, even if they had no involvement with slaves. In February 1840, Lucretia Mott, a prominent Philadelphia Quaker and Garrisonian abolitionist, undertook a religious speaking tour in Delaware. Accompanied by two elderly members of her congregation—Daniel Neal and his wife—Mott preached at Wilmington, Camden, and Dover without incident. But as she and her companions returned north, "a rumor of them being abolitionists" spread. After she spoke at Smyrna, men burst into the home where she and the Neals lodged for the night. The men "dragged" out Daniel Neal, who had not spoken publicly during the trip, "to answer" for his "disorganizing doctrines." They proceeded to tar and feather him and ride him on a rail, as Mott ineffectively offered herself as a substitute.[37]

At times, white border southerners targeted *nonabolitionist* northerners. At Warsaw, Missouri, in 1842, plantation women drove away a young white Illinois woman who taught in the town. The woman neither advocated abolition nor helped slaves escape but appeared to sympathize with those in bondage. Two years later at Parkersburg, Virginia, splintering of the Methodist Church into northern and southern organizations led to mob action. As Virginia and Ohio contested for jurisdiction in the case (discussed in chapter 3) of four white Ohioans abducted to Virginia, Methodists in Parkersburg threatened John Dillon, who had been appointed by the Ohio Methodist Conference as minister of their congregation. Following "an indignation meeting," a "committee of sixty" informed Dillon "that unless he left town before the next Saturday, he would be forcibly removed." When the minister Dillon replaced returned to help his family move, the mob threatened him as well, this time "with a coat of tar and feathers." A newspaper in nearby Marietta, Ohio, noted, "Neither of these preachers are charged with being abolitionists, but the people would not allow the church to have a preacher from Ohio." In 1846, mob violence forced northern Methodist preachers out of two other Virginia churches, one located at Salem on the state's Eastern Shore and another at Guilford in Accomack County.[38]

SOMETIMES WHITE BORDER southerners' apprehensions concerning slave revolt were as exaggerated as many of their reports of abolitionist agents. There were no major revolts in the United States after 1831, and minor revolts occurred well to the south of the borderlands. But *reports* of revolt conspiracies and abolitionist encouragement of them kept armed bands of white men on patrol.[39] Also, mass slave-escape attempts could appear much like revolt, and during the 1840s three such attempts occurred in the Border South. Two involved forceful slave action—one in Maryland in 1845, the other in Kentucky in 1848. These two were similar in origin, execution, and result, although one had free black leadership and the leadership of the other included a white man. The third began peacefully but had violent results, as well as major political repercussions.

In Maryland in July 1845, hot weather prompted between seventy and eighty overworked black men to head north from the state's southernmost counties—St. George's, Charles, and St. Mary's—toward Pennsylvania. Led by a "powerful and muscular" free black man named Bill Wheeler, the men, according to an early report, carried a few pistols, "scythe blades," and other improvised weapons. They marched "six abreast" before splitting into two groups as they approached Washington. The smaller group of about thirty headed east toward Bladensburg, where white volunteers captured at least eighteen without incident. The larger group crossed the bridge over the Anacostia River into the outskirts of the capital city and then marched north.[40]

About 300 "well armed" white men from southern Maryland and Washington pursued, on horseback, the larger group. But it was "a posse of citizens" from Rockville that caught up to the slaves at a farm about six miles north of the town. Faced with a larger, better armed, and more mobile force, the slaves refused to surrender and closed ranks. When at least one of the slaves attempted to fire a pistol, the "Rockville volunteers" unleashed "a whole volley of balls from rifles and pistols." Nine black men suffered severe wounds before surrendering. Jailed in Rockville and then "marched with ox chains, handcuffs, &c." through Washington back to their masters, most of the fugitives were sold south. Only two men stood trial. Wheeler received a prison sentence of forty years and one of the escapees, perhaps the man who attempted to fire his pistol, received a death sentence. Later that year, Governor Thomas G. Pratt commuted the sentence to life in prison.[41]

Some newspaper correspondents charged white abolitionists with instigating the escape attempt. The *Pennsylvania Freeman* accommodated them by boasting that the spread of "anti-slavery information among the slaves" inspired it. Those Marylanders attending a meeting at Port Tobacco, convened "to consider what measures were most likely to put a stop to the elopement of slaves," were less certain. They denounced "the . . . reckless efforts of fanaticism in the Northern portion of the United States, to subvert the institutions of the State, and ruthlessly to invade the peace of our people by the sacrifice of our property at the risk of our lives, and the destruction of our constitutional rights." But they put more blame on local free African Americans and the slaves themselves. They called for expelling the former group and funding an "efficient police" to better control the slave population.[42]

At least a few white Marylanders believed the Rockville posse overreacted. A correspondent of the *New York Herald* charged that drunken men from the town had shot poorly armed fugitives "down like dogs." The posse, the correspondent continued, might have achieved its purpose by loading "fine shot, or even a little coarse salt" rather than "the deadly bullet." Yet it was easy to justify excessive force. Reports of the wounds smaller bands of escapees had inflicted on their pursuers had circulated for years in Maryland. Only a month earlier, ten slaves had escaped from near Hagerstown. When they passed through Smithsburg on their way to Pennsylvania, eight white men, armed only "with bludgeons," approached them, whereupon the fugitives "drew themselves up in battle order" and attacked "with pistols and tomahawks." During a "desperate contest," which resulted in the capture of two of the fugitives, one white man had an "arm nearly severed and the bone broken, by a blow from a tomahawk." Another had a "shoulder dislocated." A third suffered a "wound in the shoulder from a tomahawk."[43]

Three years after the Maryland mass-escape attempt, the Kentucky effort, involving slaves from Fayette, Bourbon, and Mason counties, got underway. Forty to seventy-five black men, "armed with guns, pistols, knives and other warlike weapons," headed north on the morning of August 5. Edward J. "Patrick" Doyle, a young white student at Centre College, accompanied the slaves. He thereby confirmed longstanding Border South suspicions that, in the words of the *Lexington Observer and Reporter*, "there are abolitionists in our midst—emissaries from that piratical crew." But there were also black leaders among the fugitive band. [44]

By the time Doyle and the fugitives reached Cynthiana within eighteen miles of the Ohio River, a company of "about one hundred" white men, attracted in part by a $5,000 reward, launched a night attack on a "fortified" encampment of "about forty or more" of the escapees. In the ensuing "battle"—or "battles," according to some accounts—one white man suffered a mortal wound and one black man died. Later, a reinforced company of between 300 and 400 white men surrounded all of the fugitives, who took their stand in a hemp field. Following another exchange of gunfire, the slaves surrendered. Many among the white volunteers wanted to hang Doyle on the spot, but a militia general insisted he be held for trial.[45]

In contrast to Maryland in 1845, the Commonwealth of Kentucky in 1848 brought nearly fifty slaves to trial on charges of sedition and insurrection. Yet, as masters intervened to save their human property, a circuit court jury convicted only three of the leaders, all of whom were hanged. Doyle, tried separately, pleaded guilty to one of seven counts against him and received a sentence of twenty years at hard labor in the state penitentiary, where he presumably met Fairbank. During the following weeks in central Kentucky, public meetings called for stricter control of slaves and "the detection and punishment of abolitionists and others enticing slaves from their owners."[46]

The third and most influential mass-escape attempt began in Washington, D.C., in April 1848, a few months before Kentucky's, which it very likely inspired. In the Washington attempt, unarmed house servants—rather than armed field hands—sought freedom. The men, women, and children involved relied on advance planning, secrecy, and real abolitionist intervention rather than violence.

William L. Chaplin, a white abolitionist from New York who had replaced Torrey as the editor of the *Albany Patriot* and as the newspaper's Washington correspondent, led in organizing the Washington effort. Chaplin, who was nearly fifty-years-old at the time of Torrey's arrest, wrote in January 1845, "I believe that one hundred men like Charles T. Torrey, in courage and devotion to his object, would do more to deliver the slave speedily, than all our paper resolutions, windy speeches, presses and *votes* into the bargain." For some time, Chaplin feared he lacked the courage to follow Torrey's example. During his first years in Washington, he developed a relationship with the local black community and institutionalized purchases of freedom, rather than escape, as a means of destroying slavery in the Chesapeake. But in early 1848, as sales south threatened more and more families, Chaplin worked with local free black man Daniel Bell to plan mass escape. The result, though nonviolent, more than any other abolitionist initiative in the Border South down to that time, convinced leaders throughout the South that warlike conditions existed on their section's northern periphery.[47]

Working through abolitionists in Philadelphia, Chaplin contacted Daniel Drayton, a white boatman who had previously helped slaves escape from Washington. Drayton in turn paid Edward Sayres $100 to charter the schooner *Pearl*. The tiny vessel reached Washington on April 14. The following night, it sailed down the Potomac River with seventy-seven fugitive slaves in its hold. Adverse winds forced Sayres to anchor at the mouth of the Potomac. This allowed the steamer *Salem*, commanded by Washington magistrate W. C. Williams, to overtake the *Pearl* early on the morning of the seventeenth. "Armed to the teeth" with muskets, pistols, and two field pieces, Williams and thirty volunteers caught all on board by surprise. They captured the *Pearl's* passengers and crew without a fight, and towed them back to Washington. The next morning Williams paraded the would-be escapees and rescuers through the city's streets to jail.[48]

The Border South's largest antebellum mob soon gathered. For the next three days rioters—numbering as high as 3,000—controlled the city. With the *Pearl* fugitives and their abettors safely in jail, the mob vented its fury on the *National Era*, its editor Gamaliel Bailey, and Congressman Joshua R. Giddings for their alleged encouragement of or involvement in the escape attempt. On the evening of April 18, city police and a thunderstorm saved the *National Era* office from destruction. On April 19, an uproarious meeting on the steps of the U.S. Patent Office appointed a committee of fifty to call on Bailey at his nearby home to demand he cease publication. When Bailey refused, the mob again assaulted the *Era* office. The next day, rioters threatened Giddings—who had defended in Congress the right of slaves "to free themselves by any means God has put into their power"—as he visited the *Pearl* prisoners at the city jail. Hours later, a group of about 200 men from

Maryland and Virginia called Bailey out and threatened to tar and feather him.

City officials, supported by President James K. Polk, led police and deputized U.S. government employees in quelling the mob. They saved the *Era* office from destruction, and Bailey and Giddings escaped harm. Even so, angry masters sold most of the *Pearl* fugitives south, and Drayton and Sayres remained in Washington Jail until they received presidential pardons in 1852.[49]

In contrast to city officials' and Polk's moderating influence, proslavery leaders in Congress backed the mob. They did not know Chaplin had written, "If our Abolitionists will take hold, we can drive slavery out of this District at once!" But they realized that escapes, especially mass escapes, threatened slavery not only in Washington but in the tier of states stretching west from Delaware to Missouri. They responded with a torrent of warlike rhetoric.[50]

John C. Calhoun of South Carolina declared, "The crisis has come!" Holding slave escapes to be "the gravest and most vital of all questions to us and the whole Union," he interpreted the *Pearl* venture as a northern attack on a southern port. He predicted a major slave revolt unless something were done to protect slavery in the District of Columbia and counteract northern resistance to the Fugitive Slave Law of 1793. Henry Foote of Mississippi defended bloodshed in defense of slave property. He characterized the mob as "high-spirited citizens convened for the purpose of vindicating their rights thus unjustly assailed." He proclaimed the duty of the people to "inflict summary punishment if the arm of the law was too short." Robert Toombs of Georgia wanted no peace among Washington's citizens until they regained their rights. Thomas H. Bayly of Virginia contended that if laws could not protect a community in the enjoyment of its rights, that community could forcibly exercise its right of self-preservation. Frederick Stanton of Tennessee called for hanging those who helped slaves escape. Jefferson Davis of Mississippi was most emphatic. He regarded the District of Columbia as "ground upon which the people of this Union may shed blood." He asserted, "If this is to be made the centre from which civil war is to radiate here let the conflict begin."[51]

YEARS OF anger and frustration, not just the *Pearl* escape attempt, led congressmen from throughout the South to express these sentiments. They knew as well that slave unrest and abolitionist interference on the South's northern periphery existed within a context of sectionalism. The annexation of Texas in 1845 had revived the issue of slavery expansion that had emerged during the Missouri crisis of 1819. When the Mexican War—fought between May 1846 and February 1848—resulted in American acquisition of the vast territories of New Mexico and California, the status of slavery within their limits vied with slave escapes as a sectional issue.

In August 1846, David Wilmot, a Democratic congressman from Pennsylvania, introduced into the House of Representatives a proposal to ban slavery in these territories. What became known as the Wilmot Proviso caused consternation throughout the white South, as a large minority of northerners embraced the principle of stopping slavery's expansion. Proslavery forces grew more outraged when at Buffalo, New York, in August 1848 a coalition composed of Liberty abolitionists and some northern Whigs and Democrats organized the Free Soil Party, designed to enact the Proviso. In the 1848 national election, the new party gained 10 percent of the popular vote for its presidential candidate, Martin Van Buren, and elected twelve congressmen. By 1849 there were two Free Soilers in the U.S. Senate.[52]

As the territorial issue divided the country during the late 1840s, events in the Border South jurisdictions of Kentucky, Washington, D.C., Maryland, and Virginia contributed to the national crisis. In February 1849, Kentucky's legislature repealed the Act of 1833 that had banned importation of slaves into the state. This victory by the state's strongest proslavery advocates led Kentuckians who, to varying degrees, opposed perpetual slavery to place their hopes in a constitutional convention slated for that October. A group of what Cassius M. Clay called "Friends of Emancipation" organized at Frankfort on April 25 in preparation for the August 1 election of delegates. Clay, who now referred to himself as a "fanatic," led the "extremists" at Frankfort in favor of immediate adoption of a plan for gradual abolition without colonization. The majority supported prospective gradual emancipation and colonization that would begin at some unspecified time in the future. For the sake of unity, Clay acquiesced to the latter agenda.

Despite this mild platform, the campaign became violent. As Clay emerged as the emancipationists' most effective orator, his friend John G. Fee—a nonviolent abolitionist preacher—observed, "There is a good deal of the lion about Cassius. Undisturbed, he moves, speaks with mild majesty; but let them thrust him—let the smell of blood be raised, and they had better clear the ring." This proved to be an accurate description. On June 22 at a militia muster held in Foxton, Madison County, retainers of the staunchly proslavery Squire Turner attacked Clay with a knife, pistol, and club. Stabbed in the chest and badly bruised, Clay fought back with a bowie knife. He fatally eviscerated one of Turner's sons, won the fight, and gained considerable renown. Later, Gamaliel Bailey advised Clay he should rely on the law rather than concealed weapons. Clay replied that "a bowie-knife in the hands of a determined man, in a good cause" was "more terrible" to the men he faced than the "'majesty of the law'" and the "'magnanimity of the people.'"[53]

Developments in the campaign during the following months confirmed Clay's point of view. Early in July at the western Kentucky town of Paducah, perpetualist candidate Judge James Campbell shot to death emancipationist candidate Benedict Austin. On election day, there was mayhem in Louisville. As Paul Seymour—publisher of the *Louisville Examiner*—carried ballots to the polling place, a group of perpetualists "assaulted" him with "sticks." Seymour pulled "a revolver out of his pocket" and shot one of his assailants "in the breast." The rest of the perpetualists then knocked Seymour down and beat him "until he was senseless." When one of Seymour's pistol-carrying colleagues came to his rescue, a gunfight ensued in which a fourteen-year-old bystander received a bullet "through the back."[54]

The most careful analysis of the election concludes it "shored up slavery [in Kentucky] with important new constitutional buttresses." Emancipationists elected no more than two or three convention delegates and statewide had less than 10 percent of the vote. The convention strengthened slavery's legal foundations in the state and made it more difficult for the legislature to "enact a plan of emancipation." Future Supreme Court justice Samuel F. Miller believed the new constitution "fixed slavery more firmly than ever" in Kentucky. Henry Clay and Abraham Lincoln perceived wider implications in the proslavery victory. Clay, who had supported the emancipationists, assumed the results meant "no safe mode of gradual emancipation by operation of law can terminate in any one of the States the existence of slavery." Lincoln lamented, "There is no peaceful extinction of slavery in prospect for us."[55]

Calhoun had also placed the border struggle in a national perspective and suggested it posed a threat to the entire South. In his *Address of the Southern Delegates in Congress to their Constituents*, adopted on January 22, 1849, he complained, "The citizens of the South, in their attempt to recover their slaves, now meet . . . resistance in every form." There were "hostile acts of legislation . . . resistance from judges and magistrates—and . . . from mobs, comprised of whites and blacks, which, by threats or force, rescue the fugitive slave from the possession of his rightful owner." There existed, Calhoun charged, "secret combinations . . . whose object is to entice, decoy, entrap, inveigle, and seduce slaves to escape from their owners." Most dangerous was the "the employment of emissaries . . . to excite discontent among the slaves." Calhoun may have exaggerated the numbers of emissaries. Nevertheless, he echoed pronouncements from border slave-state leaders when he declared that similar actions "between independent nations [would] constitute just cause of remonstrance by the party against which the aggression was directed, and if not heeded, an appeal to arms for redress."[56]

Calhoun's remarks reflected opinion in the Lower South that it had a vital interest in the defense of slavery in the borderlands. By August 1850—four months after his death—his words seemed especially relevant to slavery's defenders. That month a series of escapes seemed, once again, to threaten slavery in the District of Columbia, Maryland, and northern Virginia. On the night of August 8, Captain John H. Goddard and a detachment of Washington police stopped Chaplin, who had never been charged in the *Pearl* case, as he drove an enclosed carriage with two fugitive slaves inside toward Maryland. The slaves, Allen and Garland, belonged respectively to Georgia congressmen Alexander H. Stephens and Robert Toombs. As Goddard halted the vehicle by jamming a fencepost through the spokes of a rear wheel, four officers and two civilian "slave-catchers" stormed it. Chaplin "fired a pistol ball" at a man who tried to "seize the reins," barely missing his target. Then "the runaways in the carriage having each a revolver, fired several times at the officers, who also fired at the Negroes." The *National Intelligencer* reported, "Not less than twenty-seven shots were fired in five or six minutes," leaving the carriage "riddled" with bullet holes. In the end, the police arrested the slaves and Chaplin. Miraculously, Allen and Garland received only minor wounds, as did Chaplin who had been thrown to the ground and beaten in a "desperate struggle."[57]

The next morning, impressions that abolitionists and slaves conspired to wreak havoc in the Chesapeake strengthened as five of eleven slaves who had escaped on August 3 "from different counties" in Maryland arrived as prisoners in Baltimore. "Certain Pennsylvanians" had captured seven of the "runaways" near Shrewsbury at "the farm of a negro, one mile across the Pennsylvania line." As the captors and slaves passed through the town, an antislavery mob led by a postmaster freed two of the slaves. On the train back to Maryland, the remaining five, who—somehow—had not been searched for concealed weapons, opened fire with pistols before being subdued.[58]

Two weeks later in Harrisburg, Pennsylvania, a party of Virginians, in an attempt to expedite legal processes, charged three fugitive slaves "with horse-stealing." When the case went to court, the judge dismissed it on the grounds that "the stealing of a horse by a slave for the purpose of escaping was not a criminal offense." As the liberated slaves left the courthouse and the Virginians attempted to seize them, a black mob intervened, "a battle ensued," and authorities arrested the Virginians "for assault and battery with intention to excite a riot." White Virginians and Marylanders responded by threatening to send *"armed band[s]* of fifty or a hundred men" in future recaption expeditions. This seemed like a threat of war to the *New York Tribune's* Baltimore correspondent, who commented, "The free States will not quietly submit to have their territory invaded by an armed posse."[59]

ANGRY OVER WHAT appeared to be a war of attrition conducted by abolitionists, free African Americans, and slaves, Border South congressmen led during the late 1840s in opposing abolition in the District of Columbia and in favoring a stronger fugitive slave law. Despite the qualified commitment of some of them to prospective gradual abolition, they sought to protect their region and their way of life against internal and external subversion. In late November 1849, Congressman Richard K. Meade of Petersburg, Virginia, justifiably conflated escape and rebellion, when he charged in a speech to a Prince George's County, Maryland, audience that abolition in the district would encourage slave escape from Maryland and "compel us to convert our dwellings into garrisons." "The incendiary's torch is brought in open day to our very hearth-stones," he complained, and demanded from the North "a peace-bond." A few days later, Governor John B. Floyd of Virginia subordinated other sectional issues, including slavery in the territories, to the safety of his constituents. "The [white] men of the South," he declared, "will not remain passive: the sword will not rest in the scabbard, whilst fanaticism is erecting . . . an alter, upon which the victims of sacrifice are to be our daughters and our wives. . . . A feeling of self preservation, and not of silly bravado, activates our course."[60]

The escape attempts of August 1850 increased this determination. So did the "Fugitive Slave Convention" held that month in Cazenovia, New York, where thirty fugitive slaves and hundreds of abolitionists endorsed Chaplin's actions. As it assessed the situation, the *Richmond Enquirer* warned its readers to be "on their guard against the designs of the Abolitionists, who may venture even into the slave States, to carry out their hellish designs." The *Enquirer* endorsed passage of a new fugitive slave law to "check the robbery of our property."[61]

# SEVEN

# Fighting over the
# Fugitive Slave Law of 1850

At the Pennsylvania Anti-Slavery Society's December 1850 meeting, Lucretia Mott asked William Elder—a white political abolitionist, journalist, and lecturer—to explain his "views on the subject of *resistance* of the people of color to the Fugitive Law and the Kidnappers." In reply, Elder observed that "life-taking" was wrong, but he "found a difficulty in applying the highest principle to practical life." As a white man, he could rely on the law to protect his rights, but African Americans, especially fugitive slaves, could not. "Slavery," he pointed out to an audience dominated by pacifists, "began in war, in man-hunting on the Coast of Africa. . . . and now comes back to man-hunting and war again." "Has not the hunted slave," he asked, "the same right that the savage African has to turn upon his pursuer?" After proclaiming "a bold periling of life . . . nobler than servility," he concluded with a Bible reference often associated with John Brown. Elder declared, "The world has been cultivated by blood. An expiatory sacrifice has ever been required for its redemption. Without the shedding of blood there is no remission of sins. There must be death for sin."[1]

Elder spoke three months after Congress passed the Compromise of 1850, designed to save the Union by ending sectional disputes over slavery. Led by Henry Clay, moderate politicians had crafted legislation to settle the issue of slavery in the territories by admitting California to the Union as a free state, allowing settlers to decide the issue in New Mexico and Utah, and ending Texas's claim to the eastern portion of New Mexico. Congress also banned the slave trade but not slavery itself in the District of Columbia. Even more closely related to the border struggle than legislation for the district, a new Fugitive Slave Law gave the national government authority to capture escaping slaves and punish resistance. The origins of this law lay in the Border South, where masters sensed they were losing the struggle and modified their commitment to state rights.[2] As it turned out, however, the major physical and political impacts of the Fugitive Slave Law of 1850 were not what most masters anticipated.

EVIDENCE OF mounting numbers of successful northward escapes during the 1840s seemed overwhelming. When, during late 1844, William L. Chaplin arrived in the Chesapeake, he reported Maryland slaves were "escaping in shoals." In early 1845, Cassius M. Clay asserted it was only a matter of time before slave labor became "utterly useless" in a tier of Kentucky counties three deep along the Ohio River. In 1846 a Connecticut native, who had purchased a farm in northern Virginia, contended, "So great is the number of escapes to the free states, that it produces an all-pervading sense of insecurity [among slaveholders]." In October 1847, the *Pennsylvania Freeman* declared, "Virginia and Maryland, and all the border slave states, will soon have no occasion for new slave markets or the aid of colonization societies for the disposal of their surplus slave populations, if the tide of North[ward] emigration continues to swell as it has done for a few years." In 1849, Kentucky abolitionist John G. Fee predicted that slavery could not long exist in any southern county bordering the North.[3]

Slavery's defenders expressed similar views. In 1845 the *Baltimore Ray* warned that "abolitionist emissaries" would soon make Maryland a free state. Two years later, a resident of the northwestern Virginia town of Martinsburg complained to John C. Calhoun that Pennsylvania's new antikidnapping law had made "slave property" in Maryland and a large portion of Virginia "utterly insecure." The law, the Virginian explained, denied masters effective legal assistance in recovering their human property, treated them as trespassers and felons, and made them liable to prosecution. He claimed that since the Pennsylvania law had gone into effect slaves in Maryland and Virginia had been escaping "in gangs of tens and twenties and the moment they reach the Pennsylvania line, all hopes of their recapture are abandoned." In January 1850, the *Baltimore Sun* charged, "Every day but swells the number of absconding slaves from Maryland," and the *Cumberland Civilian* claimed local masters who visited Pittsburgh "frequently meet with negroes belonging to themselves and neighbors." Later that year, the *Missouri Republican*, a Whig newspaper published in St. Louis, asserted, "Probably no State in the Union has suffered more by the enticing away of slaves than Missouri, and every one who has had the misfortune to lose property in this way knows how unavailing it has been to attempt their recapture."[4]

Powerful Border South politicians, including U.S. senators James M. Mason of Virginia, David Atchison of Missouri, and Henry Clay of Kentucky shared these concerns. Mason, who lived in a border county where the slave population remained stable, informed the Senate that it did not take many escapes to cost the region "hundreds of thousands of dollars" per year. "Sir," Mason declared, "it has become part of the history of the country, that, when a slave once escapes . . . you may as well go down into the sea, and endeavor to recover from his native element a fish which has escaped from you, as expect to recover such a fugitive—I mean under existing laws." Atchison charged that, although there were "very few" who helped slaves escape, "there were enough of them" to create "serious concern . . . in the border [slave] states." Clay believed resistance to slave renditions had "greatly increased during the last five years." It was, he said, "at the utmost hazard and insecurity of life itself" for a master to cross the Ohio River "and go into the interior and take back the fugitive slave to the State from which he has fled." He claimed, "Kentucky is the most suffering state."[5]

In part because abolitionists targeted the District of Columbia for underground-railroad initiatives, many Middle and Lower South congressmen shared these views. The *Pearl* escape attempt in April 1848 angered them even though their constituents lived far from the border (see chapter 6). They believed the weakening of slavery on its northern periphery spelled disaster for the entire section. In January 1849, Calhoun had made northern judicial and mob resistance to slave renditions his "grand complaint." In July 1850, David Outlaw, a North Carolina moderate, reported that northern abolitionist involvement in slave escapes "produce[d] more irritation, more heart-burning, among slaveholders, than all other causes combined." He believed, "It furnishe[d] more material for agitation than anything else, because it is a practical evil, which we suffer and a palpable wrong which the North commits, which comes home to the business and bosoms of men."[6] Therefore, considerable support existed in Congress during the late 1840s for strengthening the Fugitive Slave Law.

Yet Americans living during the sectional crisis that peaked in 1850 disagreed concerning the importance of the fugitive slave issue in comparison to the other points of sectional division. Most politicians who represented the Lower South emphasized slavery expansion. Senator Henry Foote of Mississippi spoke for many in the Lower South, when he said his constituents were not as "interested in this matter [slave escapes] as are those slave states which border the free states." Other Lower South leaders believed a stronger fugitive slave law would do no good. Jefferson Davis predicted such a law would "be a dead letter in any State where the popular opinion is opposed to such rendition." He claimed he "would sooner trust it [rendition] to . . . the sense of constitutional obligation of the States than to the enforcement of any law which Congress can enact against the popular opinion of those among whom it is executed." Many northerners, including some who opposed the expansion of slavery into western territories, were more flexible regarding the capture of fugitive slaves than Davis suggested. But he had good reason to doubt the ability of the U.S. government to enforce *any* fugitive slave law. Most historians who have studied the issue share Foote's and Davis's views. In some cases, historians barely mention the role of slave escape in the sectional crisis or in the legislation designed to end it.[7]

In contrast, politicians and journalists representing the South's northern periphery emphasized the centrality of the fugitive slave issue and demanded federal intervention. As state rights and disunion sentiment strengthened in the Lower South, white border southerners modified their commitment to state sovereignty, rejected disunion, and sought help to reduce escapes, recover escapees, and discourage conflict. In 1847 the Missouri legislature recommended, "Better treatment of rendition 'as the citizens of this State are annually subjected to heavy losses of property, by the escape of their slaves, who pass through the State of Illinois and finally find a secure place of refuge in Canada.'"[8]

In February 1850, as he introduced to the U.S. Senate his compromise plan to save the Union, Henry Clay pronounced slave renditions, "The most irritating and inflammatory [issue] to those who live in the slave States." The following month, Senator Thomas Pratt of Maryland estimated escapes cost his state $80,000 annually. He asserted, "Of all the subjects doing harm at the South, and providing excitement, the escape of fugitive slaves is doing the most harm, because it has been felt more practically, than any other of the causes of complaint." That September, the *Baltimore Sun* claimed the harboring and stealing of slaves did more to alienate the South from the North than quarrels over New Mexico and California. Opinion shapers in the southern borderlands hoped, as the *Richmond Enquirer* put it, that the new fugitive law "should naturally have the effect of inducing a better feeling and aiding the adjustment of alarming difficulties." Abolitionists in the border region, however, predicted northerners would resist such a law more strongly than they would the introduction of slavery into western territories.[9]

BORDER SLAVE STATE sentiment favoring federal intervention to help masters and their agents recover fugitive slaves from the North had existed for decades. In 1817, congressmen from Virginia and Kentucky led an unsuccessful effort to strengthen the Fugitive Slave Law of 1793. In 1822 the Maryland legislature petitioned Congress "to prevent the inconvenience from the ready protection given to escaping slaves in Pennsylvania and the difficulty thrown in the way of the recovery of slaves." In 1837 and in 1843, the same legislature called for a federal law against helping slaves escape. But it took the failure of interstate diplomacy, the *Prigg* decision, "personal liberty" legislation designed by northern state legislatures to frustrate slave catching, and escapes during the 1840s to get southern politicians and journalists to make new federal legislation a priority.[10]

At times, politicians from the Border South joined Jefferson Davis in doubting a stronger federal law could reduce escapes and assistance to the escapees. But they believed they had little choice. As historian William W. Freehling puts it, escapes threatened the "Border South's fundamental order." They might also threaten the Union. In March 1847, two months after a biracial mob in Marshall, Michigan, prevented the capture of six fugitive slaves, the Kentucky General Assembly resolved, "Outrages upon the rights and citizens of the State of Kentucky, or any other state of the Union, must necessarily . . . terminate in the breaking up and destroying the peace and harmony that is desirable [*sic*] by every good citizen of all the States of the Union." The assembly appealed to the U.S. Senate for help in recovering slaves who reached the North. In response, during the spring of 1848, the Senate Judiciary Committee, chaired by Andrew P. Butler of South Carolina, declared the North had chosen to "'to make war' on slavery." Shortly thereafter, Butler introduced a bill to strengthen the Fugitive Slave Law of 1793. Failure of this bill led a committee appointed by the Virginia House of Delegates to predict in February 1849 that unless Congress acted "the territory of the nonslaveholding states will be invaded in sudden and rapid incursions by those who have been robbed of their property." The committee warned, "Petty border warfare" could grow to threaten the "glorious Union itself" as feuds became "daily more embittered on this exciting subject." Less than a year later, Senator Mason proposed to amend the 1793 law so as to provide federal assistance in the recovery of escapees.[11]

Mason's bill recognized the right of masters and agents to seize fugitives without legal process. It provided alternatively that they might secure an arrest warrant from a federal judge or one of many new federal commissioners empowered to hear rendition cases. Such a judge or commissioner could authorize U.S. marshals, deputy marshals, and other "suitable persons" to enforce the warrants, protect claimants, and command citizens to assist them.

Once captured, an alleged fugitive slave had to be brought before a judge or commissioner for a summary hearing, at which the claimant had to provide evidence of ownership and the accused could not testify. If the judge or commissioner accepted the evidence, he could issue a certificate of removal that no other legal process would override. Anyone who interfered with either the capture or return of an alleged slave faced fines and imprisonment up to six months. As the bill progressed through the U.S. Senate during the spring and summer of 1850, southerners, supported by some northern Democrats, defeated efforts to require jury trials for, or allow writs of habeas corpus on behalf of, the accused. On August 19, Mason maintained—based on "the experience of the people of those States from whence these fugitives escape"—such provisions would defeat the purpose of the new law.[12]

Conflict along the North-South border fortified Border South determination to defeat northern modifications of the bill. As discussed in chapter 6, nearly simultaneous, high-profile slave escapes transpired in Maryland, the District of Columbia, and Virginia. These events left little doubt among the region's leaders that an escape crisis required federal action. The *Lexington Observer* stressed the importance citizens of "the border States of Kentucky, Virginia, and Maryland" placed on employing "U.S. appointees" to aid masters. Therefore, when on September 16 Congress passed the Fugitive Slave Act of 1850, and President Fillmore signed it into law two days later, most white border southerners responded with enthusiasm. Congressman Thomas H. Bayly of Virginia claimed the new law would stop the outflow of "young and most valuable" slaves. The *Missouri Republican* portrayed the law as a means of helping those who had lost slaves and suffered difficulties in recaption. The only dispute concerned how much force might be necessary to achieve the desired result. The *Washington Republic* envisioned the law having "a benign and wholesome influence." But a Baltimore correspondent of the *New York Tribune* assumed cross-border raids into the Lower North would be necessary.[13]

WITH THE federal government as their ally, the border slave states opposed disunion in 1850 and denounced what they called extremism North and South. In February 1850, Henry Clay declared southern secession "mean[t] that where one slave now deserted his master, thousands would hereafter flee." The *Lexington Observer* agreed. It rejected Lower South charges that Clay engaged in "dishonorable submission to Northern fanaticism," when he noted that disunion would not stop aid to escaping slaves. Abolitionists "would still be at work," the newspaper warned, "and all the Proclamations of the State authorities could not stop them." Only northern refusal to obey the new Fugitive Slave Law or its repeal justified secession. In October 1850, the *Petersburg Intelligencer* predicted, "The South will never secede or nullify because of the admission of California [as a free state] or the passage of the Texas Boundary Bill [eliminating that slaveholding state's claim to eastern New Mexico], but she will resist the continued nullification [of the Fugitive Slave Law] by the nonslaveholding portion of the Union." The *St. Louis Intelligencer* argued similarly, and a month later Virginia governor John Floyd counseled, "The faithful execution of this law . . . is the only means now left, by which the Union can be preserved with honor to ourselves and peace to the county."[14]

Meanwhile, the new Fugitive Slave Law pushed the Lower North, and the North generally, toward defense of state sovereignty and resistance. Governor Floyd believed northerners responded to the new law as Virginians would to "a disorganizing proclamation of an invading foe." "Public meetings," he observed, "have been called to denounce it, the newspaper press has assailed it with unusual bitterness; the preachers of the gospel have inveighed against it. . . . Opposition to it has, in many places, obliterated party lines, and men of every rank and condition of life . . . have banded themselves together with the avowed determination of resisting the law . . . and ultimately effecting its repeal."[15]

Well before Congress passed the law, abolitionists and Free Soilers in the Lower North joined their counterparts throughout the section to warn of "a dangerous reaction." In February 1850, the *Anti-Slavery Bugle* claimed capturing fugitive slaves would become "as difficult as it is infamous." In April 1850, Free Soil congressman Joshua R. Giddings called on northern states to make assisting in renditions a capital offense. Others asserted incorrectly that southerners had designed the law as a disunion measure. Calls for its repeal emerged as soon as Congress passed it.[16]

Nevertheless, many northerners supported the law, and federal magistrates, commissioners, and U.S. marshals attempted to enforce it. Support was especially strong in the Lower North.[17] John C. Wright, the moderate Whig editor of the *Cincinnati Gazette*, acknowledged that justice required jury trials for alleged fugitive slaves. But he reminded his readers that the act, "with all its imperfections," was "now the law of the land" and "we are bound as good citizens to obey it." Ohio's Democratic governor, Rueben Wood denounced opposition to the law as "nullification." Pennsylvania's Whig governor William F. Johnson opposed the law. But a large "Union" meeting in Philadelphia supported it, and that city's most distinguished statesman, former secretary of the treasury Richard Rush, warned against disobedience. In the fall 1851 election, Pennsylvania voters replaced Johnson with William Bigler, who called for noninterference with the exercise of the law so as to protect the Union. A year later, the *Maysville Eagle* noted that thirty miles north of the Ohio River, white Ohioans helped Kentucky masters recapture over thirty slaves.[18] But, as it turned out, the law's opponents in the Lower North were more influential than its supporters.

THE PASSAGE OF the Fugitive Slave Law of 1850 began a federally assisted counteroffensive that failed to achieve its objective. To a degree, the law weakened northern-based assistance to slave escapes in the Border South. This was because white abolitionists, black abolitionists, and black communities had to fight harder in the North to help fugitives who reached them. Historian David M. Potter, in his analysis of the Compromise of 1850, concludes that it amounted to a political armistice, not a real compromise regarding slavery.[19] There was, however, no armistice in the border struggle.

Instead of declining, northward escapes increased during the months and years following the new Fugitive Slave Law's passage. The Washington correspondent of the *Baltimore Sun* regarded this not so much as a reaction to the law as a product of changing circumstances. Among them were a growing slave population, more "facilities of rapid conveyance," and "increased numbers of free colored people at the North, who may be supposed to sympathize with the fugitives." In contrast, the *Detroit Democrat* linked the increase directly to the law. According to the *Democrat*, it "kindled sympathy" for slaves and "rendered pursuit by the masters a hopeless waste of time and means."[20]

Reports of slave "stampede[s]" proliferated. In November 1852, newspapers claimed that sixteen slaves from Washington County, Maryland, and thirty or more from Mason and Bracken counties, Kentucky, departed. The same month, a correspondent of the *Maysville Eagle*, who had traveled from Kentucky to northern Ohio, estimated "*over two hundred*," fugitive slaves had voyaged from Sandusky to Canada during the past two months and that forty left Cleveland in a week. Others contended large numbers of slaves from Kentucky and Maryland reached Pennsylvania and New York. In August 1853, Chicago's *Western Citizen* noted that a group of over seventy slaves arrived at Amherstburg, Canada West, after passing through Illinois during the past week. A month later, Free Soil senator Salmon P. Chase of Ohio declared, "The number of fugitives is greater than ever before. . . . There are but few captured under this law. . . . Now and then some horrible case, some

Artist Theodore Kaufman published "Effects of the Fugitive Slave Law" in 1850 as a lithograph on woven paper. Designed to provoke northern sympathy for fugitive slaves and opposition to the Fugitive Slave Law of 1850, it portrays white men firing on—rather than attempting to capture—well-dressed black men. (New York: Hoff and Bloede, 1850). Courtesy Library of Congress.

villainous transaction occurs. . . . But remember that hundreds escape where one is taken back." Regarding northward escapes from Missouri into Iowa, the *St. Louis Intelligencer* complained, "The evil has got to be an immense one, and it is daily becoming more aggravated. It threatens to subvert the institution of slavery in this State entirely. . . . There is no doubt that ten slaves are now stolen from Mo. to every one that was 'spirited' off before."[21]

While the failure of the new law to curtail escapes exasperated masters, increased activity that the law encouraged among slave catchers and kidnappers angered northerners. Assaults on black homes and abductions of free black men, women, and children occurred especially in counties close to the sectional boundary. Kidnappers from St. Louis targeted southern Illinois communities and reports of brutal actions against escaping slaves multiplied. Within a week of the new fugitive slave law's passage, white men near the border town of Bedford, Pennsylvania, seeking a $250 reward attacked ten fugitive slaves who had "lost their way on the ridge of the Alleghenies." The white men "mortally wounded" one slave, "dangerously" wounded another and captured all but two.[22]

The first arrest under the new Fugitive Slave Law occurred in New York City only a few days before the conflict near Bedford. Several newspapers in New York and the Border South hailed the capture of James Hamlet, whom a Baltimore woman claimed, as evidence that the law could be enforced without resistance. Yet in reaction to the capture, "Colored people armed themselves to the teeth, formed a thorough organization, [and] appointed vigilance committees." The commissioner who heard the case had to order a U.S. marshal "to provide a sufficient force to guard" Hamlet on his way back to Baltimore. A New York merchant stopped the process by purchasing Hamlet's freedom for $800. But the law's supporters did not regard this last reaction to be a form of resistance.[23]

As arrests continued, opposition in the North, and especially the Lower North, went beyond discussion of constitutionality, state sovereignty, civil rights, and abstract justice. Although these principles were important, the dominant theme became how the new law affected questions of personal safety, regional self-esteem, and common humanity. When that November at New Albany, Indiana, a summary hearing allowed an Arkansas claimant to take an apparently white woman, her daughter, and her grandson as slaves, concern spread that anyone could be captured. The following spring, the first rendition in Pittsburgh under the new law led Jane Gray Swisshelm, the editor of a Free Soil journal published in the city, to vow were she a man she would spit on those who had aided in it. Southern congressmen, she declared, required northern "white slaves" to capture "their black slaves." In May 1852, a deputy U.S. marshal from Baltimore, frightened by a gathering black crowd at Columbia, Pennsylvania, shot to death a fugitive slave named William Smith. A correspondent of the *Cleveland True Democrat* reported, "All the citizens were out, and as the bleeding body lay upon the ground, and his wife and children gathered round him, their anger and indignation knew no bounds. 'Murder,' was the common cry. 'The bloodiest murder,' declared the people of all sides and sects."[24]

The September 1853 attempt by several deputy U.S. marshals and a Virginia master to capture Bill Thomas at Wilkes-Barre, Pennsylvania, was not deadly but still gruesome to observe. As Thomas, a large and powerful man, served breakfast at the Phoenix Hotel, the deputies, armed with maces and pistols, "took hold of him." The ensuing struggle resulted in two wounded officers and Thomas, bloody and nearly naked, running from the hotel toward the Susquehanna River. In pursuit, the deputies fired two shots, one of which grazed Thomas's head. By the time he dove in the river and the deputies fired again, an interracial crowd had gathered, shouting, "Shame,

shame!" Commentators across the North condemned the crowd for not actively aiding Thomas. But the crowd's members disconcerted the officers enough to allow Thomas to wade up stream where a black woman helped him escape. Associate U.S. Supreme Court justice Robert C. Grier, on circuit, overruled a local indictment of the deputies for assault with intent to kill. Nevertheless, public outrage in Wilkes-Barre, as in Columbia, encouraged resistance.[25]

At times, U.S. commissioners, judges, and municipal authorities impeded recovery and punished slave catchers, much as magistrates had under the 1793 law. Justice Grier was a conservative who opposed granting habeas corpus protection, jury trials, and the right to testify to alleged fugitive slaves. But he refused to accept—in a case he heard as a Philadelphia commissioner—a Maryland claimant's affidavit regarding a black man named Henry Garnett. No Maryland court had endorsed it, Grier ruled. He also upheld Garnett's right to introduce evidence "to show that he is not the person described." He denied the law required a judge "without *trial*, [to] surrender a citizen of Pennsylvania to a kidnapper," and he released Garnett.[26]

A month later, a commissioner in Chicago demanded in fugitive slave cases "exact conformity to the letter of the law." This strictness led Zebina Eastman to conclude fugitive slaves could not be recovered in the city "under the forms of law." Swisshelm commented similarly after a Pittsburgh commissioner, following defense testimony, discharged alleged fugitive slave Oliver Jones. In October 1852, the mayor of Lancaster, Pennsylvania, personally arrested a young Maryland slaveholder who, with others, sought to recapture twenty-six slaves. The mayor claimed the Marylander had "used low and bullying language" and had engaged in a "ruffian-like display of dirks and revolvers." Although a companion paid the young master's fine so that he might be released from jail, the delay allowed the slaves to get away. Less than a year later, John Freeman, a prosperous black resident of Indianapolis, whom a man from Missouri claimed as a slave, gained court recognition of his freedom and then sued the U.S. marshal who had arrested him. In other cases, commissioners, in spite of the law's provisions, allowed writs of habeas corpus or convicted claimants and their agents as kidnappers. Neither sentiment nor regard for state rights alone influenced such rulings, since magistrates who complied with the Fugitive Slave Law could face reprisals. In an extreme instance, a Vincennes, Indiana, grand jury in March 1855 indicted a U.S. judge for enforcing the law.[27]

State legislatures in the Lower North initially acted less effectively than magistrates and local officials to hamper enforcement. In some cases, as in

Pennsylvania and Ohio, state personal liberty laws, passed earlier to protect free African Americans and, incidentally, fugitive slaves, remained in effect. But only these two states passed legislation designed specifically to counteract the new law, and they did so late in the decade. Throughout the region, Democratic politicians, especially near the southern border, tended to oppose such legislation, as did leaders in the Border South. When in March 1851 the Ohio General Assembly called for modifying or repealing the Fugitive Slave Law, the *Richmond Enquirer* responded, "They know the binding character of the Constitution, in protecting Southern property. They should be affectionate brethren and friends, instead of cold-blooded enemies and mischief makers." The next month, a Democrat-led majority in the Pennsylvania legislature passed a bill more to the *Enquirer*'s liking. It repealed the state's 1847 ban on using state jails and prisons to retain fugitive slaves, but the state's Whig governor, William F. Johnson, vetoed it.[28]

AS COMMISSIONERS, judges, legislators, and governors found ways to frustrate renditions, thousands of fugitive slaves, many of whom had lived for years in the free states, left their homes in Pittsburgh, Columbia, Cincinnati, Chicago, and other localities to seek safety elsewhere in the North or in Canada. In September 1850, Pittsburgh's *Commercial Journal* described leave-takings similar to those during invasions: "Mothers and daughters, fathers and sons, brothers and sisters were clinging to one another in despair at the thought of separation which they seemed to feel would be for life." That same month, a newspaper published in nearby Allegheny City reported that 150 local fugitive slaves had left for Canada. It claimed, "Men of stout arms are among them, and many are armed, and resolved to be free at all hazard, an attempt to arrest them would be no child's play."[29]

The plight of black refugees inspired sympathy in the Lower North. But demands for organized resistance to federal authority had emerged much earlier, as Congress began to consider Mason's bill. Most opponents endorsed peaceful noncooperation, but even they issued warnings to masters, slave catchers, and U.S. marshals. Marius R. Robinson, a white, Garrisonian pacifist, lived in the antislavery town of Salem, Ohio. In February 1850, he advised supporters of federally enforced rendition, "Those who choose to reside among us, trusting to themselves and us for protection, shall have that protection; though Congress should make every federal officer from postmaster to President, a slave-catcher." Citizens' meetings in Cleveland and Toledo skirted threats of violence when they called for resistance "by all proper means" and "by all just means."[30]

After Congress passed the new law, African Americans in the Lower North called openly for forceful resistance. On September 30, 1850, three hundred African Americans, meeting in Chicago, endorsed "self-protection," pledging, "we will stand by each other in case any attacks are made upon our liberties." Those assembled claimed they did not want to use force but if "driven to the extreme" would defend themselves "at all hazards." A few weeks later, a black group in Columbus, Ohio, advised "all colored people to go continually prepared that they may be ready at any moment to offer defense in behalf of their liberty." Shortly after the arrest of Henry Garnett in Philadelphia, local African Americans urged "the colored race to arm themselves . . . and shoot down officers of the law." In November a meeting of black residents of Bradford County, Pennsylvania, resolved, "Before we will submit to be dragged into southern bondage by the man-stealers of the South, we will die in defense of our right to liberty."[31]

In December, black underground-railroad operative Robert Purvis spoke at the same Pennsylvania Anti-Slavery Society meeting as William Elder, whose remarks open this chapter. Purvis emphasized the responsibility of black men to arm themselves, in part to prove to white people that they were not "worthy of slavery." To those who called on him to follow Jesus Christ's pacifist example, Purvis replied, "What can I do when my family are assaulted by kidnappers? I would fly, and by every means endeavor to avoid it, but when the extremity comes, I welcome death rather than slavery, and by what means God and nature have given me, I will defend myself and my family."[32]

White encouragement of black violence proliferated. Some of the earliest came from Ohio's Western Reserve, where Joshua R. Giddings had for years urged fugitive slaves to kill their pursuers. In early October, the *Ashtabula Sentinel* advised escapees to "arm yourselves at once. If the slave catcher comes, receive him with powder and ball, with dirk or bowie knife or whatever weapon may be most convenient. Do not hesitate to slay the miscreant if he comes to reenslave you or your wife or child." In Chicago, Eastman described "our colored population" as "fully prepared for any emergency." He asserted, "While they do not propose to commit any act of violence unless driven to the wall, they will not suffer the new law to be executed upon their persons. In resisting this even to the death, they will be sustained by the omnipotent sentiment of the [white] citizens of Chicago." The Wilkes-Barre, Pennsylvania, magistrate who issued a warrant for the arrest of deputy U.S. marshals in the Bill Thomas case declared, "The noble resistance and courage displayed by this man, at the time of his attempted arrest, would have made any white American the pride of his countrymen."[33]

Perhaps more significant than encouragement of violent black resistance, white leaders and communities across the Lower North pledged that African Americans would not fight alone against slave catchers and U.S. marshals. A week before Congress passed the law, the *Western Reserve Chronicle* warned, "Such a law cannot be enforced in Ohio. . . . We believe that the slave catcher will visit our soil at his peril." In a speech delivered in Congress that December, Giddings claimed to speak for the white people of northern Ohio. He warned that if President Millard Fillmore "use[d] the whole military power of the nation . . . to enforce this detestable law . . . they will hurl back defiance both at him and his army." Giddings said of Fillmore, "He may send his troops . . . he may put all the machinery of human butchery in operation; he may drench our free land with blood . . . but he will *never compel them to obey that law. . . . Our people will never be compelled by the bayonet or the cannon, or in any other manner, to extend aid or assistance in executing that infamous law.*"[34]

Others expressed similar sentiments. Shortly after the *Western Reserve Chronicle* issued its warning, Quakers, meeting at Selma, Ohio, asserted, "Those who would defend themselves by violence were bound, *by their own rule*, to use the same means in defense of their neighbors." At the end of November, a federal grand jury in Indiana reported that no overt acts of resistance to the Fugitive Slave Law had occurred in the state, but there had been "acts of public notoriety, breathing strong disaffection and opposition . . . by small bodies of persons in some several instances." As if to confirm this statement, abolitionists meeting at Camden, in the state's Jay County, resolved, "Resistance to tyrants is obedience to God, and . . . we will obey God by resisting, even unto prison and death if need be, the operation of this latest law of despotism and tyranny." The *Chicago Tribune* reported that a "spy" from Missouri had disappeared without a trace in the city after making inquiries about fugitive slaves. In September 1852, Eastman warned against "official bloodhounds" and advised "all interested to be on their guard, and ready for any emergency."[35]

Justifications of defensive violence against slave catchers, U.S. marshals, kidnappers, and militia did not *lead to* forceful clashes over the new fugitive slave law. Instead, the calls reflected a long-existing physical conflict that flourished as Congress prepared to pass the law. Just as escapes led Mason and others to demand a stronger law, violent opposition to the law encouraged antislavery leaders in the Lower North—and the North generally—to endorse resistance. The same well-publicized escapes and clashes that convinced masters they required federal intervention encouraged many people in the Lower North to fight back.

FROM EARLY 1850, through the weeks following Congress's passage of the new law, and throughout the rest of the decade, African Americans set an example of violent resistance many of their white neighbors, abolitionists, Free Soilers, and later Republicans emulated. Among the better-publicized incidents that occurred as the new fugitive slave legislation advanced through Congress were two in Ohio and one in Pennsylvania. The first Ohio incident took place near Salem. On a frigid February morning as two men from Wheeling, Virginia, approached a small house where fugitive slaves had taken refuge, "a colored woman . . . gave the alarm," and African Americans gathered in sufficient numbers to prevent capture. The second incident took place in early August. Six slaves who had escaped from Kentucky into Lawrence County, Ohio, confronted eight white men who attempted to capture them. The "well armed" slaves opened fire, "wounding several" of the would-be captors, and then "fell upon the remainder with cudgels." They "beat several until they supposed them dead, after which . . . they made their escape into the wilderness."[36] Later that month at Harrisburg, Pennsylvania, a black mob rescued two fugitive slaves from twelve Virginians. As mentioned in chapter 6, the rescue prompted warlike calls from border southerners for stringent enforcement of the proposed new law. It also encouraged more resistance.

As the law went into effect, and clashes in Boston, New York, and Detroit attracted the most press coverage, black defiance of slave catchers continued in the Lower North. In October 1850, enough African Americans gathered in Philadelphia during the Garnett hearing to lead Justice Grier to threaten to call in troops from the city's navy yard. In April 1851, following the arrest by two Marylanders of a black man, woman, and seven-year-old—all claimed by a master from Anne Arundel County, Maryland—a black crowd surrounded the home of a Harrisburg, Pennsylvania, commissioner. Three months later in Wilkes-Barre, James Whitman, described as "a large and powerful negro" used a "heavy cart whip" and "a large sheath knife" in an unsuccessful attempt to prevent his arrest by a group of slave catchers. When Whitman's captors brought him to Philadelphia en route to Baltimore, they had to fight off "colored porters, wood sawyers, stevedores, and other employees along the wharves," before they could put him on a boat. In southern Indiana during the winter of 1853, two masters from Clark County, Kentucky, recaptured ten slaves who had fled to the small settlement of Cabin Creek. But it took a gunfight in which two slaves and one master were wounded.[37]

Southeastern Pennsylvania, which had been contested territory since the 1780s, became the most dramatic and influential scene of forceful black resistance. Masters and their agents struggled in the area against fugitive slaves, free African Americans, and their white neighbors and employers. As the new law encouraged Marylanders in their slave-catching efforts, violence rose to the level of what Giddings called "civil war." This was especially the case along the boundary of Chester and Lancaster counties near "a settlement of free negroes and escaped slaves" in the "Gap Hills."[38] Among the nearby towns were Coatesville, Sadsbury, and Christiana.

Conflict began in December 1850 as a deputy U.S. marshal and a band of Marylanders forced their way into a Coatesville house in search of a fugitive slave. A black couple that resided there fought back with "axes and firearms." The man and woman's violence permitted a fugitive slave to escape but the couple suffered serious wounds in the process. Shortly thereafter, one of Giddings's white correspondents reported, "The colored people there are all well armed, and prepared to receive . . . slavehunters in a *becoming* manner. They feel that there is no other way for them than to shoot down those who seek to take their lives." At Sadsbury in January 1851, six white men, reputedly members of the "Gap gang" of criminals, entered a white man's home, found a black man named John Williams, beat him, and—without a warrant—took him toward Maryland. A "band of colored people, armed with double-barreled guns" pursued but failed to catch the kidnappers. During the following March, at least three more incidents occurred near Sadsbury, in which slave catchers broke into homes, assaulted residents, and carried black men to Maryland. In April a white man, in defiance of the Fugitive Slave Law, refused to surrender a black man to a claimant from Baltimore and the officers who accompanied him.[39]

After these encounters, African Americans at nearby Christiana were ready the following September when Maryland master Edward Gorsuch arrived, along with a deputy marshal, two assistant deputies, and five relatives, seeking four slaves who had escaped in 1849. Two of the slaves had taken refuge in a stone house owned by black underground-railroad operator William Parker. As Gorsuch and the deputy entered Parker's home, the five black men and two black women inside resisted with an axe, fish spear, and pistols. Soon about eighty well-armed black men accompanied by several white men—including two Quakers—surrounded the house. Within moments, Gorsuch was dead, his son appeared to be mortally wounded, buckshot hit two of his relatives, and two or three black men suffered wounds.[40]

Following what appeared to have been a double homicide, two wounded black men, Parker, the other men in his house, and the two slaves headed for Canada. They departed before a large armed force arrived in Christiana

In September 1851, Maryland master Edward Gorsuch was killed and his son seriously wounded when black men at Christiana, Pennsylvania, defended themselves against recapture. This drawing, entitled "The Christiana Tragedy," is from William Still, *The Underground Railroad* (Philadelphia: Porter and Coastes, 1872).

from Philadelphia. It included a U.S. marshal, a district attorney, a commissioner, forty-five U.S. marines, and a "civil posse" of fifty. Amid crowds and "intense" excitement, this federal force arrested twenty-four "colored persons," in addition to the eleven men—a few of whom were white—local authorities had detained.[41]

White southerners reacted to what they called the "Christiana Outrage" by blaming white abolitionists for encouraging "the negroes to 'stand their ground.'" They condemned the "foul murder committed" and called on Marylanders to "vindicate the dignity of the State." Widely circulated and sometimes exaggerated accounts of what happened at Christiana undermined hope in the Border South that the federal government could serve as an effective ally. Maryland governor E. Louis Lowe warned President Fillmore that his state "would not remain *one day* in the confederacy, if finally assured either that the powers of the Federal Government were inadequate, or that the public opinion of the non-slaveholding States was adverse to the protection of the rights, liberties, and lives of her citizens." In contrast, events at Christiana encouraged African Americans. Frederick Douglass found in "the Christiana conflict" an affirmation of black manhood. "If it be right for any man to resist those who would enslave them [*sic*]," he declared, "it was right for the men of color at Christiana to resist."[42]

To assuage border slave-state leaders such as Lowe and discourage abolitionists such as Douglass, a U.S. grand jury sitting in Philadelphia indicted forty-five Lower North men for treason "in the attitude of levying war against the United States." Upon learning of this charge, nonviolent Gamaliel Bailey warned, "Hang men for constructive high treason, and you will have civil war unless American citizens are bastard sons of 1776." Justice Grier agreed. He ruled the charges inappropriate, the U.S. attorney dropped them, and the accused went free.[43]

And the struggle for southeastern Pennsylvania continued. On January 1, 1852, friends of Joseph C. Miller found his body hanging from a tree along the tracks of the Pennsylvania Railroad not far from Baltimore. Miller, a white resident of West Nottingham in Chester County, had traveled with six or seven of his neighbors to Baltimore to charge Thomas McCreary of Elkton, Maryland, "with kidnapping a colored girl named Rachel Parker, who was living with him." In Baltimore, several men taunted Miller, claiming he had been involved in the Christiana battle. After Miller arranged a court date for January 7, he disappeared, either while waiting for a northbound train or after boarding it. Before long, travelers saw his body near the tracks. As suspicion fell on McCreary, the Marylander's attorney produced a witness who alleged Miller intended to sell Rachel to traders and that he hanged himself out of remorse when McCreary beat him to it. Alternatively, the attorney claimed, Miller had killed himself for fear his motives would be exposed to abolitionists. Although a Maryland court ruled Miller's death a suicide and discharged McCreary, a postmortem examination by a Pennsylvania physician determined Miller had been poisoned then hanged, suggesting murder rather than suicide. Months later, a Baltimore court ruled Rachel to be free.[44]

NOT ONLY IN southeastern Pennsylvania did white people in the border region cooperate with African Americans to threaten or implement violent resistance to the Fugitive Slave Law. When in October 1850 Ulrich Hinch of Missouri came to Chicago "in pursuit of several fugitives," a group of "respectable citizens . . . kindly informed him that he was employed in an enterprise full of personal hazard." According to Eastman, Hinch left the city, "congratulating his stars, that he had escaped with a whole skin." Eight months later in the same city, a deputy U.S. marshal arrested black man Moses Johnson on behalf of a Missouri master. As Johnson resisted arrest and screamed for help, a large crowd, composed of "white and colored, large and small, male and female" gathered and occupied the city's streets for the next four days. As efforts by the mayor, city police, "and many volunteers" failed to restore order, the U.S. commissioner who presided over Johnson's hearing called out local volunteer companies to stand between the mob and the courtroom. Finally, the commissioner ruled Johnson did not fit the master's description of the slave, and the crowd hurried Johnson away. An antislavery journalist boasted that it had taken "all the guns and bayonets, swords and cannon of the volunteer and enrolled companies" to guard "an innocent free man." The law's opponents as well as its supporters recognized how close the city had come to battle.[45]

In October 1852, a similar clash occurred in Sandusky, Ohio, as "a number of citizens of both colors" forcefully prevented a band of Kentuckians from capturing a group of fugitive slaves as they boarded a Lake Erie steamer for Canada. But it was in the border city of Cincinnati that physical interracial resistance to the Fugitive Slave Law became most common. In June 1852, black and white Cincinnatians, implementing a tactic used throughout the North, crowded a courtroom to allow a slave from Fleming County, Kentucky, to escape. In September 1853, the *Cincinnati Gazette* reported that two city police officers and others acting on behalf of a master from Covington, Kentucky, abducted a black man under pretense of arresting him for stealing a watch. When the man realized they were taking him toward the Ohio River, he yelled "murder!" Within minutes an interracial mob attacked the officers with "bricks and stones." Despite the intervention of a proslavery "party of Irish" armed with pistols as well as stones, the mob rescued the man and ruined the carriage.[46]

Three years later, the city witnessed a more tragic clash. On January 27, 1856, a group of slaves reached Cincinnati from Boone County, Kentucky. There were Robert Garner—the leader—Garner's wife, Margaret, their four young children, another man, and another woman. They were not in the city long before their owner, assisted by a deputy U.S. marshal and several others, found them at the home of free black man Elijah Kite. As the officers broke down Kite's door, he and Robert Garner opened fire with pistols, striking one of the intruders in the hand and face. During this struggle, Margaret attempted to kill her children to prevent their return to slavery. She succeeded with her two-year-old daughter. This desperate act helped convince many northerners of the horrors of slavery.

The immediate result, however, was a potentially violent dispute between Ohio and the federal government. Cincinnati authorities charged Margaret

On May 18, 1857, *Harper's Weekly* published this drawing with the caption "The Modern Medea—the Story of Margaret Garner." The previous January, Garner had killed one of her children, and attempted to kill all of them, to prevent a U.S. marshal and several other men from returning them to slavery in Kentucky. Courtesy Library of Congress.

Garner with murder and the other black adults as accessories, not to punish them but to keep them from being returned to Kentucky. As federal officials resisted this maneuver, two armed forces faced each other. The city sheriff, who had the reluctant support of Ohio's Republican governor, Salmon P. Chase, raised one. The U.S. commissioner, who had a firm endorsement from Democratic U.S. president Franklin Pierce, raised the other. Despite Pierce's threat to send troops, not until March did local authorities give way and allow the deputy to take the slaves back to Kentucky. There, despite Chase's efforts to extradite them to Ohio, their master sold them down river to New Orleans.[47]

THE ACTIONS OF THE Cincinnati and Ohio officials on behalf of Margaret Garner and her companions continued a tradition of northern governmental intervention to protect fugitive slaves against those who sought to recapture them. By 1856 the circumstances had become more volatile and the stakes higher. Border South leaders had rejected disunion and sponsored the new Fugitive Slave Law to protect slavery. But escapes appeared to have increased. Resistance to renditions in the Lower North and throughout the rest of the section continued. Defiance of the U.S. government became common. These developments *"infuriated"* public opinion throughout the South. As historian Don E. Fehrenbacher points out, "Flight . . . was a form of resistance in a society haunted by fear of rebellion, and northern violence on behalf of runaways further stimulated the apprehension of incendiary forces at work. The public excitement surrounding many escapes and rescues would scarcely fail to have a subversive effect even in remote slaveholding regions."[48]

To make matters worse for the Border South in particular and the white South in general, the fugitive slave controversy contributed to the formation of the powerful Republican Party. By the mid-1850s, this new major party had replaced the Whig Party in the North. It came to power in Ohio and ten other northern states, mounted a strong but losing campaign for the presidency in 1856, and on the state level obstructed enforcement of the Fugitive Slave Law.[49] Even more important than the fugitive slave issue in the new party's origins, however, were the consequences of an effort undertaken by Missouri slaveholders to prevent slave escapes across their state's western boundary. This defensive undertaking escalated the border struggle, revived the sectionally divisive issue of slavery expansion, and led hundreds of thousands of northerners to demand political action against the South.

# EIGHT

# Pressure on the
# Border South Increases

The most violent event in Congress's history occurred on the afternoon of May 22, 1856. Two days earlier, Charles Sumner, a Republican senator from Massachusetts, had delivered his "Crime against Kansas" speech. By "crime" Sumner meant the attempt to extend slavery into the new Kansas Territory, located west of Missouri. But, in the course of his speech, he ridiculed South Carolina and its elderly senior senator, Andrew P. Butler. Among those who heard Sumner speak was Butler's young cousin Preston Brooks, a South Carolina congressman. After reading over Sumner's speech, Brooks decided to "chastise" him, as he would a disobedient slave, for insulting the honor of his state and family. Well aware his intended victim was larger and more powerful than he, Brooks approached Sumner in a nearly empty Senate chamber as the senator sat at his desk franking copies of his speech. Standing slightly behind Sumner's right shoulder, Brooks introduced himself, stated his mission, and used a heavy wooden cane to beat his victim about the head and shoulders until he lay bleeding and unconscious.[1]

Brooks and Sumner represented states far to the south and north of the sectional line. But they clashed in a quintessential border city. A slaveholding community located near the North-South line, Washington had to deal with escapes and abolitionist interference, as did Baltimore, Parkersburg, Louisville, and St. Louis. As the seat of national government, its location interacted with sectional politics to create a particularly volatile atmosphere.

Conflict had long characterized the city. Since the 1820s, southern congressmen had threatened their northern counterparts. Nat Turner's revolt in 1831, the Snow Riot of 1836, Torrey and Smallwood's clandestine effort during the early 1840s, the large group of escaping Maryland slaves that passed through the city in 1845, the *Pearl* episode in 1848, and the sectional crisis of 1849 and 1850 kept tensions high. In early 1849, the *Richmond Republican*'s Washington correspondent predicted that, unless northern congressmen quelled their antislavery rhetoric, "there will be scenes of violence in the House." The correspondent had "heard Southern men declare that they will not much longer stand this everlasting intermeddling with their domestic institutions—this constant agitation, so well calculated to render the peace of the South insecure."[2]

Although the correspondent misjudged where the violence would occur, physical clashes between northern and southern politicians—as well as rumors of duels between them—persisted through the early 1850s. In January 1856, Congressman Albert Rust of Alabama foreshadowed Brooks's attack on Sumner by assaulting *New York Tribune* editor and Republican leader Horace Greeley. Rust only slightly injured Greeley, despite hitting him several times with a cane as the journalist walked from the Capitol.[3] The more serious attack on Sumner better symbolized the sectional divide and made it worse.

Northerners, regardless of political party, condemned Brooks for his cowardly assault on freedom of speech. In contrast, journalists and politicians in the Middle and Lower South, with notable exceptions among Whigs, praised Brooks for his manly defense of sectional honor. Most white residents of the Border South agreed with those to their south. The *South-side Democrat* of Petersburg, Virginia, found "no information more grateful to our feelings than the *classical* caning which this outrageous Abolitionist received." The *Richmond Whig* rejoiced at Brooks's "good deed," regretting only that he "did not employ a horsewhip or a cowhide upon [Sumner's] slanderous back, instead of a cane." The *Sentinel*, published in Washington, added that when Sumner insulted "his fellow senators. . . . nothing in this wide world [could be done] but cowhide bad manners *out* of him." The *Louisville Daily Courier* praised Brooks for inflicting "chastisement on Sumner, whose unresisting manhood crouched with spaniel-like spirit beneath the blows."[4]

These sentiments reflected commitment to slavery in the Border South. They reflected a defensive reaction against what residents had long regarded as northern aggression. What reservations the region's journalists expressed concerning the assault resulted from fear it would encourage, rather than alleviate, northern pressure. The *Petersburg Intelligencer* bitterly observed, "We are exceedingly sorry that Mr. Brooks dirtied his cane by laying it athwart the shoulders of the blackguard Sumner. . . . because the nasty scamp and his co-scamps will make capital for their foul camp out of the affair." The *Baltimore Patriot*, believed Brooks had been well provoked, but lamented his actions would escalate the "war of sections." And George D. Prentice, of the

*Louisville Journal*, who blamed both Brooks and Sumner for the incident, gloomily predicted it would "do injury at the North by still further inflaming the already inflamed public sentiment in that section."[5]

When Prentice mentioned inflamed sentiment, he referred to the violent northern reaction to the Fugitive Slave Law of 1850. As discussed in chapter 7, fugitive slaves and their northern defenders fought—especially in the Lower North—against masters, slave catchers, and U.S. marshals. White southerners condemned these confrontations in which northern mobs defied federal authority. But, while the Fugitive Slave Law expanded northern animosity to slavery and slaveholders, resistance to the law was *defensive*. Some of the energy that during the 1840s had been expended in support of Madison Washington, Torrey, Chaplin, and other aggressive abolitionists went after 1850 to protecting African Americans in the North.

Each side perceived the other as the offender. As the 1850s progressed, the impression spread in the North that an "aggressive slaveocracy" or "slave power" controlled the federal government. Millions of northerners believed slaveholders used aristocratic, corrupt, and antidemocratic methods to threaten the rights and undermine the interests of the North and free labor. The effort to expand slavery into the southwestern territories, the Fugitive Slave Law of 1850, and the Kansas-Nebraska Act of 1854 opening the region west of Missouri to slavery appeared to be southern attacks on northern freedom. So did a diplomatic initiative undertaken in 1854 to make Cuba a slaveholding state and the Supreme Court's 1857 *Dred Scott* decision legalizing slavery in all U.S. territories.[6]

Throughout the South, during the same span of years, northerners appeared to be the aggressors. But the Lower South had less reason to fear them than did the Border South. Lower South journalists and politicians greatly exaggerated the number of antislavery agents in their region. In contrast, the white Border South had good reason to react against assaults on its economic, social, cultural, and racial status quo. Individuals and groups, acting with support from northern antislavery organizations, challenged slavery throughout the Border South. The threat appeared greatest on the border between Kansas Territory and Missouri where war between proslavery and antislavery forces broke out.[7]

HISTORIANS HAVE PORTRAYED slavery in Missouri as a declining institution, as white laborers increased faster in the state than slave laborers. But, although slaves declined as a percentage of its population, their absolute numbers and monetary value rose during the 1840s and 1850s. Most of them cultivated hemp and tobacco on a broad east-west band of land in the center of the state, and their masters assumed that black servitude, if left alone, would dominate for the foreseeable future. The masters worried, however, because the Fugitive Slave Law of 1850 had failed to reduce escapes across Missouri's eastern and northern borders to Illinois and Iowa. In December 1853, a politician told an antiabolitionist gathering at Palmyra that hostile operations carried "off eight or ten thousand dollars worth [of slave property] at a time."[8]

To make matters worse, by that December the probability had arisen that slaves might escape across Missouri's western border as well. By 1852, several factors encouraged proposals to open Nebraska Territory, located to the west of Missouri and Iowa, to white settlement. Among them were enthusiasm for territorial expansion, demand among farmers in the Old Northwest for land, and determination among commercial interests to build a railroad to the Pacific coast. The Missouri Compromise of 1820, which allowed Missouri to enter the Union as a slave-labor state, had banned slavery in Nebraska and the rest of the old Louisiana Purchase north of the 36°30' line of latitude. But chances to extend hemp cultivation and benefit from the proposed railroad initially disposed Missourians to favor organization. So did a widespread misunderstanding of how the Missouri Compromise affected slavery. When white Missourians realized the compromise excluded slavery forever from the new territory, they opposed organization. Many of them determined to go to war if necessary to prevent the creation of a new refuge for fugitive slaves.[9]

Missourians believed the key issue was protecting slavery where it existed. They held slavery expansion to be a secondary consideration. In January 1854, future governor Claiborne F. Jackson warned that if Nebraska became a "'free nigger' territory, Missouri must become so too, for we can hardly keep our negroes here now." The *Republican*—a Whig newspaper published in St. Louis—added, "If Nebraska be made a free Territory then will Missouri be surrounded on three sides by *free territory*, where there will always be men and means to assist in the escape of our slaves." The *Republican* called organization of Nebraska in conformity with the Missouri Compromise a strategy for "abolishing Slavery in Missouri" by making "this species of property . . . insecure, if not valueless."[10]

In a speech at Weston, on the western edge of Missouri's central slaveholding area, the state's staunchly proslavery U.S. senator David Atchison charged, "[If] men . . . [from] Massachusetts and elsewhere" in the North gained control of the territory, they would threaten slavery in Missouri,

Arkansas, and Texas. There would be, "constant strife and bloodshed. . . . Negro stealing w[ould] be principle and vocation" until slaveholders surrendered. According to historian Allan Nevins, proslavery Missourians feared, "On every hand slaves would be running away, and anti-slavery sentiment rilling through the dam." As the proposed transcontinental railroad passed through the state, "every train whistle would be a salute to freedom." Even Missouri's moderate former U.S. senator Thomas Hart Benton, who supported the Missouri Compromise, feared the land west of Missouri would become an "asylum for fugitive slaves."[11]

To prevent this disaster, Atchison intervened shortly after Senator Stephen A. Douglas, the Illinois Democrat who chaired the Senate committee on territories, on January 4, 1854, introduced a new bill to organize Nebraska. Atchison, aided by James M. Mason and Robert M. T. Hunter of Virginia, Archibald Dixon of Kentucky, and Andrew P. Butler of South Carolina, convinced Douglas to change his bill. Their effort produced an amendment repealing the Missouri Compromise prohibition of slavery north of the 36°30′ line of latitude. Now settlers in the region would decide the issue. Douglas also agreed to divide Nebraska in two, with Kansas Territory west of Missouri and Nebraska Territory west of Iowa, suggesting Kansas would become a slave state. These alterations pleased most white Missourians and white southerners. But they outraged northern popular opinion, inspiring the Anti-Nebraska movement that within two years produced the Republican Party.[12]

Meanwhile, Missouri moved toward war to keep Kansas from becoming a free-labor territory and a haven for former slaves. Well before Congress passed in May 1854 what became known as the Kansas-Nebraska Act, Atchison called on white Missourians to protect slavery by capturing Kansas Territory. He told them fifty thousand slaves worth $30,000,000 lived in their western counties and "to have a free state as our western neighbor would spell disaster." During the following weeks, Missouri slaveholders pledged "to extend the institutions of Missouri over the Territory at whatever sacrifice of blood or treasure."[13]

In early July, William Walker, who claimed to be provisional governor of Kansas Territory, wrote to Atchison warning against antislavery settlers and the creation of "underground Rail Roads." He advised, "Our Southern friends must be up and stirring. Virginia, Tennessee and Kentucky ought to send her [sic] hardy sons out to claim their rights and maintain them too. Missouri, as far as she can, is doing nobly for a new State." The *Democratic Platform* of Liberty, Missouri, called for men to go to Kansas "musket in hand." Atchison asserted, "Our interests require it. Our peace through all time depends on it, and we intend to leave nothing undone that will conduce to that end and with honor can be performed." Southern support for the Missourians, however, was erratic. Leaders throughout the South recognized the importance of maintaining slavery on its northern periphery and expanding it into new territories, but most of them questioned committing political and economic resources to a region so far to their north. This meant proslavery Missourians had to rely mostly on themselves to block the creation of a free territory to their west.[14]

HISTORIAN SAMUEL A. JOHNSON comments on the fighting that began during the fall of 1855 in Kansas Territory, "Judged by the number of men engaged and the number of casualties, it was petty warfare indeed." In comparison with the mighty armies and horrible levels of death and destruction characteristic of the Civil War, Johnson is correct. Yet the magnitude of border conflict in Kansas—the numbers involved, casualties suffered, and bitterness displayed—greatly exceeded what had gone before on either side of the North-South line. Some historians have not understood that the Missouri-Kansas war was an escalation of an existing border conflict. They portray it as a violent extension of congressional debate over slavery expansion in general.[15]

But, although war in Kansas had great national significance, its cause lay in white Missourians' determination to secure their western border against slave escape. They hoped to circumvent the development of conditions there, which they and others in the Border South had experienced for decades on their borders with the Lower North. As Mary J. Klem put it in 1917, "While it has been asserted that the real motive behind settlement of Kansas was an effort by the slave States to expand their territory, slaveholding Missourians always asserted that it was merely a defensive movement to conserve existing slave property and an existing slave society." The words of the Missourians quoted in this chapter attest to this. According to Freehling, both war in Kansas and the Fugitive Slave Law—"the two most Union-shattering controversies of the 1850s"—originated in the border struggle.[16]

Northern antislavery efforts encouraged Missouri's mobilization. During March 1854, as the Kansas-Nebraska bill made its way through Congress, Eli Thayer, a Massachusetts educator and politician, brought together a group of entrepreneurs and reformers to promote free-labor migration to Kansas. Their New England Emigrant Aid Company (NEEAC) became the model for similar organizations formed across the North. As news of these organizations reached them, white Missourians decided to fight in Kansas to prevent westward escapes and protect slavery in their state.[17]

The departure for Kansas in mid-July 1854 of the NEEAC's first party of settlers, combined with four slaves' escape across the Missouri River, sparked the formation on July 29 at Weston of the Platte County Self-Defensive Association. Led by Atchison, a former general in the Missouri state militia, and Benjamin F. Stringfellow, formerly the state attorney general, the association proposed to protect slavery by a variety of means. It advocated expelling free African Americans, banning contacts "between whites and slaves," resorting to lynch law, boycotting the businesses of those who spoke against slavery, and fighting in Kansas. Militia officers at the association's initial meeting assumed there would be "wounded and dying" men. One of them declared he would go to Kansas "the first hour it shall be announced that the [northern] emigrants have come, and with my own hand help hang every one of them."[18]

Approximately one thousand men joined the Self-Defensive Association before proslavery leaders formed the more secretive Blue Lodge to send armed bands westward to vote in Kansas elections. A congressional investigating committee later concluded, "This dangerous society was controlled by men who avowed their purpose to extend slavery into the Territory at all hazards, and was altogether the most effective instrument in organizing the subsequent armed invasions and forays." The men Atchison and others recruited—whom the free-staters called "border ruffians"—were tough, unschooled, whiskey-drinking frontiersmen. They were independent, resistant to discipline, and not always well armed. They had much in common with the "border miscreants" Charles T. Torrey encountered a decade earlier along the Mason-Dixon line. [19]

On November 16, 1854, the *St. Louis Democrat* reported, "Senator Atchison is at present engaged in the upper country, banding a secret society of 5,000 persons. . . . pledged to move into Kansas on the day of the first election, to vote slavery into the Territory." On November 27, the day before Kansas held that election—one to chose a territorial delegate to Congress—the Blue Lodge sent "organized companies, well armed." At the time, Missourians constituted a majority of Kansas's residents, and the fraudulent voters only increased the margin of a proslavery victory. This was also the case during the next territorial election on March 30, 1855, when approximately 2,400 interlopers from Missouri helped choose an overwhelmingly proslavery legislature. They took control of the polls, threatened free-state voters, and generated fear and anger.[20]

As the legislature legalized slavery in the territory and made helping slaves escape a capital offense, free-staters centered in the town of Lawrence prepared to fight. On April 2, their leader Charles Robinson wrote to Thayer, "Our people have now formed themselves into four military companies, and will meet to drill till they have perfected themselves in the art. Also, companies are being formed in other places, and we want *arms*. Give us the weapons and every man from the North will be a soldier and die in his tracks if necessary, to protect and defend our rights." Robinson asked Thayer to have his "secret society" send "200 Sharps rifles. . . . [and] also a couple field-pieces." (The breach-loading Sharps carbine—manufactured at Hartford, Connecticut—fired more rapidly, with greater range and accuracy, than any weapon the Missourians had.) The first shipment of one hundred reached Lawrence on May 23. Thayer, Amos A. Lawrence, Thomas H. Webb, Samuel Cabot, and other leaders of the NEEAC secretly coordinated shipments and helped pay for the rifles.[21]

Subsequently, the free-staters sent agents east to acquire more rifles, other arms, and ammunition. In July and August 1855, Major James B. Abbott, who commanded "a military company" formed at a settlement on the banks of the Wakarusa River, traveled to Boston and New York City. After meeting Thayer, Lawrence, Horace Greeley, and Frederick Law Olmsted, Abbott purchased over 100 Sharps rifles. He also ordered "a mountain howitzer, fifty rounds of canister and shells with time fuses, five hand grenades, fifty rockets, and a half dozen swords." Thayer later provided four breach-loading cannon. In all, during 1855 and 1856, there were over 800 Sharps rifles shipped to Kansas, plus other types of rifles and muskets, small arms, and ammunition, worth over $43,000. Most of those who helped raise money for the arms—including Thayer, Lawrence, Olmsted, and famous Brooklyn, New York, preacher Henry Ward Beecher— were not technically abolitionists. But several prominent abolitionists—including Gerrit Smith, Thomas Wentworth Higginson, Wendell Phillips, and George W. Stearns—contributed. Beecher's remarks equating the free-state cause in Kansas to a holy war led the rifles to be called "Beecher's Bibles."[22]

Antipathy increased in Missouri and Kansas during the summer of 1855 as steamers moving up the Missouri River carried boxes of free-state weapons, labeled "dry goods" or "books." On July 12, a convention representing twenty-six Missouri counties denounced the NEEAC for colonizing "large armies of abolitionists upon the Territory of Kansas" with "the purpose . . . plain and obvious, whether avowed or not, of ultimately abolishing slavery in Missouri." In what historian Nicole Etcheson calls "a virtual declaration of war," those attending the convention called the free-state settlers "an army of hired fanatics," and called for "organized resistance." That July, Kansas's proslavery territorial legislature commissioned A. M. Coffey and William P. Richardson major generals and Hiram T. Strickler adjutant general in an as yet nonexistent territorial militia.[23]

In response, antislavery settlers began organizing a separate free-state government. First, a series of conventions led to the formation of the Free-State Party on June 25. Then on September 5, armed party members met fifteen miles west of Lawrence at a small settlement called Big Springs. They claimed the territorial legislature represented "lawless invaders" and vowed to oppose "foreign despotism." They declared, "Our true interests, socially, morally and pecuniarily, require that Kansas should be a free State." They pledged to resist proslavery forces "to a bloody issue" and recommended "the organization and discipline of [more] volunteer companies and the procurement and preparation of arms." The delegates denied Missourians' charges that they were aggressive abolitionists and repudiated "any attempt to encroach upon the constitutional rights of the people of any State, or to interfere with their slaves." They also pledged that masters could "recover their slaves without any molestation or obstruction from the people of Kansas." Following racial policies established in the Old Northwest, a majority promised "stringent laws excluding negroes, bond or free, from the Territory."[24]

Missourians nevertheless objected to the adoption at Topeka of a free-state constitution, plans to ratify it on December 15, and plans to elect a free-state government on January 15. A claim dispute between a free-stater and a Missourian, the murder of the free-stater on November 21, and reprisals by a free-state militia company produced a series of events that led to an advance on Lawrence. On November 26, a proslavery posse of about fifteen men, armed with shotguns and headed by county sheriff Samuel J. Jones, arrested free-stater Jacob Branson for his involvement in the reprisals. That evening, Major Abbott led at least fifteen men, some of whom carried Sharps rifles, in intercepting the posse and rescuing Branson. Jones, angry and humiliated, sent a message to territorial governor Wilson Shannon, a former Democratic governor of Ohio, claiming forty free-staters had attacked his posse. Jones declared "open rebellion" existed in and about Lawrence and asked Shannon to call out "THREE THOUSAND men to carry out the laws."[25]

Shannon, who shared proslavery fear of a free-state "military organization" that he "estimated at from one to two thousand," ordered generals Richardson and Strickler "to collect together as large a force as you can in your division" and report to Sheriff Jones. Calls to arms circulated throughout western Missouri, and within days an unruly army of about 1,500 assembled on the banks of the Wakarusa River not far from Lawrence. Some came in unorganized bands carrying obsolete weapons. Others, such as Atchison's 200-strong Platte County Rifles, had arms from state arsenals at Independence and Lexington. In Clay County on December 4, two hundred volunteers commanded by Major Ebenezer Price raided the U.S. arsenal at Liberty. Meeting no resistance, they took three cannon, an undisclosed quantity of small arms, and ammunition. The *Leavenworth Herald* declared, "To Arms! To Arms!! It is expected that every lover of *Law and Order* will rally at Leavenworth . . . to move at once to *the scene of the rebellion*. . . . the outlaws, it is said, are armed to the teeth, and number 1,000 men. Every man should bring his rifle and ammunition, and . . . two or three day's provisions"[26]

As the Missouri-dominated Kansas Militia approached Lawrence, freestaters formed a "Committee of Safety" to coordinate defense. Robinson served as commander-in-chief and Colonel James H. Lane, a former Democrat from Indiana, as second in command. By November 30, about 350 residents had enrolled in guard companies. About half received Sharps rifles and women in the town made cartridges. During early December, additional men converged on Lawrence from nearby free-state settlements, swelling the defense force to approximately 2,000. The men drilled and built earthwork fortifications seven feet high, with a placement for Abbott's howitzer. Among the last to arrive at Lawrence were five men from Osawatomie, consisting of John Brown and four of his sons. Known as Old Brown to distinguish him from his son John Jr., who had been in Kansas longer, Brown was a veteran abolitionist and underground-railroad operative who had been active in western Pennsylvania, eastern Ohio, and western New York. Shortly after Brown called for aggressive action against the Missourians, Robinson commissioned him captain of a company of twenty men in the 5th Regiment, 1st Brigade, Kansas Volunteers.[27]

The siege of Lawrence in the so-called Wakarusa War began on December 1, 1855, and lasted a week. Bands of proslavery scouts and foragers controlled the region surrounding the town, captured several free-staters, and killed one. Four developments prevented an all-out attack. First, the proslavery generals knew the town's defenders not only had superior weapons but would use them. Second, Colonel Edwin Sumner—a cousin of Charles Sumner—who commanded the U.S. Army detachment at Fort Leavenworth, refused to support the militia. Third, Shannon, hoping to avoid a proslavery disaster, negotiated the Treaty of Lawrence. Signed on December

8, it provided for the dispersal of the militia. Fourth, bitterly cold weather encouraged even the most warlike Missourians to comply.[28]

Historian James M. McPherson describes the Wakarusa War as "nothing more than a few skirmishes." It nevertheless pitted the largest American armies against each other since Patriots fought Loyalists during the War for Independence. It aroused many northerners in favor of the free-state cause and solidified white Missourian opinion that the state faced a powerful antislavery threat on its western border. Atchison spoke for Missouri slaveholders when he declared, "We must have the support of the South. We are fighting the battles of the South. . . . You far southern men are now out of the nave of the war; but if we fail it will reach your doors, perhaps your hearths. We need men—armed men." Otherwise, "civil war of the fiercest kind" would reach the entire South. A proxy war followed as groups in each section sought to raise money, arms, and troops for their side in the Kansas conflict. As Johnson notes, "Petty as it may appear [in comparison to the Civil War], this was real war. . . . Tiny armies marched, entrenched, and battled in mortal combat; guerrillas plundered; towns were sacked; prisoners were taken and exchanged." The free-staters won because they succeeded better than the Missourians in attracting assistance and settlers.[29]

Fighting resumed on January 15, 1856, when the free-state elections produced a clash near Leavenworth. It involved about thirty proslavery fighters and a free-state militia company of half that number. One proslavery man died in battle, and Missourians beat to death a free-state captive. The conflict escalated after April 19, when near Lawrence someone shot and wounded Sheriff Jones as he attempted to arrest two free-state men on charges they had months earlier helped Branson escape. Shannon supported Jones, and a U.S. marshal called on loyal citizens to quell resistance in Lawrence. Federal treason charges against free-state leaders Robinson, Lane, and Andrew Reeder had encouraged them to flee the territory. Therefore, the town's residents—leaderless and fearful of the costs of defying federal authority— did not resist on May 21 as a proslavery "posse" of 800, supported by five cannon, rode into town. In what northerners called the "Sack of Lawrence," Missouri militia, assisted by companies of volunteers from Alabama, Florida, and South Carolina, engaged in considerable mayhem. They destroyed two newspaper offices. They fired cannon at and then burned the town's Free State Hotel. And they burned Robinson's home.[30]

This invasion was the turning point in the Kansas struggle, as it led to a series of battles lasting into autumn. By circulating exaggerated accounts of the level of destruction in Lawrence, free-staters attracted more support

On May 21, 1856, a proslavery "posse" of 800 occupied Lawrence, the center of free-state power in Kansas Territory. The posse, which regarded the Free State Hotel as a political, if not military, target, fired cannon at it and then burned it. The "Sack of Lawrence" escalated fighting in the territory. The drawing is from Sara T. L. Robinson, *Kansas: Its Interior and Exterior Life* (Boston: Crosby, Nichols, 1857).

in the North and struck back at proslavery forces with great effectiveness. Free-state bands ambushed proslavery fighters and robbed, tortured, and killed proslavery settlers. The most brutal free-state attack occurred on May 24, when John Brown, four of his sons, and three other men rode to Pottawatomie Creek, dragged five proslavery men from their cabins, and either shot or hacked them to death.[31]

During the following weeks and months, proslavery forces attempted to capture or kill Brown, free-staters attacked proslavery strongholds, and Colonel Sumner vainly sought to restore order. In a struggle in which proslavery armies were larger and free-state armies better armed, each side robbed, killed, and attempted to deprive the other of food and supplies. Proslavery officials prevented Missouri River steamers from carrying northern settlers and arms to Kansas. Northerners then took an alternate route through Iowa and Nebraska. Lane led the most famous such party. Known as the Army of the North, it numbered nearly 400 and had considerable firepower.[32]

As free-state armies grew larger, proslavery fighters built log blockhouses at strategic points that became targets. On August 5, the Stubbs Militia

Company, which had formed in April 1855 to protect Lawrence, forced the evacuation of the Georgia Fort near Osawatomie. On August 12, free-state units, totaling eighty-one men under Lane's command, attacked and burned a blockhouse at Franklin, killed six Missourians, and captured eighty muskets and a cannon. On August 14, Lane, with a force of about 300, used the cannon to take Fort Saunders near the town of Marion, burn it, and capture more muskets. Two days later, sixty free-staters commanded by Captain Samuel Walker captured Fort Titus near Lecompton and thirty-four of its defenders. Only the intervention of U.S. troops prevented Walker's free-staters from conquering Lecompton, the proslavery territorial capital. Shortly thereafter, Governor Shannon resigned and fled the territory. On August 25, interim territorial governor Daniel H. Woodson declared a state of insurrection.[33]

When John W. Geary, the new governor, arrived in Lecompton on September 12, Lane's free-state army still threatened the town, and Atchison's "Grand Army," numbering about 2,700, approached Lawrence. Geary, with considerably more decisiveness than his predecessor, used U.S. troops to disperse the opposing forces. By December, he had restored order, if not peace, and inadvertently ended what hope Atchison had of making Kansas a slave state. By the following spring, as large numbers of northern settlers continued to arrive, Atchison and other proslavery leaders realized their military effort had been futile. In October 1857, free-staters took control of the territorial legislature.[34]

From 1854 through 1856, Missourians had warned that a free-state victory in Kansas meant the destruction of slavery in their state, and eventually throughout the South. The *North East Reporter* of Canton claimed in April 1855 that if the free-staters won, "the next step would . . . [be] to undermine and destroy the institution of slavery in Missouri. . . . with emissaries under the garb of religion, and co-workers with the political designation of *free-soilers*." That July, a convention held at Lexington predicted, "If Kansas is made the abode of an army of hired fanatics," the "entire slave property" of Missouri "is not merely unsafe, but valueless." Fighting in Kansas during 1856 strengthened the sense of foreboding. In August, Stringfellow declared that resisting "fanatical aggression" was "not merely a question of whether Kansas shall be a slave state or not, but a question whether the entire South shall not become the victim of misguided philanthropy." The *Missouri Democrat* observed, if Missourians did not succeed in Kansas, "Our homes must be given up to the abolition enemy."[35]

Perhaps 200 people died in Kansas warfare. The conflict destroyed

$2,000,000 worth of property. Many Missourians, besides Atchison, feared it had been in vain. The *Lexington Express* declared, "We labored honestly and zealously to make Kansas a slave state, and we acted upon the information then before us. We could do no less. But the mask is torn off and all is lost— worse than lost." Atchison gave up raising funds and blamed the rest of the South for its apathy. "I see that not even thunder and lightening will arouse the South," he wrote. "I doubt whether an earthquake—a moral and political earthquake, shaking the institution of slavery to the earth, and bringing ruin upon the whole South, would rouse her to action."[36]

Some Lower South journalists concurred in Atchison's interpretation, while not sharing his perspective. "If the people of the South," a Columbia, South Carolina editor observed, "had really believed that our fate depended on Kansas, we would have succeeded in taking the country." Instead, the editor continued, "The outposts of Kansas" were "not upon soil that we can claim truly as southern soil—and adapted for southern labor. Why should we expend out blood and treasure on an issue where our immediate interests are not concerned?" The initiation of the proslavery Buchanan presidency in March 1857 and the chance Kansas might still become a slave state under the Lecompton Constitution drafted by a proslavery convention that September revived proslavery hopes in Missouri. But, well before a territorial referendum defeated the Lecompton Constitution in August 1858, the best-informed proslavery leaders understood, lacking sufficient support from the Lower South, they had lost.[37]

White Missourians' fear of an abolitionist threat to slavery in their state approached reality. Most Kansas free-staters, like their counterparts in the Lower North, denied an intention to interfere with slavery across the sectional line or encourage slave escape. With the exception of Robinson, the free-state leaders in 1855 and 1856 were not abolitionists. The Topeka Constitution's banning of African-American settlers, suggests many of them were racially biased. In some cases, free-staters returned fugitive slaves to their masters. As late as September 1855, Lane denied that free-staters fought to free slaves. Yet, as armed conflict on the Kansas-Missouri border and increasing sales south encouraged slaves to escape westward, a minority of white settlers helped them. Like antislavery centers farther east, Lawrence became a destination for fleeing slaves, who enjoyed armed protection in the town. Organized escape networks existed by 1857, and Abbot recalled, "Hardly a week passed that some way-worn bondman did not find his way into Lawrence, the best advertised anti-slavery town in the world."[38]

Developments in southeastern Kansas were most ominous for proslavery

Missourians and the South. Well after violence had subsided elsewhere in the territory, this area witnessed small free-state and proslavery armies, supplied with cannon as well as rifles, ferociously fighting and killing. James Montgomery, who was born in Ashtabula County, Ohio, and lived in Kentucky before moving west in 1854, led antislavery forces determined to drive out proslavery settlers and protect fugitive slaves. In April 1858, troops under Montgomery's command fired on U.S. soldiers who attempted to stop their depredations on proslavery settlements. In May, Montgomery went on the offensive in Missouri. With 150 men and two cannon, he captured West Point and Barnesville.

Beginning that fall, others joined Montgomery's aggressive war. On December 20, John Brown led twenty men to Vernon County, Missouri, where they liberated eleven slaves. They also took livestock, a wagon, supplies, personal possessions, and the life of a master. By mid-March Brown had escorted the slaves to Windsor, Ontario. Thirteen other slaves who had escaped from Weston to Lawrence engaged Dr. John W. Doy and his son to transport them by wagon to Iowa. On January 25, 1859 a posse from Weston intercepted them as they traveled north, captured the slaves, and arrested the Doys for kidnapping. In June a Missouri jury sentenced the elder Doy to five years at hard labor. A month later, a band of Lawrence men invaded Missouri to rescue him.[39] These incursions, although not unprecedented in the border struggle, had dire implications for the Border South.

FREE-STATE VICTORY in Kansas disheartened slavery's Border-South advocates. In October 1856, the moderate *Louisville Courier* feared conflict might spread eastward to make the "Ohio river run blood." Four months later, the *Richmond Enquirer* published a letter asking, "Can it be that the South is going to give up that Territory, like a set of driveling imbeciles?" By late 1857, both newspapers were willing to accept Kansas as a free state in return for peace.[40]

That other northern-based initiatives targeted the Border South made the region's leaders all the more defensive. Antislavery newspapers just south of the sectional line supported fledgling political organizations that appealed to white nonslaveholders, and two overlapping efforts sent northerners southward. First, evangelical abolitionists supported missionaries in portions of the Border and Middle South. Second, some of the men who formed the NEEAC created free-labor colonies. The numbers involved in these initiatives were small. But they had impact.

By 1859, there were at least eighteen antislavery newspapers published on the South's northern periphery. They stretched from Washington to St. Louis, where B. Gratz Brown edited the *Missouri Democrat*. Most of these newspapers were, by northern antislavery standards, conservative. One, the *Daily Intelligencer* of Wheeling, Virginia, endorsed Buchanan for president in 1856. Gamaliel Bailey's *National Era* and William S. Bailey's *Newport News* of Newport, Kentucky, were exceptional in their defense of black rights. Only the *News* advocated federal action against slavery in the southern states. All of them, including the *National Era* and the *News*, emphasized the rights and interests of white nonslaveholders. They expressed varying degrees of support for plans to colonize former slaves outside the U.S. But, by insisting slavery enriched only masters, debased all who labored, undermined public education, and forced white men to compete for work against slaves, they—like Cassius M. Clay before them—raised a specter of class as well as race war. Republican support in July 1859 for the distribution in the South of a cheap edition of Hinton Rowan Helper's *Impending Crisis of the South*, which stressed the injustices suffered by white southern yeomen, posed a similar threat.[41]

As antislavery newspapers in the Border South supported state-level emancipationist politics, they aligned first with the Free Soil Party and by 1855 with the Republican Party. Tiny versions of these northern parties operated in Delaware, Maryland, Virginia, and Kentucky. Larger Free Soil and Republican organizations existed in Missouri, and northern political abolitionists occasionally ventured into the Border South. Free Soil vice-presidential candidate George W. Julian campaigned in Kentucky in 1852. Charles Sumner in 1855 and Gerrit Smith in 1857 visited Cassius M. Clay at Lexington. And in 1858, William H. Seward traveled to northern Virginia.[42]

In 1849, Kentucky's Emancipation Party conducted a vigorous, although losing, campaign to place a gradual abolition clause in the state constitution (see chapter 6). In the gubernatorial election of 1851, the party cast a disappointing 3,621 votes for Clay. But Clay and others organized a Free Soil presidential ticket in Kentucky in 1852, and Clay led a small Republican organization after 1856. During the early 1850s, Joseph Evans Snodgrass spoke in Maryland on behalf of the Free Soil Party, and thereafter David Gamble of Baltimore promoted Republican organization in the state. In Missouri, Free Soilers controlled St. Louis and in 1856 elected Francis P. Blair Jr. to Congress. The following year, James S. Rollins, running as a free-labor candidate, fell just 300 votes short of becoming governor, strengthening slaveholder fears concerning the impact of losing in Kansas. Virginia's Republican Party organized at Wheeling in August 1856 and formed a Frémont electoral ticket that September. Centered in the northwestern portion of the state, the party cast only 291 votes that November. But, because the Virginia Whigs and Democrats were so closely matched, the Republicans appeared to hold a balance of power during the early fall of 1859.[43]

Almost as long as antislavery newspapers existed in the Border South, and well before antislavery political parties emerged in the region, northern abolitionists envisioned sending missionaries southward to preach to masters and slaves the "anti-slavery part of divine truth." In 1839, Charles T. Torrey called for "a NEW MISSIONARY SOCIETY, to 'evangelize the slaveholders' and their slaves." He wanted men who "shall preach that 'the laborer is *worthy* of his hire. . . . who shall in spite of slavery and its bloody laws, *teach the slave to read the Bible*, and put Bibles and tracts in their hands." Torrey expected a few missionaries to die in the process but hoped "pure Christianity" would destroy slavery.[44]

Three northern groups—the American Wesleyan Connection, the American Missionary Association (AMA), and the American Free Baptist Missionary Society (ABFMS)—followed Torrey's advice. During the late 1840s, the Wesleyans sent Adam Crooks and Jesse McBride to North Carolina and Jarvis C. Bacon to southeastern Virginia. The much-larger AMA supported Kentucky native John G. Fee's free church in Madison County and sent ministers to help him. In 1851 the ABFMS dispatched Edward Mathews to Virginia and Kentucky. During the 1850s, the AMA assumed responsibility for the Wesleyan mission in North Carolina, expanded its effort in Kentucky, initiated other missions in Missouri and Washington, D.C., and encouraged antislavery efforts in Maryland, Virginia, and Tennessee. By 1858, abolitionists contemplated expanding missions in these states and extending them to others "groaning under the burdens and guilt of slavery." They aimed "to open the prison doors, to save the oppressed and oppressor, and the vast population of non-slaveholders. . . . prevent the effusion of rivers of blood. . . . and save our guilty nation from the fierceness of God's anger."[45]

Free-labor colonies in the Border South also began well before they peaked during the 1850s. All of the colonies sought to demonstrate the superiority of free labor and thereby encourage emancipation. Otherwise, they varied in character. Colonies in Trimble and Madison counties, Kentucky, were openly abolitionist. In Trimble in 1852, former slave rescuer Delia Webster arrived at a 600-acre farm located across the Ohio River from Madison, Indiana, where she planned to introduce free labor. Local masters, disturbed by increased escapes, threatened to "burn her buildings and destroy her crops" and had her arrested. After being jailed several times, Webster fled to Indiana. Fee had more success in Madison County, where 200 free-labor settlers resided at Berea in conjunction with his larger missionary effort.[46]

In Virginia, northerners purchased farms and employed free labor during the early 1840s. In 1846, New York abolitionist John C. Underwood launched a "free labor experiment" on property in the Shenandoah Valley he had acquired through marriage. A decade later, encouraged by events in Kansas, Underwood teamed with Thayer of the NEEAC to form the American Immigrant Aid and Homestead Company. This initiative stressed economic opportunity and regional development, masking its abolitionist goals. By attracting approximately 2,500 northern and foreign-born settlers to nearly a dozen Virginia counties, Underwood hoped to build Republican strength. For his part, Thayer established a free-labor colony of about 500 northerners at Ceredo, located in northwestern Virginia on the east bank of the Ohio River near the Kentucky line. In his public pronouncements concerning the colony, Thayer emphasized profits and peaceful coexistence. Masters, who recalled Thayer's role in sending free-state settlers to Kansas, doubted this was all he desired, even though they did not know he had armed free-staters in Kansas or that in April 1857, he had written to John Brown, "You must have a home in Western Virginia."[47]

White residents of the Border South reacted in various ways to these small and ostensibly peaceful antislavery initiatives. A few supported them. More acquiesced in what they regarded as a trend toward the eventual termination of slavery in the region. They did not object so long as they believed the process would be peaceful, drawn out, and involve removal of the black population.[48] But the majority of white border southerners, even if they supported prospective gradual emancipation, resisted. They denounced southern antislavery newspapers and political parties, missionaries, and free-labor colonies.

In 1851 the *Louisville Courier* condemned Clay and his Emancipation Party for aligning with the "vilest Disunionists of the North." According to the *Courier*, they were "disorganizers and disturbers of the peace" who risked creation of an uncontrollable free-black population. Clay encouraged such charges by avowing his commitment to "ultraism and fanaticism." By mid-decade a *Courier* correspondent claimed William S. Bailey advocated miscegenation and socialism as well as abolition. In Virginia, politicians and journalists opposed the "new idols of fanaticism and abolitionism." They pledged to stand with the Lower South in defense of slavery. In 1856 a group of Baltimore merchants, who might be expected to embrace northern interests, vowed to defend Maryland's "honor and institutions. . . . as they have been bequeathed to us." They declared, "Our loyalty to the South cannot be doubted."[49]

Abolitionist missionaries and free-labor colonists attracted more criticism than antislavery parties. Some residents of the Border South resented missionary claims that masters forbade slaves to read the Bible and denied them religious instruction. Others criticized the missionaries for using a religious venue to discuss slavery. Because missionaries met openly with slaves, the most common charge was that they encouraged slaves to escape. Free-labor colonies faced similar charges. The *Richmond Enquirer* described Thayer's effort in Virginia as designed "to elbow the institution of slavery out of the State." The newspaper correctly perceived in Thayer's colonizing "the stiletto of the assassin under the garb of the shepherd—because we think this man of peace, this husbandman with his axe and plow, is an incendiary in disguise."[50]

HIGH LEVELS of slave escapes from the Border South during the mid- to late 1850s underlay this vehement opposition to antislavery initiatives. Just as the threat of escapes on their western border led Missouri masters to wage war in Kansas, fear farther east that antislavery newspapers, parties, missionaries, and colonies encouraged escapes—and perhaps revolt—fueled resistance throughout the region. Many historians, relying on questionable census data, discount the role of slave escape in sectionalism during the 1850s. But those who lived in the borderlands believed proliferating escapes placed slavery under siege.[51]

Newspapers reported escapes of individuals, families, and groups. In September and October 1855, the *News* of Chestertown, Maryland, noted parties of seven, ten, and eleven slaves departing for the North. In December, six slaves heading north through Maryland from Virginia used pistols and knives to drive away six white men who attempted to capture them. An 1856 meeting of Kent County, Maryland, slaveholders claimed sixty had escaped during the past year. There were similar reports in Kentucky.[52]

As had been the case since the 1780s, contemporaries on both sides of the North-South line believed white abolitionists encouraged and aided escapes. In 1846, the *True Wesleyan* linked free-labor colonies in the Border South with northward escapes. As the 1850s began, white southerners claimed abolitionist missionaries in Kentucky, North Carolina, and Virginia were also involved. In Grayson County, Virginia, in September 1851, authorities charged that missionary Jarvis Bacon assisted four well-armed black men who, in attempting to reach Ohio, killed one white man and wounded four

In late December 1855, six well-armed slaves in Loudon County, Virginia, took their master's carriage and headed north. At the Maryland line, they used pistols to drive off six would-be slave catchers. The "Bold Stroke for Freedom" drawing appears in William Still, *The Underground Railroad* (Philadelphia: Porter and Coates, 1872).

others before they were captured and later executed. The Reverend George Clark reported from Cabin Creek, Kentucky, in November 1855 that "of thirty three Slaves to whom Bibles were given by one Bro. Thirty two have escaped." The thirty-third, Clark wrote, "failed & was sold down river." Antislavery politics also encouraged slave escape, especially in border counties. Fee alleged in June 1855 that following a speech by Clay, twelve slaves headed north from Jessamine County.[53]

Despite white involvement, many slaves continued to escape on their own or with the support of free African Americans. Abolitionist James Redpath's 1860 claim that 500 black men per year traveled from Canada into the South to help slaves escape is an exaggeration. But, during the 1850s, black men and women who lived just north of the sectional boundary ventured into the Border South. They came from such towns and cities as New Albany and Madison, Indiana; Cairo, Illinois; Cincinnati and Ripley, Ohio; Philadelphia; and Washington, D.C. Harriet Tubman, the best-remembered underground-railroad operative, had escaped on her own from Maryland in 1849. Thereafter, working with black abolitionist William Still of Philadelphia and white abolitionist Thomas Garrett of Wilmington, Delaware, she returned at least thirteen times to Maryland to lead groups of escapees northward.[54]

Although Tubman carried a musket during her forays into the Border South, she avoided violent confrontation. But, during the 1850s, and as had been done earlier, others—both black an white—who helped slaves reach the North relied on force and were at times the victims of it. Black abolitionist John P. Parker of Ripley *used* the weapons he carried when he helped slaves escape from Kentucky. He recalled "real warfare" with slaveholders. Seth Conklin, a young, white abolitionist from Philadelphia, died as a result of his foray into the South. During the spring of 1851, he and four other men traveled from Princeton, Indiana, to Alabama, where they rescued an enslaved family of four. As the party headed through Indiana toward Canada, slave catchers captured the family and Conklin. That April, when the Alabama master boarded an Ohio River steamer with the slaves and a manacled Conklin, a group of Ohioans demanded that at least Conklin be released. Shortly thereafter, Conklin ended his life under mysterious circumstances— he had either dived into the path of the boat's paddlewheel or been murdered—and the master continued south with the slaves.[55]

Seven months later, Kentucky marshals arrested Calvin Fairbank in Jeffersonville, Indiana, on charges he had helped a young woman escape from Louisville. Fairbank, who had served from 1845 to 1849 in the Kentucky penitentiary for a similar offense, was convicted, returned to the penitentiary, and remained there until he received a pardon in 1864. In more common but less publicized cases, captains and crews of coastal vessels from New England and New York continued, either for profit or out of sympathy, the long-established practice of hiding slaves below deck as they sailed north. In mid-1858 the arrest in Norfolk, Virginia, of captains of several coastal trading vessels, and in Petersburg of Captain William Bayliss for helping slaves escape drew attention to a long-existing network.[56]

DURING THE LATE 1850s, events in Ohio and Indiana contributed to unease in the Border South. Three times, groups of armed men challenged federal authority; once, men from Indiana invaded Kentucky. The first of the confrontations occurred in west-central and southwest Ohio in May 1857 as men, acting under local authority, fought several deputy U.S. marshals and their assistants. The conflict began at sunrise on May 21 as three deputies and five Kentuckians attempted to arrest Addison White at a Mechanicsburg farm owned by underground-railroad agent Udney H. Hyde. As White, who had fled from Flemingsburg, Kentucky, exchanged gunfire with the deputies, a crowd of about thirty neighbors arrived. They carried "all kinds of weapons from guns and pistols to pitchforks and clubs," and caused enough distraction to allow White to escape.[57]

Within a week, the deputies returned with an eleven-man federal posse and a warrant issued by U.S. district judge Humphrey H. Leavitt for the arrest of four of the men who had helped White. Again a crowd gathered, this time on behalf of the "free white men who had dared to sympathize with a bold fellow fighting and fleeing for his liberty." After the deputies and their posse placed the four men in a carriage and headed south through Champaign, Clark, and Greene counties toward Cincinnati, part of the crowd followed on horseback, firing pistols. Meanwhile, local judges issued arrest warrants for the deputies. At one point, the Clark County sheriff stopped the carriage, only to be pistol-whipped. Therefore, by the time the deputies reached Greene County, they faced an additional charge of assault with intent to kill, and their pursuers had grown to a force of 200. When caught, the deputies and their posse opened fire, but the Ohioans overwhelmed them. As the *Cincinnati Gazette* put it, "The conflict was sharp and stubborn, but superior numbers prevailed, and the deputy marshal and his posse were made prisoners."[58]

On June 9 in Cincinnati, Judge Leavitt held court on the issues presented in the case. Prominent Ohio Democrats—including U.S. senator George E. Pugh, Congressman Clement L. Vallandigham, and U.S. attorney Stanley Matthews—represented the deputy marshals. Ohio attorney general Christopher P. Walcott, a Republican, represented the Clark County sheriff who had been permanently disabled. As expected, Leavitt upheld federal authority and the deputies' use of force. Indictments followed against Ohio sheriffs, constables, and magistrates for "resisting federal officers in the discharge of their duties." But Governor Chase negotiated a compromise, which suspended charges against all who interfered with the federal officers in return for a $1,000 payment to White's master. What became known as the "Rebellion in Ohio" suggested what masters, their agents, and deputy U.S. marshals might expect in the future.[59]

During 1858 and 1859, three additional incidents confirmed an impression of persistent resistance in the Lower North to what masters in the Border South regarded as protection of their rights. In September 1858, a deputy U.S. marshal, two Kentucky slave catchers, and a deputy sheriff from Columbus captured John Price, a fugitive slave from Macon County, Kentucky, near the village of Wellington in northeastern Ohio. As they held Price in a tavern while awaiting a train to Columbus, a mob from the nearby anti-slavery center of Oberlin arrived, intending to rescue him by armed might. Among those involved in the biracial effort were Charles Mercer Langston, a prominent black abolitionist; John Anthony Copeland, a young black man who later fought beside John Brown at Harpers Ferry; and William E. Lincoln, a British theology student who attended Oberlin College. Following the deputies' refusal to release Price, Lincoln led in storming the tavern to free him. At one point, Lincoln aimed a revolver at one of the deputy marshal's party, demanding, "Quit, or I'll blow your brains out."[60]

Like the "Rebellion in Ohio," the Oberlin-Wellington rescue involved a clash between national and state authority. A federal jury in Cleveland charged thirty-seven men with violating the Fugitive Slave Law. A Loraine County grand jury indicted the deputy marshal and the three others for kidnapping. The resulting trials stretched well into 1859 and, as the rescuers refused to post bond to be released from jail, they attracted attention. Congressman Giddings praised their "forcible resistance." John Brown visited them in jail. Finally, in another negotiated settlement, Loraine County dropped the kidnapping charges against the deputies, two of the rescuers were convicted, seven others pleaded guilty in return for minimal punishments, and the U.S. government dropped its charges against the rest.[61]

A month after the Oberlin-Wellington rescue, simmering tensions between southeastern Indiana and Kentucky led to an invasion of the latter state. Cross-river escapes and recaptures had for many years alienated New Albany, Indiana, from white communities on the opposite side of the Ohio River. But a series of events beginning in early 1857 led to an escalation. A white farmer named Charles Bell, his father David Bell, and a black man named Oswald Wright helped a slave escape from Brandenburg, Kentucky, and begin his journey to Canada. That October, men working for the escapee's master lured Charles Bell to Kentucky and arrested him. Then the Kentuckians crossed to Indiana and captured David Bell and Wright, who ended up—along with Charles Bell—in Brandenburg jail. The abduction of the Bells, if not Wright, aroused anger in and about New Albany. So much talk of heading south in force circulated that Kentucky's governor called out a detachment of militia to defend Brandenburg.

High bonds and court delays kept the three Indianans in jail until the following July when Charles Bell's siblings John and Horace, "both armed with a belt of revolvers and carrying a carpet bag containing ammunition and revolvers," freed Charles and David in a midday raid. Three months later, five men from Louisville kidnapped Horace from New Albany. This time, men in the town reacted by taking "muskets, pistols, a swivel [gun], and ammunition" from the local courthouse and crossing the river into Kentucky. As the force of about 120 approached Brandenburg, the town's leaders negotiated an agreement by which the Indianans would return north and Horace Bell, but not Wright, would be freed on bond.[62]

Conflict between Ohioans and Indianans on the one side and U.S. authority and Kentuckians on the other seemed to be moving toward the level of violence that existed on the Kansas-Missouri line. In May 1859, when another state-federal jurisdictional clash occurred, this time at the central-Ohio town of Zanesville, federal authorities employed overwhelming force to achieve their goal. Early that month, a deputy U.S. marshal and his "posse" had arrested William Jackson, charging he was the human property of a Clarksburg, Virginia, master. When a Zanesville judge released Jackson on a writ of habeas corpus, the deputy rearrested him and placed him in a carriage "guarded by a large force of special deputies, all armed with loaded and cocked pistols." As this party approached the town's railroad depot, a predominantly black mob attacked with "pistols, clubs, and bricks." Thousands of people gathered to watch the fierce but brief battle. One of the witnesses commented, "Many of the assailants fought bravely." Another reported, "One Negro . . . seized the Marshall by the throat." Nevertheless the large federal force injured "several" attackers, "speedily overpowered and dispersed" the remainder, and returned Jackson to his alleged master.[63] Sufficient federal power seemed key to protecting masters' interests.

AN UNSUCCESSFUL PROSLAVERY WAR in Kansas that led to abolitionist invasions of Missouri supported perceptions that the Border South was under attack. So did well-publicized fighting between antislavery and proslavery forces in Kentucky, cases of men and women from the North going south to help slaves escape, and organized resistance in the Lower North to slave renditions. Meanwhile, ostensibly peaceful efforts involving antislavery newspapers, political parties, missionaries, and free-labor colonies encouraged conflict. These developments, and the failure of the Lower South to commit itself fully in Kansas, influenced slavery's defenders in Kentucky, Maryland, Missouri, and Virginia.[64] They wanted to protect their interests and themselves. But, as most of them looked to the national government for help, Lower South radicals concluded only secession could stop threats to slavery on their section's northern periphery or at least keep the threats from advancing toward themselves.

## NINE

## From Border War to Civil War

On October 17, 1859, Governor Henry Wise of Virginia faced a crisis. The day before, John Brown had led a biracial band of nineteen men in capturing the undefended U.S. armory at Harpers Ferry on Virginia's northern border. Brown and his men, Wise learned, came from the North, trained in western Maryland, had the support of prominent abolitionists, and intended to spark a slave rebellion that would spread throughout the South. They killed four men, took nine prisoners, and confiscated two slaves.

As wildly exaggerated reports concerning the size of Brown's force circulated, Wise called out militia units. He led two of them from Richmond and Alexandria, via the Baltimore and Ohio Railroad, to the scene of conflict. By the time he arrived, local volunteer companies had trapped the band, and a detachment of U.S. Marines—commanded by Colonel Robert E. Lee— either killed or captured most of its members. Wounded, Brown was among the captured. Within a few weeks, he and his fellow prisoners were tried on charges of treason against Virginia and convicted. Amid a display of military force, they died in early December on gallows at Charlestown.[1]

The capture, conviction, and execution of Brown and his men might be portrayed as a victory for Virginia, slavery, and the Union. The invaders failed, no slaves reached their position, U.S. troops acted decisively, and northerners—including Republicans and many abolitionists—repudiated Brown's violent tactics.[2] Yet Wise, while praising the militia's bravery, claimed the raid humbled Virginia and gravely threatened slaveholders. "Our peace has been disturbed; our citizens have been imprisoned, robbed and murdered; the sanctity of their dwellings has been violated; their persons have been outraged," he complained. Worse yet, "an entire social and sectional sympathy" had "incited" the raiders. If slaves had risen as Brown expected, Wise surmised, other "white fanatics" would have moved south.

183

This drawing, originally published in *Frank Leslie's Illustrated Newspaper* on November 5, 1859, portrays local militia—on the left—attacking John Brown's raiders, who stand before the fire-engine house that briefly became their refuge. The gate to the Harpers Ferry armory is in the background. Courtesy Library of Congress.

Although many southerners held the apparent failure of slaves to support Brown to mean they were loyal to their masters, Wise—based on years of experience—discerned a more disturbing situation. "The slaves at will can liberate themselves by running away," he asserted. "The underground rail road is at their very doors, and they may take passage when they please." Since slaves could so easily gain "exterior asylum ... *they have no need to take up arms for their own liberation.*"

Virginia, Wise lamented, had "borne and forborne" too long. As abolitionism grew stronger over many years, individuals and groups crossed the state's boundaries to help slaves escape, and northerners refused "to execute the fugitive slave laws." Now the oldest and largest slave state faced an "unparalleled border war," a "predatory war," that went well beyond John Brown's band. More than once, Wise wished the Virginia militia had captured Brown and his men *on its own*. Wise also contemplated that worsening conditions on the state's border might lead to disunion. But, because he placed Brown's raid in the context of a wider border struggle over escape and recapture, he preferred federal action over disunion as the means of protecting slavery. He realized the border slave states needed federal help and criticized proslavery president Buchanan's refusal to initiate the use of U.S. troops "to *'repel invasion,'* . . . in cases where the citizens of one State invade another State." Buchanan contended states had sole power under the U.S. Constitution to defend themselves. "Now," Wise wryly remarked, "this . . . teaches even Virginia a lesson of State Rights which destroys her constitutional guarantee of protection by the United States against invasion by abolition fanatics from other States."[3]

Well before the Harpers Ferry raid, others in the Border South reached conclusions similar to Wise's. The raid at Harpers Ferry seemed to be the logical product of years of abolitionist involvement in slave escapes and more recent assaults on the Border South stretching from Missouri's western border through Kentucky to the Chesapeake. Northern resistance to the Fugitive Slave Law of 1850 and the outcome of the war in Kansas demonstrated that federal support did not guarantee victory for slavery. But, like Wise, most Border South leaders preferred federal action to secession as a means of protecting their political, social, and racial order. In contrast, as reaction to Brown's raid spread throughout the slave states, Lower South radicals and a large minority of slavery's defenders in the Border and Middle South favored disunion as the only means of protecting slavery.

IN ADDITION TO violations of the Fugitive Slave Law, war in Kansas, and incursions into the Border South, reports of slave-revolt conspiracies contributed to proslavery defensiveness during the 1850s. The Cotton South produced unsubstantiated tales of slave unrest instigated by abolitionist agents. In the border region, where there had been violent mass-escape attempts during the 1840s, residents had better reason to assume abolitionism encouraged revolt. Joshua R. Giddings had said as much on the floor of Congress. In April 1856, William Lloyd Garrison, in response to northern efforts to arm Kansas free-staters, seemed to go further. He remarked, "If such men [in Kansas] are deserving of generous sympathy, and ought to be supplied with arms, are not the crushed and bleeding slaves at the South a million times more deserving of pity and succor? Why not, first of all, take measures to furnish them with Sharp's rifles? . . . If every 'border ruffian' invading Kansas deserves to be shot, much more does every slaveholder."[4]

Seven months after Garrison wrote, an especially widespread "negro insurrection" scare occurred in conjunction with the 1856 election campaign in which the Republican Party nominated John C. Frémont as its first presidential candidate. That September, the *Louisville Courier* claimed a black arsonist had destroyed several buildings in Frankfort, Kentucky. By December, reports of unrest among enslaved workers at the Cumberland Iron Works in Stewart County, Tennessee, inspired fear of revolt on the Tennessee-Kentucky border. Initially it seemed hundreds of black men, instigated by white abolitionists, planned "to cut the throats of all the whites," march on county seats, and open "a free path . . . on the Cumberland [River] from Nashville to the Ohio [River]." Some reports claimed slaves believed "Colonel Frémont" was in the region with an army to fight on their side.[5]

Newspapers soon characterized as exaggerated these allegations of slave conspiracies on the Tennessee-Kentucky line. Similar claims, which spread throughout the South, had even less validity. Panic nevertheless inspired vigilante action against slaves, free African Americans, and white people suspected of abolitionism. The scare enhanced an armed reaction already underway in the Border South against antislavery initiatives. Republican newspapers in the region, such as the *Wellsburg Weekly Herald* and the *St. Louis Democrat*, risked censure when they suggested that slaveholding societies were "constantly at the mercy of the evil disposed whites and brutal blacks." When William S. Bailey of the *Newport News* sympathized with the alleged slave rebels, declaring their "only crime is that of seeking liberty," he invited destruction.[6]

Well before the December 1856 revolt scare, the number and size of proslavery military and semimilitary organizations had expanded in the Border South. In 1851, Virginia encouraged formation of volunteer military companies by reducing the membership requirement to thirty-five. In that state's Grayson County, a vigilance association numbering 200 whipped and expelled John Cornutt, a local slaveholder, for defending the right of a northerner to preach against slavery. The same association pursued antislavery missionary Jarvis C. Bacon on charges he had helped slaves escape. On November 16, 1852, a mass meeting held at Minerva in Mason County, Kentucky, called for defensive action. A convention at Mayfield in the same state advocated the formation of "slave protection societies" in each county bordering the Ohio River. Similar groups organized in Missouri. In early 1856, the Virginia legislature created a system designed to provide "for the protection of every part of the state exposed to the operations of emissaries from the North." It included appointment of commissioners to search all vessels leaving port, stiffer penalties for helping slaves escape, and rewards for recapturing them. Periodically during the 1850s, Border South politicians advocated expelling free African Americans as a dangerous class.[7]

The slave revolt scare of December 1856 intensified white anxiety, vigilance, and anticipation of war. Mass arrests of slaves, whippings to force confessions, hangings, and imprisonments occurred in northern Tennessee and southern Kentucky. Suspect free African Americans and white men faced arrest. Where slave patrols had lapsed, they reorganized to monitor black communities and look out for what Edmund Ruffin of Richmond, Virginia, called "northern agents of mischief." Tennessee, Missouri, Virginia, and Alabama tightened restrictions on "the colored population." When the citizens of Hopkinsville, Kentucky, heard reports of slave revolt in the nearby town of Lafayette, "a force of 150 persons left immediately for the seat of war."[8]

Anticipating something far greater than John Brown's raid, Virginia journalists called for expanding the state militia system to protect against slave rebellion and northern invasion. Writing to the *Richmond Enquirer* on January 22, 1857, ALBEMARLE linked the policing of Virginia's slave population to an approaching war among the states that would require "all the energies that a brave and gallant people can exert, in the defense of family, fire-sides, life, liberty and property." He declared, "To be prepared for civil and domestic war is our vital necessity." Preparation, he hoped, would "open the eyes of our [northern] sister States and stay their fratricidal hands." If not, Virginia had to be ready to "roll back the tide of war. . . . to stand in the van in the impending struggle . . . to wipe the film from the eyes of aggressor States, or, as a frontier State, gallantly to stem the heady torrents of civil war." To meet the crisis, he proposed training an active militia of 57,000 backed by reserves totaling 90,000.[9]

IN 1857, most Virginians disdained ALBEMARLE's grandiose military schemes. Yet, by the time he wrote, less-structured proslavery violence had proved ineffective in Madison County, Kentucky, where a large slave population and a multifaceted abolitionist effort led by Cassius M. Clay and John G. Fee posed a threat. As Clay organized a Republican Party, Fee aligned with Gerrit Smith's radical political abolitionists in declaring slavery universally illegal. He led the AMA's largest southern missionary effort and built a free-labor colony at Berea (see chapter 8). Clay helped Fee by donating land for Berea, participating in the settlement's political and religious life, and leading bands of armed men to protect it. Fee, despite his Christian commitment to the nonviolence on which his northern AMA backers insisted, accepted Clay's use of force. Fee also acquiesced when several of his missionary associates and many Berea residents prepared to fight in his defense.[10]

During late summer 1853, slaveholders in nearby Rockcastle County warned missionaries not to preach there and arrested one of them for aiding a slave to escape. In response, Clay declared, "If the [slaveholders] . . . began violence . . . we . . . would . . . defend ourselves to the death." In a letter to Garrison, he pledged to "make eternal war" on those who would "pervert" the U.S. Constitution on behalf of slavery. He declared, "I return the war of lynchers and 'respectable' mobs! I return the war of those, however powerful, whose main business it is in these States to 'crush out abolitionism!' . . . I return the war of those, who under the hallowed names of Democracy and Republicanism . . . amid blood and prisons, bear banners inscribed with 'law and order!'"[11]

When proslavery vigilantes organized, Clay and the missionaries compared their situation to that of free-staters in Kansas, and lamented they did not attract a comparable level of northern support. In June 1855, Clay informed Salmon P. Chase, who was the Republican candidate in the Ohio gubernatorial election, "We are in a way to have trouble enough here without going to Kansas." Clay claimed there existed "a concentrated effort through all the south to crush us and the subservience of the North *has* and does encourage it!"[12] Yet, during the mid-1850s, in the heart of a slaveholding state, antislavery Kentuckians stood their ground.

Clay told abolitionists assembled at the Bush Creek Meeting House, "It need no more be asked what their plan was for setting the negro free; that their *motto was freedom on the soil*; that they [the black people] were as much entitled to it as any man or woman on that ground, and that the time was close at hand when those [masters] who contended for remuneration for [freeing] their slaves would be glad to get off even." The following month when proslavery vigilantes charged missionaries with encouraging slave violence, Fee responded, "[If] our preaching indirectly excited the slaves, then we answer . . . a wronged and outraged people will be aroused by every ray of light . . . which shows their wrongs." At a July 4, 1857, celebration, Fee's missionary associate John C. Richardson advised slaveholders in the crowd, "There are 40 thousand [black men] in Canada training daily and they will come down here & *cut your throats.*"[13]

By early 1855, the missionaries had expanded their efforts from Madison and Rockcastle counties to Garrard and Lincoln counties. In March a "band" of over thirty-five proslavery men, "armed with bowie knives and revolvers," accosted Fee near Crab Orchard on the Lincoln-Rockcastle line. According to Fee, they accused him of "rebelling against law," placed him on his horse, and drove him away. Clay then rode to Crab Orchard, "surrounded by armed followers" to overawe Fee's assailants. A few days later, Clay informed Chase, "After marshalling our forces with guns, the Lincoln Citizens have sent me a committee. We [meaning each side] have agreed to disarm and allow Fee to preach on the same ground peacefully! God defend the Right!"[14]

In June, after a mob warned Fee against speaking in Rockcastle, Clay repeated this tactic. He proposed that he and Fee, backed by "perhaps 100" well-armed supporters, speak on July 4 at Scaffold Cane, "*in behalf of human freedom*." Fee agreed to the plan, noting to an AMA official, "[The Apostle] Paul accepted the protection of 70 armed men." According to a *New York Tribune* correspondent, "Mr. Clay and his friends selected their ground on the border of Lincoln County, at a place where the cannon of the enemy could not be brought to bear upon them." Learning that Clay and Fee were "able to raise a larger force than they anticipated," slaveholders "called another meeting." With Mexican War veterans presiding, "a *peace* was agreed upon" that allowed Fee and Clay to hold a gathering at Dripping Springs. There Clay discussed "the evils of slavery politically & ecclesiastically, economically & in terms of freedom of speech." Fee analyzed the relationship of the church to slavery. They then announced their intention to speak at Scaffold Cane on July 21.[15]

When slaveholders vowed to prevent this meeting, Fee issued a broadside, advising them that, although he did "not carry weapons. . . . friends equally honest, think it right to carry weapons for self-defense—a constitutional right." He warned "slaveholders of the results of war, when, by a mobocratic course, *they should bring it on*." Clay, sounding a bit like John Brown, rallied his fighters. He declared, "We shall not have a peaceful triumph. Deity vindicates and expiates the violation of His eternal laws. Blood consecrates even the remorse of great wrong. . . . living or dying, my aspiration shall be immortal—*may our country yet be free!*" As others besides Clay and Fee predicted "scenes of blood," slaveholders backed down a third time. Fee remarked, "The men of Rockcastle threatened without doing any thing. The community look upon them as the poorest sort of filibusters." The *Cincinnati Gazette* observed more dispassionately that the slaveholders had "yielded to the superior physical and moral courage of Mr. Clay."[16]

Yet Clay was not essential to winning these bloodless battles. By the autumn of 1856, a variety of forces had driven him and Fee apart. Competition for leadership among Kentucky abolitionists and AMA pressure on Fee to condemn violence were key. So was Fee's identification with radical political abolitionists whose encouragement of slave escape galvanized proslavery opposition in central Kentucky. After Fee and Clay disagreed publicly at Slate Lick Springs, in Madison County on July 4, 1856, Clay withdrew his protection from the missionaries.[17]

During the summer of 1857, as slaveholders renewed their attacks, Clay stood aloof. That June, a mob burned one of Fee's Rockcastle churches. In mid-July at Cummins, thirty armed men captured Fee, and amid threats and abuse escorted him out of the county. When the mob captured the Rockcastle County Courthouse, a grand jury refused to indict its leaders. For over a year, Fee and others begged Clay to reconsider. But, from the start, members of Fee's churches had the weapons and the will on their own to address what one correspondent called "the rifle aspect of the slavery question." Missionary George Clark reported to an AMA official, "I never have been with Anti Slavery men who seemed to have so much *back bone* ready to die for the Cause in this State. The truth is the Pro slavery men are afraid of them."[18]

Fee asked residents of Berea not to arm themselves but took comfort in their rejection of this advice. In mid-September he reported that when a proslavery force approached his home "about 30 armed men were around . . . to defend it." Despite himself, Fee proved Clay was not the only antislavery warlord in Kentucky. Into late September 1859, Fee's supporters threatened force against slaveholders.[19]

A FEW WEEKS LATER, the raid at Harpers Ferry spread fear and loathing in the border region and throughout the South. John Brown, contemporaries asserted, had brought the savagery of Kansas warfare east. According to Governor Wise, Brown and his band had learned "the skill of the Indian in savage warfare" and turned that skill "upon the oldest and largest slaveholding State to surprise one of its strongest holds." Clay and other antislavery leaders agreed. They believed Brown and his family's suffering at the hands of Missouri border ruffians provoked him to unleash his anger against the South. Brown also diverted arms meant for use in Kansas to his invasion of Virginia.[20]

But Brown's motivation and the context within which he acted had deeper and broader roots than warfare in Kansas. Those roots lay in his involvement, well before the 1850s, in abolitionism and border conflict. Born in Connecticut in 1800, Brown observed his father helping fugitive slaves. During the 1830s and 1840s in western Pennsylvania and eastern Ohio, he engaged in underground railroading. He came to admire Charles T. Torrey and others who went south to help slaves escape. In 1847 he revealed to Frederick Douglass his desire to start a slave rebellion.[21]

By the time he spoke to Douglass, Brown had drawn close to Smith's aggressive abolitionist faction to which Torrey had belonged. A decade later, support for forays into the South had spread wider. Following Brown's incursion into Missouri in January 1859, Parker Pillsbury, a Garrisonian speaking at the Massachusetts Anti-Slavery Society's annual meeting, praised Brown as "undoubtedly the Cromwell of this generation." If Brown could not continue his attacks on slavery, Pillsbury hoped other brave men would "spring up" to "emancipate every slave in the land, before the sword of insurrection shall be sheathed." Richard J. Hinton, a British-born journalist and Brown confidant in Kansas, added, "There are men waiting both in Massachusetts and in Kansas for the time—waiting to aid the slaves in their warfare."[22]

A coterie of radical political abolitionists, Garrisonians, and Republicans—known as the "Secret Six"—raised funds for Brown and encouraged militancy among African Americans. It may be that some members of this group did not fully comprehend the extent of Brown's warlike ambitions. However, a month before the Harpers Ferry raid, Smith published his foreknowledge. In a letter to the *National Era*, he declared he had, "For many years . . . feared slavery must go out in blood;" that it was "too late to abolish it by peaceful means; too late to vote it down." African Americans, he wrote, looked to "God and insurrections," and therefore "for insurrections . . . we may look any year, any month, any day. A terrible remedy for a terrible wrong." A week later, Smith wrote of slavery, "Its violent termination is all that remains." After the raid, Wise published letters found in Brown's possession from Smith, Douglass, and other antislavery northerners.[23]

William S. Bailey, writing in Newport, Kentucky, at the time Brown invaded Virginia, proclaimed he believed the most "effectual mode of opposing slavery is by attacking it where it exists, instead of warring upon it where it may possibly exist at some future period." Bailey wrote metaphorically and later denied he had advance knowledge of Brown's plans. But what were slavery's defenders to think when they read his contention that "no enemy can be conquered until his stronghold is taken and overthrown. The stronghold of slavery is in the slave states. As long as it continues to exist and flourish there, it will be a powerful foe to free government and the rights of man. . . . The champions of freedom can never succeed against slavery as long as they suffer it to remain unmolested in its citadel."[24]

Brown's raid, its link to warfare in Kansas, its escalation of persistent clashes over slavery, produced an intense reaction. What Garrison called a "New Reign of Terror," directed often irrationally against slaves, free African Americans, northern visitors, and mildly antislavery white southerners, spread throughout the South. In the Border South, rumors of what turned out to be a real but unsuccessful plot among some of Brown's associates to rescue him kept Virginia on a military alert. Wise warned governors of Maryland, Pennsylvania, and Ohio that "in preserving the peace of our coterminous border," Virginia forces might "pursue invaders of our jurisdiction into yours." Governor Chase of Ohio rejected Wise's assertion of extraterritorial power as a potential abridgement of his state's sovereignty. Later, Chase and the Republican governor of Iowa, Ralph P. Lowe, refused new Virginia governor John Letcher's demand for the extradition of two of Brown's associates.[25]

Wise and Letcher had more success in Virginia. Wise called on the state legislature for a "guard to protect our frontier"—Virginia's "entire northern border." White Virginians crippled free-labor colonies in the state and determined "to place the Commonwealth in an attitude of defence." As volunteer companies and vigilance associations organized, former president John Tyler observed, "Virginia is arming to the teeth." The *Richmond Enquirer* asserted there was only one "means by which to check treasonable invasion—that means an ACT OF WAR." When, in January 1860, Letcher asked for additional military spending, the Assembly provided $500,000 for armaments and $20,000 to expand the Virginia Military Institute's production of officers. Within a year, Letcher boasted, "We now have in Virginia duly and legally organized, eighty-eight troops of cavalry, twenty-six companies of artillery, one hundred and nine companies of infantry and one hundred and ten companies of riflemen, uniformed and well prepared for service."[26] As the Civil War began during the spring of 1861, these forces augmented Virginia's capacity to threaten Washington, D.C.

Although other border slave states did not equal Virginia's effort, they too took or proposed military action. Maryland sent militia units to Harpers Ferry, its western counties mobilized larger slave patrols, and new volunteer rifle and cavalry units organized throughout its jurisdiction. In Kentucky, Governor Beriah Magoffin, a Democrat, blamed the Harpers Ferry raid on the Republican Party. He declared, "Our slave property is threatened, our homes are threatened, our lives, and the lives of our wives and children, are threatened . . . and reason and justice, common sense and prudence, teach us that we must adopt efficient measures of protection." Magoffin recommended "a thorough re-organization of the militia and enrollment of volunteer companies, in every portion of the commonwealth." Towns and cities enlarged police forces. Counties expanded slave patrols, and new military companies organized.[27]

Even before Magoffin spoke, rumors of slave revolt and Williams S. Bailey's ill-chosen words—quoted earlier in this chapter—led to violence. At Newport on October 25, and again on October 29, a local sheriff and prosecuting attorney led mob attacks on Bailey's printing office. A few weeks later, Fee declared at Henry Ward Beecher's Brooklyn, New York, church, "We need more John Browns—not in the manner of his action, but in his spirit of consecration." Amid reports that northern immigrants and boxes of Sharps Rifles had arrived at Berea, Fee's easily misconstrued statement produced drastic results. That December, proslavery forces finally took effective action against the antislavery center as sixty mounted men forced leading missionaries and their families to leave the state. A group of thirty-six men, women, and children from Berea took refuge in Cincinnati. Sixty other antislavery exiles soon joined them.[28]

Other missionaries and more Republicans stood firm in central Kentucky. Hundreds of them fought sporadically against slightly larger numbers of proslavery men, and Clay reemerged as leader of the antislavery forces. Facing slaveholders armed with shotguns, pistols, rifles, and cannon, he fortified his house, mounted two cannon, and talked of fighting a guerrilla war. Recalling the proslavery attack on Lawrence, he wrote, "If we had fifty or one hundred Sharpe's [sic] rifles, it would give us immense power in the mountain recesses where cannon could not touch us."[29]

In Missouri, reports circulated of a slave revolt near the town of Bolivar and fighting between African Americans and white military companies. By late 1860, James Montgomery's antislavery military campaign in Kansas led to rumors that he had invaded southwest Missouri, killed residents, burned towns, and freed slaves. Demands for defensive war followed. In December, Missouri's governor sent troops, including 600 St. Louis volunteers, to the state's western border to battle Kansas "Jay hawkers."[30]

Although Brown's raid spread fear of abolitionist-inspired slave revolt throughout the South, it had its greatest impact in the Border South. Like Governor Wise, whose remarks open this chapter, the great majority of white people in the region placed the raid in the context of a losing struggle against northern aggression. John Pendleton Kennedy of Maryland, a Whig moderate and former secretary of the navy, described the raid as an escalation of "the systematic abduction of slaves . . . [which] is already sequestering not much less than a million of Southern wealth each year." Kennedy cautioned, "The final consummation of this movement to the destruction of slavery, would . . . turn several States back into jungle for wild beasts." The *Richmond Enquirer* charged that with Brown's raid, "insult and pillage have at length given place to invasion and murder." On the floor of the U.S. Senate in January 1861, Trusten Polk of Missouri declared that underground-railroad "lawlessness is felt with special seriousness in the border slave States.

Hundreds of thousands of dollars are lost annually. And no state loses more heavily than my own. . . . But all these losses and outrages, all this disregard of constitutional obligations and social duty, are as nothing in their bearing upon the Union in comparison with the *animus*, the intent and purpose of which they are at once the fruit and the evidence."[31]

EVEN AS border slave-state leaders supported defensive measures against this threat, they disagreed among themselves concerning whether such measures were best pursued within the Union or out of it. Ten years earlier, they almost unanimously rejected disunion as a means of protecting slave property. Instead they endorsed federal government action in the form of the new Fugitive Slave Law. After 1850, most of them sought additional federal help. But continued northern resistance to slave renditions, demands for abolition in the District of Columbia, fighting in Kansas, and abolitionist endorsement of slave revolt, strengthened disunion sentiment. As James Shannon, president of Missouri's state university, indicated in 1855, disunion became a fallback position for the border slave states. Shannon told a proslavery convention, "Let us hope for the best, and prepare for the worst; and then, *having done all that men can do to save the Union*, if a dissolution is forced upon us by domestic traitors . . . then I, for one, say . . . 'having exhausted the argument, we will stand to our arms.'"[32]

Disunionists had always been stronger in the Lower and Middle South than in the Border South. But, even though the Lower South in particular had little reason to fear armed incursion from the North, Brown's raid strengthened secessionist sentiment in that region. It confirmed longstanding Lower South assumptions that if the Border South tier of slave states fell to free labor, the next tier would weaken under similar pressure and the power of slaveholders in the Union would decline. Secessionists in the Lower South had other grievances against the North, ranging from the status of slavery in the territories to what they regarded as an unfair tariff. But developments in the Border South, including economic change, emancipation sentiment, reports of abolitionist emissaries, emerging Republican parties, and especially slave escapes, had a major impact on secessionist thought.[33]

Robert Barnwell Rhett of the resolutely secessionist *Charleston Mercury* represented proslavery radicals in the Lower South. As the 1856 national election neared, he suggested that an independent South could build a chain of forts along the sectional line "to prevent the thieving North from harassing our border, kidnapping our property, and murdering our people." A year later, the *New Orleans Delta* urged Virginia to discourage free-labor colonies because "the enemy is looking over the Border . . . and organizing their forces for an early invasion." That same year, another New Orleans newspaper predicted, "Under the present Union the border [slave] States must in a short time be lost to us. [But] were the Union to end, the South would become at once a unit, and continue for perhaps a century."[34]

In 1858, Leonidas Spratt, the leading advocate for legalizing the Atlantic slave trade, worried about the dependability of the Border South in a political crisis. Two years later, when the election of a Republican president seemed likely, Rhett published an article predicting that under such an administration, "The stealing of slaves will become a trade . . . heroism in the act will be worshipped, and not alone Virginia, but every Southern State will have to record its John Brown raids." Rhett warned, "Unless some great movement . . . is made, so will the supporters of slavery be forced further and further south until they make their last Thermopilean stand on the shores of the Gulf."[35]

In April 1860, the Democratic national convention, meeting in Rhett's home town, split over endorsing popular sovereignty or federal protection of slavery in the territories. By June there were two Democratic presidential tickets. One headed by Stephen A. Douglas of Illinois appealed mainly to northern voters on a platform advocating popular sovereignty. The other headed by John C. Breckinridge of Kentucky appealed mainly to southern voters on a platform advocating a federal slave code for the territories. Well aware of the opportunity a broken Democratic Party offered, Republicans meeting at Chicago in May, nominated the relatively moderate Abraham Lincoln on a platform demanding congressional exclusion of slavery from all territories. Meanwhile, conservative Whigs from the North, Border South and Middle South organized the Constitutional Union Party and nominated John Bell of Tennessee for president.

Despite the role of territorial policy in splitting the Democratic Party, southern politicians and journalists throughout the 1860 campaign emphasized Lincoln and his party's threat to slavery itself. Based on a long border struggle, a majority of the Lower South's voters and a sizable minority of those in the Middle and Border South concluded that Republican victory justified secession. Lincoln, southern leaders predicted, would not enforce the Fugitive Slave Law. He *would* appoint Republicans to federal posts in the South and build a Republican party there. Under a Lincoln administration, first in the Border South and then in the Middle and Lower South, slave escapes would multiply. There would be more raids like Brown's, non-slaveholders would turn against slaveholders, and white supremacy would crumble.[36]

When Lincoln won the election, the cotton states prepared to leave the Union *and* convince the rest of the South that secession was the best means of preserving slavery. South Carolina led the way on December 20, 1860, as a constitutional convention meeting in Charleston voted unanimously to repeal the state's ratification of the U.S. Constitution. By February 1, 1861, conventions in the six other Lower South states had also voted overwhelmingly to withdraw. A little over a week later, delegates from the seceded states formed the Confederate States of America (CSA), with its capital at Montgomery, Alabama. Jefferson Davis of Mississippi became provisional president.

Even before the creation of the Confederacy, the seceding states sent commissioners to the Middle and Border South states to argue they must secede to avoid the danger Lincoln, Republicans, and the North in general posed to them and the white South. In February 1861, Henry L. Benning of Georgia reminded delegates to the Virginia convention who had been called to consider the secession issue that the northern threat to the Border South led masters in the region to sell their slaves south. Like Rhett, Benning predicted that under these circumstances slavery would retreat "lower and lower, until it gets to the cotton States." He warned, "If things are allowed to go on as they are, it is certain that slavery is to be abolished except in Georgia and the cotton States, and . . . ultimately in these States also." Convinced sales south would swell the Lower South's black population and encourage revolt, Benning claimed northern armed forces "would descend upon the South to assist the slaves engaged in mortal combat with their masters."[37]

Rhett, Benning, and other "fire-eaters" exaggerated the weakness of slavery in the Border South. Free labor and economic ties to the North *were* advancing as slave escapes and abolitionist incursions damaged the confidence of masters. But, in historian Michael F. Holt's words, "It is not clear that those who refused to secede were any less committed to slavery than those who did."[38] When on the South's northern periphery secessionists debated Unionists, the division was not between advocates of slave labor and advocates of wage labor. Instead two proslavery groups disagreed over whether union or disunion would best protect slavery and the existing social order against slave escape and northern interference. Each side held free-labor and their region's commercial ties to the North secondary to violent threats to slave property. Secessionists advocated leaving the Union to halt the decline of slavery in frontline counties. Unionists maintained that only federal support could achieve this goal.

In this manner, border tensions shaped the debate over secession in the

Border South during the late 1850s. Secessionists argued that, as the Union failed to protect slavery adequately against northern aggression, withdrawal and military preparation were the only safe policies. So long as the region remained in the Union, they warned, abolitionists would "operate on our slaves, to infuse discontent, and to seduce them to abscond or to rebel." But, if the North and South were "two separate political communities," there would be no such "free access." Northerners would be "foreigners in peace, or enemies in war," who could be more easily arrested and "hung." Under these altered conditions, a Virginian maintained, the "slave population of the border land would soon increase and extend, where it has been long decreasing."[39]

Brown's raid, Lincoln's victory, rumors of slave revolt in Texas, and the false reports that Montgomery had invaded Missouri strengthened Border South disunionism. In Virginia, Edmund Ruffin claimed he welcomed Brown's raid because it "stir[red] the sluggish blood of the South." Another Virginian disunionist claimed, "Armed bands of traitors, in all the panoply of war, are openly invading the State of Missouri, murdering the people, burning the towns, and proclaiming its [sic] purpose to 'free every slave in Southwestern Missouri.'" Shortly after South Carolina seceded, a correspondent of the Richmond Enquirer asked, "Have not our citizens been beaten, imprisoned and slain, in the effort to recover their property which has been enticed away from their owners? Had it not been declared, by every non-slaveholding State that we have no just title to our slaves, that the holding of them is a sin which it is the duty of the holy thieves to purge us of?" These were, the correspondent declared, "overt acts" of war, which would increase under Lincoln. Advocating immediate secession, he added, "Shall we sit down and take no adequate step to protect our people and defend our homes, until the army and navy . . . are in the hands of our enemies and used against us?"[40]

On January 3, 1861, Missouri's new governor, Claiborne F. Jackson, called on his state to "stand by" the seceding "slaveholding States, in whose wrongs she participates, and with whose institutions and people she sympathizes." A few days later, a member of Missouri's legislature claimed more specifically that the state had "$100,000,000 of slave property" and asked, "If we refuse to share our fortunes with our Southern brethren . . . what becomes of this 100,000,000?" In April 1861, former Southern Democratic presidential candidate John C. Breckinridge claimed Kentucky had to secede to protect itself. Otherwise the state "would fall beneath the aggressive power of an overwhelming party. It would become instantly a question of emancipation."[41]

When Commissioner Benning addressed the Virginia convention, he appealed to similar fears. He noted Virginia, as a state in the Union, had been ineffective in preventing slave escapes. "If you were with us," he advised, "it would become necessary, in order to collect revenue, to station police officers all along the border, and have there bodies of troops. It could be easily made part of the duty of these officers to keep strict watch along there and intercept every slave, and keep proper surveillance on all who may come within the line of particular localities. Is not that arrangement better than any fugitive slave law that you could get?"[42]

Many in the Border South, however, insisted the region had to remain in the Union to preserve slavery. The border struggle convinced them—as it had earlier Governor Wise—that their economic and social systems required federal protection. In 1857 a Virginia secessionist admitted, "most persons" in the state believed disunion would "render the preservation of our slaves . . . much more precarious than while the relation of Union continues." George W. Summers, a slaveholder from the northwestern portion of the state made the same point in early April 1861. Noting existing "constitutional and statutory provisions" protecting slavery, Summers maintained secession "so far from rendering the institution of slavery more secure in Virginia . . . will be the potent cause of insecurity." Especially in his section of the state, he warned, the loss of federal support would force masters "to sell our slaves or permit them gratuitously to run away."[43]

From the mid-1850s into early 1861, many border slave-state leaders had advocated reliance on state and federal military units to protect slavery. After the Harpers Ferry raid, they still believed such reliance would be more effective than disunion. The *Commonwealth* of Frankfort, Kentucky, predicted militia "would form a phalanx sufficiently numerous and brave to strike terror into the souls of any array of Abolitionists that could be marched into the State." Kentucky's U.S. senator John J. Crittenden maintained, "I cannot see that any evils that befall us would be less out of the Union than in it. . . . And even if the worst came to the very worst, I believe I would rather do a little fighting in the Union than out of it." In Virginia a *Richmond Enquirer* correspondent demanded that the U.S. government create "a regular force raised and stationed on the requisition of . . . [an] endangered State, within its limits, subject to be called into service by the President." A St. Louis resident, noting Missouri's exposure to "forays of fanatics and abolition outlaws," claimed the state's "people repose implicit confidence in their ability to repel invasion or suppress insurrection." In November 1860, residents of Blockersville, Virginia, rejected disunion and called for "immediate action, so far as placing the State in the best possible condition so far as defense is concerned in order to meet any emergency."[44]

Earlier, Maryland governor Thomas H. Hicks argued against South Carolina's call for a disunion convention because, he believed, it would place slavery in greater danger. Hicks asserted that the residents of his state had "more cause than the people of any other Southern State to complain of the loss and injury from conspiracies and assaults." But disunion "could only secure the continuance of them under the shelter of a *Foreign* asylum upon her borders." Following Lincoln's election, James A. Pearce, who had represented Maryland in the U.S. Senate since 1843, claimed if the Union had "not prevented the enthusiastic fanatic and the hypocritical demagogue from aiming blows at our domestic institutions, it ha[d], at least, restrained and impeded their mad efforts in some degree."[45]

The *National Intelligencer's* conservative editors warned Maryland, "It must be obvious that her situation as a *Border Slaveholding State* places upon her people the greatest caution in [undertaking] any change of relations which shall have for effect to render their slave property still more exposed to hostile aggressions from the North, without insuring them any compensating advantage in the South." A Baltimore resident, after calling on Maryland secessionists to "pause and consider that ours is a Border State," elaborated. He noted Pennsylvania was "at present restrained by law and decency from *open* warfare upon slave property." But, if Maryland seceded, "then will commence the stampede that in less than six months will either not leave a remnant of that peculiar property in the State, or make the residue of no value and evil disposed." Maryland would lose "what can hardly amount to less than fifty millions of property in value, together with about one hundred thousand servile laborers from the cultivation of the then desolate soil."[46]

Many Missourians agreed that the Border South needed federal protection. Shortly after Lincoln's election, a meeting in Boone County resolved, "In our opinion the permanent continuance of slavery in Missouri depends upon the continuance of the Union." As Montgomery encouraged slave escapes from southwestern portion of the state, the meeting called on Buchanan to take "decided and prompt action" to defend its borders. In January 1861, outgoing governor, Robert M. Stewart, noted that Missouri's "border counties have been the frequent scenes of kidnapping and violence." The state, he claimed, had "probably lost as much in the last few years, in the abduction of slaves, as all the rest of the Southern States." Disunion would only increase "battle and blood." That same month, a delegate to a "Grand Union Demonstration" held in St. Louis warned, "Going out of the Union would be the most ruinous thing Missouri could do.... Our property in this State would be in danger of destruction. There would be no Fugitive Slave Law to protect slaves . . . and Missouri would become a free State in less than five years."[47]

Just as they believed slavery in their bounds required federal protection, border slave states regarded themselves as protecting the rest of the South. The Boone County, Missouri, meeting claimed, "The ultimate peaceful and profitable continuance of slavery in the Southern States depends upon the continuance of the barrier which the border slave States now afford them against Northern aggression." The *Statesman* of Lexington, Kentucky, opposed immediate secession while portraying Kentuckians as "gallant and spirited" defenders of slavery. Sounding very much like the Boone meeting, the *Statesman* declared, "Our state is a barrier of protection to the Cotton States against anti-slavery aggressions. Our friends to the South can certainly bear the administration of Lincoln as long as we can." The prosecession *Richmond Enquirer*, also liked the noble image of the Border South saving its sister states from federal "coercion." But Virginia unionist George W. Summers approached the issue differently. He insisted that the cotton states desired Virginia "to become, to use a homely phrase, the outside row in the corn field. We are to protect the slave property in the States south of us, but lose our own."[48]

Former post master general, Amos Kendall, writing in Washington, D.C., summed up the Border South unionist position. "The cry of disunion," he wrote, came most insistently from states that suffered least "from Northern outrages," because "other slave-holding States [stood] between them and the free States." Federal protection of slavery was "imperfect," and the border slave states lost "a hundred slaves by Abolition thieves where [the cotton] States lose one." But secession would allow "the John Browns of the North [to be] let loose . . . with no other restraints than the laws of war between independent nations." The border struggle had taught Kendall and many others in the Border South that limited U.S. government help in defense of human property was better than none. "They prefer[red] to fight the Abolitionists, if fight they must, within the Union."[49]

DIVISION OVER the best means of protecting slavery distinguished opinion in the Border South from opinion in the Lower South during the 1860–61 secession winter. In the Lower South, the threat to slavery *in the Border South* helped create near unanimity among white residents in favor of disunion. But, as this chapter indicates, many in the Border South feared immediate secession would make the situation worse. Even leaders, such as Wise, who by early 1861 favored secession recognized the power of the Union to protect as well as threaten slavery. Therefore, with the exception of Delaware whose legislature on January 3, 1861, voted overwhelmingly to reject secession, the contests in the Border South on the issue were close, nuanced, and contentious. Politicians, journalists, and public meetings considered a wide range of options: unconditional unionism, conditional unionism, qualified disunionism, and unconditional secession. All involved in the debate invoked honor, history, the Constitution, and the relationship of the Border South to the rest of the South. In addition to protecting slavery, each side presented other compelling arguments. Secessionists appealed to shared southern values and the importance of the domestic slave trade, which could be disrupted if the Border South remained in the Union. Unionists noted commercial ties to the North and the likelihood secession would turn their region into a battleground. Unionist loyalty to the U.S. government, however, did not extend to support for coercion of seceded states or the dismantling of slavery and white supremacy.[50]

Despite the existence of a well-organized secession movement within its borders, conditional unionism flourished in Virginia in early 1861. Unionists won a January 14 election that chose delegates for a state constitutional convention. The Virginia legislature led in calling a national "peace conference" that met in Washington, D.C., on February 4. Although the conference failed to achieve its goal, the state convention voted ninety to forty-five on April 4 against immediate secession.

To a greater degree than in other border states, intrastate regionalism complicated Virginia's debate as its northwestern counties were more pro-Union than the rest of the state. In particular, slave escape and incursions from the North bred a sense of exposure in northwestern Virginia. George W. Summers told the Virginia convention that, unlike eastern Virginia, the northwestern portion of the state had no mountain barrier to stand between it and northern abolitionists or northern armies. "It was better," he said, "to protect slavery in Western Virginia than in New Mexico," but it could not be done after secession. Other northwestern Virginians favored separating their region from the rest of the state. Decades of underrepresentation in the Virginia legislature, a lack of state funding for education and roads, and a relatively small slave population encouraged this sentiment. So did commercial ties to western Pennsylvania and eastern Ohio.[51]

Even more than western Virginians, white Marylanders during late 1860 and early 1861 fearfully contemplated their long and "defenseless" northern border. The prospect of losing what protection the Fugitive Slave Law provided inclined Maryland toward unionism. So did railroad connections to the Northwest and Baltimore's commercial ties to the Northeast. Other issues kept disunionism strong in the state. Among them were Baltimore's role as the port of entry for much of the South, a tendency to look to Virginia for leadership, and emotional solidarity with the Cotton South. Republican rejection of compromise, threats to coerce seceded states, and disregard for the Fugitive Slave Law also contributed. Amid this controversy, Governor Hicks, who sought accommodation with the incoming Lincoln administration, nurtured a "fragile" unionism.[52]

In Kentucky there had been a longstanding consensus among the great majority of white residents that northern abolitionists *and* Lower South nullifiers threatened the Union. By the late 1850s, local Whigs and Democrats agreed that antislavery efforts constituted the graver danger. Abolitionist activity in the heart of the state, slave escapes, John Brown's raid, and Lincoln's election prodded Kentucky leaders to seek greater protection for slavery. But, like most Virginians and Marylanders, they believed their state's exposed location precluded immediate secession. In early December 1860, Governor Beriah Magoffin, who personally sympathized with secessionists, emphasized cooperation, within the Union, among slave states to strengthen the Fugitive Slave Law. Other Kentucky leaders, ranging from unionist John J. Crittenden to secession-leaning John C. Breckinridge, supported the Washington Peace Conference and a proposed border-state conference as the best means of protecting slavery. Nevertheless, Kentucky reorganized and expanded its militia in anticipation of having to defend itself against northern aggression.[53]

Of all the border slave states, Missouri experienced the most pronounced polarization of sentiment during the secession winter, as its extreme unionists and disunionists dominated discussion. Immediately following Lincoln's election, proslavery unionists dominated. A correspondent of the *Missouri Republican* advised, "If fight we must, we intend doing so under the stars and stripes." Continued confrontations with antislavery forces on the state's western border contributed to concerns that Missouri required national assistance in defending itself. But, during early 1861, antislavery unionists centered in St. Louis and determined disunionists centered in Jefferson City shaped Missouri's reaction to the secession crisis. Led by incoming governor Claiborne F. Jackson, the state's disunionist legislature voted on January 18 to hold a general election on February 18 for delegates to a state convention. Meanwhile, Francis P. Blair Jr. organized St. Louis unionists politically and militarily. He also arranged for federal reinforcements to hold the city arsenal. Blair's preparations and an overwhelming unionist victory in the February election put the secessionists on the defensive and prepared the way for armed conflict between the two groups.[54]

FROM THE TIME OF the Harpers Ferry raid and into early 1861, many Americans presumed to know where civil war would begin. By late December 1860, Fort Sumter, at Charleston, South Carolina, had emerged as a likely candidate. On January 9, 1861, state shore batteries drove away a U.S. ship carrying reinforcements and supplies for the fort. Although the Buchanan administration henceforth avoided provocative actions, journalists and politicians continued to suspect war would begin there. But before the Charleston incident, and for some time thereafter, the North-South line seemed to be an equally likely location.

Wise, in his initial response to Brown's raid, had suggested civil war would begin along the North-South border. A month later, reports circulated that 750 men from northern Ohio had organized to invade Virginia as part of the plan to rescue Brown. Wise reacted by sending 1,000 militiamen to the state's northern frontier, and South Carolina offered military aid. Just prior to Lincoln's election, militia rallied in Cumberland and other Virginia counties "to meet the first attack and not sit back and watch the people's property destroyed." Proslavery "minutemen" organized in Virginia, Maryland, and Missouri. As the cotton states seceded between December 1860 and February 1861, border slave-state residents worried about "hostile aggressions" from the states of the Lower North.[55]

By then, the region's leaders had long since ceased threatening to send bands north to chastise those who violated the Fugitive Slave Law. But they advocated offensive as well as defensive warfare. Beginning in November 1860, Wise, supported by the *Richmond Enquirer*, threatened to seize federal arms and ships within Virginia's jurisdiction and use them to control Washington, D.C. Governor Hicks of Maryland suspected a plot existed in his state to raise a force of 8,000 men "to seize Washington." On January 1, 1861, the *New York Herald* reported that militia from Maryland and Virginia—which had been augmented in response to Brown's raid—planned to capture the capital and prevent Lincoln's inauguration.[56] Others supposed the plotters hoped to create a situation that would push Maryland into secession.

In February, U.S. general-in-chief Winfield Scott began to station troops to defend Washington. The *Enquirer* claimed these troops constituted a

"Federal army of coercion" aimed against Virginia. "Among independent nations," the newspaper observed, "the collection of large armaments upon the frontiers, is a just cause of apprehension. How much more threatening, is such an army immediately upon the borders of Virginia."[57] In view of physical proximity and the preexisting border struggle, it made sense to expect the Civil War would begin there.

But, in regard to military engagement if not bloodshed, the war began with the Confederate bombardment of Fort Sumter on the morning of April 12, 1861. Lincoln's attempt to assert U.S. authority over the fort, through what he termed a peaceful effort to deliver provisions by sea, provoked the attack. The clash at Fort Sumter and Lincoln's subsequent call on governors of the loyal states to raise 75,000 volunteers to fight against the Confederacy broke the stalemate between unionists and secessionists in the Middle and Border South. Five days after Confederate cannon fired on Fort Sumter, the Virginia convention voted eighty-eight to fifty-five in favor of immediate secession. Battles between Virginia and Union forces followed as on April 18–19 state militia captured the Harpers Ferry arsenal, seized the U.S. Navy yard at Norfolk, and threatened Washington. On July 21 at Manassas Junction, a few miles to the city's southwest, a Confederate army—in the first major battle of the Civil War—stopped a Union advance toward Richmond. Even then, opinion in the Border South remained divided. The Middle South states of Arkansas, North Carolina, and Tennessee had seceded on May 6, May 20, and June 8 respectively. But, after considerable turmoil, Delaware, Maryland, Kentucky, Missouri, and the western part of Virginia remained in the Union.[58]

There was no chance Delaware would secede. But in Maryland, events unfolded much as leaders of all persuasions had feared. As Governor Hicks refused to send troops from his state to fight against other southerners, and threats to Washington proliferated, on April 19 a Baltimore mob attacked a Massachusetts militia regiment on its way to protect the capital. Following the "first real bloodshed of the war," secessionists burned bridges north of the city in an attempt to keep troops from passing through. Lincoln responded by sending thousands of federalized militia from Harrisburg and Philadelphia to occupy Maryland. On April 26, General Scott ordered General Benjamin O. Butler of Massachusetts to dissolve the Maryland assembly if it voted to secede. Under the circumstances, the assembly demonstrated considerable obstinacy. It denounced the occupation and called for Union recognition of Confederate independence before it declined to endorse secession. In the end, proslavery unionism *and* northern troops held Maryland in the Union.[59]

Northern armies also helped keep western Virginia and Missouri in the Union, although not so decisively as in Maryland. When the Virginia convention endorsed secession, most of the delegates from the state's northwestern counties voted "no," especially those who represented border counties. There were, nevertheless, large secessionist minorities in other parts of the area. In May, when unionists centered in Wheeling prepared to establish a separate state government, Confederate forces attempted to take control. Union general George B. McClellan, commanding 20,000 Ohio militia, counterattacked and, by late 1861, had driven out the Confederate army. Much of what became central, southern, and eastern West Virginia, however, harbored pro-Confederate sentiment. Guerrilla warfare persisted into 1865.[60]

In Missouri the unionist victory in electing delegates to the state convention forestalled Governor Jackson's organization of a secessionist state militia. Still, eighty-eight of the ninety-nine convention delegates owned slaves. Even though they voted overwhelmingly in mid-March to remain in the Union, they condemned coercion of seceded states. Secessionist sentiment strengthened after Fort Sumter and Lincoln's call for troops, but U.S. Army support gave the unionists an advantage. On May 10, unionist militia commanded by Captain Nathaniel Lyon captured a secessionist force of 1,000 as it attempted to take control of the federal arsenal at St. Louis. In June, Lyon advanced on Jefferson City, forcing Jackson and the state government to retreat toward the southwest. Meanwhile, Montgomery led 200 Kansas militia into western Missouri. During the final months of 1861, Union generals John C. Frémont and Henry W. Halleck drove organized Confederate forces out of the state. But guerrilla warfare continued for years.[61]

Compared to other border slave states, Kentucky in 1861 had the mildest internal divisions. Leading unionists and disunionists in the state joined in rejecting Lincoln's call for troops and "agreed upon armed neutrality," a policy Governor Magoffin made official on May 20. Although Kentucky unionists and secessionists each organized militias, they did not fight each other. Also, because Lincoln was less sure he could control Kentucky than he could Maryland, he risked no precipitate military action that might drive Kentucky into the Confederacy. Instead, during the summer of 1861, a Confederate invasion of the extreme western portion of the state prompted its legislature to align with the Union. Even so, Confederate armies controlled the southern quarter of Kentucky until early the following year.[62]

As soon as it began, the Civil War accelerated and enlarged the long-existing phenomenon of northward slave escapes. In this drawing, published in *Frank Leslie's Illustrated Weekly Newspaper* on June 8, 1861, Virginia slaves crowd into Union-controlled Fortress Monroe on the state's coast.

BORDER SOUTH unionists and secessionists hoped their policies would protect slavery in the region. But the Civil War accelerated the key component of the long border struggle. Slave escapes peaked during the war. As fugitives headed toward Union lines, northern soldiers replaced free African Americans and abolitionists as their aids and abettors. Neither unionism in Maryland, West Virginia, Kentucky, and Missouri nor secession in Virginia could stop them.[63]

Early in the war, it had seemed unionism might save slavery in most of the Border South. Journalists published reassuring accounts of people in the Lower North complying with the Fugitive Slave Law. Unionist politicians in Missouri, in particular, emphasized the willingness of their northern neighbors to apprehend fugitive slaves. Plenty of Democrats, and some Republicans, in the Lower North sought to reassure white border southerners. President Lincoln and Secretary of State William H. Seward added their voices.

In his April 15 appeal for troops, Lincoln pledged "to avoid any destruction of, or interference with, [human] property." Seward announced, "The condition of slavery in the several states will remain just the same whether [the rebellion] shall succeed or shall fail." During the early weeks of the war, Union military officers promised to return to their masters' slaves who reached their lines *and* to help put down slave revolts.[64]

Yet escapes increased. On April 9, the *Cleveland Herald* reported that 1,000 slaves had reached Chicago since the previous fall. The same day, the *New York Herald* noted that 300 recently left Detroit for Canada. A wire story from Harrisburg maintained that 500 Maryland slaves had passed through Pennsylvania's York, Franklin, and Adams counties. The escapes increased again as Union troops, many of whom were recruited in the Lower North, occupied the border slave states and points farther south. On May 23, at Fortress Monroe in northern Virginia, General Butler began to define slaves who reached his lines as contraband of war who would not be returned to their masters. Within six months, there were 900 "contrabands," with more arriving daily. In Missouri, Montgomery announced that his army fought for abolition. When, on August 30, Frémont proclaimed all the slaves in that state to be free, Lincoln countermanded the general's order. Within a year, however, Lincoln began to change his mind about emancipation. In a war in which northern soldiers marched to a song proclaiming, "John Brown's body lies a-moldering in the grave [but] his soul is marching on," neither secession nor loyalty to the Union allowed border slave states to avoid what they had fought against for so long.[65]

# CONCLUSION

In early June 1863, a variety of considerations led the Confederate Army of Northern Virginia to invade Pennsylvania. Robert E. Lee, who commanded the army, hoped to weaken northern morale, relieve Union pressure on Richmond, cut Washington off from the North, force the Union to pull back troops on the Mississippi River, and encourage Britain and France to recognize the Confederacy. Lee also envisioned a massive foraging expedition to strip the Pennsylvania countryside of horses, cattle, pigs, and produce, and the state's towns of shoes, clothing, and money. Lee's ranking officers, if not the general himself, intended as part of the foraging operation to capture fugitive slaves and kidnap free African Americans in retaliation for decades of slave escapes and northern aid to them. This objective and rumors that the invasion's target was Harrisburg eerily echoed the *Richmond Enquirer*'s threat thirteen years earlier of a "fierce border war," involving "burnings to the ground of a few such towns as Harrisburg."[1]

Lee's army of 75,000 men moved north through Virginia's Shenandoah Valley, crossed the Potomac River into Maryland, and reached Pennsylvania by mid-June. Immediately, Confederate cavalry, infantry, and irregulars began to capture African Americans indiscriminately and send them south by wagon or on foot. Most of the captives ended up in Shenandoah Valley or Richmond jails. Slave traders purchased others. Black people in the southern Pennsylvania towns of Mercersburg, Chambersburg, Greencastle, Waynesboro, York, and Gettysburg suffered the most. At Greencastle, a Confederate captain captured two and warned residents that after the conquest of Pennsylvania he "would return . . . and take off every neager." An infantry sergeant serving in Confederate general Richard Ewell's Second Corps informed his family, "I do not think our Generals intend to invade except to get some of our Negroes back which the Yankees have stolen and let them know something about . . . war." Others claimed "they were only reclaiming their property which . . . had [been] stolen and harbored."[2]

Estimates vary regarding the numbers of African Americans taken or displaced during the campaign. David G. Smith, who has studied the issue most thoroughly, contends that, if black civilians captured in Virginia and Maryland are included, the total may have been over 1,000. Confederate troops probably took between 200 and 300 in southern Pennsylvania and about 1,000 African Americans fled north through Harrisburg. Since 1862, Lee's headquarters had officially endorsed using the Army of Northern Virginia to recapture fugitive slaves, and, according to Smith, most of the soldiers involved in the captures came from Virginia, "where many Union depredations had taken place." Lincoln's Emancipation Proclamation of January 1, 1863, and Union recruitment of black troops also helped prompt the soldiers' attempts to capture African Americans. Historian Kent Masterson Brown notes that Lee's invading forces included thousands of slaves to assist in foraging. He suspects that "some of the African American" captives "were actually runaways from" the Confederate army.[3] This recalls earlier escapes of slaves in transit. In either case, the abductions during the Pennsylvania campaign echoed prewar practices, although carried out on a larger scale in a limited area.

In June 1863, as during the antebellum decades, white Pennsylvanians divided in their response to slave catching and kidnapping. Many in the path of southern forces, either out of fear or for profit, helped apprehend African Americans. Others sympathized with the captives, and some resisted abductors. After observing black men, women, and children driven through Chambersburg's streets, Rachel Cormany—the wife of a Union soldier—reported, "O! How it grated on our hearts to have to sit quietly & look at such brutal deeds." At Greencastle, as a detachment of Lee's troops commanded by a chaplain escorted thirty or forty black women and children through the town, local white men confronted and disarmed the soldiers, jailed them, and freed their prisoners. In several other instances, black captives escaped on their own.[4]

Had the Army of Northern Virginia somehow won the great battle at Gettysburg, fought July 1–3 against a substantially larger Union force, slave catching and kidnapping—as well as introduction of slaves into the North—would have spread. Instead, disastrous defeat, resulting in the loss of one-third of Lee's army in killed and wounded, marked the turning point in the Civil War. Lee never again went on the offensive. This Union victory, followed on July 4 by the capture of Vicksburg—the Confederacy's last stronghold on the Mississippi River—settled the South's fate. It was only matter of time before the North's superior resources overwhelmed the Confederacy and ended slavery.

IN VIEW OF THE long border struggle preceding the Civil War, it makes sense that during the Confederacy's only major invasion of the Lower North its military commanders diverted limited resources from its major objectives to recapture or kidnap African Americans. After all, the conflict in the borderlands had been the most enduring, emotional, and violent of the issues driving the sections apart.

The border struggle had also been crucial in keeping most of the Border South in the Union. William W. Freehling maintains that, had slavery been stronger in the Border South, the Civil War may have turned out differently because more states in the region would have seceded.[5] Freehling is correct regarding how the loss of the Border South hurt the Confederacy. But, in the minds of border slave-state leaders, it was not so much the weakness of slavery in the region as the threat to it from the Lower North that determined their course of action. The threat convinced most of them that remaining in the Union, and securing improved federal protection, was better than secession as a means of saving slavery and white supremacy.

Even after the Union decided to end slavery in the Confederacy, most white people in the Border South clung to human bondage. Despite—or perhaps because of—the relatively strong pre-war antislavery efforts in Delaware and Kentucky, these states held out longest against emancipation. Freeing the few hundred slaves who remained in Delaware would not affect the state's economy. But, for fear of black equality and violence, the state's voters overwhelming rejected the gradual emancipation plan Lincoln offered in 1862. In Kentucky, proslavery unionists remained in control, despite occupation by Union armies. Motivated by fears similar to those of their Delaware counterparts and by a far greater economic interest, the Kentuckians despised Lincoln, denounced black enlistment, and opposed the Emancipation Proclamation. They still held 65,000 African Americans in bondage at war's end. It took the Thirteenth Amendment, ratified in December 1865 without Delaware and Kentucky's support, to end slavery in these states.[6]

In West Virginia, Maryland, and Missouri, only the absence of men who fought for the Confederacy, disfranchisement of pro-Confederate voters, and the votes of occupying Union soldiers allowed state-level emancipation legislation to pass. West Virginia, which entered the Union in July 1862 with a gradual abolition provision in its constitution, adopted immediate emancipation in February 1865. But, although African Americans constituted a very small portion of the state's population, it limited their rights. In Maryland, as the war encouraged escape and black enlistment in Union armies, conservative unionists who dominated the state's politics moved toward emancipation. A referendum held in October 1864 ended slavery in the state. But had many proslavery Marylanders not been absent or disfranchised, the outcome would have been different. Missouri's internal civil war and mass slave escapes produced a more decisive victory for antislavery forces and a larger step toward black legal—if not voting—rights. Assisted by disfranchisement of their opponents, radical Republicans centered in St. Louis held an emancipation convention in January 1865 that abolished slavery.[7]

FROM THE late eighteenth century and into the Civil War years, the physical struggle over slavery along the North-South line helped shape the course of American history. It produced the Fugitive Slave Law of 1793, the underground railroad, white southern fear of an abolitionist-slave alliance, interstate disputes and diplomacy, the revised Fugitive Slave Law of 1850 and resistance to it, Bleeding Kansas, and John Brown's raid. The struggle promoted antagonism between the Lower North and Border South, kept most of the Border South in the Union, and helped push the Lower South into secession.

Intrusions of slave catchers, kidnappers, and slavery itself into the Lower North produced violent reactions and affected popular opinion. Despite their prejudice, many white people in the region sympathized with African Americans in their determination to be free. Despite commercial ties to the South, the states of the Lower North became, over time, more opposed to slavery, more tolerant of abolitionism, and less likely to sympathize with white southerners. During the same period, slave escape and northern support for it convinced majorities in the Border South they were losing the struggle. By 1850 they placed their trust in federal assistance to keep African Americans in bondage. In contrast, bloody resistance to the new Fugitive Slave Law, defeat in Kansas Territory, and aggressive antislavery tactics in the borderlands encouraged Lower South leaders to threaten secession to protect slavery. When it appeared that a Republican president might allow the border conflict to expand, they carried out the threat.

Had the Border South been more successful in defending slavery, Lower South radicals would have had less reason to leave the Union. Had all the Border South, not just most of Virginia, joined the Confederacy, the Civil

War would have gone differently. Especially in Maryland, federalized northern militia helped keep border slave states, or portions of them, in the Union. But it was the long border struggle that predisposed Maryland, Delaware, western Virginia, Kentucky, and Missouri to remain loyal to the U.S. government. In 1861, most of their leaders bet this course would preserve slavery within their jurisdiction for the foreseeable future. Instead, slavery lasted just four years. The outcome of the Civil War finally ended the border struggle.

# NOTES

## ABBREVIATIONS

| | |
|---|---|
| *AWP* | *Albany Weekly Patriot* |
| AFASS | American and Foreign Anti-Slavery Society |
| AASS | American Anti-Slavery Society |
| AMA | American Missionary Association |
| AMAA | American Missionary Association Archives |
| *CDG* | *Cincinnati Daily Gazette* |
| *CG* | *Congressional Globe* |
| *CWHP* | *Cincinnati Weekly Herald and Philanthropist* |
| *DNI* | *Daily National Intelligencer* |
| *FDP* | *Frederick Douglass' Paper* |
| *GUE* | *Genius of Universal Emancipation* |
| HSP | Historical Society of Pennsylvania |
| LC | Library of Congress |
| *LPA* | *Louisville Public Advertiser* |
| *LOR* | *Louisville Observer and Reporter* |
| MASS | Massachusetts Anti-Slavery Society |
| *NASS* | *National Anti-Slavery Standard* |
| NEASS | New England Anti-Slavery Society |
| *NYDT* | *New York Daily Tribune* |
| NYHS | New York Historical Society |
| OHS | Ohio Historical Society |
| PASP | Pennsylvania Abolition Society Papers |
| *PF* | *Pennsylvania Freeman* |

## PREFACE

1. Breckinridge to John C. Breckinridge, January 9, 1860, in *New York Times*, January 20, 1860. I follow William W. Freehling's method in *The South vs. the South* of using "Lower South," "Middle South," and "Border South," rather than "Deep South" and "Upper South" to designate southern regions. The Middle South included North Car-

olina, Tennessee, and Arkansas. The Lower South included South Carolina, Georgia, Florida, Alabama, Mississippi, Louisiana, and Texas. I use the term "Upper North" to refer to New England, New York, Michigan, and Wisconsin.

INTRODUCTION

1. *Richmond Enquirer*, quoted in *Liberator*, October 11, 1850 (1st–8th quotations); *NYDT*, August 27, 1850; IAGO [to editor], August 26, [1850], *NYDT*, August 29, 1850 (9th quotation). As early as 1837, a Cincinnati weekly used the term "border warfare" to describe conditions in southern Ohio. See *Philanthropist*, October 6, 1837.

2. *Baltimore Patriot*, quoted in *Philanthropist*, January 16, 1838.

3. *PF*, February 14, 1839.

4. Wilbur Zelinsky, "Cultural Geography," in Miller, *A Geography of Pennsylvania*, 136–37; Etcheson, *Emerging Midwest*, 2–4 (quotation), 94–98; Hensel, *Christiana Riot and the Treason Trial of 1851*, 14–18; Berwinger, *Frontier against Slavery*, 8, 18–26; Gruenwald, *River of Enterprise*, 141–43.

5. Brugger, *Maryland*, 152–55; Fields, *Slavery and Freedom on the Middle Ground*, 42; Gruenwald, *River of Enterprise*, 104–5; Williams, *West Virginia: A History*, 50; Aron, *How the West Was Lost*, 124, 141–42.

6. Bruger, *Maryland*, 186, 251–52; Williams, *West Virginia: A History*, 31; Aron, *How the West Was Lost*, 135–36; Fields, *Slavery and Freedom on the Middle Ground*, 41. On the role of the Cumberland Road (also known as the National Road), see Hubert C. H. Wilhelm, "The Road as a Corridor for Ideas," in Raitz, *National Road*, 267; Harned to George Whipple, December 26, 1853, AMAA (quotation).

7. *CDG*, October 13, 1838; *Philanthropist*, September 22, 1841 (quotation).

8. Ayers, *In the Presence of Mine Enemies*, xviii–xix (quotations); Berlin, *Slaves Without Masters*, 26–27; Fields, *Slavery and Freedom on the Middle Ground*, 4–5; Gudmestad, *A Troublesome Commerce*; Clark, *A History of Kentucky*, 192–93; Staudenraus, *African Colonization Movement*; Campbell, *Maryland in Africa*; Tallant, *Evil Necessity*, 27–58.

9. Daniel Justin Herman, review of Freehling, *South vs. the South*, in *South Carolina Historical Magazine* 103 (July 2002): 271.

10. Williams, *West Virginia: A Bicentennial History*, 42–43; Aron, *How the West was Lost*, 124, 129 (quotation); Phillips, "'Crime against Missouri,'" 63–66.

11. The percentages in this and the preceding paragraph are derived from the 1850 U.S. Census figures, available online at the University of Virginia Historical Census Browser, http://fisher.lib.virginia.edu/collections/stats/histcensus/php (accessed February 20, 2010). See also Phillips, "Crime Against Missouri," 65–66; Thomas, "Border South."

12. Clark, *History of Kentucky*, 194–96; Tallant, *Evil Necessity*, 8–10; Gruenwald, *River of Enterprise*, 144–5; Eaton, "Minutes and Resolutions of an Emancipation Meeting," 543; Ryle, *Missouri*, 25–27; Phillips, "Crime against Missouri," 65–66.

13. Berwanger, *Frontier against Slavery*, 8–17, 22–51; Simeone, *Democracy and Slavery in Frontier Illinois*; Pocock, "Slavery and Freedom in the Early Republic," 3–6; Winch,

*Philadelphia's Black Elite*, 17–20, 174; Nash, *Forging Freedom*, 172–83; *Ohio Statesman*, November 4, 1840; Middleton, *Black Laws in the Old Northwest: A Documentary History*; Middleton, *Black Laws: Race and the Legal Process in Early Ohio*; *CG*, 30th Cong., 1st sess., June 22, 1848, Appendix, 727 (quotation).

14. *Philanthropist*, November 14, 1837; Hart, *Slavery and Abolition*, 277–78.

15. Martineau, *Retrospect of Western Travel*, 141–45; Swisshelm to Horace Greeley, April 10, [1850], *NYDT*, April 12, 1850 (1st quotation); Dixon, *Personal Narrative of a Tour through a Part of the United States and Canada*, 70–71 (2nd quotation); David W. Aiken, "Autobiography," (1848) Wilson Library, University of North Carolina, Chapel Hill, quoted in Franklin, *Southern Odyssey*, 162 (3rd quotation).

16. Melish, quoted in *GUE* 3 (October 1823): 57.

17. Tocqueville, *Democracy in America*, 332–33.

18. *Lexington Intelligencer*, October 26, 1838 (1st quotation); *Philanthropist*, April 30, 1839 (2nd quotation).

19. *American Farmer*, quoted in *GUE* 6 (April 28, 1827): 196 and (November 17, 1827): 155; Thomas Marshall, in *PF*, February 17, 1841; Kentucky woman in *Freeman*, December 4, 1845; Tallant, *Evil Necessity*, 9–10, 81–89; *Lexington Intelligencer*, October 26, 1838; Utter, *Frontier State*, 397 (quotations); Current, *Northernizing the South*, 42; *LPA*, January 8, 1841. Historians also regard the Ohio River as a boundary "between freedom and slavery, between North and South." See Gruenwald, *River of Enterprise*, xi; Darrel E. Bigham, "River of Opportunity: Economic Consequences of the Ohio," in Reid, *Always a River*, 154.

20. *National Enquirer*, quoted in *Philanthropist*, February 3, 1837; A BALTIMOREAN, in *PF*, July 4, 1844 (quotation).

21. Morris, quoted in *Tocsin of Liberty*, November 24, 1842 (quotation); Middleton, *Black Laws in the Old Northwest: A Documentary History*, 27–30.

22. "Address of the Liberty State Convention, Held at Peterboro, January 19, 20, 1842," *Emancipator*, March 10, 1842.

23. Aptheker, "Negro in the Abolitionist Movement," 15; Freehling, *Road to Secession*, 1:502; *Western Citizen* (Chicago), October 14, 1842; *PF*, July 4, 1844; Harrold, *Rise of Aggressive Abolitionism*, 107–14; Von Holst, *Constitutional and Political History of the United States*, 3: 429–30 (1st quotation); Fields, *Slavery and Freedom on the Middle Ground*, 38–39 (2nd quotation); Mallory, *Life and Speeches of Henry Clay*, 2:374 (3rd–5th quotations).

24. *Virginian*, quoted in *Louisville Daily Journal*, December 3, 1842, and in *AWP*, January 19, 1843 (1st and 2nd quotations); Maryland to Greeley, August 1, 1843, quoted in *PF*, August 14, 1843 (3rd quotation).

25. [Giddings to Henry] Fassette, February 5, 1852, *Ashtabula Sentinel*, February 14, 1852 (1st–3rd quotations); Daniel H. Hise, diary entry, October 30, 1855, Hise Diaries, OHS, Columbus (4th and 5th quotation).

26. The role of the Border South in the secession movement and its contribution to Confederate defeat is most concisely presented in Freehling, *The South vs. the South*.

27. McPherson, *This Mighty Scourge*, 3–4, 10–12; Foner, *Free Soil, Free Labor, Free Men*,

11–148; Ellis and Wildavsky, "A Cultural Analysis of the Role of Abolitionists in the Coming of the Civil War," 89–116; *CG*, 30th Cong., 1st sess., April 20, 1848, Appendix, 502, 508; *CG*, 36th Cong., 2nd sess., March 2 1861, 1375–80; *New York Herald*, November 13, 1860.

28. Thomas Pressly, *Americans Interpret Their Civil War*; Foner, "Causes of the American Civil War," 197–214; Perman, *Coming of the American Civil War*, xviii; McPherson, *Ordeal by Fire*, 5–58; Richards, *Slave Power*; Holt, *Political Crisis of the 1850s*; Gienapp, *Origins of the Republican Party*. Recently, Marc Egnal has objected to regarding slavery as the central cause of the war. See Egnal, *Clash of Extremes*, 4–7.

29. Fehrenbacher, *Slaveholding Republic*, 253–94; Morrison, *Slavery and the American West*; McPherson, *This Mighty Scourge*, 13–17; Beard and Beard, *Rise of American Civilization*, 1:667, 1:698–99, 1:710, 2:3–10, 2:51–53; Foner, *Free Soil, Free Labor, Free Men*, 11–148; Huston, *Calculating the Value of the Union*; Link, *Roots of Secession*; Dew, *Apostles of Disunion*, 1–2.

30. Freehling, "Editorial Revolution," 64–72; Freehling, *Road to Disunion*, 1:473–74, 2:203–67; Freehling, *South vs. the South*, 26–32.

31. Ayers, *In the Presence of Mine Enemies*, xviii–xix (1st quotation); *Maysville Eagle*, June 22, 1839; Siebert, *Underground Railroad*, 358 (2nd quotation); Freehling, *South vs. the South*, 26–32; Freehling, *Road to Disunion*, 2:67, 532; Griffler, *Front Line of Freedom*, 126–30.

32. Griffler, *Front Line of Freedom*; Fields, *Slavery and Freedom on the Middle Ground*, 16–17; Franklin and Schweninger, *Runaway Slaves*, 109, 116, 122–24. Gerald Mullin notes that before 1775 many more Virginia slaves escaped south than north. See Mullin, *Flight and Rebellion*, 111.

33. Harrold, *Abolitionists and the South*, 78–79; Joshua Leavitt to Piercy and Reed, February 15, 1841, *Emancipator*, February 25, 1841; *Washington Patriot*, quoted in *Liberator*, July 31, 1846 (quotation); *Pittsburgh Gazette*, September 22, 1850; *Cleveland True Democrat*, quoted in *Western Citizen* (Chicago), July 8, 1851.

34. Still, *Underground Railroad*, 155; *Philanthropist*, November 11, 1836 (1st quotation); X.Z. to Editor, April 10, 1836, *Philanthropist*, May 6, 1836; *Western Citizen* (Chicago), August 14, 1845 (2nd quotation).

35. *New York Daily Sentinel*, quoted in *GUE*, 2, series 3 (September 1831): 77–78; *Pennsylvania Freeman*, July 25, 1839; [Nathaniel E. Johnson], "Rights of a Fugitive Slave," *New York Evangelist*, February 24, 1842; *Philanthropist*, May 11, 1852.

36. Giddings, *Speeches in Congress*, 175; *CG*, 30th Cong., 1st sess., April 20, 1848, 654; Correspondence of the *Journal of Commerce*, quoted in *Albany Evening Journal*, April 24, 1848 (1st quotation); *Gazette*, quoted in *Pittsburgh Saturday Visiter*, October 12, 1850 (2nd quotation).

37. *PF*, June 27, 1839 (1st and 2nd quotations); *Philanthropist*, July 21, 1841 (3rd and 4th quotations). William Ellery Channing made a similar point long ago. See Channing, *A History of the United States*, 5:141.

38. Holt, *Rise and Fall of the American Whig Party*, 982.

1. This account synthesizes of the following: *Western Luminary*, September 27, October 4, 1826; *Kentucky Reporter*, quoted in *Maryland Gazette*, October 18, 1826 (1st quotation); *Kentucky Advertiser*, quoted in *Richmond Enquirer*, October 17, 1826 (2nd and 3rd quotations). *Western Citizen* (Paris), quoted in *Niles Register* 27 (November 18, 1826): 192 (4th and 5th quotations). See also Aptheker, *American Negro Slave Revolts*, 277–78.

2. *Niles Register* 37 (December 29, 1829): 277 (quotations); *Portsmouth Times*, quoted in *Richmond Enquirer*, January 28, 1830. On Gabriel, see Egerton, *Gabriel's Rebellion*.

3. Winks, *Blacks in Canada*, 142–58; *Annals of Congress*, 16th Cong., 2nd sess., January 24, 1821, col. 941.

4. Finkelman, "Evading the Ordinance," 21–51; *GUE* 3 (February 1824): 113.

5. Berwanger, *Frontier Against Slavery*, 11, 13–15, 17; Simeone, *Democracy and Slavery in Frontier Illinois*, 131–41 (quotation).

6. Berwanger, *Frontier Against Slavery*, 17–18.

7. *GUE* 3 (February 1824): 115 (quotation). Historian Paul Finkelman modifies an interpretation popular among historians during the mid-twentieth century that portrayed white northerners—especially those in the Old Northwest—as unrelentingly racist. See Finkelman, "Fugitive Slaves, Midwestern Racial Tolerance," 92.

8. James H. Dickey to [a friend], September 30, 1824, *Western Luminary*, October 4, 1826. See also *Western Citizen* (Paris), quoted in *GUE* 2 (October 1822): 59. On white Kentuckians' ambivalent views regarding slavery, see Tallant, *Evil Necessity*, 1–26.

9. Fehrenbacher, *Slaveholding Republic*, 206.

10. Ibid., 206–9.

11. Ibid., 209; Finkelman, *Slavery and the Founders*, 85; Palmer and McRae, *Calendar of Virginia State Paper*, 5:396–98, 402–3 (quotations). Historian Richard S. Newman portrays the PAS as less involved in direct action than this account of its involvement with Davis indicates. See Newman, *Transformation of American Abolitionism*, 4–5.

12. John McCree and William Rogers to Thos. Mifflin, June 4, 1791, in Palmer and McRae, *Calendar of Virginia State Papers*, 5:320 (1st quotation); John Purdon, ed., *Digest of the Laws of Pennsylvania* (Philadelphia: Philip H. Nicklin, 1818), 482, quoted in Leslie, "A Study in the Origins of Interstate Rendition," 67n (2nd quotation); Mifflin to Pennsylvania Assembly, August 24, 1791, in Reed, *Pennsylvania Archives, Fourth Series*, 4:179–81.

13. Palmer and McRae, *Calendar of Virginia State Papers*, 5:343–4, 402 (1st and 2nd quotations) 396–97 (3rd and 4th quotations), 402–3 (5th and 6th quotations); Leslie, "Origins of Interstate Rendition," 67–70; Finkelman, *Slavery and the Founders*, 85.

14. Finkelman, *Slavery and the Founders*, 98–99; Fehrenbacher, *Slaveholding Republic*, 212–15.

15. Fehrenbacher, *Slaveholding Republic*, 212–13.

16. For Washington's views on the intractability of the problem, see Fitzpatrick, *Writings of George Washington*, 36:123–24, 36:148, 37:578.

17. Wilson, *Standard History of Pittsburgh, Pennsylvania*, 810; Philip Hickey to Joseph Watson, June 14, 1827 (quotation) and Joseph Watson to Duncan S. Walker and B. J. Walker, January 26, 1828, in Watson Correspondence, Hill Memorial Library, Louisiana State University, Baton Rouge; American Convention, *Minutes of . . . Fifteenth Convention* (1817), 18–19; Dunn, *Indiana and Indianans*, 1:352–53; Jesse Torrey, *A Portraiture of Slavery*, 80–98. Wilson also notes peaceful rendition of slaves in Allegheny County in "early years."

18. Maryland, *Votes and Proceedings of the House of Delegates of the State of Maryland, November 29, 1796*, in *Archives of Maryland Online*, 105:96 (1st quotation); Brackett, *Negro in Maryland*, 85 (2nd and 3rd quotations), 87.

19. Maryland, *Votes and Proceedings of the House of Delegates*, 1815–16 sess. (January 11, 1816): 228–57 (1st and 2nd quotations); Ridgely to Findley, February 24, 1818, in Reed, *Pennsylvania Archives, Fourth Series*, 4:81–82 (3rd quotation).

20. "Resolutions, Passed February 16, 1821," in Maryland, *Session Laws, 1820*, in *Archives of Maryland Online*, 625:175.

21. "Resolutions, Passed February 23, 1822," in Maryland, *Session Laws, 1821*, in *Archives of Maryland Online*, 626:179–80 (1st–5th quotations); *Niles Register* 50 (August 20, 1836): 424 (6th quotation). See also Ripley, *History of the General Assembly of Maryland*, 330.

22. Schwartz, *Slave Laws*, 126–27, 129–31; Egerton, *Gabriel's Rebellion*, 148; *Annals of Congress*, 17th Cong., 1st sess. March 27, 1822, col. 1380.

23. Hurt, *Ohio Frontier*, 95–141; Etcheson, *Emerging Midwest*, 67–68; E. B. Nixon, "The Underground Railroad in Southern Indiana," seminar paper, Siebert Papers, reel 3, Ohio Historical Society, Columbus.

24. Middleton, *Black Laws: Race and the Legal Process in Early Ohio*, 47 (quotations); Pocock, "Slavery and Freedom in the Early Republic," 4–8. Middleton contends the court provisions of the 1804 statute were "merely procedural," but, as in Pennsylvania, they could be used against masters and their agents.

25. Middleton, *Black Laws: Race and the Legal Process in Early Ohio*, 47–51.

26. Beeson to Huntington, February 24, 1810, in Smith, "First Fugitive Slave Case," 93–100. Beeson later regained custody of Jane as a fugitive from justice and returned her to slavery.

27. McDonald, "Negro in Indiana before 1800," 294–95; Dunn, *Indiana and Indianans*, 1:341–44 (quotations).

28. Reed, *Pennsylvania Archives, Fourth Series*, 4:219–20.

29. Preston, "Underground Railroad in Northwestern Ohio," 409; Wilson, *History of the Rise and Fall of the Slave Power*, 1:63 (1st quotation); Channing, *History of the United States*, 5:141 (2nd and 3rd quotations); Griffler, *Front Line of Freedom*, 38 (4th quotation); Winks, *Blacks in Canada*, 142–58.

30. *Anti-Slavery Bugle*, February 27, 1846 (1st and 2nd quotations); *Annals of Congress*, 16th Cong., 2nd sess., January 24, 1821, col. 941 (3rd quotation); Siebert, "The Underground Railroad: A Description of It and Its Effects," Siebert Papers, Reel 9, OHS, Columbus. The speaker ruled Brown's presentation of the memorial out of order,

but the state department later unsuccessfully attempted to get a commitment from Canada to extradite fugitive slaves.

31. Hagedorn, *Beyond the River*, 56–57; Coffin, *Reminiscences of Levi Coffin*, 106–116 (quotations). See also Bordewich, *Bound for Canaan*, 95–96.

32. *Niles Register* 21 (December 1, 1821): 214; Anonymous, "What Right Had a Fugitive Slave of Self-Defense against His Maser?" 106–20 (quotations); Leslie, "Pennsylvania Fugitive Slave Act of 1826," 434.

33. Dunn, *Indiana and Indianans*, 1:347.

34. Hardesty, *Historical and Geographical Encyclopedia*, 273–75; Larkin, *Pioneer History of Meigs County, Ohio*, 148–153; Governor Jeremiah Morrow to Governor James Pleasants, August 30, 1825, in Governor James Pleasants Executive Papers 1822–1825, Library of Virginia, Richmond.

35. Berlin, *Slaves without Masters*, 99–100.

36. Warville, "On the Blacks of North America," in *GUE*, December 8, 15, 1827; Winch, "Philadelphia and the Other Underground Railroad," 6 (1st quotation); American Convention, *Minutes of . . . Seventh Convention* (1801), 40 (2nd quotation). Similar conditions existed in Boston. See Wilson, *Freedom at Risk*, 105–6.

37. *NASS*, October 29, November 5, 1840; Nash and Soderlund, *Freedom by Degrees*, 198–200; Winch, "Other Underground Railroad," 7, 9; Dunn, *Indiana and Indianans*, 1:341–43; *Niles Register*, quoted in Wilson, *Freedom at Risk*, 96 (1st quotation); *GUE*, February 25, August 26, 1826; *GUE*, February 24, April 21, 28, July 28, 1827; *GUE*, August 30, 1828; *Freedom's Journal*, quoted in *GUE*, April 1, 1826; *African Observer* 1 (August 1827): 139–40; Du Bois, *Philadelphia Negro*, 25 (2nd quotation).

38. Tyson to Hopper, July 10, 1811; Tyson to J. Ridgeway, July 25, 1811; Tyson to William Masters, December 12, 1811, April 9, August 20, November 11, 1812, Pennsylvania Abolition Society Papers, HSP, Philadelphia; Hopper, "Tales of Oppression," *NASS*, October 29, November 5, 1840. See also Graham, *Baltimore*, 53–60; Whitman, *Price of Freedom*, 80–81.

39. Wilson, *Freedom at Risk*, 92–93, 106–7; Winch, "Other Underground Railroad," 7; Child, *Hopper*, 84–86 (1st quotation); Tyson, *Tyson*, 80–82 (2nd quotation); Sturge, *Visit to the United States*, 22 (3rd and 4th quotations). See also Bordewich, *Bound for Canaan*, 133–34, 137–38.

40. Wilson, *Freedom at Risk*, 19–37; J. Watson to Gentlemen, March 20, 1826, Watson Correspondence, Louisiana State University, Baton Rouge; Watson to David Holmes and J. E. Davis, January 20, 1827, *GUE*, April 28, 1827; Winch, "Other Underground Railroad," 9–24.

41. American Convention, *Minutes of . . . Eleventh Convention*, (1806), 5–6; American Convention, *Minutes of . . . Thirteenth Convention* (1812), 9, 14, 27; American Convention, *Minutes of . . . Fourteenth Convention* (1816), 17–19; American Convention, *Minutes of . . . Fifteenth Convention*, 13–14; Dunn, *Indiana and Indianans*, 1:352–53; Bordewich, *Bound for Canaan*, 137; Smedley, *History of the Underground Railroad*, 26, 29 (quotation).

42. *Niles Register* 14 (July 4, 1818): 328 (1st–4th quotations); Morris, *Free Men All*,

28–29; Dunn, *Indiana and Indianans*, 1:341–44 (5th and 6th quotations 144); *GUE*, July 18, 1823; Wilson, *Freedom at Risk*, 67–76. In 1824 the Illinois legislature defeated an anti-kidnapping bill.

43. *Philanthropist* (Mt. Pleasant), June 3, 1820.

44. Dunn, *Indiana and Indianans*, 1:343 (1st quotation); *Advertiser*, quoted in *GUE*, September 24, 1825 (2nd–6th quotations).

45. *Advertiser*, quoted in *GUE*, September 24, 1825.


CHAPTER TWO

1. *Louisville Journal*, quoted in *LOR*, June 1, 1842.

2. Egerton, *Gabriel's Rebellion*, 148; Berlin, *Slaves without Masters*, 89–91; Hadden, *Slave Patrols*, 57; Garrison and Garrison, *Garrison*, 1:236–42, 311; Schwartz, *Slave Laws*, 131–34; Coleman, *Slavery Times in Kentucky*, 87–88; John Floyd to Governor of New York, December 3, 1831, Simon Gratz Collection, HSP, Philadelphia.

3. George Drinker to Joseph Bringhurst, December 10, 1804, PASP, Philadelphia (quotation); Dillon, *Slavery Attacked*, 140, 145–59, 178–81; *Liberator*, October 8, 15, 1831; *Liberator*, January 14, 1832; Abzug, *Cosmos Crumbling*, 154; Garrison and Garrison, *Garrison*, 1:236–40; Eaton, "Mob Violence" 355; McMaster, *History of the People of the United States*, 5:272; Wyatt-Brown, "Postal Campaign," 227–38; Stewart, *Holy Warriors*, 70–71; Grimsted, *American Mobbing*, 17–19.

4. Eaton, "Mob Violence," 359–61; Harrold, *Abolitionists and the South*, 64–83; Freehling, *Road to Secession*, 1:113–17, 455–74.

5. Harrold, *Rise of Aggressive Abolitionism*, 6–7, 71–72; Wyatt-Brown, "Postal Campaign," 228–29; *National Enquirer*, August 4, 1835; *National Enquirer*, January 25, 1838; *Commonwealth*, April 18, 1838 (quotation); *Philanthropist*, April 10, 1838; *PF*, April 15, 1847; *PF*, January 6, May 4, June 15, 1848; *Colored American*, March 7, 1840; Charles T. Torrey to Sir, January 24, 1842, *Emancipator*, February 4, 1842; Nancy Day to George T. Downing, June 18, 1855, Myrtilla Miner Papers, LC, reel 1, Washington, D.C.

6. *Enquirer*, quoted in *Philanthropist*, February 3, 1837 (1st quotation); *Commonwealth*, April 18, 1838 (2nd quotation); *Commonwealth*, March 13, 1839; *American*, quoted in *PF*, February 13, 1840 (3rd quotation); *Baltimore American*, quoted in *PF*, February 13, 1840 (4th quotation); Clay quoted in Harrison, *Antislavery Movement in Kentucky*, 48 (5th quotation). See also Nye, *Fettered Freedom*, 23–25, 42–45. The impact of such claims on popular opinion was so strong that as late as 1940 a Kentucky historian used "fanatic" to describe those who helped slaves escape. See Coleman, *Slavery Times in Kentucky*, 27, 89–91

7. Wood, *Black Majority*, 239; Kolchin, *American Slavery*, 158–59; Franklin and Schweninger, *Runaway Slaves*, 97–130 (1st quotation); Whitman, "Slavery, Manumission, and Free Black Workers," 216 (2nd quotation). See also Whitman, *Price of Freedom*, 69–71.

8. Wilson, *Standard History of Pittsburgh*, 817; Clark, *History of Kentucky*, 206–7; Dillon, *Slavery Attacked*, 206; Griffler, *Front Line of Freedom*, 48; Brugger, *Maryland*, 245–47; *Philanthropist*, November 11, 1836; *Philanthropist*, November 14, 1837; White, "Minute

Book," June 1839, HSP, Philadelphia; *Cleveland Agitator*, quoted in *PF*, December 31, 1840; *Labor Advocate and Anti-Slavery Chronicle*, March 8, 1841; *PF*, September 1, 1841; *Western Citizen* (Chicago), September 16, 1842; *National Era*, August 22, 1850.

9. *LOR*, July 24, 1841; *Richmond Enquirer*, quoted in *PF*, August 11, 1841; *Spirit of Liberty*, October 31, 1841; *North Star*, April 14, 1848; *North Star*, September 9, 1850; Potter, *Impending Crisis*, 136. In 1837 the *Maysville Eagle* reported Kentucky had lost millions of dollars in pursuit of fugitive slaves in Ohio. In 1859 the Kentucky governor estimated that the state had lost $100,000 in slave escapes per year. See *Eagle*, October 18, 1837; Turner, "Kentucky Slavery," 301.

10. *National Era*, August 22, 1850; Franklin and Schweninger, *Runaway Slaves*, 279–80.

11. Hart, *Slavery and Abolition*, 230–31; Preston, "Underground Railroad in Northwestern Ohio," 412; Clark, *History of Kentucky*, 206–7; Potter, *Impending Crisis*, 135–37; Franklin and Schweninger, *Runaway Slaves*, 282; Freehling, *South vs. the South*, 27; Fehrenbacher, *Slaveholding Republic*, 246–7; Ewing, *Northern Rebellion and Southern Secession*, 247–54; Dunn, *Indiana and Indianans*, 1:530–33. There is a long tradition of questioning the accuracy of the 1850 and 1860 Census figures. See Ewing, *Northern Rebellion*, 247–54.

12. *National Enquirer*, quoted in *Philanthropist*, February 3, 1837; Harrold, *Subversives*, 6–8; Gudmestad, *A Troublesome Commerce*, 8–34; Wickliffe quoted in Clark, "Slave Trade," 333; *PF*, July 4, 1844 (1st and 2nd quotations); [Giddings] to Sentinel, February 6, 1851, *Ashtabula Sentinel*, February 15, 1851 (3rd quotation).

13. Deyle, *Carry Me Back*, 283–89; Turner, "Kentucky Slavery," 299–30. In 1847, Joseph E. Snodgrass reported from Maryland Eastern Shore that most slaves had "disappeared" due to (1) emancipation by will, (2) assisted escape, (3) "transfers to the South" either with owners or by sale to traders. See J. E. S. to [Gamaliel Bailey], August 12, 1847, *National Era*, August 19, 1847. On the relationship between the fear that slaves might escape and sale south see John G. Fee to Lewis Tappan, October 30, 1849, AMAA, New Orleans; *New York Evening Post*, August 12, 1850; Jesse McBride to Luther Lee, August 23, 1851, *True Wesleyan*, September 13, 1851; Gara, *Liberty Line*, 158. In 1839, Robert W. Walker, a former U.S. senator from Mississippi, claimed 400,000 slaves had been sent south from Maryland, Virginia, and Delaware during the past eight years. See *Pennsylvania Freeman*, June 13, 1839.

14. Statistics compiled from Historical Census Browser, Geospatial & Statistical Data Center, University of Virginia, http://fisher.lib.virginia.edu/collections/stats/histcensus/php/county.php (accessed February 20, 2010). See also Trexler, *Slavery in Missouri*, 113.

15. *Commonwealth*, November 28, 1838 (1st quotation); *Enquirer*, quoted in *Emancipator*, October 1835 (2nd and 3rd quotations); *Louisville Journal*, February 4, 1841 (4th quotation).

16. Eaton, *Freedom of Thought*, 194 (1st quotation); Drake, *Quakers and Slavery*, 185–87; Potter, *Impending Crisis*, 478 (2nd quotation); Gara, *Liberty Line*, 156 (3rd quotation); Franklin and Schweninger, *Runaway Slaves*, 274–79 (4th and 5th quotations).

David Brion Davis argues that "detection of supposed abolition agents" was part of "an attempt at ideological discipline within the Southern community." See Davis, *Slave Power Conspiracy*, 37.

17. Bordewich, *Bound for Canaan*, 46–80, 92–96; Griffler, *Front Line of Freedom*, 58–80; Harrold, *Rise of Aggressive Abolitionism*, 18–20 (quotations), 41–42, 111–14; Thomas Morris, quoted in *Philanthropist*, February 17, 1841. The *Louisville Journal* published portions of Smith's address; see *Louisville Journal*, February 4, 1842. The widely publicized 1841 arrest, sentencing, and execution of three free black men in St. Louis for murdering two white men added to white insecurity in the region. See *Louisville Journal*, June 5, July 7, 1841; *Commonwealth*, July 6, 1841.

18. Hagedorn, *Beyond the River*, 86–89; Griffler, *Frontline of Freedom*, 46–49; *Lynchburg Democrat*, quoted in *Niles Register* 49 (October 3, 1835): 76–77 (quotation); White, "Minute Book," [June 1839], 3, HSP, Philadelphia; Harrold, *Rise of Aggressive Abolitionism*, 108.

19. Brown, *Memoir of Abel Brown*, 83–84 (1st quotation), 87 (2nd quotation). Brown's *Memoir* quotes a letter from Brown to Joshua Leavitt regarding fugitive slaves in Beaver. It also includes an undated statement "by a gentleman from Virginia" concerning his trip to Baltimore.

20. Franklin, *Southern Odyssey*, 152; *Norfolk Beacon*, quoted in *Liberator*, January 14, 1842; Washington correspondence of the *New York Commercial*, quoted in *Western Citizen* (Chicago), November 12, 1842 (quotations).

21. *DNI*, May 23, 1833; *Patriot*, quoted in *National Enquirer*, November 2, 1837.

22. Wyatt-Brown, "Postal Campaign," 230 and Wyatt-Brown, *Lewis Tappan*, 149–51; *Eagle*, October 18, 1837 (1st quotation); *Commonwealth*, November 28, 1838 (2nd quotation); *LPA*, quoted in *CG*, 25th Cong., 3rd sess., Appendix, February 9, 1839, 168 (3rd quotation); *Lexington Intelligencer*, February 26, 1839 (4th and 5th quotations).

23. *Enquirer*, quoted in *Emancipator*, Oct. 1835 (1st and 2nd quotations); *Gazette*, quoted in *Philanthropist*, August 28, 1838 (3rd and 4th quotations); *Times*, quoted in *PF*, November 28, 1839 (5th quotation); *American*, quoted in *PF*, February 13, 1840 (6th–8th quotations).

24. Wise, *Life of Wise*, 50 (1st quotation); "Preamble and Resolutions Respecting Slavery," February 12, 1839, Illinois Anti-Slavery Concert for Prayer, *Narrative of Facts*, 36–37 (2nd–5th quotations); *Pennsylvania Freeman*, February 28, 1839 (6th quotation).

25. *American Farmer*, quoted in *Pennsylvania Freeman*, February 13, 1840.

26. *Virginian*, quoted in *AWP*, January 19, 1843.

27. Walter Johnson, review of *Slave Patrols: Law and Violence in Virginia and the Carolinas*, in *William and Mary Quarterly* 69 (July 2002): 798–801 (1st quotation); Hadden, *Slave Patrols*, 41–47; Eaton, *Growth of Southern Civilization*, 80; Franklin, *Militant South*, 73–74 (2nd quotation), 179–82; Trexler, *Slavery in Missouri*, 182–3; Younger, "Southern Grand Juries and Slavery," 175–76; *Louisville Daily Journal*, August 20, 1845; Stafford, "Slavery in a Border City," 149–50, 154–55; *GUE*, quoted in *Liberator*, June 2, 1832 (3rd quotation); *Louisville Courier*, quoted in *Anti-Slavery Bugle*, January 17, 1852, quoted in

Nye, *Fettered Freedom*, 179n (4th quotation); *Liberator*, March 27, 1840 (5th–7th quotations). Franklin regards slave patrols as an arm of the military.

28. Clephane, "Local Aspects of Slavery," 226; *Pennsylvania Inquirer*, quoted in *PF*, April 12, 1838; CTT to ———, April 2, 1842, *Emancipator*, April 14, 1842; Samivel Weller Jr. to Mr. Editor, November 15, 1842, *Tocsin of Liberty*, December 15, 1842; Weller to Mr. Printer, June 11, 1843, *AWP*, August 11, 1843; "Negro Stealer," *AWP*, February 7, 1844; Franklin, *Militant South*, 74; *Richmond Enquirer*, April 28, 1848 (quotations).

29. *Baltimore Sun*, July 8, September 14, 1844 (1st–4th quotations); *LPA*, quoted in *Commonwealth*, June 29, 1841 (5th–7th quotations); Mahon, *History of the Militia*, 83–85; *Philanthropist*, February 12, 1836 (8th quotation); "Negro Stealer," *AWP*, March 6, 1844 (9th quotation); *DNI*, July 10, 1845.

30. *Maysville Eagle*, July 11, 1827 (1st quotation); *Philanthropist*, November 14, 1837 (2nd quotation); Nye, *Fettered Freedom*, 182–84.

31. *Alexandria Gazette*, August 29, 1835, quoted in Eaton, "Mob Violence," 358 (1st quotation); *Richmond Enquirer*, August 4, 1835 (2nd quotation); *Niles Register* 49 (October 3, 1835): 78; *Parkersburg Gazette*, quoted in *Philanthropist*, November 14, 1837 (3rd and 4th quotations); *Richmond Enquirer*, September 17, 1844 (5th and 6th quotations).

32. *Lexington Observer and Reporter*, November 17, 1841 (1st and 2nd quotations); *AWP*, March 23, 1843 (3rd quotation); Grimsted, *American Mobbing*, 129 (4th quotation).

33. Dillon, *Lovejoy*, 65–67; Trexler, *Slavery in Missouri*, 121–22 (quotation); Gara, *Liberty Line*, 157.

34. Trexler, *Slavery in Missouri*, 185 (quotations).

35. Torrey to ———, April 2, 1842, *Emancipator*, April 14, 1842.

36. Elijah P. Lovejoy to Brother, November 2, 1835, in Lovejoy and Lovejoy, *Memoir of Lovejoy*, 155 (quotation); Nye, *Fettered Freedom*, 176–79; Grimsted, *American Mobbing*, 115, 125–26; Eaton, "Mob Violence" 369. Nye does not distinguish between vigilance committees and mobs.

37. *Lexington Intelligencer*, quoted in Dumond, *Antislavery*, 203 (quotation); Fladeland, *Birney*, 113–24. See also Nye, *Fettered Freedom*, 128–29; Freehling, *Road to Disunion*, 1:115–17. Freehling contends Birney could have published in Danville. Richard Grimsted reports there were a half-dozen antiabolition mobs in Virginia in 1835. See Grimsted, *American Mobbing*, 125.

38. Nye, *Fettered Freedom*, 177; *Niles Register* 48 (August 15, 1835): 410 (1st quotation); Kramer, "Trial of Reuben Crandell," 123–25 (2nd and 3rd quotations); Grimsted, "Rioting in Its Jacksonian Setting," 377–78; Harrold, *Subversives*, 33. When Crandall's case finally went to trial eight months later, a jury acquitted him

39. *Lynchburg Democrat*, quoted in *Niles Register*, 49 (October 3, 1835): 76–77 (1st–3rd quotations); Lovejoy and Lovejoy, *Memoir of Lovejoy*, 155 (4th–6th quotations); Dillon, *Lovejoy*, 65.

40. Dillon, *Lovejoy*, 65, 68–74, 81–88, 169; Trexler, *Slavery in Missouri*, 117–19; Grimsted, *American Mobbing*, 103–4.

41. A. C. Garratt to Joshua Leavitt, May 21, 1836, in *Friend of Man*, June 23, 1836.

Contemporary reports of these events are confused and this is reflected in the second-ary literature. This account relies heavily on Garratt because he provides details and chronology that clarify other sources. See *Emancipator*, June 16, July 7, 14, 1836; Trexler, *Slavery in Missouri*, 120; Dillon, *Lovejoy*, 86.

42. Dillon, *Lovejoy*, 86; *Philanthropist*, June 10, 1836; *Emancipator*, June 16, 1836 (quotations).

43. *Emancipator*, June 16, 1836 (quotation); *Illinois Patriot*, quoted in *Kentucky Gazette*, June 13, 1836; Trexler, *Slavery in Missouri*, 120; Dillon, *Lovejoy*, 86; David Nelson to Those of Marion County who threaten me, *Emancipator*, July 7, 14, 1836; *Philanthropist*, June 10, 1836; Nelson to New York Evangelist, January 27, 1837, *Evangelist*, March 4, 1837.

44. Thompson, *Prison Life*, 18–22, 30–31 (1st quotation), 45, 52, 55, 83–85 (3rd quotation), 90–91, 357–58; Alvan Stewart to *Friend of Man*, *PF*, December 15, 1841; Charles T. Torrey to Gerrit Smith, August 3, 1844, Smith Papers, Syracuse University Library, Syracuse, N.Y.; *Liberator*, October 11, 1844 (2nd quotation); *Republican*, quoted in *Liberator*, August 27, 1841 (4th quotation); *Public Advertiser*, August 2, 1841 (5th quotation).

### CHAPTER THREE

1. "Negro Stealer," *AWP*, February 7, 1844 (1st–6th quotations); Samivel Weller Jr., "Notes on Southern Travel," *AWP*, May 1, 1844 (7th–13th quotations). Smallwood used "Samivel Weller Jr.," the name of a character in Charles Dickens's *The Pickwick Papers*, as a pseudonym.

2. Watson to David Holmes and J. E. Davis, January 20, 1827, *GUE*, April 28, 1827 (1st quotation); *Baltimore Sun*, quoted in *Liberator*, February 21, 1840 (2nd quotation); *PF*, April 16, 1846 (3rd and 4th quotations); Hensel, *Christiana Riot*, 15–17.

3. Johnson, *State of Ohio vs. Forbes and Armitage*, 19–20. See also Berlin, *Slaves without Masters*, 99; Turner, "Kentucky Slavery," 295.

4. Dunn, *Indiana and Indianans*, 1:347 (quotation); Wilson, *Freedom at Risk*, 50–52.

5. "Negro Stealer," *AWP*, February 7, 1844 (1st quotation); Fellman, *Inside War*, 19 (2nd quotation); Thomas Whitson, "Early Abolitionists of Lancaster County," paper read before the Lancaster County Historical Society, March 3, 1911, in Seibert Papers, Reel 14, OHS, Columbus (3rd quotation). Whitson suggests that his paper was based on "recall."

6. *Spirit of Liberty*, February 25, April 15, 1843; *Western Citizen* (Chicago), July 23, 1844 (quotation), July 28, 1846; *Anti-Slavery Bugle*, January 30, 1846.

7. *Quincy Argus*, quoted in *Philanthropist*, July 31, 1838; PHILO PATRIDOS to Dr. Bailey, *Philanthropist*, June 23, 1840; *Cincinnati Herald*, quoted in *Anti-Slavery Bugle*, August 22, 1845.

8. Gamaliel Bailey to James G. Birney, March 31, 1843, in Dumond, *Letters of Birney*, 2:726; R. M. Pearson to Editor, October 30, 1838, *PF*, November 29, 1838; *Gazette*, November 20, 1838; *Enquirer*, September 12, 1856.

9. *Cazenovia Abolitionist*, quoted in *Philanthropist*, August 27, 1842 (1st and 2nd quotations); Smith to G. Bailey Jr., September 13, 1842, *Philanthropist*, October 15, 1842 (3rd quotation); Morris to the Legislature and People of Ohio on Slavery, November 23, 1838, *CDG*, November 26, 1838 (4th quotation); *PF*, February 7, 1839. See also Volpe, *Forlorn Hope of Freedom*, 2, 104.

10. *Philanthropist*, October 7, 1836; *Philanthropist*, December 19, 1837; *Philanthropist*, February 27, June 26, August 7, 14, 28, 1838; *Philanthropist*, December 23, 30, 1840; Lesick, *Lane Rebels*, 89–90; *Signal of Liberty*, December 11, 1841; *Signal of Liberty*, December 17, 1842; *Western Citizen* (Chicago), August 5, October 7, 1842; *Western Citizen* (Chicago), June 17, 1843; George W. Clark to Sir, June 16, 1845, *Liberty Press*, June 28, 1845. Clark mentions that many of the delegates visited black schools in Cincinnati.

11. Smith, *Liberty and Free Soil Parties*, 41–42; "Morris to the Legislature and People of Ohio," *CDG*, November 26, 1838 (quotation); *Western Citizen* (Chicago), October 21, 1852.

12. *National Enquirer*, January 14, 1837 (1st quotation); *Gazette*, quoted in Hagedorn, *Beyond the River*, 224 (2nd quotation); *Freeman*, October 21, 1847 (3rd quotation).

13. *Freedom's Journal*, February 15, 1828; *Freedom's Journal*, March 7, 1829; *National Enquirer*, January 14, 1837; *Philanthropist*, August 25, 1837; *Philanthropist*, August 28, 1838; Berlin, *Slaves without Masters*, 160–61; Wilson, *Freedom at Risk*, 10–11; Laprade, "Domestic Slave Trade," 20–21. Berlin concludes the extent of kidnapping in antebellum American is "impossible to determine."

14. *National Enquirer*, November 5, 12, December 3 (2nd quotation), 24 (1st quotation), 1836; *Spirit of Liberty*, May 14, 1842; *Philanthropist*, June 17, 1836; R. M. Pearson to Editor, October 30, 1838, *PF*, November 29, 1838; *Western Citizen* (Chicago), June 20, 1848; *Sagamon Journal*, quoted in *ASB*, July 6, 1849.

15. *Philanthropist*, August 25, 1837 (1st and 2nd quotations); *Journal and Luminary*, quoted in *Philanthropist*, October 6, 1837 (3rd and 4th quotations); *Maysville Eagle*, October 18, November 4, 1837; *Eagle* and *Cincinnati Journal*, quoted in *Philanthropist*, November 14, 1837. The *Journal* reported that the kidnappers "threatened to shoot her." See also Hagedorn, *Beyond the River*, 123–27.

16. *Pittsburgh Christian Witness*, quoted in *Philanthropist*, June 28, 1838 (quotation); A. D. Barber to Gamaliel Bailey, *Philanthropist*, January 8, 1839; *Philanthropist*, May 12, 1841.

17. Hagedorn, *Beyond the River*, 123–38, 141–43; *Ohio Statesman*, February 5, 1838; *Cleveland Observer*, March 1, 1838; *Philanthropist*, March 6, 13, 1838; *Philanthropist*, December 21, 1842.

18. *Eagle* (1st–3rd quotations), *Journal* (4th and 5th quotations), quoted in *Philanthropist*, November 14, 1837; *PF*, August 14, 1845. One need not oppose slavery or the lawful rendition of fugitive slaves to condemn kidnapping. Nor need one be a northerner. Throughout the antebellum period, some slaveholders in the Lower South sacrificed financially to help return kidnapping victims to their families. See Wilson, *Freedom at Risk*, 30.

19. *Philanthropist*, June 10, 1836 (1st and 2nd quotations); *Philanthropist*, November

12, 1839 (3rd quotation); *WC*, September 4, 1845 (4th quotation). On views of southern licentiousness, see Walters, *Antislavery Appeal*, 72–78.

20. *National Inquirer*, December 24, 1836.

21. Mary A. Thomas to Friend, April 19, 1848, *Anti-Slavery Bugle*, May 5, 1848 (1st–5th quotations); *Columbus Standard*, quoted in *Anti-Slavery Bugle*, March 2, 1850 (6th–11th quotations).

22. *Cleveland Herald*, December 20, 1838; *Augusta Colonizationist*, quoted in *PF*, January 24, 1839 (1st and 2nd quotations); *Scioto Gazette*, September 4, 1845 (3rd quotation); Grimsted, *American Mobbing*, 126. One disputed report claimed the victim of the Guyandotte vigilantes died the next day. See *Emancipator*, March 14, 1839.

23. *Ohio Statesman*, December 13, 1842; *Philanthropist*, December 21, 1842; *Philanthropist*, March 8, April 12, 1843; *Philanthropist*, May 17, 1845; Morris to Dr. Bailey, *Tocsin of Liberty*, November 24, 1842 (quotations). See also Hagedorn, *Beyond the River*, 223–22.

24. *PF*, August 14, 1845

25. Griffler, *Front Line of Freedom*, 18, 105–6.

26. *National Enquirer*, October 26, 1839 (1st quotation); Phebe Ann Lindsley to J. S. Lindsley, May 11, 1848, Siebert Papers, Reel 9, OHS, Columbus (2nd quotation); Aaron Benedict [to Wilber Siebert], July 3, 1894, in Siebert Papers, Reel 9, OHS, Columbus; D. to Editor, October 22, 1838, *Philanthropist*, November 27, 1838 (3rd quotation). On rewards, see Schwartz, *Slave Laws*, 135.

27. For examples of peaceful renditions see *PF*, August 29, 1839; *PF*, March 5, 26, June 25, 1840; *PF*, September 1, 1841.

28. *PF*, March 28, 1844.

29. *PF*, May 23, June 6 (quotation), July 7, 1844; Edward H. Magill, "The Underground Railroad in Bucks County," *Bucks County Intelligencer*, February 3, 1898, Siebert Papers, Reel 12, OHS, Columbus. Based on the Consumer Price Index, $700 in 1844 equals about $20,019 in 2007 currency.

30. D—— to Editor, quoted in *Emancipator*, February 21, 1839 (1st quotation); *Philanthropist*, November 19, 1839 (2nd quotation); *Western Citizen* (Chicago), January 20, 1843 (3rd quotation). On September 4, 1845, after a master used a pistol to apprehend a fugitive slave in Chicago, Eastman asked, "Are the laws of Kentucky in force here?"

31. Abraham Allen to Dr. Bailey, November 3, 1838, *Philanthropist*, November 20, 1838 (quotation); Samuel D. Cochran to Bailey, February 27, 1841, *Philanthropist*, March 24, 1831; Joseph Fell to [?], April 22, 1844, *PF*, May 9, 1844; *South Bend Register*, quoted in *Anti-Slavery Bugle*, September 17, 1847; *Butler Whig*, quoted in *Anti-Slavery Bugle*, October 22, 1847.

32. Henry C. Wright to Benjamin Lundy, *National Enquirer*, October 26, 1837 (1st quotation); J. to [?], July 18, 1838, *PF*, August 2, 1838 (2nd–6th quotations). On Shipley, see Parrish, *Brief Memoirs of Thomas Shipley and Edwin P. Atlee*.

33. X, Y, Z to Editor, October 4, 1841, *Spirit of Liberty*, October 9, 1841 (1st–3rd quotations); *Spirit of Liberty*, October 16, 1841 (4th and 5th quotations).

34. *Indiana Freeman*, November 23, 1844. The *Freeman* noted that officers could call

on a citizen "posse comitatas" to invade the homes of those who sheltered fugitive slaves. See also *Western Citizen* (Chicago), October 21, 1842.

35. Harrold, *Rise of Aggressive Abolitionism*, 71–72; *Philanthropist*, June 25, 1838.

36. Lewis to [Lundy], *National Enquirer*, May 6, 1837.

37. CITIZEN to [*Observer*], *Philanthropist*, September 1, 1837 (quotations); *Philanthropist*, June 12, 1838.

38. *Philanthropist*, June 26, 1838.

39. Ibid., September 3, 1839; ibid., November 11, 1840.

40. Middleton, "Fugitive Slave Issue," 285–310; Finkelman, *Imperfect Union*, 47–48 (1st quotation), 94–95 (2nd quotation), 155; *CDG*, March 23, 1837.

41. *Philanthropist*, February 20, 1838 (1st quotation); *Free Press*, quoted in *PF*, October 5, 1839 (2nd quotation); *CDG*, September 14, 1838 (3rd quotation).

42. *PF*, December 19, 1839; *PF*, November 26, 1840; Finkelman, *An Imperfect Union*, 164–66; *LPA*, May 29, 1841 (quotations). The official name of the case was *State v. Farr*. But it was known as the Raines Case, after Bennett Raines, the master who lost his slaves.

43. *LPA*, May 29, 1841; *Philanthropist*, June 16, 30, 1841; Richards, "*Gentlemen of Property and Standing*," 92–100; Finkelman, *An Imperfect Union*, 148–55, 167–77; *Spirit of Liberty*, May 20, 1843; *Anti-Slavery Bugle*, April 24, 1846; *Anti-Slavery Bugle*, July 7, 1848.

44. Grimsted, *American Mobbing*, 59–61; Fladeland, *Birney*, 136–42; *Philanthropist*, quoted in *National Enquirer*, October 8, 1836 (quotation).

45. A Christian to the Editors of the Philanthropist, August 29, 1837, *Philanthropist*, September 8, 1837 (1st quotation); *National Gazette*, quoted in *National Enquirer*, November 23, 1837 (2nd quotation). The best account of Lovejoy and the mob is in Dillon, *Lovejoy*, 159–76.

46. Richards, "*Gentlemen of Property and Standing*," (1st quotation); Stewart, *Holy Warriors*, 65–73; *Cleveland Daily Herald*, June 15, 25, 1839; *Philanthropist*, February 17, 1841 (2nd and 3rd quotations); *PF*, June 20, 1839; Dillon, *Lovejoy*, 176–77.

47. *Compiler* and *Whig*, quoted in *Philanthropist*, June 12, 1838.

48. Morris to William J. McKinney, February 10, 1841, *Philanthropist*, February 17, 1841 (1st quotation); Morris to Samuel Webb et al., January 30, 1838, *CDG*, June 22, 1838 (2nd–5th quotations); Foner, *Free Soil, Free Labor, Free Men*, 97–98, 100–2; "Address of the Liberty Party of Pennsylvania, of 1845," *AWP*, August 6, 1845 (6th quotation).

49. *Sentinel*, May 23, 1844.


CHAPTER FOUR

1. Clark, "Annual Message," *Maysville Eagle*, December 5, 1838.

2. Birney, *Birney*, 166 (quotation); Hagedorn, *Beyond the River*, 87–89, 144–65, 186–87; *Maysville Eagle*, November 21, 1838.

3. *Philanthropist*, February 12, 1839.

4. Hamilton, *Prologue to Conflict*; Campbell, *Slave Catchers*; Fehrenbacher, *Slavehold-*

*ing Republic*, 205–51. Paul Finkelman and William W. Freehling analyze the impact of interstate disputes stemming from the fugitive slave laws. See Finkelman, "Protection of Black Rights in Seward's New York," 211–34; Finkelman, "Kidnapping of John Davis and the Adoption of the Fugitive Slave Law of 1793," 397–422; Finkelman, "Fugitive Slaves, Midwestern Racial Tolerance, and the Value of Justice Delayed," 89–141; Freehling, *Road to Disunion*, 1:455–474, 502–5.

5. *Niles Register* 29 (February 25, 1826): 419; *Maryland Gazette*, January 12, 1826 (quotations).

6. McMaster, *History of the People of the United States*, 5:218; Morris, *Free Men All*, 47 (1st quotation); *Maryland Gazette*, February 16, 1826 (2nd–4th quotations); Leslie, "Pennsylvania Fugitive Slave Act," 437. Despite the Maryland commissioners' failure to visit Trenton, the following December New Jersey passed a law dealing with fugitive slaves. See Finkelman, "Chief Justice Hornblower of New Jersey and the Fugitive Slave Law of 1793," in Finkelman, *Slavery and the Law*, 120–21.

7. *GUE*, February 4, 1826.

8. *National Gazette and Literary Register*, February 4, 10 (quotation), 1826; Leslie, "Pennsylvania Fugitive Slave Act," 438–40; Morris, *Free Men All*, 47–53. The interpretation here differs from that of Leslie and Morris.

9. William M. Meredith to Henry J. Williams, February 14, 1826, Pennsylvania (box) — Legislature, New York Public Library , quoted in Morris, *Free Men All*, 51.

10. Leslie, "Pennsylvania Fugitive Slave Act," 440, 443–45 (1st quotation); Thomas Shipley to Isaac Barton, February 15, 1826, PASP, HSP, Philadelphia, 9:216 (2nd quotation); Robert H. Goldsborough to W. W. Meredith, March 29, 1826, Meredith Papers, HSP, Philadelphia, quoted in Morris, *Free Men All*, 53 (3rd quotation); James T. Morehead and J. Speed Smith, *Special Message*, in Ohio, *Executive Documents*, 37 G.A., Document 37, 5–6 (4th and 5th quotations).

11. Nogee, "Prigg Case and Fugitive Slavery 1842–1850: Part I," 185; *National Enquirer*, January 18, 1838 (quotation); Ritner to Henry Hannen, April 5, 1838, *Liberator*, August 10, 1838. See also Finkelman, "*Prigg v. Pennsylvania* and Northern State Courts," 6–8.

12. *Philanthropist*, January 30, 1838; Veazey, *Annual Message*, 9 (quotations)

13. Veazey, *Annual Message*, 9.

14. Veazey, *Annual Message*, 9 (quotations); Nogee, "Prigg Case," 185; Fehrenbacher, *Slaveholding Republic*, 219.

15. George R. Gilmer to Joseph Vance, August 21, 1838, in Ohio, *Executive Documents, Documents . . . Thirty-Seventh General Assembly* (1838), *Executive Document #8*; Patrick Noble to [Wilson Shannon], January 25, 1840, in Ohio, *Executive Documents, Documents . . . Thirty-Eighth General Assembly* (1840), *Executive Document #89*; *Emancipator*, quoted in *PF*, August 9, 1838 (quotation); *PF*, May 9, 1839.

16. Gilmer to Vance, August 21, 1838, in Ohio, *Executive Documents*, 37 G.A., #8 (1st–4th quotations); *Annual Report of the Maine Anti-Slavery Society*, quoted in *Pennsylvania Freeman*, May 9, 1839 (5th quotation).

17. *Philanthropist*, January 21, 1840 (1st and 2nd quotations); *American Farmer*, quoted in *PF*, February 13, 1840 (3rd quotation).

18. *New Era*, quoted in *PF*, August 29, 1835 (quotations). See also Finkelman, "Protection of Black Rights in Seward's New York," 215. Finkelman's account of the arrest of the sailors differs slightly from that presented here.

19. *PF*, August 29, 1839; *PF*, January 16, 1840; Finkelman, "Protection of Black Rights," 216–19; Seward to Hopkins, September 16, 1839, quoted in Finkelman, "Protection of Black Rights," 217 (quotations).

20. Hopkins to Seward, October 4, 1839, quoted in Finkelman, "Protection of Black Rights," 219 (1st quotation); *PF*, January 9 (2nd quotation), 16, 1840; Ohio, *Executive Documents*, 39 G.A. (1840–1841) #25, 17–19 (3rd quotation). See also Finkelman, "Protecting Black Rights," 220n and *Philanthropist*, March 10, 1840.

21. Seward to New York Legislature, March 26, 1841, in *LPA*, April 9, 1841; Finkelman, "Protecting Black Rights," 223–24, 231–34; *DNI*, February 17, 1842.

22. *Pennsylvania Freeman*, January 9, 1840 (1st quotation); *Spirit of Liberty*, December 11, 1841 (2nd quotation); *Richmond Enquirer*, January 20, 1841 (3rd quotation); *LPA*, May 24, 1841 (4th quotation).

23. G. T. Stewart, "Ohio's Fugitive Slave Law," [1], (published in *Firelands Pioneer*, July 1888), Siebert Papers, OHS, Columbus (quotations); Griffler, *Front Line of Freedom*, 107 (quotations); Middleton, *Black Laws: Race and Legal Process in Early Ohio*, 164; Middleton, *Black Laws in the Old Northwest*, 26–27.

24. Martin, *Antislavery Movement in Kentucky Prior*, 110n; JUSTICE to Mr. Collins, October 9, 1837, *Eagle*, November 1, 1837 (quotations); *Eagle*, October 10, 1838; *Philanthropist*, December 21, 1842.

25. *Maysville Eagle*, November 1, 1837 (quotations).

26. *Philanthropist*, October 2, December 18 (quotation), 1838.

27. *CDG*, October 6, 11, 24 (1st and 2nd quotations), 25, 1838; *Pennsylvania Freeman*, October 11, 1838; *Maysville Eagle*, October 10, 1838; *Statesman*, quoted in *PF*, October 11, 1838 (3rd quotation). Vernon L. Volpe contends historians have exaggerated the impact of Mahan's arrest on the 1838 Ohio election. Volpe claims that other issues, such as banking, were more important. Contemporary sources suggest that the arrest had a significant impact. See Volpe, "The Ohio Election of 1838," 85–100.

28. *Ohio State Journal* (Semi-Weekly), October 26, 1838; Vaughan, *Argument at Trial*; *Maysville Eagle*, November 14, 1838 (quotation); *Philanthropist*, May 21, 1839; *Maysville Monitor*, quoted in *Philanthropist*, January 1, 1839; James Byers to Citizens of Mason and Bracken Counties, February 1, 1839, *Eagle*, February 13, 1839.

29. *Maysville Eagle*, November 14, 1838 (1st quotation); *Commonwealth*, November 28, 1838 (2nd and 3rd quotations); *Patriot*, quoted in *Philanthropist*, January 8, 1839 (4th quotation).

30. Mahan to *Zion's Watchman*, quoted in *Philanthropist*, December 11, 1838. On Mahan's involvement in the underground railroad, see Hagedorn, *Beyond the River*, 88–89. Henry Bibb, who escaped from Kentucky slavery during the late 1830s, claimed not to have been aware of the existence of abolitionists until he reached Cincinnati. Gamaliel Bailey, writing in 1838, simultaneously denied Cincinnati abolitionists went into Kentucky to help slaves escape *and* regretted that they

did. See Bibb, *Narrative of Life and Adventures*, xxi; *Philanthropist*, November 20, 1838.

31. *CDG*, November 20 (quotations), November 26, 1838; *Cincinnati Advertiser and Journal*, quoted in *CDG*, November 26, 1838.

32. Ohio, *Executive Documents*, 37 G.A. (1838), 19–20 (quotations); *Maysville Eagle*, December 12, 1838. The Georgia-Maine dispute very likely influenced Vance's message. See "Special Message from the Governor," in Ohio, *Executive Documents*, Document 8, 37 G.A. (December 7, 1838), 1–15.

33. Clark, *Annual Message*, December 5, 1837, in *Kentucky Gazette*, December 7, 1837.

34. On failure of earlier resolutions, see *Commonwealth*, December 28, 1838. On Whig control, see *Lexington Intelligencer*, January 18, 1839. On the Kentucky General Assembly's actions, see *Maysville Monitor*, quoted in *CDG*, December 27, 1838; *Philanthropist*, January 1, 8, 1839 (quotations); *Commonwealth*, January 9, 1839. Some Kentuckians wanted, in addition, that the Ohio legislature ban entry of free African Americans into the state, make color "prima facie evidence of slavery," and allow owners to recover twice the value of lost slave property in civil suits. See *Louisville City Gazette*, quoted in *Philanthropist*, January 8, 1839.

35. *Philanthropist*, January 15, 1839; *Lexington Intelligencer*, January 18, 1839; *Commonwealth*, December 28, 1838 (quotation), January 9, 1839.

36. *Ohio Statesman* and *Cincinnati Daily Gazette*, quoted in *Philanthropist*, January 1, 1839 (1st–5th quotations); *Ohio State Journal*, January 14, 1839 (6th quotation).

37. *Maysville Monitor*, quoted in *Philanthropist*, January 1, 1839 (1st quotation); *Commonwealth*, January 2 (2nd quotation), 9 (3rd quotation), 1839; *City Gazette*, quoted in *Philanthropist*, February 5, 1839 (4th quotation); *LPA*, February 9, 1839 (5th quotation).

38. Columbia Correspondence of the *Cincinnati Gazette*, quoted in *Lexington Intelligencer*, January 24, 1839; Ohio, *Ohio Senate Journal*, 37 G.A. (January 21, 1839), 192 (January 26, 1839), 224; Ohio, *Ohio House Journal*, 37 G.A. (January 17, 1839), 253 (January 22, 1839), 285–86; Ohio, *Executive Documents*, 37 G.A., Document 84 (January 21, 1839), 1–4; Morehead and Speed [to Ohio General Assembly], January 26, 1839, in Wilson Shannon to Ohio General Assembly, January 26, 1839, in Ohio, *Executive Documents*, 37 G.A., Document 37; *Maysville Eagle*, February 2, 1839; Galbreath, "Ohio's Fugitive Slave Law," 217.

39. *Eagle*, February 2, 1839; *Observer*, quoted in *Ohio State Journal* (Tri-Weekly), February 4, 1839. For a milder reaction, see *Lexington Intelligencer*, February 5, 1839.

40. *Ohio State Journal* (Tri-weekly), February 4, 1839; *Louisville Public Advertiser*, February 9, 1839 (1st, 3rd, and 4th quotations); *Cincinnati Gazette*, quoted in *Lexington Intelligencer*, January 29, 1839 (2nd quotation); *Commonwealth*, February 6, 1839 (5th and 6th quotations).

41. Wilson Shannon to General Assembly, January 21, 1839, in Ohio, *Executive Documents*, 37 G.A., Document 84, 1–4 (quotations); Morehead and Smith to Shannon, January 26, 1839, in Shannon to General Assembly of Ohio, January 26, 1839, in Ohio, *Executive Documents*, 37 G.A., Document 37, 2–11; Ohio, *Senate Journal*, 37 G.A.,

224–25, 271–74, 385–94; Ohio, *House Journal*, 37 G.A., 325, 345; *Lexington Intelligencer*, February 12, 1839; Galbreath, "Ohio's Fugitive Slave Law," 218. Other sources report the vote as fifty-three to fifteen in the house and twenty three to eleven in the senate. See *Maysville Eagle*, March 2, 1839. Wade's nineteenth-century biographer suggests the bill passed the senate on February 23. See Riddle, *Wade*, 134–44.

42. "An act relating to fugitives from labor or service," February 26, 1839, in Middleton, *Black Laws in the Old Northwest*, 111–16 (quotations); *Philanthropist*, March 24, 1840; Ohio, *House Journal*, 39 G.A. (January 18, 1841), 214–15. The *Ohio State Journal* reported it did not know whether the term *Black Law* was used for the Ohio fugitive slave law "because its provisions were of a heinous and reprehensible nature, or only because it related to persons whose complexion was of that color." See *Ohio State Journal* (daily), December 13, 1842.

43. *Ohio State Journal* (tri-weekly), February 25, 1839 (1st–3rd quotations); *Ohio Statesman*, quoted in *Commonwealth*, March 6, 1839 (4th–6th quotations); *Standard*, quoted in *Maysville Eagle*, February 27, 1839 (7th–9th quotations).

44. *Eagle*, March 2, 1839 (1st–3rd quotations); *Western Citizen* (Paris), March 8, 1839 (4th quotation); "An act relating to Fugitives from labor," in Middleton, *Black Laws in the Old Northwest*, 111–61 (5th quotation).

45. E. S. to W. L. G., July 24, 1839, *PF*, September 12, 1839; *Philanthropist*, December 4, 1838 (quotation); *LPA*, February 9, 1839.

46. *Philanthropist*, December 4, 18 (1st and 2nd quotations), 1838, January 1, 15, 22, February 12, 1839; *Cleveland Observer*, quoted in *PF*, February 28, 1839; *Cincinnati Daily Gazette*, December 14, 1838; A. A. Guthrie to Goodard and Chambers, January 19, 1839, *Philanthropist*, February 5, 1839 (3rd–6th quotations). Ann Hagedorn, in contrast, maintains without evidence that "Ohioans were largely indifferent to the law because it did not affect them. Few, after-all, were engaged in the business of transporting runaway slaves through the state." An earlier historian perceived that the Kentucky commissioners and passage of the law caused public opinion in the state to become more antislavery. See Hagedorn, *Beyond the River*, 182; Hickok, *Negro in Ohio*, 170–71.

47. [?] to Gamaliel Bailey, January 30, 1839, *Philanthropist*, February 12, 1839 (1st quotation); "Speech of Mr. Wade, on the bill relating to fugitives from labor . . . in the Senate of Ohio, February 22, 1839," *Philanthropist*, April 30, 1839 (2nd–9th quotations).

48. *Philanthropist*, May 7, 1839; J. Cable to [?], March 1, 1839, *PF*, April 11, 1839 (1st and 2nd quotations); *Philanthropist*, quoted in *PF*, May 2, 1839 (3rd quotation); *PF*, May 30, 1839 (4th and 5th quotations); J. H. B. to Brother Murray, June 5, 1839, *PF*, June 27, 1839 (6th quotation).

49. *Ohio State Journal*, quoted in *Philanthropist*, March 12, 1839 (1st–3rd quotation); *Philanthropist*, quoted in *LPA*, May 22, 1839 (4th quotation); Jay to [?], June 1839, quoted in *Philanthropist*, November 12, 1839 (5th–7th quotations).

50. A. D. Barber to Dr. Bailey, *Philanthropist*, January 8, 1839; *Philanthropist*, May 7, 1839; *PF*, August 1, 1839; *Observer* and *Republican*, both quoted in *PF*, August 1, 1839 (1st and 2nd quotations); *Colored American*, August 31 (3rd and 4th quotations), November

16, 1839; *Colored American*, March 21, 1840; *Aurora*, quoted in *PF*, January 16, 1840 (5th quotation).

51. *Lexington Intelligencer*, September 17, 1839; *Maysville Eagle*, quoted in *Philanthropist*, October 8, 1839; A Listener to Dr. Bailey, March 16, 1840, *Philanthropist*, March 24, 1840 (quotation).

52. Brooke to Dr. Bailey, October 6, 1840, *Philanthropist*, October 28, 1840; *Philanthropist*, quoted in *PF*, November 5, 1840; *Philanthropist*, March 24, 1841; *Lebanon Star*, quoted in *PF*, June 10, 1841 (quotation).

53. *Commonwealth*, June 25, 1839 (1st and 2nd quotations); *Maysville Eagle*, December 4, 1839 (3rd and 4th quotations).

54. *Philanthropist*, December 16, 1840 (1st quotation); *LPA*, May 22, 1839; *Western Citizen* (Paris), June 28, 1839 (2nd quotation).

55. Martin, *Antislavery Movement in Kentucky*, 95–96; *LOR*, November 17, 1841 (3rd and 4th quotations); *Philanthropist*, September 3, 1839; *Philanthropist*, September 1, 1841 (5th quotation), December 21, 1842; *CDG*, December 6, 1842.

56. *Telegraph*, quoted in *Philanthropist*, October 8, 1839 (1st quotation); *Philanthropist*, December 23, 1840 (2nd and 3rd quotations).

57. [?] to Dear Sir, March 2, 1839, *Philanthropist*, April 9, 1839; Ohio Anti-Slavery Society Resolutions, *Philanthropist*, June 18, 1839; James A. Thome to Dr. Bailey, May 23, 1839, *Philanthropist*, June 25, 1839; Morgan County Anti-Slavery Society, August 1, 1839, *Philanthropist*, September 3, 1839; Report, February 20, 1840, *Philanthropist*, March 24, 1840 (quotation); Ohio, *House Journal*, 39 G.A., 212–33, 650–51; Ohio, *Senate Journal*, 39 G.A., 478, 493–94, 548. The committee used racist terminology but truthfully reported the petitioners did "not specify a single instance of injustice that has occurred under" the law.

58. *Philanthropist*, September 3, 1839; *Philanthropist*, March 24, 1841; *Philanthropist*, March 30, 1842; *Lebanon Star*, quoted in *PF*, June 10, 1841 (quotation); Cover, *Justice Accused*, 166–68; *CDG*, November 21, 1842. Bliss's report raised some of the same constitutional issues addressed in *Prigg*. See Ohio, *House Journal*, 39 G.A., 216–21. See also Middleton, *Black Laws: Race and the Legal Process in Early Ohio*, 116–28.

59. *LPA*, October 10, 1839; *LPA*, February 29, April 18, 1840; *CDG*, August 7, 1840; *Ohio Statesman*, October 14, 1840; *LOR*, July 31, 1841.

60. *Philanthropist*, October 13, 1840 (1st quotation); *Emancipator*, quoted in *Pennsylvania Freeman*, October 29, 1840 (2nd and 3rd quotations); *LPA*, February 4 1841; Holt, *Whig Party*, 112–13, 141–42.

61. *Ohio Statesman*, September 29, October 12 (1st quotation); *Philanthropist*, October 8, 1842 (2nd and 3rd quotations); *Kentucky Gazette*, October 22, 1842; *Ohio Statesman*, December 6, 1842. The Dayton event received extensive press coverage. Estimated attendance ranged from 130,000 to 250,000. See *Western Citizen* (Paris), September 9, 1842; *Commonwealth*, September 13, 1842; *CDG*, September 21, 1842; *Louisville Daily Journal*, September 24, 1842; *LOR*, October 5, 1842; *Ohio State Journal* (weekly edition), October 5, 1842.

62. *Ohio Statesman*, December 9 (2nd quotation), December 13 (1st quotation), 1842;

Ohio, *House Journal*, 41 G.A., 19, 34–35; Ohio, *Senate Journal*, 41 G.A., 65–67, 72, 231; *Globe*, December 17, 1842; *Ohio State Journal* (daily), December 13, 1843. The *Philanthropist* has slightly different figures for the vote. See *Philanthropist*, December 14, 1842.

63. *Ohio State Journal* (daily), December 13, 1842; *Philanthropist*, December 14, 21, 1842; *Philanthropist*, January 11, 1843; *Niles Register* 69 (September 20, 1845): 41–42; Ohio, *House Journal*, 41 G.A., 35–36; *Ohio Statesman*, December 13, 1842 (quotation); Stewart, "Ohio's Fugitive Slave Act," 12–15, Siebert Papers, OHS, Columbus.

64. *Enquirer*, quoted in *Liberator*, October 11, 1850 (quotation). On stringent measures, see Morris, *Free Men All*, 131–47; Freehling, *Road to Disunion*, 1:501–3. On guaranteeing northern resistance, see Hamilton, *Prologue to Conflict*, 168–72; Potter, *Impending Crisis*, 130; Fehrenbacher, *Slaveholding Republic*, 231–33.

CHAPTER FIVE

1. *Telegraph*, quoted in *Liberator*, December 20, 1844. See also Hagedorn, *Beyond the River*, 226–27.

2. *Liberator*, December 20, 1844 (1st quotation); *Sun*, quoted in *NASS*, January 30, 1845 (2nd quotation); *Observer*, quoted in *Louisville Daily Journal*, December 16, 1844 (3rd and 4th quotations).

3. Emma Chapin to Wilber Siebert, January 11, 1896 and James Buswell to [Siebert], March 13, 1896, Siebert Papers, Reel 2, OHS, Columbus; *National Enquirer*, December 17, 1836 (quotation); *Baltimore Patriot*, October 6, 1837, quoted in *Philadelphia Saturday Chronicle*, October 1837; *PF*, June 10, 1846; *Columbia Spy*, quoted in *Anti-Slavery Bugle*, November 19, 1847; *Evansville Journal*, quoted in *Philanthropist*, October 21, 1836; *Western Citizen* (Paris), July 9, 1841; *Spirit of Liberty*, January 8, 1842.

4. Bordewich, *Bound for Canaan*, 171–72; R. J. M. Blackett, "'Freedom, or the Martyr's Grave,'" 118–19; *Colored American*, February 20, 1841; Pease and Pease, *They Who Would Be Free*, 211–12; Griffler, *Front Line of Freedom*, 87; *Spirit of Liberty*, February 18, April 15, 1843; Louis Tappan to William Lloyd Garrison, December 15, 1837, *Liberator*, January 5, 1838; Dillon, *Lovejoy*, 159, 164; JULIUS to Frederick Douglass, September 30, 1849, *North Star*, October 12, 1849.

5. *Evansville Journal*, quoted in *Philanthropist*, October 21, 1836; *National Enquirer*, December 17, 1836; *Quincy Argus* quoted in *Philanthropist*, July 31, 1838; Samuel D. Cochran to [Gamaliel] Bailey, February 27, 1841, *Philanthropist*, March 24, 1841; *Western Citizen* (Paris), July 9, 1841; *National Enquirer*, December 17, 1836; *PF*, May 30, 1839; *PF*, June 30, 1841; *PF*, June 10, 1847; *NYDT*, August 27, 1850. On slave-catcher casualties, see *Philanthropist*, October 21, 1836; *Philanthropist*, July 31, 1838; *Philanthropist*, August 20, 1842; *PF*, May 30, 1839; *PF*, June 30, November 3, 1841; *PF*, April 11, 1844; *PF*, June 10, 1847; *Anti-Slavery Bugle*, August 10, 1850; *NYDT*, August 27, 1850.

6. Richards, *"Gentlemen of Property and Standing,"* 131–55 (1st quotation); Grimsted, *American Mobbing*, 46–49; McKivigan, *War against Proslavery Religion*, 27–28, 51–52; Stewart, *Holy Warriors*, 67; *PF*, February 28 (3rd quotation), May 30, 1839 (2nd quotation); J. Cross to Leavitt, December 14, 1839, *PF*, January 16, 1840; F.J. [to editors],

April 7, 1844, *PF*, April 11, 1844; James Buswell to [Siebert], [March 13, 1896], Siebert Papers, OHS, Columbus.

7. On abolitionists and Quakers, see *Philanthropist*, March 24, 1841; *Western Citizen* (Chicago), August 28, 1845; *PF*, February 28, 1839; *PF*, April 11, 1844; *Telegraph*, quoted in *Liberator*, December 20, 1844.

8. D—— to Editor, October 22, 1838, *PF*, February 28, 1839; In regard to cases in which both sides had "legal process," see *Niles Register* 50 (August 20, 1836), 423–24; J. P. Jr. [to *PF*], June 30, 1838, *PF*, July 12, 1838; J. Cross to [Joshua] Leavitt, December 13, 1839, *PF*, January 16, 1840; Samuel D. Cochran to [Gamaliel Bailey], February 27, 1841, *Philanthropist*, March 24, 1841; *Cleveland Advertiser*, quoted in *LPA*, March 30, 1841; *Philanthropist*, August 20, 1842; *Rochester Daily Advertiser*, quoted in *Globe*, December 15, 1842; *CDG*, December 6, 1842 (quotation).

9. *PF*, February 28, 1839; *PF*, April 11, 1844; *CDG*, December 6, 1842 (quotations).

10. *Anti-Slavery Bugle*, July 7, 1840; *Anti-Slavery Bugle*, August 11, 1848; *Witness*, quoted in *PF*, September 26, 1839 (1st quotation); Horace Nye to Gamaliel Bailey, August 30, 1838, *Philanthropist*, September 13, 1838 (2nd and 3rd quotations).

11. *Niles Register* 50 (August 20, 1836): 423–24; *Philanthropist*, July 31, August 28 (1st quotation), 1838; Putnam County Anti-Slavery Society Resolutions, July 4, 1843, Siebert Papers, OHS, Columbus (2nd quotation); *Van Metre v. Mitchell* (1853), in Catterall, *Judicial Cases*, 4:305–6 (3rd quotation); N. Walton to Editors, February 8, 1846, *PF*, February 19, 1846 (4th and 5th quotations).

12. *PF*, June 6, 1839 (1st and 2nd quotations); *Western Citizen* (Chicago), October 21, 1842 (3rd and 4th quotations); *Western Citizen* (Chicago), February 3, 1843 (6th quotation); Thomas Morris to Dr. Bailey, *Tocsin of Liberty*, November 24, 1842 (5th quotation); *Ohio Statesman*, January 3, 1843.

13. *Press*, quoted in *Spirit of Liberty*, October 16, 1846 (1st and 2nd quotations); *Spirit of Liberty*, October 29, 1842 (3rd quotation).

14. Wm. Henderson, JP, et al., to Sir, January 31, 1846, *ASB*, April 24, 1846 (quotations); *Chester Republican*, quoted in *Boston Daily Atlas*, August 22, 1844; *PF*, June 19, 1845; *PF*, January 15, 1846; "Negro Stealer," *AWP*, February 14, 1844.

15. *National Enquirer*, December 17, 1836 (quotations); *Tocsin of Liberty*, December 1, 1842; *AWP*, March 2, 1843; *Spirit of Liberty*, January 8, November 19, 1842; Hagedorn, *Beyond the River*, 221–22. See also Mabee, *Black Freedom*, 275–90. The *Spirit of Liberty* (January 8, 1842) estimated that 90 percent of Christian ministers shared Rankin's views on the use of force. On Quaker violence, see Preston, "Fugitive Slave Law in Ohio," 343–44; *Baltimore Sun*, August 8, 1848.

16. Samuel D. Cochran to [Gamaliel] Bailey, February 27, 1841, *Philanthropist*, March 24, 1841; *Spirit of Liberty*, November 6, 1841 (1st and 2nd quotations); *Anti-Slavery Bugle*, May 11, 1847 (3rd–6th quotations); *Vaughan v. Williams*, U.S. Circuit Court, Indiana, May 1845, in McLean, *Reports of Cases*, 3:530. In 1850, abolitionists at Salem, Ohio, used a similar tactic. See M. R. Robinson to Brother Johnson, February 8, 1850, in *Anti-Slavery Bugle*, February 16, 1850.

17. *Evansville Journal*, quoted in *Philanthropist*, October 21, 1836 (1st quotation);

*Baltimore Patriot*, quoted in *Philadelphia Saturday Chronicle*, [October 1837], in *Franklin County School Annual*, November 14–18, 1927, in Siebert Papers, reel 14, OHS, Columbus (2nd quotation); *National Enquirer* November 2, 1837; *Quincy Argus*, quoted in *Philanthropist*, July 31, 1838 (3rd quotation); *Washington Patriot*, quoted in *Liberator*, July 31, 1846 (4th quotation).

18. Emphasis added. James Shaw to Dr. Bailey, May 8, 1839, *Philanthropist*, May 21, 1839 (1st, 3rd, and 4th quotations) and *Ohio Freeman*, quoted in the same issue of *Philanthropist* (2nd quotation); *PF*, May 30, 1839. The *Ohio Freeman* was not an antislavery newspaper.

19. Shaw to Bailey, May 8, 1839, *Philanthropist*, May 21, 1839 (quotation); *PF*, May 30, 1839; Hagedorn, *Beyond the River*, 186–87.

20. Shaw to Bailey, May 8, 1839, *Philanthropist*, May 21, 1839 (quotations); *Philanthropist*, June 18, 1839; Hagedorn, *Beyond the River*, 188–90.

21. F.J. [to Editors], April 7, 1844, *PF*, April 11, 1844.

22. *Cincinnati Herald*, quoted in *Louisville Daily Journal*, July 25, 1845 (1st and 2nd quotations); *ASB*, May 7, 1847 (3rd and 4th quotations); William Henry Egle, "An Underground Route," Siebert Papers, reel 13, OHS, Columbus (5th quotation); Godcharles, *Chronicles of Central Pennsylvania*, 2:146–47 (5th quotation); *Cincinnati Herald*, quoted in *Anti-Slavery Bugle*, July 7, 1848 (6th quotation).

23. John Rankin to Edwards, September 13, 1841, quoted in *PF*, November 3, 1841 (quotations); Hagedorn, *Beyond the River*, 219–22.

24. *Anti-Slavery Bugle*, October 22, 1847 (1st–4th quotations); [no name] to Editor, June 2, 1848, *Western Citizen* (Chicago), June 20, 1848 (5th and 6th quotations).

25. Samuel D. Cochran to [Gamaliel] Bailey, February 27, 1841, *Philanthropist*, March 24, 1841 (1st and 2nd quotation); *Cleveland Advertiser*, quoted in *LPA*, March 30, 1841 (3rd quotation).

26. *LPA*, March 30, 1841 (all quotations are from the *LPA*).

27. *PF*, June 30, 1841 (1st and 2nd quotations); Julius A. Willard to [Zebina Eastman], October 6, 1843, *Western Citizen* (Chicago), October 12, 1843 (3rd–7th quotations). The *PF* regarded an earlier account of the Chester County incident published in the *NYDT* to be exaggerated.

28. *Evansville Journal*, quoted in *Philanthropist*, October 21, 1836.

29. D—— to Editor, October 22, 1838, *Philanthropist*, quoted in *PF*, February 28, 1839.

30. David Grimsted notes Pennsylvania's predominance. See Grimsted, *American Mobbing*, 73–74.

31. *Niles Register* 50 (August 20, 1836): 423–24. The quotations are from the judge's charge to the jury at Heath and Steedman's trial held two years later. See also Hart, *Slavery and Abolition*, 281; and Grimsted, *American Mobbing*, 75. Grimsted maintains the masters were briefly jailed for violating "Sunday travel laws." The *Register* reports Heath and Steedman only considered charging the masters with this offense.

32. W. H. J. to Friend, August 1, 1837, *National Enquirer*, August 10, 1837 (1st quotation); Bean, *History of Montgomery County, Pennsylvania*, 311–13; *Spirit of Liberty*, quoted

in *PF*, June 19, 1845 (2nd–4th quotations). For examples of acceptance by courts of the argument that claimants of slaves failed to prove slavery legally existed in their state, see W. H. J. to Friend, August 1, 1837, *National Enquirer*, August 20, 1837; *Philanthropist*, March 24, 1840; *Maysville Eagle*, March 22, 1845.

33. *New York Daily Herald*, August 18, 1836; *PF*, January 15, 1846; *NYDT*, quoted in *ASB*, November 19, 1847 (quotations).

34. *Village Herald*, quoted in *National Enquirer*, December 17, 1836; *Woodbury Herald*, quoted in *New York Spectator*, December 15, 1836.

35. *PF*, June 10, 1847 (quotations); *ASB*, September 10, 1847; Crooks, *Life and Letters of Rev. John McClintock*, 143–81, in "Dickinson College Digital Collections," http://deila.dickinson.edu/cdm4/document.php?CISOROOT=/buchan&CISOPTR=673 (accessed March 19, 2010); Godcharles, *Chronicles of Central Pennsylvania*, 2:148–49. The *PF* copied several newspapers, including one from Maryland. They each struggled to get an accurate account of what had happened. See also Grimsted, *American Mobbing*, 74; *Ohio Observer*, July 7, 1847; *Mississippian*, October 1, 1847.

36. *NYDT*, August 27, 1850 (quotations); Grimsted, *American Mobbing*, 75.

37. *Marion Visiter*, quoted in *PF*, September 19, 1839 (quotations); *Philanthropist*, August 7, October 8, 1839; *Philanthropist*, March 10, 1840; *Maysville Eagle*, quoted in *Lexington Intelligencer*, September 17, 1839; *Cincinnati Gazette*, quoted in *Emancipator*, September 19, 1839. See also Preston, "Fugitive Slave Acts in Ohio," 437–56.

38. *Norris v. Newton* (1850), in Catterall, *Judicial Cases*, 5:35–37; Dunn, *Indiana and Indianans*, 1:527; Furlong, "South Bend Fugitive Slave Case," 7–24; *Norris v. Newton* (1850), in Catterall, *Judicial Cases*, 5:36–38 (quotations); Paul Finkelman, "'The Law and Not Conscience, Constitutes the Rule of Action': The South Bend Fugitive Salve Case and the Value of Justice Delayed," in Nieman, *Constitution, Law, and American Life*, 23–51.

39. Cross to [Joshua] Leavitt, December 14, 1839, *PF*, January 16, 1840.

40. W. H. J. to Friend, August 1, 1837, *National Enquirer*, August 10, 1837 (1st and 2nd quotations); Cross to Leavitt, December 14, 1839, *PF*, January 16, 1840 (3rd quotation); *PF*, October 21, 1847 (4th and 5th quotations); *Anti-Slavery Bugle*, April 13, 1850 (6th quotation).

41. [?] to Editor, December 4, 1839, *Philanthropist*, December 17, 1839.

42. Ibid. (1st quotation); *PF*, December 19, 1839 (2nd quotation), November 26, 1840; *LPA*, May 29, 1841 (3rd quotation); *Lebanon Star*, quoted in *PF*, June 10, 1841; Wright, "A Station on the Underground Railroad," 164–69; Finkelman, *An Imperfect Union*, 165. Wright's article contains transcripts of court records.

43. *LPA*, May 29 (1st quotation), 31, August 17, 1841; *Lexington Gazette*, quoted in *Western Citizen* (Paris), August 20, 1841; *Philanthropist*, June 30, 1841 (2nd–4th quotations); *Cincinnati Enquirer*, quoted in *Western Citizen* (Paris), August 20, 1841. At the time, only Massachusetts and Connecticut had taken similar positions on slaves in transit. The *Philanthropist* quoted John C. Vaughan, formerly of South Carolina, concerning friendly relations. The call for manliness is the *Philanthropist*'s.

44. *Republican*, quoted in *Western Citizen* (Paris), July 9, 1841; *Philanthropist*, June 30, 1841; *Philanthropist*, April 12, 1843; Griffler, *Front Line of Freedom*, 53–54.

45. *Louisville Journal*, June 19, 1841; *Western Citizen* (Paris), August 20, 1841; *PF*, August 25, 1841; *Cincinnati Enquirer*, quoted in *Western Citizen* (Paris), August 20, 1841 (quotations).

46. *Cincinnati Republican*, quoted in *Louisville Journal*, September 6, 1841 (1st quotation); *Times*, September 6, 1841, quoted in Griffler, *Front Line of Freedom*, 55 (2nd quotation); Grimsted, *American Mobbing*, 62–63 (3rd quotation); Folk, "Queen City of Mobs," 333–51; Richards, *"Gentlemen of Property and Standing,"* 40–43. Griffler, relying on John Mercer Langston's autobiography, contends the mob fired the cannon three times and forced African Americans to retreat. Grimsted, relying on contemporary sources, argues not only that black men took the cannon but won the battle.

47. Griffler, *Front Line of Freedom*, 56; Harrold, *Bailey*, 43 (1st quotation); Grimsted, *American Mobbing*, 62–63 (2nd quotation).

48. *Philanthropist*, August 20, 1842; Grimsted, *American Mobbing*, 64.

CHAPTER SIX

1. David Grimsted provides a summary of the literature on Clay. See Grimsted, *American Mobbing*, 314–15. See also Harrold, "Cassius M. Clay on Slavery and Race," 42–56; Harrold, "The Intersectional Relationship between Cassius M. Clay and the Garrisonian Abolitionists," 101–119; Harrold, "Violence and Nonviolence in Kentucky Abolitionism," 15–38; Tallant, *Evil Necessity*, 115–23.

2. Clay, *Life of Cassius Marcellus Clay*, 175 (quotation); Marshall, *Speeches and Writings*, 207.

3. Clay, *Writings*, 285 (1st quotation); *Cincinnati Herald*, quoted in *NASS*, September 11, 1845 (2nd quotation); SCOBLE to Joshua Leavitt, August 16, 1845, *Emancipator*, August 20, 1845; *Louisville Daily Journal*, August 20, 21, 1845; *Liberator*, August 29, 1845; *Niles Register* 68 (August 30, 1845): 409; *Lexington Observer*, quoted in *Western Citizen* (Chicago), September 11, 1845; *Maysville Eagle*, October 15, 1845. Clay told Salmon P. Chase, "You see my appeals are directed to the non-slaveholders—men as a mass never have and never will yield, resign power and money *willingly*—we must force slavery or she will never yield!" See Clay to Chase, July 3, 1845, Chase Papers, HSP, Philadelphia.

4. *Niles Register* 68 (August 30, 1845): 408 (1st quotation); Marshall, *Speeches and Writings*, 187–210 (2nd–10th quotations).

5. Marshall, *Speeches and Writings*, 205–7 (1st, 2nd, and 4th quotations); Clay, *Writings*, 295 (3rd quotation); *Cincinnati Herald*, quoted in *NASS*, September 11, 1845 (5th–7th quotations); *LOR*, quoted in *DNI*, August 26, 1845; *Maysville Eagle*, August 37, 1845; *Lexington Inquirer*, quoted in *Niles Register*, 68 (August 30, 1845): 408–9 (8th quotation).

6. Smiley, *Lion of White Hall*, 98 (1st quotation); Marshall, *Speeches and Writings*, 207 (2nd quotation).

7. *Baltimore Saturday Visiter*, August 5–December 30, 1843; *Baltimore Saturday Visiter*, February 10, 24, April 13, 1844; *Baltimore Saturday Visiter*, January 25, June 14, 1845;

*NYDT*, January 31, 1846; Harrold, *Abolitionists and the South*, 29–30, 42; Harrold, *Bailey*, 90. More ephemeral abolitionist newspapers published in the Border South during the late 1840s included the *Crisis* of Moundsville, Virginia, the *Delaware Abolitionist*, and *Daily Enterprise* of Wheeling, Virginia. See *PF*, May 25, 1848; *Western Citizen* (Chicago), June 6, 1848; *National Era*, January 25, 1849.

8. *Western Citizen* (Chicago), June 6, 1848 (1st quotation); *Baltimore Saturday Visiter*, February 14, 1846 (2nd quotation); *Examiner*, July 3, 1847 (3rd quotation). On freedom of the press, see Eaton, *Freedom of Thought*; *NASS*, June 18, 1845; *Examiner*, July 3, 1847.

9. *True American*, June 3, 1845, in Clay, *Writings*, 213 (1st quotation), 217 (2nd quotation); Smiley, *Lion of White Hall*, 84 (3rd quotation).

10. *National Era*, January 7 (1st quotation), February 25, August 26 (2nd quotation) 1847; *National Era*, November 16, 1848; *National Era*, May 10, 1849; *Baltimore Patriot*, quoted in *Emancipator*, December 23, 1845 (3rd quotation); *Daily True Democrat*, January 22, 1847 (4th quotation).

11. Floan, *South in Northern Eyes*, 6–7; Dillon, *Lundy*, 71, 76–77, 112–16; Birney to Smith, September 13, 1835, in Dumond, *Letters of Birney*, 1:243 (quotation). Smiley, *Lion of Whitehall*, 4, 37, 43, 59; Stampp, "Fate of the Southern Anti-Slavery Movement," 19–22; Clay, *Writings*, 72–74, 123, 127–28, 140–41, 176–89, 204–5, 224–25, 338; *True American* (with Vaughan as editor), July 16, August 5, September 9, 30, 1846; *Louisville Examiner*, June 19, July 3, 10, September 11, 1847.

12. Freehling, *Road to Disunion*, 1:162–209, 455–74; Harrison, *Antislavery Movement in Kentucky*, 46–48; Fields, *Slavery and Freedom on the Middle Ground*, 1–89; Tallant, *Evil Necessity*, 2003), 7–8 (quotations), 91–114; Whitman, *Price of Freedom*,; Illinois Anti-Slavery Concert, *Narrative of Facts*, 36–37.

13. Chase to Lewis Tappan, February 15, 1843, Chase Papers, LC, Washington, D.C.; David Johnson to Calhoun, October 18, 1848, in Boucher, "Correspondence of Calhoun," 481–82 (2nd quotation). On the unanimity of opinion concerning the fate of slavery in the Border South, see Theodore Weld to James G. Birney, June 19, 1834, in Dumond, *Letters of Birney*, 119–21; NEASS, *Third Annual Report*, 13–14; *Emancipator*, April 5, June 14, 1838; MASS, *Annual Reports, Eleventh Annual Report* (1843), 20; Gamaliel Bailey to John Scoble, January 19, 1845, in Abel and Klingberg, *A Side-Light on Anglo-American Relations*, 202–4; A Citizen of Maryland to Editor, February 14, 1845, *AWP*, February 26, 1845; *True American*, May 13, 1846; *Baltimore Saturday Visiter*, quoted in *Emancipator*, August 13, 1845; Iago to Tribune, April 22, [1850], in *NYDT*, April 24, 1850; AFASS, *Annual Reports, Thirteenth Annual Report* (1853), 29.

14. Harrison, *Antislavery Movement in Kentucky*, 49; Freehling, *Road to Disunion*, 1:469; Tallant, *Evil Necessity*; Whitman, *Price of Freedom*, 3, 67, 140–57. Freehling regards this as a weak proslavery position.

15. *Centreville Times*, quoted in *PF*, November 28, 1839; *CWHP*, October 22, 1845; *Richmond Enquirer*, December 28, 1849; Bruce, *Violence and Culture*, 132; Johnson, "Charles Osborne's Place," 192; Freehling, *Road to Disunion*, 1:455, 462, 469–70, 505; Smiley, *Lion of White Hall*, 92. Although he lived in the Lower South, J. D. B. De Bow well stated the views of white Kentuckians: "Yet Kentucky is by no means prepared for emancipa-

tion; with such a proportion of blacks it is impossible that she can be. She would not incur the perilous risk of retaining in her midst such an army of lazy, worthless *free negroes* as would result. It would be a blight which no wealth could sustain." See *De Bow's Review* 7 (September 1849): 205. For Maryland, see McDonald, "Prelude," 19–21.

16. Gowdey to Lummins, November 5, 1831, *Liberator*, December 3, 1831; [?] to Editors of *Courier and Enquirer*, quoted in *Liberator*, January 7, 1832; J. J. S. to *\*\*\*\*\**, *Kentucky Gazette*, April 30, 1842; Greenberg, *Masters and Statesmen*, 99; Barney, *Road to Secession*, 152–53; *PF*, June 13, 1839, August 29, 1850. Abolitionists often claimed that without the hope they held out to slaves of peaceful emancipation, revolt was inevitable. See *PF*, June 13, 1839; Alvan Stewart to Samuel Webb, June 25, 1840, Stewart Papers, NYHS, Albany, N.Y.; Henry Highland Garnet, *Emancipator*, March 4, 1842; Walters, *Antislavery Appeal*, 25–26.

17. *LPA*, January 21 (1st–3rd quotations), February 1, 1841 (5th–7th quotations); Wickliffe to John C. Calhoun, February 26, 1849, in Boucher, "Correspondence Addressed to Calhoun," 499 (4th quotation).

18. Fairbank, *Rev. Calvin Fairbank during Slavery Times*, 12–24 (quotation), 35, 45–57; Runyon, *Delia Webster*, 64–67, 121–24.

19. *Emancipator*, December 25, 1844; Isaac Wade to Editor of *Anti-Slavery Bugle*, *NASS*, October 29, 1846; *Gazette*, October 5, 1844 (1st quotation) and *Observer and Reporter*, October 2, 1844 (2nd quotation), both quoted in Runyon, *Webster*, 42; *Observer and Reporter*, January 1, 1845, quoted in Coleman, *Slavery Times in Kentucky*, 202 (3rd quotation).

20. Harrold, *Subversives*, 64–93; Smallwood, *Narrative of Thomas Smallwood*, 20 (quotation).

21. S.P.A. to *NYDT*, August 26, [1850], *PF*, September 5, 1850 (1st quotation); P.P. to Sirs, February 7, 1842, *New York Evangelist*, February 10, 1842; *Tocsin of Liberty*, October 27, 1842; Samivel Weller Jr. to Nevy, November 9, 1842, *Tocsin of Liberty*, November 17, 1842; Weller to Printer, November 19, [1842], *Tocsin of Liberty*, December 1, 1842; Weller to Editor, November 15, 1842, *Tocsin of Liberty*, December 14 1842; Weller to Printer, November 19, 1842, *Tocsin of Liberty*, December 1, 1842; Weller to Editor, November 19, 1842, *Tocsin of Liberty*, December 8, 1842; Weller to Printer, April 17, 1843, *AWP*, April 27, 1843; Weller to Printer, June 6, 1843, *AWP*, June 15, 1843; *AWP*, April 27, 1843; *AWP*, February 14, 1844 (2nd quotation). Samivel Weller Jr. was Smallwood's pen name. On the practice of sending letters or newspaper stories to slaveholders, see *Centreville Times* quoted in *PF*, November 28, 1839; *Western Citizen* (Chicago), November 12, 1842.

22. Harrold, *Subversives*, 82–90; William L. Chaplin to J. C. Jackson, December 30, 1844, *AWP*, January 8, 1845; MARYLAND to H. Greeley, August 1, 1845, *PF*, August 14, 1845; *Baltimore Ray*, quoted in *Baltimore Saturday Visiter*, July 19, 1845; *Emancipator*, January 7, June 1, 1846; J. E. S. to [Gamaliel Bailey], September 20, 1847, *National Era*, September 23, 1847.

23. Torrey to Gerrit Smith, August 3, 1844, Smith Papers (1st quotation); Harrold, *Subversives*, 90, 92; Lovejoy, *Memoir of Torrey*, 345–46 (2nd quotation); *Emancipator*,

July 1, 1846; *Emancipator*, May 26, 1847; *Anti-Slavery Bugle*, November 17, 1848 (3rd quotation). See also J. E. S[nodgrass] to [Editor], September 20, 1847, *National Era*, September 23, 1847.

24. Harrold, *American Abolitionists*, 67 (1st quotation); *Parkersburg Gazette*, quoted in *Philanthropist*, August 28, 1838; W. B. Burnell to Gerrit Smith, *AWP*, February 18, 1846 (2nd quotation).

25. *Baltimore Saturday Visiter*, May 23, 1846; Lovejoy, *Torrey*, 146, 315, 330–31, 357; *Emancipator*, July 1, 846; A Citizen of Fauquier County to Gales and Seaton, July 27, 1833, *DNI*, August 3, 1833 (1st and 2nd quotations); White, "Minute Book," [June 1839] and December 14, 1840 to March 11, 1844, HSP, Philadelphia; Griffler, *Frontline of Freedom*, 46–80 (3rd quotation); *PF*, February 13, 1840, February 29, 1844; Cecelski, "Shores of Freedom," 174–206 (4th quotation); Grover, *Fugitives' Gibraltar*, 67–93.

26. *Philanthropist*, August 8, 1838; *Peoria Register*, quoted in *Western Citizen* (Chicago), September 16, 1842; *Spirit of Liberty*, November 5, 1842 (1st quotation); Thomas J. Moore to Editor, March 15, 1843, *Western Citizen* (Chicago), March 30, 1843; *Philanthropist*, August 27, 1842 (2nd and 3rd quotations); Elder to Chase, May 25, 1845, Chase Papers, HSP, Philadelphia (4th quotation). According to Calvin Fairbank, Bailey's household and those of other Liberty leaders in Cincinnati sheltered fugitive slaves. See Fairbank, *Fairbank*, 21.

27. *Peoria Register*, quoted in *Western Citizen* (Chicago), September 6, 1842 (1st and 2nd quotations); *Emancipator*, June 29, 1843 (3rd and 4th quotations); *New Era*, quoted in *True Wesleyan*, October 23, 1847 (5th and 6th quotations).

28. *PF*, October 21, 1847 (1st quotation); *Human Rights*, quoted in *Philanthropist*, December 9, 1836 (2nd quotation).

29. Illinois Anti-Slavery Concert, *Narrative of Facts*, 36–37.

30. *Louisville Daily Journal*, August 21, 1845. On Clark, see chapter 4.

31. SCOBLE to Leavitt, August 6, 1845, *Emancipator*, August 20, 1845 (1st–4th quotations); *Christian Advocate*, quoted in *Liberator*, May 22, 1846 (5th quotation); *Western Citizen* (Paris), June 25, 1841; P. [to editor], August 15, 1845, *Louisville Daily Journal*, August 18, 1845.

32. *Louisville Weekly Courier*, February 10, 1849.

33. *Maysville Eagle*, May 14, 1845, November 19, 1846; *Emancipator*, January 27, 1842 (1st–5th quotations); Brackett, *Negro in Maryland*, 80–81. Robert J. Breckinridge's mildly antislavery Baltimore magazine contended the slaveholders' initiative was "part of a concerted plan covering all of the boarder Slave States." See *Emancipator*, quoted in *Spirit of Liberty*, June 25, 1844 (6th quotation);

34. Brackett, *Negro in Maryland*, 91 (1st quotation); J. E. S. to Editor, October 18, 1847, in *National Era*, October 21, 1847; *NASS*, quoted in *Anti-Slavery Bugle*, January 19, 1849 (2nd quotation); *NYDT*, August 18, 1850 (3rd and 4th quotations); *New York Tribune*, quoted in *PF*, September 5, 1850 (5th and 6th quotations).

35. *Philanthropist*, March 24, 1841.

36. *Niles Register* 68 (August 30, 1846): 408–0; *AASS*, September 4, September 11, 1845; *AASS*, April 23, 1846; *CWHP*, March 18, April 15, 1846; Wade to Editor of *Anti-*

*Slavery Bugle*, quoted in *NASS*, October 29, 1846; E. Mortimer Bye to Friend, *PF*, September 9, 1847.

37. *PF*, March 5, 1840.

38. Grimsted, *American Mobbing*, 123–27; *CWHP*, October 1, 15, 1845; *Marietta Intelligencer*, quoted in *Niles Register* 69 (October 11, 1845): 90 (quotations); Eaton, "Mob Violence," 363.

39. Eaton, *Freedom of Thought*, 116; Wyatt-Brown, *Southern Honor*, 402–34; Grimsted, *American Mobbing*, 135–36; *Kentucky Gazette*, January 9, 1836; *Evansville Journal*, quoted in *CDG*, November 1, 1838; *Western Citizen* (Paris), quoted in Coleman, *Slavery Times*, 88; Nye, *Fettered Freedom*, 133. There was a major revolt/escape scare in Kentucky in November 1838. See *New York Spectator*, November 13, 1838; Coleman, *Slavery Times*, 88.

40. *Daily Union*, quoted in *Richmond Enquirer*, July 11, 1845 (1st quotation); *Baltimore Sun*, July 9, 10 (2nd–4th quotations), 1845. The account in this paragraph and those that follow of the July 1845 Maryland mass-escape attempt is a composite based—in addition to those sources already cited—on: *Baltimore Sun*, July 14, 18, 22, 30, 1845; *Port Tobacco Times*, quoted in *Richmond Enquirer*, July 15, 1845; *Richmond Enquirer*, July 18, 1845; *Niles Register* 68 (July 12, 1845): 293; (July 26, 1845): 332; *PF*, July 17, 31, 1845; *Baltimore Saturday Visiter*, July 19, 1845; *Liberator*, August 1, 15, 1845. Herbert Aptheker includes the Maryland and Kentucky mass-escape attempts in his pioneering study of slave revolts. See Aptheker, *American Negro Slave Revolts*, 337–38.

41. *Baltimore Sun*, July 9 (2nd quotation), July 10 (1st quotation), 1845; *Daily Union*, quoted in *PF*, July 17, 1845 (3rd and 4th quotations); *New York Herald*, quoted in *PF*, July 17, 1845 (5th quotation); Maryland, *Annual Message of the Executive to the General Assembly*, 25–26.

42. *PF*, July 17, 1845 (1st quotation); *Baltimore Sun*, quoted in *Liberator*, August 1, 1845 (2nd and 3rd quotations).

43. *Herald*, quoted in *PF*, July 17, 1845 (1st and 2nd quotations); *Western Citizen* (Chicago), November 12, 1842; *PF*, June 5, 1845 (3rd–9th quotations). In Maryland, reports of frequent escapes of slaves in groups of five to thirty continued through the 1850s. See *Liberator*, May 12, 1848; Brackett, *Negro in Maryland*, 89–90; Fields, *Slavery and Freedom on the Middle Ground*, 67.

44. *Commonwealth of Kentucky v. Slaughter et al.*, quoted in Coleman, *Antislavery Times*, 91 (1st quotation); Tallant, *Evil Necessity*, 146; *LOR*, (2nd and 3rd quotations) quoted in Coleman, *Slavery Times*, 88–91.

45. *LOR*, August 12, 1848; *Lexington Atlas*, quoted in *Baltimore Sun*, August 17, 1848; *Lexington Atlas*, quoted in *North Star*, August 25, 1848 (quotation); Coleman, *Slavery Times*, 90. Frederick Douglass, commenting in the *North Star*, denied that white men led the slaves.

46. Coleman, *Slavery Times*, 91–92; Runyon, *Delia Webster*, 123; Tallant, *Evil Necessity*, 146 (quotation), 249n.

47. Chaplin to James C. Jackson, January 3, 1845, *AWP*, January 8, 1845 (quotation); Harrold, *Subversives*, 98–115, 128.

48. Harrold, *Subversives*, 116–18, 128.

49. Harrold, *Subversives*, 124–41; Harrold, "*Pearl* Affair," 150–152; *CG*, 30th Cong., 1st sess., April 20, 1848, 654 (quotation).

50. Chapin to Smith, May 17, 1848, Smith Papers, Syracuse University, Syracuse, N.Y. (quotation); Harrold, *Subversives*, 142–43.

51. *CG*, 30th Cong., 1st sess., Appendix, April 20, 1848, 501–4 (quotations); *CG*, 30th Cong., 1st sess., April 21, 1848, 657, 662; *CG*, 30th Cong., 1st sess., April 25, 1848, 665–66; Correspondence of the *Boston Daily Whig*, quoted in *Liberator*, April 28, 1848. Foote and other southern senators described helping the *Pearl* slaves escape as mob action, which required a response in kind.

52. Potter, *Impending Crisis*, 1–89; Sewell, *Ballots*, 131–69; Blue, *Free Soilers*, 137–143.

53. Clay, *Life*, 491–92 (1st quotation); Clay, *Writings*, 430 (2nd quotation); "Convention of the Friends of Emancipation," *National Era*, May 10, 17, 1849; Smiley, *Lion of White Hall*, 133–37 (3rd quotation); Fee to Gamaliel Bailey, June 13, 1849, *National Era*, June 28, 1849 (4th quotation Clay to [Bailey], August 4, 1849, *National Era*, August 16, 1849 (5th–8th quotations). Recent studies of the 1849 emancipationist effort in Kentucky are Freehling, *Road to Disunion*, 1:467–71 and Tallant, *Evil Necessity*, 137–58.

54. Tallant, *Evil Necessity*, 147–48; Tapp, "Breckinridge," 142; *Louisville Weekly Courier*, August 11, 1849 (quotations).

55. Tallant, *Evil Necessity*, 149–51, 157–60.

56. Cralle, *Works of John C. Calhoun*, 6:295–98.

57. Harrold, *Subversives*, 146–47.

58. *Baltimore Sun*, August 10, 12, 1850; *NYDT*, August 13, 1850 (quotations); *Richmond Enquirer*, August 10, 1850.

59. *Philadelphia Bulletin*, quoted in *National Era*, August 29, 1850 (1st–4th quotations); *NYDT* correspondence, quoted in *PF*, September 5, 1850 (5th and 6th quotations). See also *Baltimore Sun*, August 22, 26–29, 1850.

60. Freehling, *Road to Secession*, 503; *Richmond Enquirer*, November 30 (1st–3rd quotations), December 4 (4th quotations), 25, 1849.

61. *Richmond Enquirer*, August 27, 1850. See also *Baltimore Sun*, August 26, 1850.


CHAPTER SEVEN

1. "Report of the Anti-Slavery Convention, December 20, 1850 (concluded)," *PF*, January 9, 1851. The Bible reference is to Hebrews 9:22.

2. On changing southern views concerning state rights, see Gara, "Fugitive Slave Law," 229–40; Schwartz, *Slave Laws*, 121–22; Keller, "Extraterritoriality and the Fugitive Slave Debate," 113–14. In January 1850, a member of Kentucky's General Assembly declared, "The time for state legislative action on the issue "was speedily passing away." See *Lexington Observer*, February 6, 1850.

3. Chaplin to James C. Jackson, December 30, 1844, *AWP*, January 8, 1845 (1st quotation); *Emancipator*, February 19, 1845 (2nd quotation); *True Wesleyan*, quoted in *Eman-*

*cipator*, May 26, 1846 (3rd quotation); *PF*, October 21, 1847 (4th quotation); Fee to Louis Tappan, October 30, 1849, AMAA, New Orleans.

4. *Ray*, quoted in *Baltimore Saturday Visiter*, July 19, 1845 (1st quotation); C. J. Franklin to Calhoun, July 15, 1847, Boucher, "Correspondence to Calhoun," 386–87 (2nd–4th quotations); *Sun*, quoted in Berlin, *Slaves without Masters*, 247 (5th quotation); *Civilian*, quoted in *North American and United States Gazette*, January 21, 1850 (6th quotation); *Daily Missouri Republican*, October 22, 1850 (7th quotation). A week after the *Republican* published its lament, it claimed 18,000 slaves, worth at total of $2,000,000, had escaped to the free states since 1793. See *Republican*, October 30, 1850.

5. Freehling, *Road to Disunion*, 1:503–4 (1st, 4th, 5th, and 9th quotations); *CG*, 31st Cong., 1st sess., August 19, 1850, 1583 (2nd quotation); Preston, "Fugitive Slave Acts in Ohio," 430–31 (3rd quotation); Clay, quoted in *Anti-Slavery Bugle*, March 2, 1850 (6th quotation); *CG*, 31st Cong., 1st sess., Appendix, February 6, 1850, 123 (6th–8th quotations); *CG*, 31st Cong., 1st sess., Appendix, May 13, 1850, 571 (10th quotation).

6. Harrold, *Subversives*, 142–43; *United States Gazette*, March 2, 1849 (1st quotation); Outlaw to wife, July 29, 1850, Outlaw Papers, Southern Historical Collection, Wilson Library, University of North Carolina, Chapel Hill (2nd and 3rd quotations).

7. Freehling, *Road to Disunion*, 1:502–3 (1st quotation); *CG*, 31st Cong., 1st sess., Appendix, February 13, 1850, 150 (2nd quotation). Allen Nevins in the first volume of his multi-volume history of the Civil War era and David M. Potter in his magisterial study of antebellum sectionalism barely mention the fugitive slave issue as part of the debate over the Compromise of 1850. See Nevins, *Ordeal of the Union*, 1:341; Potter, *The Impending Crisis*, 112–13. See also Hamilton, *Prologue to Conflict*, 17. A few historians regard the Fugitive Slave Law of 1850 as key to southern acquiescence in legislation that limited slavery's prospects in the West and threatened to end the slave trade in the District of Columbia. See Morris, *Free Men All*, 131–47.

8. Potter, *Impending Crisis*, 122–30; Trexler, *Slavery in Missouri*, 185 (quotation). Border South leaders held the new Fugitive Slave Law to be a practical measure. They distrusted Lower South leaders who used it to promote disunion sentiment. See discussion of the views of the *St. Lewis Union* in *Daily Missouri Republican*, October 30, 1850.

9. *CG*, 31st Cong., 1st sess., Appendix, February 6, 1850, 122–24 (1st quotation); *CG*, 31st Cong., 1st sess., March 14, 1850, 524 (2nd quotation); *Sun*, September 16, 1850; *Enquirer*, quoted in Gara, "Fugitive Slave Law," 234 (3rd quotation); *Anti-Slavery Bugle*, February 9, 1850; *National Era*, October 24, 1850.

10. Leslie, "Pennsylvania's Fugitive Slave Law," 431, 435 (1st quotation); Brackett, *Negro in Maryland*, 88; Keller, "Extraterritoriality," 115; Fehrenbacher, *Slaveholding Republic*, 225–26; Morris, *Free Men All*, 131–45 (2nd quotation).

11. *NYDT*, August 29, 1850; Keller, "Extraterritoriality," 115–16; Preston, "Ohio Fugitive Slave Law," 430–31; Freehling, *Road to Disunion*, 1:503 (1st quotation); "Resolutions of the Legislature of Kentucky," 1–5 (2nd and 3rd quotations); Virginia, *Report of a Select Committee*, 10 (4th–7th quotations), 18–20.

12. "An Act to amend . . . the Act entitled 'An Act respecting Fugitives from Jus-

tice, and Persons escaping from the Service of their Masters,'" 462–65; *CG*, 31st Cong., 1 sess., Appendix, August 19, 1850, 1583 (quotation).

13. *Observer*, September 9, 1850 (1st and 2nd quotations); Bayly to "My Constituents," October 7, 1850, *Richmond Enquirer*, October 12, 1850 (3rd quotation); *Daily Missouri Republican*, October 19, 22, 1850; *Republic*, quoted in *LOR*, September 9, 1850 (4th quotation); IAGO to [editor], August 26, [1850], *NYDT*, August 29, 1850. Of Border South newspapers, the *Union* of St. Louis was exceptional in worrying that a too-strong Fugitive Slave Law would threaten the Union. See *Union*, quoted in *Daily Missouri Republican*, October 30, 1850.

14. *Daily Missouri Republican*, August 19, September 23, 1850; *Baltimore Sun*, September 11, 1850; *DNI*, December 9, 1850; Clay, quoted in Bugg, "Political Career of James Murray Mason," 381 (1st quotation); *LOR*, February 6 (2nd quotation), October 16 (3rd quotation), 1850; *Petersburg Intelligencer*, quoted in *DNI*, December 17, 1850 (4th quotation); *St. Louis Intelligencer*, quoted in Gara, "Underground Railroad in Illinois," 523–24; *Richmond Enquirer*, December 3, 1850 (5th quotation). E. Louis Lowe, governor of Maryland, and former Governor Thomas Metcalfe of Kentucky issued similar statements. See *DNI*, January 9, 1851; *Maysville Eagle*, quoted in *Vermont Chronicle*, April 2, 1851.

15. *Richmond Enquirer*, December 3, 1850.

16. *National Era*, May 25, 1858 (1st quotation); *Bugle*, February 9 (2nd quotation), April 13, August 10, 1850. *Western Citizen* (Chicago), October 29, 1850; *Western Citizen* (Chicago), January 21, 1851; *National Era*, January 24, October 10, 24, November 21, 1850; *National Era*, January 22, May 6, June 3, November 24, 1852; *National Era*, May 12, 1853; *PF*, June 19, 1851; *Daily Missouri Republican*, August 5, 1852; *FDP*, May 5, 1854. See also Preston, "Fugitive Slave Law in Ohio," 470–74.

17. Campbell, *Slave Catchers*, 199–201; Fehrenbacher, *Slaveholding Republic*, 233–35; *Pennsylvanian*, quoted in *Richmond Enquirer*, October 11, 1850; H. C. Wright to Garrison, November 2, 1850, *Liberator*, November 22, 1850; [?] to Gales and Seaton, November 28, 1850, *DNI*, December 7, 1850; Potter, *Impending Crisis*, 137–38. Fergus M. Bordewich contends there had been "at least sixty . . . attempted arrests in the North" by February 1851. Stanley Campbell, who is concerned with "cases" rather than arrests, lists only fifteen as having occurred during the same period. See Bordewich, *Bound for Canaan*, 323; Campbell, *Slave Catchers*, 199.

18. *CDG*, October 17, 1850 (1st–3rd quotations); *CDG*, January 9, 1851 (4th quotation); *LOR*, December 18, 1850; *Richmond Enquirer*, January 14, 1851 (5th quotation); *Liberator*, November 21, 1851; *Baltimore Sun*, January 22, 1852; *Eagle*, [October 9, 1852], quoted in *FDP*, November 19, 1852.

19. Potter, *Impending Crisis*, 90–120.

20. ION [to editors], October 14 [sic], 1850, *Sun*, October 12, 1850 (1st and 2nd quotations); *Democrat*, quoted in *Pittsburgh Saturday Visiter*, September 17, 1853 (3rd and 4th quotations).

21. *Ohio Observer*, November 3, 1852; *Mississippian*, November 5, 1852 (1st quotation);

*Maysville Eagle*, quoted in *FDP*, November 19, 1852; John G. Fee to George W. Julian, November 9, 1852, Joshua R. Giddings-George W. Julian Papers, LC, Washington, D.C.; *Eagle*, quoted in *North American and United States Gazette*, November 23, 1852 (2nd quotation); *FDP*, December 3, 1852; *Western Citizen* (Chicago), August 16, 1853; Chase speech "at a Mass Meeting in Syracuse," August 31, 1853, *FDP*, September 16, 1853 (3rd quotation); *St. Louis Intelligencer*, quoted in *Independent*, January 18, 1855 (4th quotation).

22. *Cleveland True Democrat*, quoted in *Ashtabula Sentinel*, April 5, 1851; *Pennsylvania Freeman*, quoted in *Liberator*, October 17, 1851; *Independent*, quoted in *Frederick Douglass' Paper*, June 17, 1852; [Joshua R. Giddings] to Gentlemen, February 3, 1853, *Ashtabula Sentinel*, February 10, 1853; *DNI*, February 6, 1856, December 17, 1859; *Liberator*, February 8, 1856; *Richmond Times*, quoted in *Fayetteville Observer*, February 10, 1852; *Maysville Eagle*, quoted in *Daily Cleveland Herald*, September 26, 1853; *Ripley Bee*, November 18, 1854; *Daily Cleveland Herald*, March 14, 1856; Aristides [to editors], *Pittsburgh Saturday Visiter*, March 5, 1853; telegraph report, October 1, 1850, *Anti-Slavery Bugle*, October 5, 1850.

23. *Baltimore Sun*, September 30, October 5, 1850; *New York Journal of Commerce*, quoted in *DNI*, October 1, 1850; *Richmond Enquirer*, October 1, 1850; *New York Herald*, quoted in *Richmond Enquirer*, October 2, 1850; *LOR*, October 9, 1850 (1st quotation); *Western Citizen* (Chicago), October 8, 1850 (2nd quotation); *Louisville Courier*, quoted in *FDP*, December 3, 1852. See also [Tappan], *Fugitive Slave Bill*.

24. Bordewich, *Bound for Canaan*, 323; Campbell, *Slave Catchers*, 115–16; *New Albany Ledger*, quoted in *North Star*, December 5, 1850; Money, "Fugitive Slave Law of 1850 in Indiana," 270–71; *Western Citizen* (Chicago), January 21, April 22, 1851; Salmon P. Chase, *Daily Ohio Statesman*, March 4, 1851; *Liberator*, April 4, 11, 1851; *North American and United States Gazette*, March 17, 1851; *Pittsburgh Saturday Visiter*, June 11, 1853 (1st and 2nd quotations); *True Democrat*, quoted in *Western Citizen* (Chicago), May 11, 1852 (3rd quotation). Citizens of New Albany saved the family captured there by purchasing its freedom. At Columbia, the deputy, a deputy from Harrisburg who had assisted him, and the claimant had to flee for their lives. Columbia had a large black population and had a reputation as a "rendezvous of the runaways." See *Baltimore Sun*, April 28, 1851; *Liberator*, May 7, 1852 (quotation).

25. *Ohio Observer*, September 28, 1853 (1st quotation); *New York Tribune*, quoted in *FDP*, September 30, 1853 (2nd quotation); *North American and United States Gazette*, October 6, 1853; *Carson League*, quoted in *Liberator*, November 4, 1853; *New York Tribune*, quoted in *Ripley Bee*, November 26, 1853; W. C. Gildersleeve to Judge Grier, *FDP*, December 30, 1853.

26. *Philadelphia American*, quoted in *Daily National Intelligencer*, October 30, 1850. David M. Potter, following Stanley Campbell, writes, "the picture of overwhelming defiance must be qualified. There were after all, in the first six years of the law, only three cases of forcible and successful rescue. During the same time, it is estimated that two hundred Negroes were arrested." Unless Potter refers only to "cases" that went to

court, this is an extreme understatement concerning resistance. See Potter, *Impending Crisis*, 138; Campbell, *Slave Catchers*, 167n. For a different interpretation see Fehrenbacher, *Slaveholding Republic*, 233, 235.

27. *Western Citizen*, November 5, 1850 (1st and 2nd quotations) August 16, 1853; *New York Tribune*, quoted in *FDP*, May 27, 1853; *Pittsburgh Saturday Visiter*, July 23, 1853; E. C. D. to Editor, October 17, 1852, *FDP*, December 3, 1852 (3rd and 4th quotations); *Richmond Enquirer*, November 18, 1853; Dunn, *Indiana and Indianans*, 1:506–8; *Liberator*, February 14, 1851; Preston, "Fugitive Slave Laws in Ohio," 465–66; *Baltimore Sun*, April 24, 1851; *Independent*, quoted in *FDP*, April 22, 1853; John Law to President [Franklin Pierce], March 15, 1855 and Law to Caleb Cushing, March 16, 1855, in Letters Received by the Attorney General, reel 5, Bethesda, Md. Freeman charged the marshal with assault and sued for $10,000 but lost the suit in Indiana court on the grounds that state law did not apply to U.S. officials.

28. Morris, *Free Men All*; *Richmond Enquirer*, April 3, 1851 (quotation); *Boston Daily Atlas*, April 16, 1851; *Baltimore Sun*, April 25, 1851; *Philadelphia North American*, quoted in *FDP*, January 22, 1852; Preston, "Fugitive Slave Laws in Ohio," 472–73.

29. *Commercial Journal*, quoted in Wilson, *Standard History*, 820–21 (1st quotation); *New York Herald*, quoted in *Richmond Enquirer*, October 2, 1850; *New York Tribune*, quoted in *Daily Missouri Republican*, October 12, 23, 1850; *Western Citizen* (Chicago), November 5, 1850; Middleton, "Fugitive Slave Crisis in Cincinnati," 22; *Baltimore Sun*, September 30, 1850 (2nd quotation). It seems likely that much of the increase in slave escapes claimed by southerners following the passage of the new law rested on the refugee movement. See *Daily Missouri Republican*, October 30, 1850; Winks, *Blacks in Canada*, 237. Fergus Bordewich estimates that "as many as three thousand fugitives crossed into Canada within three months of the passage of the Fugitive Slave Law." See Bordewich, *Bound for Canaan*, 324.

30. Chris Padget, "Comeouterism and Antislavery Violence in Ohio's Western Reserve," in McKivigan and Harrold, *Antislavery Violence*, 206–7; *North Star*, December 5, 1850; Benjamin Wade, quoted in Preston, "Fugitive Slave Laws in Ohio," 465–56; Robinson to Johnson, February 8, 1850, *Anti-Slavery Bugle*, February 16, 1850 (1st quotation); Preston, "Fugitive Slave Laws in Ohio," 467–68 (2nd and 3rd quotations). During the 1850s, the term "underground railroad" lost its implication of secrecy. In 1852, Jane Gray Swisshelm reported, "A gang of runaway slaves" had openly passed through her village near Pittsburgh, "accompanied by an escort of the managers." Similar reports circulated in Chicago and Cleveland. See *Pittsburgh Saturday Visiter*, January 31, 1852. See also James Evans Snodgrass to R. R. Raymond, September 27, 1852, *Liberator*, October 22, 1852; J. McBride to Editor, October 4, 1852, *Liberator*, October 29, 1852.

31. *Western Citizen* (Chicago), October 8, 1850 (1st–4th quotations); *Daily Missouri Republican*, October 9, 1850; Preston, "Fugitive Slave Laws in Ohio," 472 (5th quotation); *Philadelphia Ledger*, October 18, [1850], quoted in *New York Weekly Herald*, October 19, 1850 (6th quotation); *Liberator*, November 15, 1850 (7th quotation). African

Americans in New York and New England reacted similarly to the new law. See Horton and Horton, *In Hope of Liberty*, 253.

32. *Pennsylvania Freeman*, January 9, 1851.

33. *Ashtabula Sentinel*, October 6, 1850, quoted in Preston, "Fugitive Slave Laws in Ohio," 463 (1st quotation); *Western Citizen* (Chicago), October 22, 1850 (2nd and 3rd quotations); Gildersleeve to Grier, *FDP*, December 30, 1853 (4th quotation).

34. "Speech of Hon. J. R. Giddings, of Ohio . . . made December 9, 1850," *National Era*, December 26, 1850. See also *Ashtabula Sentinel*, September 28, 1850.

35. Henry C. Wright to Garrison, November 2, 1850, *Liberator*, November 22, 1850 (1st quotation); *DNI*, December 11, 1850 (2nd quotation); *National Era*, December 19, 1850 (3rd quotation); *Tribune*, quoted in *Daily Missouri Republican*, October 22, 1850 (4th quotation); *Western Citizen* (Chicago), September 28, 1852 (5th and 6th quotations).

36. *Anti-Slavery Bugle*, February 9, 1850 (1st quotation); *Lebanon Star*, quoted in *ASB*, August 10, 1850 (2nd–5th quotations); *North American*, quoted in *NYDT*, August 27, 1850; *Daily Missouri Republican*, August 27, 1850. See also D. H. Hise, diary entry, February 5, 1850, Hise Papers, OHS, Columbus.

37. *New York Weekly Herald*, October 19, 1850; *Baltimore Sun*, April 25, 28, 1851; *Philadelphia Gazette*, and *Philadelphia Ledger*, quoted in *Boston Daily Atlas*, June 27, 1851 (quotations); *Nashville Whig*, quoted in *FDP*, April 15, 1853. On the memory of this event, see Griffler, *Front Line of Freedom*, 111. On mobs in New England and New York, see *Emancipator*, October 10, 1850; *Cleveland Herald*, October 16, 1850; *New York Weekly Herald*, October 19, 1850; *Richmond Enquirer*, October 11, 1850.

38. [Giddings] to Mr. Sentinel, January 2, [1851], *Ashtabula Sentinel*, January 1, 1851 (1st quotation); *Lancaster Union*, quoted in *Liberator*, January 13, 1851; *North American and United States Gazette*, September 13, 1851 (2nd and 3rd quotations); Hensel, *Christiana Riot*, 18.

39. *Philadelphia Ledger*, quoted in *Boston Daily Atlas*, January 3, 1851 (1st quotation); *Cincinnati Gazette*, January 4, 1851, quoted in Middleton, "Fugitive Salve Crisis," 25; [Giddings] to Mr. Sentinel, January 16, 1851, *Ashtabula Sentinel*, February 1, 1851 (2nd quotation); *Lancaster Union*, quoted in *Liberator*, January 31, 1851 (3rd quotation); *Cleveland True Democrat*, quoted in *Ashtabula Sentinel*, April 5, 1851; *Baltimore Sun*, April 25, 1851. Later accounts, based largely on memory, mention other incidents at about the same time. See Grimsted, *American Mobbing*, 78.

40. Grimsted, *American Mobbing*, 79–80; *North American and United States Gazette*, September 13, 1851; *Baltimore Sun*, September 16, 1851; J. S. Corsuch to Editors, September 17, 1851, *Baltimore Sun*, September 18, 1851. See also *U.S. v. Hanaway* (1851), in Catterall, *Judicial Cases*, 4:301–4.

41. *New York Tribune*, quoted in *CDG*, September 18, 1851 (quotations); *North American*, quoted in *Baltimore Sun*, September 16, 1851.

42. *Baltimore Sun*, September 13, 15 (3rd quotation), 16 (1st quotation), 1851; *North American and United States Gazette*, September 13, 1851 (2nd quotation); *Lexington*

*Observer*, September 24, 1851; Lowe to Fillmore, September 15, 1851, *Baltimore Sun*, September 19, 1851 (4th quotation); *FDP*, September 25, 1851 (5th quotation).

43. *North American and United States Gazette*, September 13, 1851 (1st quotation); *National Era*, October 23, 1851 (2nd quotation); Campbell, *Slave Catchers*, 101; Slaughter, *Bloody Dawn*, 123–35.

44. *North American and United States Gazette*, January 3, 8, 1852; *New York Weekly Herald*, January 10, 1852; *Boston Daily Atlas*, January 13, 14, 15, 1852; *FDP*, February 19, 1853; *National Era*, quoted in *Pittsburgh Saturday Visiter*, January 29, 1853.

45. *Western Citizen* (Chicago), October 22, 1850 (1st–3rd quotations), June 10, 1851 (6th and 7th quotations); *Milwaukee Daily Sentinel*, June 4, 1851 (4th and 5th quotations); *Cleveland Herald*, June 10, 1851.

46. *Ohio Observer*, November 3, 1852 (1st quotation); *Mississippian*, November 5, 1852; Middleton, "Fugitive Slave Crisis," 26; *Gazette*, quoted in *FDP*, September 30, 1853 (2nd and 4th quotations); *Pittsburgh Saturday Visiter*, September 17, 1853 (3rd quotation).

47. *Cincinnati Gazette*, January 29, 1856, quoted in *National Era*, February 7, 1856; *National Era*, January 31, 1856; *Daily Cleveland Herald*, February 28, 1856; Weisenburger, *Modern Medea*; Yanuck, "Garner Fugitive Slave Case," 47–66; Bordewich, *Bound for Canaan*, 401–5; Campbell, *Slave Catchers*, 144–47.

48. Freehling, *Reinterpretation of American History*, 262–64 (1st quotation); Fehrenbacher, *Slaveholding Republic*, 246–47, 250–51 (2nd quotation); Nevins, *Ordeal of the Union*, 2:382.

49. Fehrenbacher, *Slaveholding Republic*, 245; Foner, *Free Soil, Free Labor, Free Men*, 134–37, 209–10.

CHAPTER EIGHT

1. Donald, *Sumner*, 282–308.

2. *Richmond Enquirer*, quoted in *Anti-Slavery Bugle*, February 2, 1849.

3. *Richmond Enquirer*, October 1, 1850; Etcheson, *Bleeding Kansas*, 19; Van Deusen, *Greeley*, 201–2.

4. *South-side Democrat*, May 24, 1856 (1st quotation); *Richmond Whig* (2nd and 3rd quotations), both quoted in *National Era*, June 5, 1856; *Sentinel*, quoted in *Liberator*, June 13, 1856 (4th quotation); *Courier*, February 3, 1857 (5th quotation).

5. *Petersburg Intelligencer*, quoted in *National Era*, June 6, 1856 (1st quotation); *Patriot*, quoted in *National Era*, June 19, 1856 (2nd quotation); *Louisville Journal*, May 24, 1856 (3rd quotation).

6. Boucher, "In Re: That Aggressive Slavocracy," 13–79 (1st quotation); Foner, *Free Soil, Free Labor, Free Men*, 9 (2nd quotation); May, *Southern Dream of a Caribbean Empire*, 46–76.

7. Freehling, *Road to Disunion*, 2:63–64.

8. *Whig Messenger*, December 15, 1853, quoted in Merkel, "Underground Railroad and the Missouri Borders 1840–1860," 278; Phillips, "'Crime against Missouri,'" 65–66.

9. Nevins, *Ordeal of the Union*, 2:80–87; Potter, *Impending Crisis*, 145–51. In late

1852, at least some Missourians did not believe the Missouri Compromise prevented the extension of slavery into Nebraska. See Ray, *Repeal of the Missouri Compromise*, 164–73.

10. Jackson to David R. Atchison, January 18, 1854, Atchison Papers, State Historical Society of Missouri, Columbia (1st quotation); *Republican*, quoted in *NYDT*, January 30, 1854 (2nd–4th quotations).

11. Cutler, *History of the State of Kansas*, 93 (1st quotation); Nevins, *Ordeal of the Union*, 2:92 (2nd and 3rd quotations); *CG*, 33rd Cong., 1st sess., Appendix, April 25, 1854, 559 (4th quotation).

12. Nevins, *Ordeal of the Union*, 2:92–93; Potter, *Impending Crisis*, 160; Wolff, *Kansas-Nebraska Bill*; Gienapp, *Origins of the Republican Party*, 69–78.

13. Nichols, *Bleeding Kansas*, 9 (1st quotation); *Platte Argus*, quoted by James R. Doolittle in *CG*, 35th Cong., 1st sess., March 8, 1858, 986 (2nd quotation); Atchison to Jefferson Davis, September 24, 1854, Davis Papers, Rare Book and Special Collections Library, Duke University, Durham, N.C.

14. William Walker to Atchison, July 6, 1854, Atchison Papers, State Historical Society of Missouri, Columbia (1st and 2nd quotations); *Democratic Platform*, quoted in Shoemaker, "Missouri's Proslavery Fight for Kansas," part 1: 233–34 (3rd quotation); Atchison quoted in Phillips, "Crime against Missouri," 73 (4th quotation); Nevins, *Ordeal of the Union*, 2:81; Etcheson, *Bleeding Kansas*, 11, 16.

15. Johnson, *Battle Cry of Freedom*, 181. David M. Potter writes that the Kansas-Nebraska Act "transplanted the controversy from the halls of Congress to the plains of Kansas." See Potter, *Impending Crisis*, 199. See also Charles Robinson, *The Kansas Conflict* (New York: Harper and Brothers, 1892), 6, quoted in Klem, "Missouri in the Kansas Struggle," 393.

16. Klem, "Missouri in the Kansas Struggle," 394–95 (1st quotation); Freehling, *Road to Disunion*, 2:62–67 (2nd quotation). See also Freehling, *Road to Disunion*, 1:550–51.

17. Johnson, *Battle Cry of Freedom*, 16–17; Potter, *Impending Crisis*, 199–200; Sanborn, *Brown*, 163; *FDP*, May 26, 1854.

18. Cutler, *History of the State of Kansas*, 90 (quotations); Nichols, *Bleeding Kansas*, 15; Freehling, *Road to Secession*, 2:67; Etcheson, *Bleeding Kansas*, 31–33.

19. Cutler, *History of the State of Kansas*, 91 (1st quotation); Klem, "Missouri in the Kansas Struggle," 396–98; Craik, "Southern Interest," 388; Wilson, *With the Border Ruffians*, 83–85; "Negro Stealer," *AWP*, February 7, 1844 (2nd quotation); Isely, "Sharps Rifle Episode" 553–54; Nichols, *Bleeding Kansas*, 60; Tindle, *Opothleyahola and the Loyal Muskogee*, 108.

20. *Democrat*, quoted in Cutler, *History of the State of Kansas*, 90–91 (1st quotation), 93–94 (2nd quotation); Etcheson, *Bleeding Kansas*, 31, 54. Klem, "Missouri in the Kansas Struggle," 399–400; Gienapp, *Rise of the Republican Party*, 170; Potter, *Impending Crisis*, 201; Etcheson, *Bleeding Kansas*, 54–60. Reports of election figures vary. Historians have estimated that as many as 10,000 men belonged to Missouri's secret societies. See Phillips, "Crime against Missouri," 75.

21. Klem, "Missouri in the Kansas Struggle," 403n; Isely, "Sharps Rifle Episode,"

551 (quotations) 553–61, 565. The free-staters had earlier formed the Kansas Legion, which, according to historian Nicole Etcheson, "was a combination of fraternal order . . . and free state army." See Etcheson, *Bleeding Kansas*, 56–59, 76.

22. Isely, "Sharps Rifle Episode," 554–65; Etcheson, *Bleeding Kansas*, 76–77 (1st quotation); Johnson, *Battle Cry of Freedom*, 173 (2nd quotation).

23. Etcheson, *Bleeding Kansas*, 76–77 (1st and 2nd quotations); *Lexington Weekly Express*, quoted in *New York Herald*, July 20, 1855 (3rd and 4th and 6th and 7th quotations); Johnson, *Battle Cry of Freedom*, 135 (5th quotation); Cutler, *History of Kansas*, 105–6.

24. Cutler, *History of Kansas*, 108–9 (quotations); Etcheson, *Bleeding Kansas*, 71–72.

25. Etcheson, *Bleeding Kansas*, 72–76, 80; Cutler, *History of Kansas*, 116–17 (quotation); Johnson, *Battle Cry*, 138–39.

26. Shannon to William P. Richardson and H. J. Strickler, November 27, 1855, Shannon to President of the U.S. [Franklin Pierce], November 28, 1855 (quotations), "Executive Minutes," 3:289–94; Johnson, *Battle Cry of Freedom*, 141–42; Etcheson, *Bleeding Kansas*, 82; Klem, "Missouri in the Kansas Struggle," 404–5; Isely, "Sharps Rifle Episode," 564; Mullis, *Peacekeeping on the Plains*, 161.

27. Johnson, *Battle Cry of Freedom*, 139–44 (quotations); List of Companies, November–December 1855, in Kansas State Historical Society, *Territorial Kansas Online*, Topeka; Klem, "Missouri in the Kansas Struggle," 404–5; Etcheson, *Bleeding Kansas*, 82–83; Cutler, *History of the State of Kansas*, 118–21; Reynolds, *Brown*, 146–47.

28. Cutler, *History of the State of Kansas*, 118–20; Johnson, *Battle Cry*, 141–44; Etcheson, *Bleeding Kansas*, 77, 82–88; Nichols, *Bleeding Kansas*, 60–61; Isely, "Sharps Rifle Episode," 553.

29. McPherson, *Ordeal by Fire*, 104 (1st quotation); Klem, "Missouri in the Kansas Struggle," 406–8; Craik, "Southern Interest," 359–60 (2nd and 3rd quotations); Johnson, *Battle Cry of Freedom*, 181 (4th quotation), 208–17.

30. Nichols, *Bleeding Kansas*, 105–9 (1st quotation); Etcheson, *Bleeding Kansas*, 89–91, 104–5 (2nd quotation); Johnson, *Battle Cry*, 145, 148–59.

31. Johnson, *Battle Cry*, 158–60, 181–85.

32. Johnson, *Battle Cry*, 185–97; Cutler, *History of Kansas*, 141.

33. Stubbs Militia Company Constitution, By-laws, and Charter, April 16, 1855, in Kansas State Historical Society, *Territorial Kansas Online*, Topeka; Cutler, *History of Kansas*, 141–43; Mullis, *Peacekeeping on the Plains*, 218–19; Johnson, *Battle Cry of Freedom*, 196–202; Etcheson, *Bleeding Kansas*, 122; "Executive Minutes," 4:325. On free-state immigrants 1856–1857, see Craik, "Southern Interest," 434, 443.

34. Parrish, *Atchison*, 206–9; Johnson, *Battle Cry of Freedom*, 231–34; Etcheson, *Bleeding Kansas*, 131–35, 153–55; Craik, "Southern Interest," 380–83, 433–34, 438.

35. *Reporter*, April 5, 1855, quoted in Shoemaker, "Missouri's Pro-Slavery Fight for Kansas," 331 (1st quotation); *New York Herald*, July 21, 1855 (2nd and 3rd quotations); Craik, "Southern Interest," 359–66; Baltimore, "Stringfellow," 26 (5th and 6th quota-

tions); W. H. Russell et al., to the People of the South, *DeBow's Review* 20 (May 1856): 635–37; *Democrat*, quoted in Etcheson, *Bleeding Kansas*, 121 (7th quotation).

36. Klem, "Missouri in the Kansas Struggle," 409; *Express*, quoted in Craik, "Southern Interest," 433 (1st quotation); Atchison, quoted in Parrish, *Atchison*, 208 (2nd quotation). Etcheson accepts the figure for property losses but estimates deaths at only thirty-eight. See Etcheson, *Bleeding Kansas*, 135.

37. *Missouri Democrat*, in Craik, "Southern Interest," 434 (quotations); Etcheson, *Bleeding Kansas*, 158.

38. Cutler, *History of the State of Kansas*, 105, 109; Etcheson, *Bleeding Kansas*, 55, 71–72, 75, 78, 113–14, 120, 192, 205. Craik, "Southern Interest," 363–64; Sheridan, 29–30; Abbott, "Rescue of Dr. John W. Doy," 4:312–13; Sheridan, "From Slavery in Missouri to Freedom in Kansas," 31.

39. Holloway, *Kansas*, 517–18; Etcheson, *Bleeding Kansas*, 191–97, 201–4; Reynolds, *Brown*, 278–79; Abbott, "Rescue of Dr. John W. Doy," 312–23. Reynolds reports seven raids from Kansas into Missouri before Brown's.

40. *Louisville Daily Courier*, October 6, 1856 (1st quotation); *Louisville Daily Courier*, December 21, 1857; D. R. H. to Gentlemen, February 5, 1857, *Richmond Enquirer*, February 5, 1857 (2nd quotation), December 21, 1857.

41. *Missouri Democrat* and *Kentucky News*, quoted in *Radical Abolitionist* 3 (March 1858): 57–58 and 4 (April 1858): 6–7; *National Era*, December 23, 1858; *National Era*, October 13, 20, 1859; *Wheeling Daily Intelligencer*, September 9, 10, 1856; *Newport News*, January 3, 1856; Francis P. Blair Jr. to C. W. White, September 6, 1858, *National Era*, September 30, 1858; John G. Fee to S. S. Jocelyn, July 7, 1859, AMAA, New Orleans; Brown, *Southern Outcast*, 69–90, 152–88; Freehling, *Road to Disunion*, 2:242–45. William S. Bailey changed the name of his paper to *Kentucky News* and later *Free South*. Helper's book originally appeared in June 1857. On northern financial support, see Salmon P. Chase to Gerrit Smith, September 1, 1846, Smith Papers, Syracuse University, Syracuse, N.Y.; Lewis Tappan to Gamaliel Bailey, November 6, 1848, letter book copy, Tappan Papers, LC, Washington, D.C.; Charles F. Harvey to Charles Francis Adams, January 15, 1859, Adams Papers, Massachusetts Historical Society, Boston; Hickin, "Underwood," 160.

42. On antislavery parties in the Border South, see Sewell, *Ballots for Freedom*, 314–20; Freehling, *Road to Secession*, 2:227–45; Harrold, *Abolitionists and the South*, 112, 127–28. On northern political abolitionists in the Border South, see John G. Fee to Julian, August 31, 1852, September 1852, November 9, 1852, Giddings-Julian Papers, LC, Washington, D.C.; Palmer, *Selected Letters of Charles Sumner*, 1:435n; *FDP*, June 29, 1855; Cassius M. Clay to Gerrit Smith, June 14, 1858, Smith Papers, Syracuse University, Syracuse, N.Y.; John C. Underwood to Seward, January 26, 1858, Seward Papers, University of Rochester, Rochester, N.Y. Historian Philip J. Schwarz has a copy of *Speeches of Gerrit Smith in Congress* (New York: Mason Brothers, 1855) inscribed, "Cassius M. Clay from his friend Gerrit Smith, Whitehall, June 1, 1857."

43. Fee to Clay, September 18, 1849, Fee-Clay Correspondence, Berea College, Berea, Ky.; Martin, *Antislavery Movement in Kentucky*, 130–32; Tallant, *Evil Necessity*, 159–63;

Harrison, *Antislavery Movement in Kentucky*, 66–68; Harrold, *Abolitionists and the South*, 128–29; Sewell, *Ballots for Freedom*, 318–20; Freehling, *Road to Disunion*, 2:77–78; William H. Seward to John C. Underwood, November 20, 1858, February 13, 1858, March 19, 1859, Underwood Papers, LC, Washington, D.C.; Lowe, "Republican Party in Antebellum Virginia," 261; Link, *Roots of Secession*, 202.

44. *Emancipator*, November 18, 1846 (1st quotation); Lovejoy, *Memoir of Torrey*, 68 (2nd–4th quotations). For extended discussions of the abolitionist missionaries, see Mabee, *Black Freedom*, 235–41, Harrold, *Abolitionists and the South*, 84–106, and Harrold, *Rise of Aggressive Abolitionism*, 98–101.

45. Harrold, *Abolitionists and the South*, 87–89; AFASS, *11th Annual Report* (1851), 68; AMA, *13th Annual Report* (1859), 56 (quotations).

46. Money, "Fugitive Slave Law in Indiana," 283–87 (quotation); Harrold, *Abolitionists and the South*, 120–25. After Webster left her farm, Lewis Tappan and other abolitionists tried without success to revive her free-labor project. During the late 1820s, British reformer Frances Wright's short-lived utopian community at Nashobia, Tennessee, transcended the border region and sought to prepare slaves for freedom. See *GUE*, December 3, 1825–June 10, 1826; *GUE*, July 28, 1827–April 26, 1828.

47. Abbott, "Yankee Farmers in Northern Virginia," 56–63; Hickin, "Antislavery in Virginia," 609–16; Harrold, *Abolitionists and the South*, 107–20 (1st quotation); Rice, "Eli Thayer and the Friendly Invasion of Virginia," 575–96; Smith, "Ante-Bellum Attempts of Northern Business," 190–213; Hickin, "Underwood," 156–68; Lowe, "Republican Party in Antebellum Virginia," 270; Thayer to Brown, April 17, 1857, in Sanborn, *Life and Letters of John Brown*, 383 (2nd quotation).

48. *Norfolk Herald*, quoted in *National Era*, November 18, 1847; J. H. D. to William S. Bailey, *Liberator*, May 28, 1858; *Richmond Whig*, quoted in *Louisville Examiner*, March 31, 1849.

49. *Courier*, quoted in *Lexington Observer and Reporter*, March 5, 1851 (1st quotation); Clay to Cincinnati Anti-Slavery Convention, April 15, 1852, *Liberator*, June 4, 1852 (2nd quotation); SE DE KAY to [editor], *Courier*, May 22, 1855 (3rd quotation); *South-side Democrat*, quoted in *National Era*, May 7, 1857 (4th quotation); Baltimore Merchants' Meeting, February 27, 1856, *National Era*, March 6, 1856 (5th and 6th quotations).

50. *Louisville Examiner*, July 31, August 7, 1847; AFASS, *Tenth Annual Report* (1850), 59; Mathews, *Autobiography of the Rev. E. Mathews*, 368–69; William Kendrick to S. S. Jocelyn, March 8, 1858, G. H. Pool to Jocelyn, July 5, 1859, AMAA, New Orleans; *Enquirer*, March 17, 1857 (quotations). See also Eaton, "Resistance of the South to Northern Radicalism," 277–28; Abbott, "Yankee Farmers," 62–63. Some Virginia newspapers were not so worried. See *Southern Argus*, in *Wellsburg Weekly Herald*, May 1, 1857.

51. Campbell, *Slave Catchers*, 110–47, 195–96; Gara, *Liberty Line*, 36–40, 152–59. For an early challenge to the census data from a pro-southern perspective see Ewing, *Northern Rebellion and Southern Secession*, 247–54. Harold D. Tallant maintains that assisted escapes on Kentucky's borders increased during the 1850s. See Tallant, *Evil Necessity*, 163, 254, 55n.

52. Brackett, *Negro in Maryland*, 88–90; McDonald, "Prelude," 200–1; *Cincinnati Gazette*, quoted in *FDP*, November 5, 1852; *National Era*, February 14, 1850; Correspondence of the *New York Tribune*, quoted in *PF*, September 5, 1850; *NASS*, July 31, 1851; Gara, *Liberty Line*, 18.

53. *True Wesleyan*, quoted in *Emancipator*, May 27, 1846; Kentucky: John G. Fee to Editors, *Pennsylvania Freeman*, August 8, 1850; Fee to Editors, June 26, 1850, *Anti-Slavery Bugle*, August 10, 1850. On North Carolina, see *National Era*, October 17, 1850; Harrold, *Abolitionists and the South*, 101. On Virginia, see *Baltimore Sun*, October 6, 1851; *Richmond Times*, quoted in *Daily Missouri Republican*, April 15, 1852; Hickin, "Anti-slavery in Virginia," 401. On Kentucky, see Fee to George W. Julian, November 9, 1852, Giddings-Julian Papers, LC, Washington, D.C.; Clark to S. S. Jocelyn, November 19, 1855 (quotations), Fee to Jocelyn, June 23, 1855, AMAA, New Orleans. A jury exonerated the North Carolina missionaries. Arrests of white men and women for enticing away slaves figure prominently in contemporary reports. See *North American and United States Gazette*, September 20, 1853; Fields, *Middle Ground*, 63–65; *National Era*, November 25, 1858; Schwartz, *Slave Laws*, 136–45. On black-white cooperation, see Aidt-Guy, "Persistent Maryland," 23–25; *Shelby News*, quoted in *Pennsylvania Freeman*, February 9, 1856; McDonald, "Prelude," 200–1, 250–51.

54. Still, *Underground Railroad*, 124–26; Siebert, *Underground Railroad*, 151–53; Griffler, *Front Line of Freedom*, 10–11, 80–82; Redpath, *Brown*, 229; Coffin, *Reminiscences*, 206–16; *Louisville Daily Courier*, December 16, 18, 1856; *New York Herald*, December 19, 1856; George Burroughs to [Wilber Siebert], January 16, 1896, Siebert Papers, OHS, Columbus; *National Era*, November 5, 1857; J. W. Loguen to Frederick Douglass, *FDP*, April 6, 1855; Hiram Wilson to Henry Bibb, January 1, 1853, *FDP*, February 4, 1853; Still, *Underground Railroad*, 155–58; Thomas Garrett to Eliza Wigham, October 24, 1856, December 27, 1856, March 29, 1857, Quaker Collection, Haverford College Library, Haverford, Pa.; Rossbach, *Ambivalent Conspirators*, 205–6; Griffler, *Front Line of Freedom*, 114–17. Among recent biographies of Tubman are Jean McMahon Humez, *Harriet Tubman: The Life and the Life Stories* (Madison: University of Wisconsin Press, 2003); Beverly Lowry, *Harriet Tubman: Imagining a Life* (New York: Doubleday, 2007); Milton C. Sernett, *Harriet Tubman: Myth, Memory, and History* (Durham, N.C.: Duke University Press, 2007).

55. Parker, *His Promised Land*, 74–75; Weeks, "Parker," 156–57; Dunn, *Indiana and Indianans*, 1:518–24; Still, *Underground Railroad*, 30–31, 35; Pickard, *The Kidnapped and the Ransomed*, 32–85. The family was that of Peter Still, William Still's brother.

56. Fairbank, *Fairbank*, 85–149; Fairbank to [Frederick Douglass], November 13, 1851, *FDP*, November 20, 1851; *Baltimore Sun*, September 3, 1850; Report of Investigating Committee, Portsmouth, Virginia, March 13, 1856, in Frederick S. Calhoun, ed., *Letters Received by the Attorney General 1809–1870* (Bethesda, Md.: University Publishers of America, 1995–2003), Reel 6; Grover, *Fugitive's Gibraltar*, 67–93, 238–56; Schwartz, *Slave Laws*, 143–44.

57. *Cincinnati Gazette*, May 28, [1857], quoted in *Fayetteville Observer*, June 4, 1857;

Lena Hyde, "True Story of the Underground Railroad," *Tribune* (Maysville, Ohio), September 29, 1897, Siebert Papers, Reel 9, OHS, Columbus; Prince, "Rescue Case of 1857," 293, 295 (quotations); Campbell, *Slave Catchers*, 162.

58. AASS, *Fugitive Sale Law and Its Victims*, 86–73; *New York Tribune*, quoted in *National Era*, June 11, 1857 (quotation); *Cincinnati Gazette*, quoted in *Fayetteville Observer*, June 4, 1857; Prince, "Rescue Case of 1857," 296; *Cincinnati Gazette*, quoted in *Fayetteville Observer*, June 4, 1857.

59. Matthews, *Slave Catchers*, 163–64 (1st quotation); Prince, "Rescue Case of 1857," 299–308; *New York Herald*, June 1, 1857 (2nd quotation).

60. Campbell, *Slave Catchers*, 164–65, 193–94; Chris Padget, "Comeouterism and Antislavery Violence in Ohio's Western Reserve," in McKivigan and Harrold, *Antislavery Violence*, 193–95 (quotation); Brandt, *Town that Started the Civil War*, 51–64.

61. *New York Herald*, June 1, 1857 (1st quotation); Campbell, *Slave Catchers*, 165–67; Chris Padget, "Comeouterism and Antislavery Violence in Ohio's Western Reserve," in McKivigan and Harrold, *Antislavery Violence*, 195 (2nd quotation).

62. On 1850s clashes in the region, see *Louisville Daily Courier*, May 15, 1855; *Louisville Daily Courier*, December 4, 1856. This account is based on Money, "Fugitive Slave Law in Indiana," 287–297 (quotation). For slightly different accounts, see *LOR*, October 27, 1858 and Gresham, *Gresham*, 78–91. In May 1859, a Kentucky jury convicted Wright of slave stealing. Gresham holds that Wright soon had his sentence reversed on a technicality and returned to Corydon, Indiana. More recently, Darrell E. Bigham contends that Wright remained in a Kentucky prison for five years. See Bigham, *On Jordon's Banks*, 46–47.

63. *DNI*, May 12, 1859 (1st, 3rd, and 5th quotations); *Daily Cleveland Herald*, May 4, 1859 (2nd quotation); Campbell, *Slave Catchers*, 134–35; Henry C. Brown to Cousin Clara, May 5, 1859, typed copy, Siebert Papers, reel 9, OHS, Columbus; *Newark Advocate*, May 11, 1859 (4th quotation).

64. *Richmond Enquirer*, September 3, 1850; *Shelby News*, quoted in *PF*, February 9, 1856; *Enquirer*, quoted in *Louisville Daily Courier*, June 16, 1857; William Kendrick to S. S. Jocelyn, March 8, 1858, AMAA, New Orleans.

CHAPTER NINE

1. Oates, *To Purge This Land with Blood*, 290–306; Reynolds, *Brown*, 288–333 (290 quotation).

2. Henry Winter Davis, quoted in *National Era*, March 1, 1860; *Richmond Enquirer*, November 30, 1860.

3. "Speech of Governor Wise at Richmond," *New York Herald*, October 26, 1859; "Governor's Message to the Legislature of Virginia," *Richmond Enquirer*, December 6, 1859 (quotations); Shanks, *Secession Movement*, 95–96.

4. Wyatt-Brown, *Southern Honor*, 402–34; Giddings, *Speeches in Congress*, 484–85; *Liberator*, April 4, 1856 (quotation).

5. *Louisville Daily Courier*, September 17, December 8, 16, 29, 1856; *Cleveland Daily*

*Herald*, December 10, 1856; *Wellsburg Weekly Herald*, December 19, 1856; *Louisville Journal* and *Nashville Gazette*, quoted in *Milwaukee Sentinel*, December 23, 1856; *National Anti-Slavery Standard*, January 3, 7, 1857; Dew, "Black Ironworkers," 321–38; Wish, "Slave Insurrection Panic of 1856," 206–22.

6. *Nashville Union*, quoted in *Louisville Daily Courier*, December 16, 1856; *New York Herald*, December 22, 1856; Ruffin, *Diary*, 1:19–20; *Louisville Courier*, quoted in *New York Weekly Herald*, January 3, 1857; Barney, *Secession Impulse*, 163–88; *Democrat*, quoted in *Daily Cleveland Herald*, December 10, 1856; *Wellsburg Weekly Herald*, December 19, 1856 (1st quotation); *Newport News*, quoted in *NASS*, January 3, 1857 (2nd quotation).

7. Nye, *Fettered Freedom*, 182, 187–88; Eaton, "Mob Violence," 363–64; *New York Daily Tribune*, August 13, 1850 (quotation); Hickin, "Antislavery in Virginia," 2:401–2; AFASS, *Thirteenth Annual Report* (1853), 146–47; *Richmond Times*, quoted in *Daily Missouri Republican*, April 15, 1852; Jesse McBride to Mr. Editor, June 11, 1852, *Liberator*, July 23, 1852; *North American and United States Gazette*, November 23, 1852; *Cleveland Herald*, November 30, 1852 (1st quotation); *St. Louis Republican*, quoted in *Richmond Enquirer*, November 25, 1853; Schwartz, *Slave Laws*, 140–41 (2nd quotation); Berlin, *Slaves without Masters*, 360–64, 371–74. Accounts of the Grayson County committee's activities vary.

8. *Louisville Daily Courier*, December 8, 16, 29, 1856; Ruffin, *Diary*, 1:18–19 (1st quotation); *Cleveland Daily Herald*, December 10, 1856 (2nd and 3rd quotations); *Louisville Journal*, quoted in *Milwaukee Sentinel*, December 23, 1856; *New York Weekly Herald*, January 3, 1857.

9. ALBEMARLE [to editors], January 22, 1857, *Richmond Enquirer*, February 10, 1857.

10. Harrold, *Abolitionists and the South*, 88, 101–2; Smiley, *Clay*, 154; Harrold, "Violence and Nonviolence in Kentucky Abolitionism," 15–38; Sears, *Day of Small Things*, 1–54; Fee to Clay, June 31, 1849, in Clay, *Life*, 373–75; Fee to S. S. Jocelyn, September 4, 1853, July 29, 1857, August 1857; Peter H. West to George Whipple, December 25, 1853, Francis Hawley to Jocelyn, September 29, 1854, J. B. Mallet to Jocelyn, December 6, 1857, Fee, "Free Speech and Free Churches in Kentucky," unpublished manuscript, September [1855], AMAA, New Orleans.

11. Fee to A. G. W. Parker, August 15, 1853, in R. G. Williams to Editors, August 27, 1853 (clipping), Fee to George Whipple, August 26, 1853, AMAA, New Orleans; Clay, "To the People of Kentucky," *Liberator*, September 30, 1853 (1st quotation); Clay to Garrison, November 21, 1853, *Liberator*, December 9, 1853 (2nd quotation).

12. Clay to Chase, June 4, 1855, Chase Papers, HSP, Philadelphia (quotation); Correspondence of the *New York Tribune*, August 20, [1855], *FDP*, October 5, 1855.

13. W. H. Kirtley to Col. Johnson, July 2, 1855, *Anti-Slavery Bugle*, July 28, 1855 (1st quotation); Fee, *Mt. Vernon Resolutions vs. Free Speech*, broadside, July 18, 1855, AMAA, New Orleans (2nd quotation); Fee to S. S. Jocelyn, July 15 1857, AMAA, New Orleans (3rd quotation).

14. Fee to S. S. Jocelyn, March 24, (1st and 3rd quotations), June 7, 1855, July 15, 1857 (2nd quotation), AMAA, New Orleans; Sears, *Day of Small Things*, 38–39; Clay to M. Burton, March 29, 1855, Fee-Clay Correspondence, Berea College, Berea, Ky.; Clay,

*Life*, 75–76 (4th quotation); Clay to Salmon P. Chase, July 5, 1855, Chase Papers, HSP, Philadelphia (5th quotation).

15. Fee to S. S. Jocelyn, June 7, 1855, AMAA, New Orleans (1st and 3rd quotations); AMA, *Ninth Annual Report* (1855), 76–77 (2nd, 8th, and 9th quotations); *Liberator*, August 3, 1856; Clay to Salmon P. Chase, June 4, 1855, Chase Papers, HSP, Philadelphia; Correspondence of the *New York Tribune*, August 20, [1855], *FDP*, October 5, 1855 (4th–6th quotations).

16. Fee, *Mt. Vernon Resolutions vs. Free Speech* (1st quotation), AMAA, New Orleans; Clay to Editors of the *Cincinnati Gazette*, quoted in *Anti-Slavery Bugle*, July 28, 1855 (2nd quotation); Clay, *Life*, 76–77; *Kentucky News*, quoted in *Anti-Slavery Bugle*, August 1, 1855; *Bangor Daily Whig and Courier*, August 11, 1855 (3rd quotation); Fee to S. S. Jocelyn, August 3, 1855, AMAA, New Orleans (4th quotation); *CDG*, quoted in *Daily Scioto Gazette*, July 26, 1855 (5th quotation).

17. [Fee to Lewis Tappan], September [1855], Fee to S. S. Jocelyn, July 16, 1856, James Scott Davis to Jocelyn, July 29, 1856, all located in AMAA, New Orleans; *NASS*, November 17, 1855; Tappan to Fee, February 29, 1856, letter-book copy, Tappan Papers, LC, Washington, D.C.; Fee to William Goodell, January 10, 1856, *Radical Abolitionist* 1 (March 1856): 57; Fee to Clay, April 18, 1856, Fee-Clay Correspondence, Berea College, Berea, Ky.; Fee to Clay, May 10, 1856, Fee Papers, Berea College, Berea, Ky.; Clay to G. W. Brown, February 12, 1856, *Liberator*, April 18, 1856; Fee, *Autobiography*, 102–5.

18. Fee to Clay, September 1, November 26, 1856, July 28, 1857, Fee-Clay Correspondence, Berea College, Berea, Ky.; Sears, *Day of Small Things*, 39, 43; Clark to S. S. Jocelyn, November 19, 1855 (2nd quotation), Fee to Jocelyn, July 28, August 14, 1857 (1st quotation), J. M. McLean to Jocelyn, August 13, 1857, James S. Davis to Jocelyn, May 2, 1858, AMAA, New Orleans; McLean to Editor (from *Free Presbyterian*), *Liberator*, August 14, 1857; Fee to Clay, August 27, 1857, Fee Papers, Berea College Berea, Ky.; James S. Davis to Clay, October 2, 1857, in Clay, *Life*, 237; Fee to Gerrit Smith, April 12, 1858, Smith Papers, Syracuse University, Syracuse, N.Y.; Mabee, *Black Freedom*, 237.

19. Fee to Jocelyn, July 29, August, September 16 (1st and 2nd quotations), 1857, J. B. Mallet to Jocelyn, December 6, 1857, Otis B. Waters to Jocelyn, January 19, 1858, Richardson to Jocelyn, March 31–April 24, [1858], J. S. Davis to Jocelyn, June 6, 1859, Fee to Jocelyn, July 7, 1859, Richardson to Jocelyn, September 30, 1859 (3rd quotation), all located in AMAA, New Orleans; AMA, *Eleventh Annual Report* (1857), 63; *CDG*, quoted in *NASS*, September 5, 1857.

20. *Richmond Enquirer*, December 6, 1850 (quotation); *Boston Daily Advertiser*, November 23, 1859; *National Era*, February 2, March 8, 1860; Etcheson, *Bleeding Kansas*, 190, 211–12; Reynolds, *Brown*, 237, 244–45, 266.

21. Griffler, *Front Line of Freedom*, 122–23; Boyer, *Brown*, 87, 351–52; Reynolds, *Brown*, 103–4.

22. Stauffer, *Black Hearts of Men*, 168–72; "Annual Meeting of the Massachusetts Anti-Slavery Society," January 27–28, 1859, *Liberator*, February 4, 1859 (quotations); Dillon, *Slavery Attacked*, 234–37.

23. Rossbach, *Ambivalent Conspirators*, 1982 (1st quotation); Smith, circular letter,

*National Era*, September 15, 1859 (2nd–4th quotations); Smith to Editor, September 19, 1859, *National Era*, September 29, 1859 (5th quotation); Channing, *Crisis of Fear*, 19.

24. *Free South*, quoted in *Anti-Slavery Bugle*, October 29, 1859.

25. Garrison, *New "Reign of Terror,"* (1st quotation); Mabee, *Black Freedom*, 240–41; Eaton, "Mob Violence," 336–67; *National Era*, January 5, 19, 1860; Dillon, *Slavery Attacked*, 238–41; Potter, *Impending Crisis*, 478–79; Barney, *Secession Impulse*, 165–66; Grimsted, *American Mobbing*, 127–28; *Wellsburg Weekly Herald*, November 25, 1859; Wise to Chase, November 25, 1859, and Chase to Wise, December 1, 1859, quoted in *Liberator*, December 30, 1859 (2nd and 3rd quotations); Link, *Roots of Secession*, 180–82; Oates, *To Purge this Land with Blood*, 320–24; Shanks, *Secession in Virginia*, 90–92.

26. "Governor Wise's Message to the Legislature of Virginia," *Richmond Enquirer*, December 6, 1859 (1st and 2nd quotations); *New York Herald*, December 1, 1859; Wise, "Thayer," 594; Hickin, "Underwood," 164; *National Era*, January 19, 1860; *New York Herald*, December 1, 1859 (3rd quotation); Link, *Roots of Secession*, 180–85; Tyler, *Letters and Times of the Tylers*, 2:555 (4th quotation); *Richmond Enquirer*, November 30, 1860 (5th quotation); Shanks, *Secession Movement*, 89–96; Letcher to Jas. S. Brisbane, November 19, 1860, *Enquirer*, November 23, 1860 (6th quotation).

27. Evitts, *A Matter of Allegiance*, 126–27; Brackett, *Negro in Maryland*, 97–98; *Daily Mississippian*, December 13, 1859 (2nd and 3rd quotations); *New York Herald*, December 1, 1859.

28. *Cincinnati Commercial*, quoted in *Anti-Slavery Bugle*, November 5, 1859; X to Editor, *NASS*, November 12, 1859; *Louisville Courier*, quoted in *New York Herald*, December 1, 1859; Bailey to Fellow-Citizens of Kentucky, *Liberator*, January 27, 1860; Sears, *Day of Small Things*, 272–74 (quotation), 277–88; Mrs. M. H. Fee to Jocelyn, November 29, 1859, J. S. Davis to Jocelyn, December 11, 1859, both located in AMAA, New Orleans; *Cincinnati Gazette*, quoted in *Anti-Slavery Bugle*, January 14, 1860; William Kendrick to [Jocelyn], December 13, 1859, [Candee to Jocelyn], December 26, 1859, both in AMAA, New Orleans; AMA, *Fourteenth Annual Report* (1860), 49–55. When Fee attempted to resettle in Bracken County, Kentucky, he claimed 800–1,000 men gathered to drive him out. See Fee to Jocelyn, January 25, 1860, AMAA, New Orleans.

29. Coleman, *Slavery Times*, 112–13; Sears, *Day of Small Things*, 321–35; Clay to Jocelyn, December 17, 1859, Fee to Jocelyn, January 16, 1860, both located in AMAA, New Orleans; [David Preston to J. S. Rogers, March 27, 1860, George Candee to Jocelyn], June 9, July 4, 17, 1860, AMAA, New Orleans; *NASS*, April 7, 14, 1860; Clay, *Life*, 236–49, 355; Clay to [?], *NASS*, April 7, 1860; *Anti-Slavery Bugle*, April 14, 1860 (quotation).

30. *Warsaw Dispatch*, quoted in *New York Herald*, December 30, 1859; *Daily Missouri Republican*, December 5, 6, 7, 27, 1860; Neely, *Border between Them*, 91–95; Phillips, "Crime against Missouri," 80; Montgomery to George L. Stearns, November 27, December 12, 14, 1860; Montgomery to F. B. Sanborn, January 14, 1861, in Kansas State Historical Society, *Territorial Kansas Online*, Topeka.

31. Kennedy, "The Border States: Their Power and Duty in the Present Disordered Condition of the Country," in Wakelyn, *Southern Pamphlets on Secession*, 242–43 (1st

quotation); *Richmond Enquirer*, December 6, 1859 (2nd quotation); *CG*, 36th Cong., 2nd sess., January 14, 1861, 356 (3rd quotation).

32. *Louisville* Daily *Courier*, July 9, 11, 14, 16, 1856; Dillon, *Abolitionists*, 235–36; Dillon, *Slavery Attacked*, 241; ION [to Editors], October 14, 1850, in *Baltimore Sun*, October 12, 1850; *Richmond Enquirer*, October 18, 1850; *Baltimore Sun*, September 19, 1851; [Shannon], *An Address Delivered before the Pro-Slavery Convention*, 32 (quotation).

33. Dillon, *Slavery Attacked*, 241; Harrold, *Abolitionists and the South*, 22, 152–61; *Charleston Mercury*, quoted in Dumond, *Southern Editorials on Secession*, 50–55; Reynolds, *Brown*, 422–26, 439. William W. Freehling contends that slave escapes, by weakening slavery in the Border South, contributed to secession in the Lower South. See Freehling, *South Versus the South*, 26–27, 32, 37–38; Freehling, *Road to Disunion*, 2:67–68, 532–33. Steven Deyle argues that sales south—the mirror image of northward escapes—from the Border South helped push the Lower South toward secession. See Deyle, *Carry Me Back*, 84–93.

34. *Charleston Mercury*, October 4, 1856 (1st quotation); *Delta*, quoted in Rice, "Thayer," ch. 21, 6–7 (2nd quotation); *New Orleans Crescent*, quoted in Deyle, *Carry Me Back*, 91 (3rd quotation).

35. Deyle, *Carry Me* Back, 86; *Charleston Mercury*, October 11, 1860 (1st quotation); *New York Herald*, quoted in *Charleston Mercury*, September 8, 1860 (2nd quotation). In 1857 the *Mercury* contended even Virginia was unreliable and, therefore, there had to be a cotton South confederacy. See *Southside Democrat*, quoted in *National Era*, May 7, 1857.

36. Freehling, *Road to Disunion*, 2:369, 451, 530–31; Dumond, *Secession Movement*, 117n Crafts, *Reluctant Confederates*, 154; Holt, *Political Crisis*, 223–25; Foner, *Free Soil, Free Labor, Free Men*, 313–16; Reynolds, *Brown*, 426, 439.

37. Dew, *Apostles of Disunion*, 18, 64–66.

38. Holt, *Political Crisis*, 228.

39. *Richmond Enquirer*, quoted in *Wellsburg Weekly Herald*, October 17, 1856; *Enquirer*, January 2, 1857 (quotations). See also Ryle, *Missouri*, 208–10.

40. Shanks, *Secessionist Movement*, 93, 96 (1st quotation), 100–1; *Richmond Enquirer*, November 30 (2nd quotation), December 25 (3rd–5th quotations), 1860.

41. Ryle, *Missouri*, 179–80 (1st quotation); *Daily Missouri Republican*, January 14, 1861 (2nd and 3rd quotations); *New York Herald*, April 8, 1861 (4th quotation).

42. *Richmond Enquirer*, February 22, 1861.

43. SENEX, *Richmond Enquirer*, January 2, 1857 (1st and 2nd quotations); Crofts, *Reluctant Confederates*, 109–11; Shanks, *Secessionist Movement*, 131; Ayers, *In the Presence of Mine Enemies*, 99–100; *Daily Register*, April 3, 1861 (3rd–5th quotations).

44. *Commonwealth*, October 28, 1859 (1st quotation); *New York Herald*, December 22, 1859 (2nd quotation); J. R., "The Wrong and the Remedy," *Richmond Enquirer*, December 6, 1859 (3rd quotation); St. Louis Correspondence, February 1, 1860, *Herald*, February 19, 1860 (4th and 5th quotation); Blockersville, Cumberland County, Maryland, Resolutions, November 29, 1860, *Fayetteville Observer*, December 3, 1860 (6th quotation).

45. *National Era*, February 16, 1860 (1st and 2nd quotations); *Daily Evening Bulletin*, December 18, 1860 (3rd quotation).

46. *DNI*, December 31, 1860.

47. *Missouri Statesman*, quoted in Ryle, *Missouri*, 171–72 (1st quotation); *Richmond Enquirer*, November 17, 1860 (2nd quotation); Ryle, *Missouri*, 178–79 (3rd–5th quotations); *Daily Missouri Republican*, January 13, 1861 (6th and 7th quotations).

48. *Missouri Statesman*, November 23, 1860, quoted in Ryle, *Missouri*, 171–72 (1st quotation); *Statesman*, quoted in *Daily Evening Bulletin*, December 18, 1860 (2nd and 3rd quotations); *Daily Register*, April 3, 1861 (4th quotation); *Richmond Enquirer*, January 1, 1861 (5th quotation).

49. Kendall to Orr, September 10, 1860, *DNI*, September 26, 1860.

50. Hancock, "Civil War Comes to Delaware," 29–46; *Baltimore Exchange*, quoted in *DNI*, November 9, 1860.

51. Gunderson, *Old Gentlemen's Convention*, (1st quotation); Nevins, *Emergence of Lincoln*, 2:397–402; Link, *Roots of Secession*, 228–39; Crofts, *Reluctant Confederates*, 160; Shanks, *Secession Movement*, 137–38, 211; *Daily Register*, April 3, 1861 (2nd quotation). Out of Virginia's slave population of about 500,000 in 1860, only about 8,000 lived in the northwestern portion of the state. See Link, *Roots of Secession*, 238.

52. William H. Collins, quoted in *Bangor Whig*, January 18, 1861 (1st quotation); A[nthony] Kennedy, "The Position of Maryland," *New York Herald*, February 7, 1861; Henry Winter Davis, quoted in *Daily Evening Bulletin*, January 29, 1861; Evitts, *Matter of Allegiance*, 155–72 (2nd quotation 172).

53. *Louisville Daily Courier*, July 9, 11, 14, September 16, 1856; Magoffin to S. F. Hale, December 27, 1860; *Daily Missouri Republican*, January 6, 1861 (quotation); Harrison and Klotter, *New History of Kentucky*, 186–88, 190.

54. Ryle, *Missouri*, 169–72, 181–93, 208–10; LINN to Editor Republican, November 30, 1860, *Daily Missouri Republican*, December 6, 1860 (quotation); *Daily Missouri Republican*, December 6, 7, 8, 27, 1860; Harvey, "Missouri," 36–37.

55. *Wellsburg Weekly Herald*, November 25, 1859; *Richmond Whig*, quoted in Evitts, *Maryland*, 157 (1st quotation); Shanks, *Secession Movement in Virginia*, 114–15, 122 (2nd quotation); Ryle, *Missouri*, 185–86; *Richmond Enquirer*, January 25, February 8, 1861; *DNI*, December 31, 1860; Harrison and Klotter, *New History of Kentucky*, 187; "Message of Governor Stewart," *Milwaukee Daily Sentinel*, January 4, 1861; *Richmond Whig*, quoted in *Fayetteville Observer*, February 14, 1861 (3rd quotation).

56. Shanks, *Secession Movement*, 125; *DNI*, January 3, 1861; Evitts, *Maryland*, 162–63 (quotation); Denton, *Southern Star for Maryland*, 67–68; *Herald*, January 1, 1861.

57. *Boston Daily Atlas*, January 8, 1861; *Richmond Enquirer*, February 12, 1861 (quotation).

58. Shanks, *Secession Movement*, 198–204.

59. Denton, *Southern Star for Maryland*, 55–165 (quotation 69–70); Brown, *Baltimore and the Nineteenth of April, 1861*, 48–59; Manakee, *Maryland in the Civil War*, 24–59; *New York Herald*, April 22, 23, May 4, 17, 1861; Nevins, *War for the Union*, 1:77–89.

60. *Boston Daily Atlas*, January 8, 1861; C. Stuart McGehee, "The Tarnished Thirty-

Fifth State," in Davis and Robertson, *Virginia at War: 1861,* 149; Curry, *A House Divided,* 77; Kenneth N. Noe, "Exterminating Savages," in Noe and Wilson, *Civil War in Appalachia,* 104–30; O'Brien, *Guerrilla Warfare in the Southern Appalachians.*

61. Ryle, *Missouri,* 211–13, 229–31; Lyon, "Claiborne Fox Jackson and the Secession Crisis in Missouri," 422–41; Phillips, *Damned Yankee,* 212–14; Harvey, "Missouri from 1849 to 1861," 39–40; Neely, *Border between Them,* 101–31.

62. Harrison and Klotter, *New History of Kentucky,* 187–91 (quotation); Harrison, *Civil War in Kentucky,* 14–32.

63. Dillon, *Slavery Attacked,* 248; Freehling, *Reintegration of American History,* 265–66; Freehling, *Road to Disunion,* 2: 63–64 Hall, *Appalachian Ohio in the Civil War,* 178–9; Foner, *Reconstruction,* 42; Harrold, *Subversives,* 239. On the significance of slave escapes in causing the Civil War, see also Starr, "Secession Speeches," 135–36; Fehrenbacher, *Slaveholding Republic,* 246–47; Ashworth, *Slavery, Capitalism, and Politics,* 496.

64. *Alexandria Gazette,* quoted in *DNI,* April 12, 1861; *Cumberland Civilian,* quoted in *Virginia Free Press,* April 18, 1861; *Daily Missouri Republican,* March 8, 1861; Hubbart, *Older Middle West,* 146–71; Lincoln and Seward, quoted in McPherson, *Struggle for Equality,* 56 (quotations); *Liberator,* May 10, 1861.

65. *Daily Cleveland Herald,* April 9, 1861; *New York Herald,* April 9, 1861; *Boston Investigator,* May 1, 1861; McPherson, *Struggle for Equality,* 69–73; McPherson, *Ordeal by Fire,* 290 (1st quotation); Commager, *Blue and Grey,* 1:556 (quotation).

CONCLUSION

1. McPherson, *Ordeal by Fire,* 350; Brown, *Retreat from Gettysburg,* 12–33; Ayers, *In the Presence of Mine Enemies,* 400; *Richmond Enquirer,* quoted in *Liberator,* October 11, 1850 (quotations).

2. David G. Smith, "Race and Retaliation: The Capture of African Americans during the Gettysburg Campaign," in Wallenstein and Wyatt-Brown, *Virginia's Civil War,* 137–43 (quotations); Saple, *Writing and Fighting the Confederate War,* 158.

3. Smith, "Race and Retaliation," 137–39, 144–46; Alexander, "A Regular Slave Hunt," 87–88; Coddington, *Gettysburg Campaign,* 150; Brown, *Retreat from Gettysburg,* 31–32. See also the testimony of Major Charles Blacknall of North Carolina and Colonel William Christian of Virginia, quoted in Brown, *Retreat from Gettysburg,* 32. Brown is much less certain than Smith concerning where the captives ended up.

4. Mohr, *Cormany Diaries,* 329–30 (quotation); Alexander, "Regular Slave Hunt," 86–87.

5. Freehling, *South vs. the South,* 14–20, 25–29, 201–2.

6. Essah, *House Divided;* Howard, *Black Liberation in Kentucky,* 5–28; Townshend, *Lincoln and the Bluegrass,* 322–23; Harrison, *Civil War in Kentucky,* 87–94; Foner, *Reconstruction,* 37.

7. Richard O. Curry, "Crisis Politics in West Virginia 1861–1870," in Curry, *Radicalism, Racism, and Party Realignment,* 80–92; Wagandt, *Mighty Revolution,* 210–11, 246–63; Foner, *Reconstruction,* 41–42; Peterson, *Freedom and Franchise,* 106–16, 121–34; Barclay, *Liberal Republican Movement in Missouri,* 5–7.

# BIBLIOGRAPHY

MANUSCRIPT COLLECTIONS

Albany, New York
  New York Historical Society
    Alvan Stewart Papers
Baton Rouge, Louisiana
  Hill Memorial Library, Louisiana State University
    Joseph Watson Correspondence
Bethesda, Maryland
  University Publications of America
    Letters Received by the Attorney General, 1809–1870
Berea, Kentucky
  Berea College Archives
    John G. Fee–Cassius M. Clay Correspondence
    John G. Fee Papers
Boston, Massachusetts
  Massachusetts Historical Society
    Charles Francis Adams Papers
Chapel Hill, North Carolina
  Southern Historical Collection, Wilson Library, University of North Carolina
    David Outlaw Papers
Columbia, Missouri
  State Historical Society of Missouri
    David R. Atchison Papers
Columbus, Ohio
  Ohio Historical Society
    Daniel H. Hise Diaries
    Wilbur H. Siebert Papers
Durham, North Carolina
  Rare Book and Special Collections Library, Duke University
    Jefferson Davis Papers

Haverford, Pennsylvania
  Haverford College Library
    Quaker Collection
New Orleans, Louisiana
  Amistad Research Center, Tulane University
    American Missionary Association Archives
Philadelphia, Pennsylvania
  Historical Society of Pennsylvania
    Salmon P. Chase Papers
    Simon Gratz Autograph Collection
    Pennsylvania Abolition Society Papers
    Jacob C. White Sr. "Minute Book of the Vigilant Committee of Pennsylvania."
Providence, Rhode Island
  Brown University Library
    Eli Thayer Papers
Richmond, Virginia
  Library of Virginia
    Governor James Pleasants Executive Papers 1822–1825
Rochester, New York
  University of Rochester
    William H. Seward Papers
Syracuse, New York
  Syracuse University Library
    Gerrit Smith Papers
Topeka, Kansas
  Kansas State Historical Society, Territorial Kansas Online 1854–1861
    Stubbs Militia Company Constitution, By-laws, and Charter, April 16, 1855
Washington, D.C.
  Library of Congress
    Salmon P. Chase Papers
    Joshua R. Giddings-George W. Julian Papers
    Myrtilla Miner Papers
    Lewis Tappan Papers
    John C. Underwood Papers


### PUBLISHED DOCUMENTS, LETTERS, AND PAPERS

Abel, Annie H., and Frank J. Klingberg, eds. *A Side-Light on Anglo-American Relations 1839–1850*. Lancaster, Pa.: Association for the Study of Negro Life and History, 1927.

American and Foreign Anti-Slavery Society. *Annual Reports*. New York: AFASS, 1849–1853.

American Convention for Promoting the Abolition of Slavery. *Minutes of the Proceedings of the Seventh Convention.* Philadelphia: American Convention, 1801.

———. *Minutes of the Proceedings of the Eleventh Convention.* Philadelphia: American Convention, 1806.

———. *Minutes of the Proceedings of the Thirteenth Convention.* Philadelphia: American Convention, 1812.

———. *Minutes of the Proceeding of the Fourteenth Convention.* Philadelphia: American Convention, 1816.

———. *Minutes of the Proceedings of the Fifteenth Convention.* Philadelphia: American Convention, 1818.

"An Act to amend . . . the Act entitled 'An Act respecting Fugitives from Justice and Persons escaping from the Service of their Masters." *Statutes at Large of the United States of America* 9 (1862).

American Missionary Association. *Annual Reports.* New York: AMA, 1857–1860.

*Annals of Congress.* 1821–1822.

Boucher, Chauncey S., ed. "Correspondence Addressed to John C. Calhoun 1837–1849." 2 vols. *Annual Report of the American Historical Association for the Year 1929.* Washington, D.C.: Government Printing Office, 1930.

Catterall, Helen T. ed. *Judicial Cases Concerning American Slavery and the Negro.* 5 vols. Washington, D.C.: Carnegie Institute of Washington, 1926–1937.

Clay, Cassius Marcellus. *The Writings of Cassius Marcellus Clay.* Edited by Horace Greeley. 1849. Reprint, New York: Negro Universities Press, 1969.

Commager, Henry Steele, ed. *The Blue and the Gray: The Story of the Civil War as Told by Participants.* 2 vols. Revised and abridged edition. New York: Mentor, 1973.

*Congressional Globe.* 1833–1861.

Cralle, Richard K., ed. *The Works of John C. Calhoun.* 6 vols. New York: Appleton, 1874–1888.

"Executive Minutes Recorded in the Governor's Office during the Administration of Governor Wilson Shannon." In *Kansas Historical Collections.* 17 vols. Topeka: Kansas State Historical Society, 1875–1910.

Dumond, Dwight L., ed. *The Letters of James G. Birney.* 2 vols. New York: Appleton-Century, 1938.

———, ed. *Southern Editorials on Secession.* New York: Century, 1931.

Eaton, Clement. "Minutes and Resolutions of an Emancipation Meeting in Kentucky 1894." *Journal of Southern History* 14 (November 1948): 541–45.

Fitzpatrick, John C., ed. *The Writings of George Washington from the Original Manuscript Sources 1745–1799.* 39 vols. Washington, D.C.: Government Printing Office, 1931–1944.

Giddings, Joshua R. *Speeches in Congress.* 1853. Reprint, New York: Negro Universities Press, 1964.

Goodell, John, ed. *Diary of William Sewall 1797–1846.* Beardstown, Ill.: privately printed, 1930.

Kansas State Historical Society. *Territorial Kansas Online 1854–1861.* http://www
.territorialkansasonline.org (accessed February 20, 2010).

Mallory, Daniel, ed. *Life and Speeches of Henry Clay.* 2 vols. New York: Robert P. Bixby,
1844.

Marshall, Thomas F. *Speeches and Writings of Hon. Thomas F. Marshall.* Edited by W. L.
Barre. Cincinnati: Applegate, 1858.

Maryland. *Annual Message of the Executive to the General Assembly of Maryland, December
Session 1845.* Annapolis: State of Maryland, 1845.

———. *Session Laws, 1820–1821.* In *Archives of Maryland Online.* Annapolis: Maryland
State Archives, 2004. http://aomol.net (accessed February 20, 2010).

———. *Votes and Proceedings of the House of Delegates of the State of Maryland 1796–1816.*
In *Archives of Maryland Online.* Annapolis: Maryland State Archives, 2004. http://
aomol.net (accessed February 20, 2010).

Massachusetts Anti-Slavery Society. *Annual Reports.* Boston: MASS, 1843 and 1848.

McLean, John. *Reports of Cases Argued and Decided in the Circuit Court of the United
States for the Seventh Circuit.* 6 vols. Cincinnati: various publishers, 1850–1856.

Merrill, Walter M., and Louis Ruchames, eds. *The Letters of William Lloyd Garrison.*
6 vols. Cambridge, Mass.: Harvard University Press, 1971–1981.

Middleton, Stephen. *The Black Laws in the Old Northwest: A Documentary History.*
New York: Greenwood, 1992.

Mohr, James, ed. *The Cormany Diaries: A Northern Family during the Civil War.*
Pittsburgh: University of Pittsburgh Press, 1982.

New England Anti-Slavery Society. *Third Annual Report.* Boston: NEASS, 1835.

Ohio. *Executive Documents,* 37 G.A. (1838–1839), no. 37; 38 G.A. (1839–1840), no. 8;
39 G.A. (1840–1841), no. 25.

———. *Journal of the House of Representatives.* 37–41 G.A. (1838–1843).

———. *Journal of the Senate of Ohio.* 37–41 G.A. (1838–1843).

Palmer, Beverly Wilson, ed. *The Selected Letters of Charles Sumner.* 2 vols. Boston:
Northeastern University Press, 1990.

Palmer, William P., and Sherman McRae, eds. *Calendar of Virginia State Papers and
Other Manuscripts.* 11 vols. 1875. Reprint, New York: Kraus Reprints, 1968.

Parker, John P. *His Promised Land: The Autobiography of John P. Parker, Former Slave and
Conductor on the Underground Railroad.* Edited by Stuart Seely Sprague. New York:
Norton, 1996.

Pennsylvania. *Pennsylvania Archives.* 119 vols. Philadelphia and other locations:
Pennsylvania, 1852–1935.

Reed, George Edward, ed. *Pennsylvania Archives, Fourth Series.* 12 vols. Harrisburg:
Commonwealth of Pennsylvania, 1900.

"Resolutions of the Legislature of Kentucky." *U.S. Senate Reports,* 30th Cong., 1st sess.,
No. 143 (serial set 512).

Ripley, C. Peter et al. eds. *The Black Abolitionist Papers.* 5 vols. Chapel Hill: University
of North Carolina Press, 1985–1992.

Ruffin, Edmund. *The Diary of Edmund Ruffin*. Edited by William K. Scarborough. 3 vols. Baton Rouge: Louisiana State University Press, 1972.

Saple, William B., ed. *Writing and Fighting the Confederate War: The Letters of Peter Wellington Alexander, Confederate War Correspondent*. Kearney, N.J.: Belle Grove, 2002.

[Shannon, James]. *An Address Delivered before the Pro-Slavery Convention of the State of Missouri, Held at Lexington, July 13, 1855, on Domestic Slavery*. St. Louis: the Convention, 1855.

Tyler, Lyon Garner, ed. *The Letters and Times of the Tylers*. 3 vols. 1884. Reprint, New York: DaCapo, 1970.

Veazey, Thos. W. *Annual Message from the Governor to the Legislature of Maryland, December Session 1838*. Annapolis: Maryland, 1839.

Virginia. *Report of a Select Committee . . . to Enquire into the Existing Legislation of Congress upon the Subject of Fugitive Slaves, and to Suggest Such Additional Legislation as May Be Proper*. Virginia General Assembly (House of Delegates). Document Number 50. Richmond: Commonwealth of Virginia, 1849.

Wakelyn, Jon L., ed. *Southern Pamphlets on Secession, November 1860–April 1861*. Chapel Hill: University of North Carolina Press, 1996.

### NEWSPAPERS AND PERIODICALS

*African Observer* (Philadelphia), 1827–1828

*Albany Evening Journal* (Albany, New York), 1848

*Albany Weekly Patriot* (Albany, New York), 1843–1846

*Anti-Slavery Bugle* (Salem, Ohio), 1846–1859

*Ashtabula Sentinel* (Jefferson, Ohio), 1851–1852

*Baltimore Saturday Visiter*, 1843–1845

*Baltimore Sun*, 1844–1861

*Bangor Whig* (Bangor, Maine), 1855–1861

*Boston Advertiser*, 1859

*Boston Atlas*, 1844–1851

*Boston Investigator*, 1861

*Charleston Mercury*, 1860

*Cincinnati Gazette*, 1838–1851

*Cincinnati Weekly Herald and Philanthropist*, 1845–1846

*Cleveland Herald*, 1838–1861

*Cleveland Observer*, 1838

*Colored American* (New York), 1839–1841

*Commonwealth* (Frankfort, Kentucky), 1838–1859

*Daily National Intelligencer* (Washington, D.C.), 1842–1860

*De Bow's Review* (New Orleans), 1849–1856

*Emancipator* (New York and Boston), 1839–1845

*Evening Bulletin* (San Francisco), 1860

*Fayetteville Observer* (Fayetteville, North Carolina), 1852–1860

*Frederick Douglass' Paper* (Rochester, New York), 1852

*Free West* (Chicago), 1853

*Freedom's Journal* (New York), 1828–1829

*Friend of Man* (Utica, New York), 1836

*Genius of Universal Emancipation*
(Jonesboro, Tennessee, and
Baltimore), 1823–1831
*Globe* (Washington, D.C.), 1842
*Independent* (New York), 1855
*Indiana Freeman* (Indianapolis), 1844
*Indiana State Sentinel* (Indianapolis),
1844
*Kentucky Gazette* (Lexington), 1836–
1842
*Labor Advocate and Anti-Slavery Chronicle*
(New Garden, Indiana), 1841
*Lexington Intelligencer* (Lexington,
Kentucky), 1838–1839
*Lexington Observer and Reporter*
(Lexington, Kentucky), 1850–1858
*Liberator* (Boston), 1831–1860
*Liberty Press* (Utica, New York), 1845
*Louisville Courier*, 1849–1857
*Louisville Examiner*, 1847
*Louisville Daily Journal*, 1842–1846
*Louisville Public Advertiser*, 1826–1841
*Maryland Gazette* (Annapolis), 1826
*Maysville Eagle* (Maysville, Kentucky),
1837–1846
*Milwaukee Sentinel*, 1856
*Mississippiani* (Jackson), 1847–1859
*Missouri Republican* (St. Louis),
1850–1861
*National Anti-Slavery Standard*
(New York), 1840–1860
*National Enquirer* (Philadelphia),
1835–1839
*National Era* (Washington, D.C.),
1847–1860
*National Gazette* (Philadelphia), 1826
*Newark Advocate* (Newark, Ohio),
1859–1861
*Newport News* (Newport, Kentucky),
1856
*New York Evangelist*, 1837–1842
*New York Evening Post*, 1850

*New York Herald*, 1836–1861
*New York Spectator*, 1836–1838
*New York Times*, 1860
*New York Tribune*, 1850
*Niles Register* (Baltimore), 1821–1845
*North American and United States Gazette*
(Philadelphia), 1850–1853
*North Star* (Rochester, New York), 1848
*Ohio Observer* (Hudson, Ohio), 1847–1853
*Ohio State Journal* (Columbus), 1838–1851
*Ohio Statesman* (Columbus), 1838–1842
*Pennsylvania Freeman* (Philadelphia),
1839–1856
*Philadelphia Saturday Chronicle*, 1837
*Philanthropist* (Cincinnati), 1837–1841
*Philanthropist* (Mount Pleasant, Ohio),
1820
*Pittsburgh Saturday Visiter*, 1850–1853
*Radical Abolitionist* (New York),
1856–1858
*Register* (Raleigh, North Carolina), 1861
*Richmond Enquirer*, 1826–1861
*Ripley Bee* (Ripley, Ohio), 1853–1854
*Scioto Gazette* (Chillicothe, Ohio),
1845–1855
*Signal of Liberty* (Ann Arbor, Michigan),
1841–1842
*Spirit of Liberty* (Pittsburgh), 1841–1843
*Tocsin of Liberty* (Albany, New York),
1842
*True Democrat* (Cleveland), 1847
*True Wesleyan* (New York), 1851
*Vermont Chronicle* (Bellows Falls), 1851
*Virginia Free Press* (Charlestown), 1861
*Wellsburg Weekly Herald* (Wellsburg,
Virginia), 1856–1859
*Western Citizen* (Chicago), 1842–1853
*Western Citizen* (Paris, Kentucky),
1839–1842
*Western Luminary* (Lexington,
Kentucky), 1826
*Wheeling Daily Intelligencer*, 1853–1856

Abbott, James B. "The Rescue of Dr. John W. Doy." *Transactions of the Kansas Historical Society* 4 (1890): 312–23.

Abbott, Richard H. "Yankee Farmers in Northern Virginia 1840–1860." *Virginia Magazine of History and Biography* 76 (January 1968): 56–63.

Abzug, Robert H. *Cosmos Crumbling: American Reform and the Religious Imagination.* New York: Oxford University Press, 1995.

Aidt-Guy, Anita Louise. "Persistent Maryland: Antislavery Activists between 1850 and 1864." Ph.D. diss., Georgetown University, 1994.

Alexander, Ted. "A Regular Slave Hunt: The Army of Northern Virginia and Black Civilians in the Gettysburg Campaign." *North and South* 4 (September 2001): 82–89.

American Anti-Slavery Society. *The Fugitive Slave Law and Its Victims, Anti-Slavery Tracts, No. 15.* Revised and enlarged edition. New York: AASS, 1861.

Anonymous. "What Right Had a Fugitive Slave of Self-Defense against His Master?" *Pennsylvania Magazine of History and Biography* 13 (April 1889): 106–9.

Aptheker, Herbert. *American Negro Slave Revolts.* 1943. Reprint, New York: International, 1969.

———. "The Negro in the Abolitionist Movement." *Science and Society* 5 (Winter 1941): 2–23.

Aron, Stephen. *How the West Was Lost: The Transformation of Kentucky from Daniel Boone to Henry Clay.* Baltimore: Johns Hopkins University Press, 1996.

Ashworth, John. *Slavery, Capitalism, and Politics in the Antebellum Republic.* 2 vols. New York: Cambridge University Press, 1995 and 2007.

Ayers, Edward L. *In the Presence of Mine Enemies: War In the Heart of America, 1859–1863.* New York: Norton, 2003.

———. *Vengeance and Justice: Crime and Punishment in the Nineteenth Century American South.* New York: Oxford University Press, 1984.

Baltimore, Lester B. "Benjamin F. Stringfellow: The Fight for the Missouri Border." *Missouri Historical Review* 62 (October 1967): 14–29.

Barclay, Thomas S. *The Liberal Republican Movement in Missouri 1865–1871.* Columbia: State Historical Society of Missouri, 1926.

Barney, William T. *The Road to Secession: A New Perspective on the Old South.* New York: Praeger, 1972.

———. *Secession Impulse: Alabama and Mississippi in 1860.* Princeton, N.J.: Princeton University Press, 1974.

Bean, Theodore Weber, ed. *History of Montgomery County, Pennsylvania.* Philadelphia: Everts and Peck, 1884.

Beard, Charles A., and Mary R. Beard. *The Rise of American Civilization.* 2 vols. New York: Macmillan, 1927.

Berlin, Ira. *Slaves without Masters: The Free Negro in the Antebellum South.* New York: Pantheon, 1974.

Berwanger, Eugene H. *The Frontier against Slavery: Western Anti-Negro Prejudice and the Slavery Extension Controversy*. Urbana: University of Illinois Press, 1967.

Bibb, Henry. *Narrative of the Life and Adventures of Henry Bibb, an American Slave*. New York: Bibb, 1849.

Bigham, Darrell E. *On Jordon's Banks: Emancipation and Its Aftermath in the Ohio Valley*. Lexington: University Press of Kentucky, 2006.

Birney, William. *James G. Birney and His Times*. 1890. Reprint, New York: Negro Universities Press, 1969.

Blackett, R. J. M. "'Freedom of the Martyr's Grave': Black Pittsburgh's Aid to the Fugitive Slave." *Western Pennsylvania Historical Magazine* 61 (April 1978): 117–34.

Blue, Frederick J. *The Free Soilers: Third Party Politics 1848–54*. Urbana: University of Illinois Press, 1973.

Bordewich, Fergus M. *Bound for Canaan: The Underground Railroad and the War for the Soul of America*. New York: Amistad, 2005.

Boritt, Gabor S., ed. *Why the Civil War Came*. New York: Oxford University Press, 1996.

Boucher, Chauncey. "In Re: That Aggressive Slavocracy." *Mississippi Valley Historical Review* 8 (June–September 1921): 13–79.

Boyer, Richard O. *The Legend of John Brown: A Biography and a History*. New York: Knopf, 1973.

Brackett, Jeffrey R. *The Negro in Maryland: A Study of the Institution of Slavery*. 1889. Reprint, New York: Negro Universities Press, 1969.

Brandt, Nat. *The Town that Started the Civil War*. 1990. Reprint, New York: Dell, 1991.

Brown, Catherine S. *Memoir of Abel Brown, by His Companion*. Worcester, Mass.: Brown, 1849.

Brown, David. *Southern Outcast: Hinton Rowan Helper and The Impending Crisis*. Baton Rouge: Louisiana State University Press, 2006.

Brown, George W. *Baltimore and the Nineteenth of April, 1861: A Study of the War*. 1887. Reprint, Baltimore: Johns Hopkins University Press, 2001.

Brown, Kent Masterson. *Retreat from Gettysburg: Lee, Logistics, and the Pennsylvania Campaign*. Chapel Hill: University of North Carolina Press, 2005.

Bruce, Dickson D. *Violence and Culture in the Antebellum South*. Austin: University of Texas Press, 1979.

Brugger, Robert J. *Maryland: A Middle Temperament 1634–1988*. Baltimore: Johns Hopkins University Press, 1988.

Bugg, James L., Jr. "The Political Career of James Murray Mason: The Legislative Phase." Ph.D. diss., University of Virginia, 1950.

Burton, Orville Vernon. *The Age of Lincoln*. New York: Hill and Wang, 2007.

Campbell, Penelope. *Maryland in Africa: The State Colonization Society 1831–1857*. Urbana: University of Illinois Press, 1971.

Campbell, Stanley W. *Slave Catchers: Enforcement of the Fugitive Slave Law 1850–1860*. Chapel Hill: University of North Carolina Press, 1968.

Cecelski, David S. "The Shores of Freedom: The Maritime Underground Railroad in North Carolina 1800–1861." *North Carolina Historical Review* 71 (April 1994): 174–206.

Channing, Edward P. *A History of the United States*. 6 vols. New York: Macmillan, 1905–1932.

Channing, Stephen A. *Crisis of Fear: Secession in South Carolina*. New York: Simon and Schuster, 1970.

Child, Lydia Maria. *Isaac T. Hopper: A True Life*. Boston: J. P. Jewett, 1853.

Clark, Thomas D. *A History of Kentucky*. Lexington, Ky.: John Bradford, 1960.

———. "The Slave Trade between Kentucky and the Cotton Kingdom." *Mississippi Valley Historical Review* 21 (December 1934): 331–42.

Clay, Cassius Marcellus. *The Life of Cassius Marcellus Clay*. 1886. Reprint, New York: Negro Universities Press, 1969.

Clephane, Walter C. "Local Aspects of Slavery in the District of Columbia." *Records of the Columbia Historical Society* 3 (October 1926): 224–50.

Coddington, Edwin B. *The Gettysburg Campaign: A Study in Command*. New York: Charles Scribner's Sons, 1984.

Coffin, Levi. *Reminiscences of Levi Coffin, the Reputed President of the Underground Railroad*. 3rd ed. Cincinnati: Robert Clark, 1898.

Coleman, J. Winston. *Slavery Times in Kentucky*. Chapel Hill: University of North Carolina Press, 1940.

Cover, Robert M. *Justice Accused: Antislavery and the Judicial Process*. New Haven, Conn.: Yale University Press, 1975.

Craik, Elmer Leroy. "Southern Interest in Territorial Kansas 1854–1858." *Kansas Historical Collections* 15 (1919–1921): 376–95.

Crofts, Daniel W. *Reluctant Confederates: Upper South Unionists in the Secession Crisis*. Chapel Hill: University of North Carolina Press, 1989.

Crooks, George R. *The Life and Letters of Rev. John McClintock*. New York: Nelson and Philips, 1876.

Current, Richard N. *Northernizing the South*. Athens: University of Georgia Press, 1983.

Curry, Richard O. *A House Divided: A Study of Statehood Policy and the Copperhead Movement in West Virginia*. Pittsburgh: University of Pittsburgh Press, 1964.

———, ed. *Radicalism, Racism, and Party Realignment: The Border States during Reconstruction*. Baltimore: Johns Hopkins University Press, 1969.

Cutler, William B. *History of the State of Kansas*. Chicago: A. T. Andreas, 1883.

Davis, David Brion. *The Slave Power Conspiracy and the Paranoid Style*. Baton Rouge: Louisiana State University Press, 1970.

Davis, William C., and James I. Robertson Jr., eds. *Virginia at War: 1861*. Lexington: University Press of Kentucky, 2005.

Denton, Lawrence M. *A Southern Star for Maryland: Maryland in the Secession Crisis 1860–1861*. Baltimore: Publishing Concepts, 1995.

Dew, Charles B. *Apostles of Disunion: Southern Secession Commissioners and the Causes of the Civil War*. Charlottesville: University of Virginia Press, 2001.

———. "Black Ironworkers and the Slave Insurrection Panic of 1856." *Journal of Southern History* 41 (August 1975): 321–38.

Deyle, Steven. *Carry Me Back: The Domestic Slave Trade in American Life*. New York: Oxford University Press, 2005.

Dillon, Merton L. *Benjamin Lundy and the Struggle for Negro Freedom*. Urbana: University of Illinois Press, 1966.

———. *Elijah P. Lovejoy, Abolitionist Editor*. Urbana: University of Illinois Press, 1961.

———. *Slavery Attacked: Southern Slaves and Their Allies 1619–1860*. Baton Rouge: Louisiana State University Press, 1990.

Dixon, James. *Personal Narrative of a Tour through a Part of the United States and Canada*. 2nd ed. New York: Lane and Scott, 1849.

Donald, David Herbert. *Charles Sumner and the Coming of the Civil War*. Chicago: University of Chicago Press, 1960.

Drake, Thomas E. *Quakers and Slavery in America*. New Haven, Conn.: Yale University Press, 1950.

Du Bois, W. E. B. *The Philadelphia Negro: A Social Study*. 1899. Reprint, New York: Schocken Books, 1967.

Dumond, Dwight L. *Antislavery: The Crusade for Freedom in America*. New York: Norton, 1961.

———. *The Secession Movement 1860–1861*. 1931. Reprint, New York: Negro Universities Press, 1968.

Dunn, Jacob Piatt. *Indiana and Indianans: A History of Aboriginal and Territorial Indiana and the Century of Statehood*. 5 vols. Chicago: American Historical Association, 1919.

Eaton, Clement. *Freedom of Thought in the Old South*. Durham, N.C.: Duke University Press, 1940.

———. *The Freedom of Thought Struggle in the Old South*. New York: Harper, 1964.

———. *The Growth of Southern Civilization 1790–1860*. New York: Harper and Row, 1961.

———. "Mob Violence in the Old South." *Mississippi Valley Historical Review* 29 (December 1942): 351–70.

Egerton, Douglas R. *Gabriel's Rebellion: The Virginia Slave Conspiracies of 1800 and 1802*. Chapel Hill: University of North Carolina Press, 1993.

Egnal, Marc. *Clash of Extremes: The Economic Origins of the Civil War*. New York: Hill and Wang, 2009.

Ellis, Richard, and Aaron Wildavsky. "A Cultural Analysis of the Role of Abolitionists in the Coming of the Civil War." *Comparative Studies in Society and History* 32 (January 1990): 89–116.

Essah, Patience. *A House Divided: Slavery and Emancipation in Delaware*. Charlottesville: University of Virginia Press, 1996.

Etcheson, Nicole. *Bleeding Kansas: Contested Liberty in the Civil War Era*. Lawrence: University Press of Kansas, 2004.

———. *The Emerging Midwest: Upland Southerners and the Political Culture of the Old Northwest, 1787–1861*. Bloomington: Indiana University Press, 1996.

Evitts, William J. *A Matter of Allegiance: Maryland from 1850 to 1861*. Baltimore: Johns Hopkins University Press, 1974.

Ewing, E. W. R. *Northern Rebellion and Southern Secession*. Richmond, Va.: J. L. Hill, 1904.

Fairbank, Calvin. *Rev. Calvin Fairbank during Slavery Times*. 1890. Reprint, New York: Negro Universities Press, 1969.

Fee, John G. *The Autobiography of John G. Fee*. Chicago: National Christian Association, 1891.

Fehrenbacher, Don E. *The Slaveholding Republic: An Account of the United States Government's Relationship to Slavery*. New York: Oxford University Press, 2001.

Fellman, Michael. *Inside War: The Guerrilla Conflict in Missouri during the American Civil War*. New York: Oxford University Press, 1989.

Fields, Barbara Jeanne. *Slavery and Freedom on the Middle Ground: Maryland during the Nineteenth Century*. New Haven: Yale University Press, 1985.

Finkelman, Paul. "Evading the Ordinance: the Persistence of Bondage in Indiana and Illinois." *Journal of the Early Republic* 9 (Spring 1989): 21–51.

———. "Fugitive Slaves, Midwestern Racial Tolerance, and the Value of 'Justice Delayed.'" *Iowa Law Review* 78 (October 1992): 89–141.

———. *An Imperfect Union: Slavery, Federalism, and Comity*. Chapel Hill: University of North Carolina Press, 1981.

———. "The Kidnapping of John Davis and the Adoption of the Fugitive Slave Law of 1793." *Journal of Southern History* 56 (August 1990): 397–422.

———. "*Prigg v. Pennsylvania* and Northern State Courts: Anti-Slavery Use of a Pro-Slavery Decision." *Civil War History* 25 (March 1975): 5–35.

———. "The Protection of Black Rights in Seward's New York." *Civil War History* 34 (September 1988): 211–33.

———. *Slavery and the Founders: Race and Liberty in the Age of Jefferson*. Armonk, N.Y.: M. E. Sharpe, 1996.

———, ed. *Slavery and the Law*. Madison, Wis.: Madison House, 1997.

Fladeland, Betty. *James Gillespie Birney: Slaveholder to Abolitionist*. Ithaca, N.Y.: Cornell University Press, 1955.

Floan, Howard R. *The South in Northern Eyes 1831–1861*. Austin: University of Texas Press, 1958.

Foner, Eric. "Causes of the American Civil War: Recent Interpretations and New Directions." *Civil War History* 20 (September 1974): 197–214.

———. *Free Soil, Free Labor, Free Men: The Ideology of the Republican Party before the Civil War*. New York: Oxford University Press, 1970.

———. *Reconstruction: America's Unfinished Revolution, 1863–1877*. New York: Oxford University Press, 1988.

Folk, Patrick A. "The Queen City of Mobs: Riots and Community Reaction in Cincinnati 1788–1848." Ph.D. diss., University of Akron, 1978.

Franklin, John Hope. *The Militant South 1800–1861*. Cambridge, Mass.: Harvard University Press, 1956.

———. *A Southern Odyssey: Travelers in the Antebellum North.* Baton Rouge: Louisiana State University Press, 1976.

Franklin, John Hope, and Loren Schweninger. *Runaway Slaves: Rebels on the Plantation.* New York: Oxford University Press, 1999.

Freehling, William W. "The Editorial Revolution, Virginia, and the Coming of the Civil War: A Review Essay." *Civil War History* 16 (March 1970): 64–77.

———. *The Reintegration of American History: Slavery and the Civil War.* New York: Oxford University Press, 1994.

———. *The Road to Disunion.* 2 vols. New York: Oxford University Press, 1990 and 2007.

———. *The South vs. the South: How Anti-Confederate Southerners Shaped the Course of the Civil War.* New York: Oxford University Press, 2001.

Furlong, Patrick J. "The South Bend Fugitive Slave Case." In *We the People: Indiana and the United States Constitution.* Indianapolis: Indiana Historical Society, 1987.

Galbreath, C. B. "Ohio's Fugitive Slave Law." *Ohio Archaeological and Historical Quarterly* 34 (1925): 216–40.

Gara, Larry. "The Fugitive Slave Laws: A Double Paradox." *Civil War History* 10 (September 1964): 229–40.

———. *Liberty Line: The Legend of the Underground Railroad.* Lexington: University of Kentucky Press, 1961.

———. "The Underground Railroad in Illinois." *Journal of the Illinois State Historical Society* 56 (Autumn 1963): 508–28.

Garrison, Wendell Phillips, and Francis Jackson Garrison. *William Lloyd Garrison, 1805–1889: The Story of His Life Told by His Children.* 4 vols. New York: Century, 1883–1889.

Garrison, William Lloyd. *The New "Reign of Terror" in the Slaveholding States, 1859–1860.* 1860. Reprint, New York: Arno, 1969.

Gienapp, William E. *The Origins of the Republican Party 1852–1856.* New York: Oxford University Press, 1987.

Godcharles, Frederick A. *Chronicles of Central Pennsylvania.* 4 vols. New York: Lewis Historical Publishing, 1944.

Graham, Leroy. *Baltimore: Nineteenth Century Black Capital.* Washington, D.C.: University Press of America, 1982.

Greenberg, Kenneth S. *Masters and Statesmen: The Political Culture of American Slavery.* Baltimore: Johns Hopkins University Press, 1985.

Gresham, Matilda. *Life of Walter Quintin Gresham, 1832–1895.* Chicago: Rand McNally, 1919.

Griffler, Keith P. *Front Line of Freedom: African Americans and the Forging of the Underground Railroad in the Ohio Valley.* Lexington: University Press of Kentucky, 2004.

Grimsted, David. *American Mobbing, 1828–1861: Toward Civil War.* New York: Oxford University Press, 1998.

———. "Rioting in Its Jacksonian Setting." *American Historical Review* 77 (April 1972): 361–90.

Grover, Kathryn. *The Fugitive's Gibraltar: Escaping Slaves and Abolitionism in New Bedford, Massachusetts.* Amherst: University of Massachusetts Press, 2001.

Gruenwald, Kim W. *River of Enterprise: The Commercial Origins of Regional Identity in the Ohio Valley, 1790–1850.* Bloomington: Indiana University Press, 2002.

Gudmestad, Robert H. *A Troublesome Commerce: The Transformation of the Interstate Slave Trade.* Baton Rouge: Louisiana State University Press, 2003.

Gunderson, Robert Gray. *Old Gentlemen's Convention: The Washington Peace Conference of 1861.* Madison: University of Wisconsin Press, 1961.

Hadden, Sally E. *Slave Patrols: Law and Violence in Virginia and the Carolinas.* Cambridge, Mass.: Harvard University Press, 2001.

Hagedorn, Ann. *Beyond the River: The Untold Story of the Heroes of the Underground Railroad.* New York: Simon and Schuster, 2002.

Hall, Susan G. *Appalachian Ohio in the Civil War, 1862–1863.* Jefferson, N.C.: McFarland, 2000.

Hamilton, Holman. *Prologue to Conflict: The Crisis and Compromise of 1850.* Lexington: University Press of Kentucky, 1964.

Hancock, Harold. "Civil War Comes to Delaware." *Civil War History* 2 (December 1956): 29–41.

Hardesty, H. H. *Historical and Geographical Encyclopedia . . . Outline Map and History of Meigs County, Ohio.* Toledo, Ohio: Hardesty, 1883.

Harrison, Lowell H. *The Antislavery Movement in Kentucky.* Lexington: University Press of Kentucky, 1978.

———. *The Civil War in Kentucky.* Lexington: University Press of Kentucky, 1975.

Harrison, Lowell H., and James C. Klotter. *A New History of Kentucky.* Lexington: University Press of Kentucky, 1997.

Harrold, Stanley. *The Abolitionists and the South 1831–1861.* Lexington: University Press of Kentucky, 1995.

———. "Cassius M. Clay on Slavery and Race: A Reinterpretation." *Slavery and Abolition* 9 (May 1989): 43–56.

———. *Gamaliel Bailey and Antislavery Union.* Kent, Ohio: Kent State University Press, 1986.

———. "The Intersectional Relationship between Cassius M. Clay and the Garrisonian Abolitionists." *Civil War History* 35 (January 1989): 101–19.

———. "The *Pearl* Affair: The Washington Riot of 1848." *Records of the Columbia Historical Society* 50 (1980): 140–60.

———. *The Rise of Aggressive Abolitionism: Addresses to the Slaves.* Lexington: University Press of Kentucky, 2004.

———. *Subversives: Antislavery Community in Washington, D.C., 1828–1865.* Baton Rouge: Louisiana State University Press, 2003.

———. "Violence and Nonviolence in Kentucky Abolitionism." *Journal of Southern History* 57 (February 1991): 15–38.

Hart, Albert Bushnell. *Slavery and Abolition 1831–1841.* 1906. Reprint, New York: Negro Universities Press, 1968.

Harvey, Charles M. "Missouri from 1849 to 1861." *Missouri Historical Review* 2 (October 1907): 23–41.

Hensel, William Uhler. *The Christiana Riot and Treason Trial of 1851*. 1911. Reprint, New York: Negro Universities Press, 1969.

Hickin, Patricia P. "Antislavery in Virginia 1831–1861." 3 vols. Ph.D. diss., University of Virginia, 1968.

———. "John C. Underwood and the Antislavery Movement in Virginia." *Virginia Magazine of History and Biography* 73 (April 1965): 156–68.

Hickok, Charles T. *The Negro in Ohio, 1802–1870*. 1896. Reprint, New York: Ams, 1975.

Holloway, J. N. *History of Kansas from the First Exploration of the Mississippi Valley to Its Admission to the Union*. Lafayette, Ind.: James, Emmons, 1868.

Holt, Michael F. *The Political Crisis of the 1850s*. New York: Wiley, 1978.

———. *The Rise and Fall of the American Whig Party: Jacksonian Politics and the Onset of the Civil War*. New York: Oxford University Press, 1993.

Horton, James Oliver, and Lois E. Horton. *In Hope of Liberty: Culture, Community, and Protest among Northern Free Blacks, 1700–1860*. New York: Oxford University Press, 1997.

Howard, Victor B. *Black Liberation in Kentucky: Emancipation and Freedom, 1862–1884*. Lexington: University Press of Kentucky, 1983.

Hubbart, Henry C. *The Older Middle West, 1840–1880*. 1936. Reprint, New York: Russell and Russell, 1963.

Hurt, R. Douglas. *The Ohio Frontier: Crucible of the Old Northwest, 1720–1830*. Bloomington: Indiana University Press, 1996.

Huston, James L. *Calculating the Value of the Union: Slavery, Property Rights, and the Economic Origins of the Civil War*. Chapel Hill: University of North Carolina Press, 2003.

———. "The Experiential Basis of the Northern Antislavery Impulse." *Journal of Southern History* 56 (November 1990): 609–40.

Illinois Anti-Slavery Concert for Prayer. *Narrative of Facts Respecting Alanson Work, Jas. E. Burr, and Geo. Thompson*. Quincy, Ill.: Quincy Whig, 1842.

Isely, W. H. "The Sharps Rifle Episode in Kansas History." *American Historical Review* 12 (April 1907): 546–66.

Johnson, Oliver. "Charles Osborne's Place in Anti-Slavery History." *International Review* 13 (September 1882): 191–206.

Johnson, Samuel A. *The Battle Cry of Freedom: The New England Emigrant Aid Company in the Kansas Crusade*. Lawrence: University of Kansas Press, 1954.

Johnson, William. *State of Ohio vs. Forbes and Armitage*. Ithaca, N.Y.: Cornell University Library, 1846.

Keller, Ralph A. "Extraterritoriality and the Fugitive Slave Debate." *Illinois Historical Journal* 78 (Summer 1985): 113–28.

Klem, Mary J. "Missouri in the Kansas Struggle." *Mississippi Valley Historical Association Proceedings* 9 (1917–1918): 397–413.

Kolchin, Peter. *American Slavery 1619–1877*. New York: Hill and Wang, 1993.

Kramer, Neil S. "The Trial of Reuben Crandell." *Records of the Columbia Historical Society* 50 (1980): 123–39.

Laprade, William T. "The Domestic Slave Trade in the District of Columbia." *Journal of Negro History* 11 (January 1926): 17–34.

Larkin, Stillman C. *Pioneer History of Meigs County, Ohio*. Columbus: Berlin Printing, 1908.

Lesick, Lawrence. *The Lane Rebels: Evangelicalism and Antislavery in Antebellum America*. Metuchen, N.J.: Scarecrow, 1980.

Leslie, William R. "The Pennsylvania Fugitive Slave Act of 1826." *Journal of Southern History* 18 (November 1952): 429–45.

———. "A Study in the Origins of Interstate Rendition: the Big Beaver Creek Murders." *American Historical Review* 57 (October 1951): 63–76.

Link, William A. *Roots of Secession: Slavery and Politics in Antebellum Virginia*. Chapel Hill: University of North Carolina Press, 2003.

Lovejoy, Joseph C. *Memoir of Rev. Charles T. Torrey*. 1847. Reprint, New York: Negro Universities Press, 1969.

Lovejoy, Joseph C., and Owen Lovejoy. *Memoir of the Rev. Elijah Lovejoy*. 1838. Reprint, Freeport, N.Y.: Books for Libraries, 1970.

Lowe, Richard G. "The Republican Party in Antebellum Virginia 1856–1860." *Virginia Magazine of History and Biography* 81 (July 1973): 259–79.

Lyon, William H. "Claiborne Fox Jackson and the Secession Crisis in Missouri." *Missouri Historical Review* 58 (July 1964): 422–41.

Mabee, Carleton. *Black Freedom: The Nonviolent Abolitionists from 1830 through the Civil War*. London: Macmillan, 1970.

Mahon, John K. *History of the Militia and the National Guard*. New York: Macmillan, 1983.

Manakee, Harold R. *Maryland in the Civil War*. Baltimore: Maryland Historical Society, 1961.

Martin, Asa Earl. *The Anti-Slavery Movement in Kentucky Prior to 1850*. 1918. Reprint, New York: Negro Universities Press, 1970.

Martineau, Harriet. *Retrospective of Western Travel*. New York: Lohman, 1838.

Mathews, Edward. *Autobiography of the Rev. E. Mathews*. 1866. Reprint, Miami: Mnemosyne, 1969.

May, Robert E. *The Southern Dream of a Caribbean Empire*. Baton Rouge: Louisiana State University Press, 1973.

McDonald, Earl E. "The Negro in Indiana before 1800." *Indiana Magazine of History* 27 (December 1931): 291–306.

McDonald, Lawrence H. "Prelude to Emancipation: The Failure of the Great Reaction in Maryland 1831–1850." Ph.D. diss., University of Maryland, 1974.

McKivigan, John R. *The War against Proslavery Religion: Abolitionism and the Northern Churches 1830–1865*. Ithaca, N.Y.: Cornell University Press, 1984.

McKivigan, John R., and Stanley Harrold, eds. *Antislavery Violence: Sectional, Racial, and Cultural Conflict in Antebellum America*. Knoxville: University of Tennessee Press, 1999.

McMaster, John Bach. *History of the People of the United States, from the Revolution to the Civil War*. 8 vols. New York: Appleton, 1883–1913.

McPherson, James M. *This Mighty Scourge: Perspectives on the Civil War*. New York: Oxford University Press, 2007.

———. *Ordeal by Fire: The Civil War and Reconstruction*. 3rd ed. Boston: McGraw Hill, 2001.

———. *The Struggle for Equality: Abolitionism and the Negro in the Civil War and Reconstruction*. Princeton, N.J.: Princeton University Press, 1964.

Merkel, Benjamin G. "The Underground Railroad and the Missouri Borders, 1840–1860." *Missouri Historical Review* 37 (April 1943): 271–85.

Middleton, Stephen. *The Black Laws: Race and the Legal Process in Early Ohio*. Athens: Ohio University Press, 2005.

———. "The Fugitive Slave Crisis in Cincinnati 1850–1860: Resistance, Enforcement, and Black Refugees." *Journal of Negro History* 72 (Winter–Spring 1987): 20–32.

———. "The Fugitive Slave Issue in Southwest Ohio: Unreported Cases." *Old Northwest* 14 (Winter 1988–1989): 285–310.

Miller, E. Willard, ed. *A Geography of Pennsylvania*. University Park: Pennsylvania University Press, 1995.

Morris, Thomas D. *Free Men All: The Personal Liberty Laws of the North, 1780–1861*. Baltimore: Johns Hopkins University Press, 1974.

Morrison, Michael A. *Slavery and the American West: The Eclipsing of Manifest Destiny and the Coming to the Civil War*. Chapel Hill: University of North Carolina Press, 1997.

Money, Charles H. "The Fugitive Slave Law of 1850 in Indiana." *Indiana Magazine of History* 17 (June, September 1921): 159–98, 257–97.

Mullin, Gerald. *Flight and Rebellion: Slave Resistance in Eighteenth Century Virginia*. New York: Oxford University Press, 1972.

Mullis, Tony R. *Peacekeeping on the Plains: Army Operations in Bleeding Kansas*. Columbia: University of Missouri Press, 2004.

Nash, Gary B. *Forging Freedom: The Formation of Philadelphia's Black Community, 1720–1840*. Cambridge, Mass.: Harvard University Press, 1981.

Nash, Gary B., and Jean R. Soderlund. *Freedom by Degrees: Emancipation in Pennsylvania and Its Aftermath*. New York: Oxford University Press. 1991.

Neely, Jeremy. *The Border between Them: Violence and Reconciliation on the Kansas-Missouri Line*. Columbia: University of Missouri Press, 2007.

Nevins, Allan. *The Emergence of Lincoln*. 2 vols. New York: Charles Scribner's Sons, 1950.

———. *Ordeal of the Union*. 2 vols. New York: Charles Scribner's Sons, 1947.

———. *The War for the Union*. 2 vols. New York: Charles Scribner's Sons, 1959.

Newman, Richard S. *The Transformation of American Abolitionism: Fighting Slavery in the Early Republic*. Chapel Hill: University of North Carolina Press, 2002.

Nichols, Alice. *Bleeding Kansas*. New York: Oxford University Press, 1954.

Nieman, Donald G., ed. *The Constitution, Law, and American Life: Critical Aspects of the Nineteenth Century Experience*. Athens: University of Georgia Press, 1992.

Noe, Kenneth N., and Shannon H. Wilson, eds. *The Civil War in Appalachia: Collected Essays*. Nashville: University of Tennessee Press, 1997.

Nogee, Joseph. "The Prigg Case and Fugitive Slavery, 1842–1850: Part I." *Journal of Negro History* 39 (July 1954): 185–205.

Nye, Russell B. *Fettered Freedom: Civil Liberties and the Slavery Controversy, 1830–1860*. Rev. ed. East Lansing: Michigan State University Press, 1963.

Oates, Stephen B. *To Purge this Land with Blood: A Biography of John Brown*. 2nd ed. Amherst: University of Massachusetts Press, 1984.

O'Brien, Michael. *Guerrilla Warfare in the Southern Appalachians 1861–1865*. Westport, Conn.: Praeger, 1991.

Parrish, Isaac. *Brief Memoirs of Thomas Shipley and Edwin P. Atlee, Read before the Pennsylvania Society for Promoting the Abolition of Slavery*. Philadelphia: PAS, 1838.

Parrish, William E. *David Rice Atchison of Missouri, Border Politician*. Columbia: University of Missouri Press, 1961.

Pease, Jane H., and William H. Pease. *They Who Would Be Free: Blacks' Search for Freedom 1830–1861*. New York: Athenaeum, 1974.

Perman, Michael, ed. *The Coming of the American Civil War*. Lexington, Mass.: Heath, 1993.

Peterson, Norma L. *Freedom and Franchise: The Political Career of B. Gratz Brown*. Columbia: University of Missouri Press, 1965.

Phillips, Christopher. "'The Crime against Missouri': Slavery, Kansas, and the Cant of Southernness in the Border Wests." *Civil War History* 48 (March 2002): 60–81.

———. *Damned Yankee: The Life of General Nathaniel Lyon*. Baton Rouge: Louisiana State University Press, 1996.

Pickard, Kate E. R. *The Kidnapped and the Ransomed: Recollections of Peter Still and His Wife "Vina" after Forty Years of Slavery*. Syracuse, N.Y.: William T. Hamilton, 1856.

Pocock, Emil. "Slavery and Freedom in the Early Republic: Robert Patterson's Slaves in Kentucky and Ohio, 1804–1819." *Ohio Valley History* 6 (Spring 2006): 3–26.

Potter, David M. *The Impending Crisis, 1848–1861*. New York: Harper and Row, 1976.

Pressly, Thomas. *Americans Interpret Their Civil War*. 2nd ed. New York: Free Press, 1962.

Preston, Emmett D. "The Fugitive Slave Acts in Ohio." *Journal of Negro History* 28 (October 1943): 422–77.

———. "The Underground Railroad in Northwestern Ohio." *Journal of Negro History* 17 (October 1932): 409–36.

Prince, Benjamin F. "The Rescue Case of 1857." *Ohio Archaeological and Historical Publications* 16 (January 1907): 292–309.

Raitz, Karl, ed. *National Road*. Baltimore: Johns Hopkins University Press, 1991.

Ray, Pearly Ormond. *The Repeal of the Missouri Compromise, Its Origin and Authorship*. Cleveland: Arthur H. Clark, 1909.

Redpath, James. *The Public Life of Capt. John Brown*. Boston: Thayer and Eldridge, 1860.

Reid, Robert L., ed. *Always a River: The Ohio River and the American Experience*. Bloomington: Indiana University Press, 1991.

Reynolds, David S. *John Brown: Abolitionist*. New York: Knopf, 2005.

Rice, O. K. "Eli Thayer and the Friendly Invasion of Virginia." *Journal of Southern History* 37 (November 1971): 575–96.

Richards, Leonard R. *"Gentlemen of Property and Standing": Anti-Abolition Mobs in Jacksonian America*. New York: Oxford University Press, 1970.

———. *The Slave Power: The Free North and Southern Domination, 1780–1860*. Baton Rouge: Louisiana State University Press, 2000.

Riddle, Albert G. *The Life of Benjamin F. Wade*. Cleveland: William W. Williams, 1886.

Ripley, Elihu S. *History of the General Assembly of Maryland, 1635–1904*. Baltimore: Nunn, 1905.

Rossbach, Jeffrey S. *Ambivalent Conspirators: John Brown, the Secret Six, and a Theory of Slave Violence*. Philadelphia: University of Pennsylvania Press, 1982.

Runyon, Randolph Paul. *Delia Webster and the Underground Railroad*. Lexington: University Press of Kentucky, 1996.

Ryle, Walter Harrington. *Missouri: Union or Secession?* Nashville, Tenn.: George Peabody College for Teachers, 1931.

Sanborn, Franklin B. *The Life and Letters of John Brown*. 1885. Reprint, New York: Negro Universities Press, 1969.

Schwartz, Philip J. *Slave Laws in Virginia*. Athens: University of Georgia Press, 1996.

Sears, Richard D. *The Day of Small Things: Abolitionism in the Midst of Slavery, Berea, Kentucky, 1854–1864*. Lanham, Md.: University Press of America, 1986.

Sewell, Richard D. *Ballots for Freedom: Antislavery Politics in the United States, 1837–1860*. New York: Oxford University Press, 1976.

Shanks, Henry Thomas. *The Secession Movement in Virginia, 1847–1861*. 1934. Reprint, New York: Ams, 1971.

Sheridan, Richard B. "From Slavery in Missouri to Freedom in Kansas, 1854–1865." *Kansas History* 12 (Spring 1989): 28–47.

Shoemaker, Floyd C. "Missouri's Proslavery Fight for Kansas, 1854–1855." *Missouri Historical Review* 48 (April, July 1954): 221–36, 325–40 and 49 (October 1954): 41–54.

Siebert, Wilbur H. *The Underground Railroad from Slavery to Freedom*. New York: Macmillan, 1898.

Simeone, James. *Democracy and Slavery in Frontier Illinois: The Bottomland Republic*. DeKalb: Northern Illinois University Press, 2000.

Slaughter, Thomas P. *Bloody Dawn: The Christiana Riot and Racial Violence in the Antebellum North*. New York: Oxford University Press, 1991.

Smallwood, Thomas. *A Narrative of Thomas Smallwood (Colored Man)*. Toronto: J. Stephens, 1851.

Smedley, Robert C. *History of the Underground Railroad in Chester and Neighboring Counties of Pennsylvania.* Lancaster, Pa.: Office of the Journal, 1883.

Smiley, David. *Lion of White Hall: The Life of Cassius M. Clay.* Madison: University of Wisconsin Press, 1962.

Smith, George Winston. "Ante-Bellum Attempts of Northern Business to 'Redeem' the Upper South." *Journal of Southern History* 11 (May 1945): 190–213.

Smith, Theodore Clark. *The Liberty and Free Soil Parties in the Northwest.* 1897. Reprint, New York: Arno, 1969.

Smith, William Henry. "The First Fugitive Slave Case of Record in Ohio." *Annual Report of the American Historical Association for 1893.* Washington, D.C.: Government Printing Office, 1894.

Stafford, Hanford Dozier. "Slavery in a Border City: Louisville 1790–1860." Ph.D. diss., University of Kentucky, 1982.

Stampp, Kenneth M. "The Fate of the Southern Anti-Slavery Movement." *Journal of Negro History* 28 (January 1943): 10–22.

Staudenraus, Philip J. *The African Colonization Movement.* New York: Columbia University Press, 1960.

Stauffer, John. *Black Hearts of Men: Radical Abolitionists and the Transformation of Race.* Cambridge, Mass.: Harvard University Press, 2002.

Stewart, James Brewer. *Holy Warriors: The Abolitionists and American Slavery.* Revised ed. New York: Hill and Wang, 1997.

Still, William. *The Underground Railroad.* 1871. Reprint, Chicago: Johnson Publishing, 1970.

Sturge, Joseph. *Visit to the United States in 1848.* London: Hamilton, Adams, 1842.

Tallant, Harold D. *Evil Necessity: Slavery and Political Culture in Antebellum Kentucky.* Lexington: University Press of Kentucky, 2003.

Tapp, Hambleton. "Robert J. Breckinridge and the Year 1849." *Filson Club History Quarterly* 12 (July 1938): 125–50.

[Tappan, Lewis]. *The Fugitive Slave Bill: Its History and Unconstitutionality, with an Account of the Seizure and Enslavement of James Hamlet.* 3rd ed. New York: William Harned, 1850.

Thomas, William G., III. "The Border South." *Southern Spaces: an Interdisciplinary Journal* April 16, 2004. www.southernspaces.org/contents/2004/thomas/1a.htm.

Thompson, George. *Prison Life and Reflections.* 1847. Reprint, New York: Negro Universities Press, 1969.

Tindle, Lela J. McBride Brockway. *Opothleyahola and the Loyal Muskogee: Their Flight to Kansas in the Civil War.* Lincoln: University of Nebraska Press, 1992.

Tocqueville, Alexis de. *Democracy in America.* Translated and edited by Harvey C. Mansfield and Delba Winthrop. Chicago: University of Chicago Press, 2000.

Torrey, Jesse. *A Portraiture of Slavery, in the United States.* Philadelphia: Torrey, 1817.

Townshend, William H. *Lincoln and the Bluegrass: Slavery and Civil War in Kentucky.* Lexington: University Press of Kentucky, 1955.

Trexler, Harrison Anthony. *Slavery in Missouri, 1804–1865.* Johns Hopkins University

Studies in Historical and Political Science, ser. 32, no. 2. Baltimore: Johns Hopkins Press, 1914.

Turner, Wallace B. "Kentucky Slavery in the Last Ante Bellum Decade." *Register of the Kentucky Historical Society* 58 (October 1960): 291–307.

Utter, William T. *The Frontier State, 1803–1825.* In *The History of the State of Ohio.* 6 vols. edited by Carl Wittke. Columbus: Ohio State Archaeological and Historical Society, 1942.

Van Deusen, Glyndon G. *Horace Greeley: Nineteenth-Century Crusader.* 1953. Reprint, New York: Hill and Wang, 1964.

Vaughan, John C. *Argument at the Trial of Rev. John B. Mahan, Nov. 10, 1838.* Cincinnati: Samuel A. Alley, 1838.

Volpe, Vernon L. *Forlorn Hope of Freedom: The Liberty Party in the Old Northwest.* Kent, Ohio: Kent State University Press, 1990.

———. "The Ohio Election of 1838: A Study in the Historical Method." *Ohio History* 95 (Summer–Autumn 1986): 85–100.

Von Holst, Hermann E. *The Constitutional and Political History of the United States.* 8 vols. Chicago: Callaghan, 1877–1902.

Wagandt, Charles L. *The Mighty Revolution: Negro Emancipation in Maryland 1862–1864.* Baltimore: Johns Hopkins University Press, 1964.

Wallenstein, Peter, and Bertram Wyatt-Brown, eds. *Virginia's Civil War.* Charlottesville: University of Virginia Press, 2005.

Walters, Ronald L. *The Antislavery Appeal: American Abolitionism after 1830.* Baltimore: Johns Hopkins University Press, 1976.

Weeks, Louis. "John P. Parker: Black Abolitionist Entrepreneur 1827–1900." *Ohio History* 80 (Spring 1971): 155–67.

Weisenburger, Steven. *Modern Medea: A Family Story of Slavery and Child-Murder from the Old South.* New York: Hill and Wang, 1998.

Whitman, T. Stephen. *Challenging Slavery in the Chesapeake: Black and White Resistance to Human Bondage, 1775–1865.* Baltimore: Maryland Historical Society, 2007.

———. *The Price of Freedom: Slavery and Manumission in Baltimore and Early National Maryland.* Lexington: University Press of Kentucky, 1997.

———. "Slavery, Manumission, and Free Black Workers in Early National Baltimore (Maryland)." Ph.D. diss., Johns Hopkins University, 1993.

Williams, John A. *West Virginia: A Bicentennial History.* New York: Norton, 1976.

———. *West Virginia: A History.* 2nd ed. Morgantown: University of West Virginia Press, 2001.

Wilson, Carol. *Freedom at Risk: The Kidnapping of Free Blacks in America 1780–1865.* Lexington: University Press of Kentucky, 1994.

Wilson, Erasmus, ed. *Standard History of Pittsburgh, Pennsylvania.* Chicago: H. R. Cornell, 1898.

Wilson, Henry. *The Rise and Fall of the Slave Power.* 3 vols. 3rd ed. Boston: James R. Osgood, 1876.

Wilson, R. H. *With the Border Ruffians: Memories of the Far West, 1852–1868*. London: John Murray, 1908.

Winch, Julie. "Philadelphia and the Other Underground Railroad." *Pennsylvania Magazine of History and Biography* 111 (January 1987): 3–25.

———. *Philadelphia's Black Elite: Activism, Accommodation, and the Struggle for Autonomy*. Philadelphia: Temple University Press, 1998.

Winks, Robin W. *The Blacks in Canada, a History*. New Haven: Yale University Press, 1971.

Wise, Barton H. *The Life of Henry A. Wise of Virginia, 1806–1876*. New York: Macmillan, 1899.

Wish, Harvey. "The Slave Insurrection Panic of 1856." *Journal of Southern History* 5 (May 1939): 206–22.

Wolff, Gerald W. *The Kansas-Nebraska Bill: Party, Section, and the Coming of the Civil War*. New York: Revisionist, 1977.

Wood, Peter. *Black Majority: Negroes in South Carolina from 1670 through the Stono Rebellion*. New York: Knopf, 1974.

Wright, Florence Bedford. "A Station on the Underground Railroad." *Ohio History* 14 (April 1905): 164–69.

Wyatt-Brown, Bertram. "The Abolitionists' Postal Campaign of 1835." *Journal of Negro History* 50 (October 1965): 227–38.

———. *Lewis Tappan and the Evangelical War against Slavery*. Cleveland: Press of Case Western Reserve University, 1969.

———. *Southern Honor: Ethics and Behavior in the Old South*. New York: Oxford University Press, 1982.

Yanuck, Julius. "The Garner Fugitive Slave Case." *Mississippi Valley Historical Review* 40 (June 1953): 47–60.

Younger, Richard D. "Southern Grand Juries and Slavery." *Journal of Negro History* 40 (April 1955): 166–78.

# INDEX

Abbott, James B., 166, 167, 172

Abolition: gradual, 120–22, 126–27, 134–35; proposed for District of Columbia, 137

"Abolitionist emissaries," 42, 44, 139

Abolitionist missionaries, 175, 177–78, 193

Abolitionist organizations, xiii, 30, 175

Abolitionist propaganda, 37–39

Abolitionists: and African Americans, 116–17, 119; and Border South, 35–39, 116–18, 120–21, 174; in border struggle, 2; and John Brown, 183, 190–91; caution among, 33–34; and Cassius M. Clay, 116–17; and contacts with slaves, 44–45; described, xiii; and fugitive slave laws, 21–22, 141; Garrisonian, xiii, 116; Liberty (*see* Liberty Party); in Lower North, 86–87, 98, 114; mob attacks on, 67–70; radical political, 116, 187, 189; and slave escapes, 14, 15, 20, 39–40, 42–45, 72, 130, 140; on slaves, 117; and slaves in transit, 66–67; and violence, 38, 95, 99–100, 241 (n. 16); white, 56, 58, 97, 112–13, 177–78

African Americans: and abolitionists, 116–17, 119; aid fugitive slaves, 27–28; and black manhood, 15; and border struggle, xiii, 2, 6–7, 12, 14; in Border South, 38, 212; during Civil War, 209–11; defensive measures among, 28, 95–96; and Fugitive Slave Law of 1850, 147, 150; and kidnappers, 32, 57–59; and Lower North, 75–75, 84, 99; mob attacks on, 67–70; and slave catchers, 62, 96; and violence, 95–96, 98, 100–11, 114, 152–56, 182; white attitudes toward, 7, 20, 56, 70, 118, 121, 172

—free: and Border South, 4, 6, 20, 36; and fugitive slaves, 42–45, 124, 130, 178; southern threats to, 186–87

Anti-Nebraska Movement, 163

Antislavery Missionaries. *See* Abolitionist missionaries

Army of Northern Virginia, 209–11

Atchison, David, 140, 162–65, 168–69, 171–72

Ayers, Edward L., 4

Bacon, Jarvis C., 175, 177, 186

Bailey, Gamaliel: on black rights, 174; on Border South, 47–48; on Cassius M. Clay, 135; on Cincinnati, 4; on kidnapping, 59; and *National Era*, 11–20; on North-South controversies, 77–78, 86, 155; on slave escapes, 40, 124, 231 (n. 30); on slaves in Ohio, 65–66; on violence, 98, 114, 132–33

Bailey, William S., 174, 176, 186, 191–93

Baltimore, 3–4, 7–8, 31, 204

Bayley, Thomas H., 133, 143

Bartley, Mordecai, 60, 99

Beecher, Henry Ward, 166, 193

Bell, Charles, 181–82

Bell, David, 181–82

Benning, Henry L., 196, 198

Berea, Ky., 139, 176, 178, 187–90, 193

Birney, James G., 49, 59, 68, 118, 120

Black Act. *See* Ohio Fugitive Slave Law

"Black Laws," 7, 25–26, 56

Black people. *See* African Americans

Blair, Francis P., 174, 202–3

Blue Lodge, 165

Border clashes. *See* Border struggle

Border conflict. *See* Border struggle

Border gangs, 53–54

Borderlands, xii, 2–4, 203

"Border miscreants," 53–54, 57

Border North. *See* Lower North

Border northerners, 149–50, 153–56

Border ruffians, 54, 165

Border slave states. *See* Border South

Border South: and abolitionists, 51–52, 118–20, 131; border counties in, 41; defensive measures in, 11–12, 192; defensiveness in, 35–36, 126–27, 129, 160–61, 193, 208; defined, xi–xii, 4–5; and federal support, 23, 118, 143–44, 154–55, 182, 185, 202; and Fugitive Slave Law of 1850, 11–12, 141–43, 149, 245 (n. 8); and kidnapping, 30; and Lower North, 3, 120–21; and Lower South, 13, 140, 211; mobs in, 49–50, 69; racial prejudice in, 7; and secession debate, 194–98, 200–204; in sectional struggle, 2; and slave escapes, 11, 41–42; and slavery, 4–6, 20, 38–39, 41, 44–46, 121, 211; threats to, 70–71, 118, 161, 173, 182, 193–94; unionism in, 143–44, 198–201

Border southerners, 9, 44–45, 176–77

Border struggle: John C. Calhoun on, 135–36; and causes of Civil War, 2; described, xii–xiii; development of, 10–11, 15; and Fugitive Slave Law of 1850, 151; Kentucky and Ohio in, 72–73, 79–85, 94; in Lower North, 18, 53–71, 88–90, 100–115; and secession, 196–97, 211; and U.S. history, 212

Bordewich, Fergus M., 246 (n. 29), 248 (n. 290)

Breckinridge, John C., 195, 197, 202, 242 (n. 33)

Breckinridge, Robert J., xii

Brooke, Abram, 88, 112–13

Brooks-Sumner incident, 159–61

Brown, Abel, 43, 123

Brown, John: and Harpers Ferry raid, 12, 183–84, 190; in Kansas, 168, 170, 173; on Oberlin-Willington rescue, 181; song about, 207; Eli Thayer on, 176; on Charles T. Torrey, 124

Brown, Kent Masterson, 210

Brown County, Ohio, 101–2

Brush Creek, Ohio, 101–2

Buchanan, 172, 174, 185, 203

Burnett, Cornelius, 58, 113, 115

Burr, James E., 51–52

Butler, Andrew P., 142, 163, 159

Butler, Benjamin O., 204, 207

Calhoun, John C., 133, 135–36, 140

Campbell, Stanley, 246 (n. 17), 247 (n. 26)

Canada, 14, 18, 27, 125, 141, 145, 149

Cannon-Johnson gang, 31–32, 53

Carberry, Valentine, 101–2

Carlisle, Pa., 109–10

Chaplin, William L., 131–33, 136–37, 139

Chase, Salmon P., 67, 145–46, 157, 180, 188, 192

Chester County, Pa., 98, 102–3, 106, 153, 155

Chicago, 148, 150–51, 155–56

Christiana, Pa., 153–55

Cincinnati, 3–4; antislavery in, 8, 56, 128; and kidnapping, 33, 57–58; mobs in, 67–69; riots in, 67–68, 112–15; and slave catchers, 103, 156–57; slaves in, 65–66;

Civil War: and borderlands, 203–4; causes of, xii, 2, 4, 12–13, 16; and slave escapes, 206–7

Clark, James, 72, 81–82

Clay, Cassius M.: and antislavery efforts, 116–18, 134–35, 139, 174, 189–90, 193, 239 (n. 3); condemned, 176; described, 116, 119–20; and fighting in Kentucky, 187–90; on proslavery efforts, 4; and slaves, 126, 178

Clay, Henry, 65, 91, 116; and Compromise of 1850, 138; on secession, 143; on slave renditions, 141; on slavery, 70; on threat of war, 11, 135

Coffin, Levi, 28

Colonization movement, xiv, 121, 174

Columbia, Pa., 32, 147, 247 (n. 24)

Common law, 20–21

Compromise of 1850, 138

Confederate States of America, 196

Confrontations, 94–95, 103–5, 188–89

Crisis of 1850, 1, 137, 139–41

Crittenden, John J., 198, 202

Cumberland Iron Works, 186

Davis, Jefferson, 133, 140–41, 196

Davis, John, 21–22, 29

Dayton, Ohio, 25

De Bow, J. D. B., 40, 240–41 (n. 15)

Delany, Martin R., 96

Delaware, 5, 73–74, 204, 211

Democratic Party, xiv, 81, 90, 149, 195

Diplomacy, interstate, 72–77, 79–85

District of Columbia. *See* Washington, D.C.

Disunionism, 141, 143–44, 194, 197–98

Dixon, James, 7–8

Domino theory, 12, 194–96, 200

Douglas, Stephen A., 163, 195

Douglass, Frederick, 38, 154–55, 190

Dorsey, Basil, 108

Doy, John W., 173

Drayton, Daniel, 132–33

Eastman, Zebina: on abolitionist newspapers, 119; on fugitive slave laws, 63,
150–51; on Lower North, 55–57; on slave
escapes, 15, 98

Elder, William, 125, 138

Emancipation Party, 176

Emancipation Proclamation, 210–11

Escape networks, 11, 122–26, 179. *See also*
Underground railroad

Etcheson, Nicole, 166–67

Fairbank, Calvin, 121–22, 242 (n. 26)

Federal action, 184–85, 198–200, 202

Federal government, 143–44

Fee, John G.: and abolitionist organizations,
175, 187; and Cassius M. Clay, 134, 189–90;
expulsion of, 259 (n. 28); and free labor
colonies, 176; and fighting in Kentucky,
187–90; on Harpers Ferry Raid, 193; and
slave escapes, 139, 178

Fehrenbacher, Don E., 20, 158

Fields, Barbara Jeanne, 11

Finkelman, Paul, 219 (n. 7)

"Fire-eaters," 196

Floyd, John B., 137, 144

Foote, Henry, 133, 140, 244 (n. 51)

Fort Sumter, 203–4

Franklin, John Hope, 40, 42, 46

Freehling, William W., 13, 40, 142, 164, 211,
225 (n. 37)

Free labor, 13, 65

Free labor colonies, 175–77

Freeman, John, 148, 248 (n. 27)

Free Soil Party, xiv, 134, 174

Free-staters in Kansas Territory: and African Americans, 172; impact on Border
South, 173; organize, 167, 172; seek arms,
166–67; take offensive, 170. *See also* Kansas
Territory

Frémont, John C., 174–75, 185–86, 205, 207

Fugitive Slave Convention, 137

Fugitive Slave Law of 1793, 12; condem-
nation of, 57; enforcement of, 97; and
Fugitive Slave Law of 1850, 12; and Lower
North, 63–64; origins of, 21–22; and
*Prigg v. Pennsylvania*, 76–77; resistance to,
23–25; and slaves in transit, 66–67

Fugitive Slave Law of 1850: arrests under,
147; and Border South, 83, 137–39, 142–43,
202; and border war, 1; during Civil War,
206; debate over, 15, 140–41, 245 (n. 7); and
escapes from Missouri, 162; reaction to,
138, 141, 144–58, 161; shaping of, 73, 77, 143;
support for, 140–41; and threat of civil
war, 16; and Union, 246 (n. 13)

Fugitive slaves: and Border South, 141;
capture of, 10; and crisis of 1850, 140; and
Lawrence, Kans. Terr., 172; and Lee's invasion of Pennsylvania, 209–11; and Lower
North, 7, 14–15, 23, 27–28, 75, 85, 88, 149;
numbers of, 39–42; and resistance to
rendition, 62, 87; and slavery, 12

Gabriel revolt conspiracy, 18, 36

"Gap Gang," 54, 153

Gara, Larry, 42

Garner, Margaret, 156–57

Garnett, Henry, 150, 152

Garret, Thomas, 179

Garrison, William Lloyd, xiii, 94–95, 185, 191

"Gentlemen of property and standing," 69, 97

Gettysburg, battle of, 210

Giddings, Joshua R.: on "civil war" in Pennsylvania, 153; on Fugitive Slave Law of
1850, 12, 144, 150–51; on resistance to rendition, 15, 27, 112, 181; and slave revolt, 185;
on slaves "sent south," 41; on Washington,
D.C., mob, 132–33

Great Postal Campaign, 38–39

Greeley, Horace, 160, 166

Grier, Robert C., 148, 152, 155

Griffler, Keith P., 14, 27, 239 (n. 46)

Grimsted, David, 114, 225 (n. 37), 237
(nn. 30–31), 239 (n. 46)

Hagedorn, Ann, 233 (n. 46)

Haitian Revolution, 36

Hamlin, Edwin S., 105

Hammond, Charles, 55, 66–67, 90
Harned, William, 4
Harpers Ferry, 4, 190–94, 204. *See also* Brown, John
Harrisburg, Pa., 1, 74, 76, 110, 136–37, 152
Hart, Albert Bushnell, 40
Hayden, Lewis, 122
Helper, Hinton Rowan, 174, 253 (n. 41)
Hicks, Thomas H., 199, 202–4
Historians, 40, 42, 141
Holt, Michael F., 16, 196
Hopper, Isaac, 31
Hudson, Sally, 101–2
Hunter, Robert M. T., 163

Illinois, 7, 19, 25, 27–28, 65–67
Indiana, 7, 19, 25–28, 32–37, 66–67
Intersectional economics, 3–4
Interstate controversies, 77–79
Interstate diplomacy, 72–93
Interstate war, predicted, 72, 79, 80

Jackson, Claiborne F., 162, 202, 205
Johnson, Eliza Jane, 58–59, 80
Johnson, Samuel A., 164, 169
Johnson, William F., 144, 149
Jones, Benjamin "Big Ben," 62, 123
Jones, Samuel J., 167–69
Journalism, American, xiii–xiv
Jury trials, 22, 75, 85, 143–44

Kansas Territory, 163, 164–71. *See also* Free-staters in Kansas Territory
Kennedy, John Pendleton, 193
Kennett Township, Pa., 28
Kentuckians, white, 83–86, 89, 114
Kentucky: and abolitionists, 35, 38, 44, 187–90, 193; and African Americans, 118; and Cotton South, 5; defensive measures in, 46, 48; and emancipation, 211; and Harpers Ferry raid, 192; and Indiana, 26, 181–82; and kidnapping, 57–58; and Ohio, 25–26, 28–29, 72–73, 82; secession debate in, 197–98, 202, 204; and slave escape, 72, 131, 223 (n. 9); and slave trade, 17, 40; threats to slavery in, 134, 139, 174
Kentucky commissioners, 82–86
Kentucky-Ohio controversy, 72–73
Kidnappers, 10, 32, 57–58, 138, 146

Kidnapping: and African Americans, 29–33, 57–59; and Fugitive Slave Law of 1793, 23–24; and Lee's invasion of Pennsylvania, 209–11; and Lower North, 26, 32–33, 57–61, 75, 92, 139; as sectional issue, 30; and slave trade, 10, 30; southern help to victims of, 227 (n. 18)
Klem, Mary J., 164

Lancaster County, Pa., 106, 153
Lane, James H., 168–72
Law officers, 35–36, 46, 97
Lawrence, Amos A., 166
Lawrence, Kans. Terr., 166–70, 172
Lawrence, Treaty of, 168–69
Leavitt, Humphrey H., 180
Leavitt, Joshua, 38–39
Lecompton Constitution, 172
Lee, Robert E., 183, 209–10
Letcher, John, 192
Lexington, Ky., 3, 116–17, 126
Liberty Party: described, xiii–xiv; New York wing of, 10–11, 42, 116; in Ohio, 56; in Pennsylvania, 70
Lincoln, Abraham, 135, 195–97, 203–7, 210–11
Louisville, Ky., 3, 135
Lovejoy, Elijah P., 50, 65, 68–69, 95
Lovejoy, Owen, 125
Lower North: assisted escapes in, 75; and Border South, 3, 211–12; and border struggle, 1, 34, 53–71; character of, 4–5; and causes of Civil War, xii; defined, xi; and fugitive slave laws, 63–64, 144–59, 179–82; and fugitive slaves, 18, 23–25, 27–28, 42–43, 62–64, 149; and kidnapping, 32–33, 57–61; masters' view of, 111; mobs in, 67–70; and racial prejudice, 7, 55–57, 70; "slave catchers" in, 61–64, 75; and slavery, 6–7, 20, 23, 95–115; and slaves in transit, 112–31; threat to, 59–60, 71
Lower South: and abolitionists, 38, 42; and Border South, 121, 136, 140, 212; and causes of Civil War, xii; and Henry Clay, 143; and issues in sectional struggle, 140; and kidnapping, 30; and secession, 13, 141, 185, 200; and slave escapes, 12; and war in Kansas, 172
Lundy, Benjamin: on African Americans, 20, 99; and *Genius of Universal Emancipation*,